WRITING
with INTENT

ALSO BY MARGARET ATWOOD

FICTION

The Edible Woman (1969)
Surfacing (1972)
Lady Oracle (1976)
Dancing Girls (1977)
Life Before Man (1979)
Bodily Harm (1981)
Murder in the Dark (1983)
Bluebeard's Egg (1983)
The Handmaid's Tale (1983)
Cat's Eye (1988)
Wilderness Tips (1991)
Good Bones (1992)
The Robber Bride (1993)
Alias Grace (1996)
The Blind Assassin (2000)
Good Bones and Simple Murders (2001)
Oryx and Crake (2003)

POETRY

Double Persephone (1961)
The Circle Game (1966)
The Animals in That Country (1968)
The Journals of Susanna Moodie (1970)
Procedures for Underground (1970)
Power Politics (1971)
You Are Happy (1974)
Selected Poems (1976)
Two-Headed Poems (1976)
True Stories (1981)
Interlunar (1984)
Selected Poems II: Poems Selected and New, 1976–1986 (1986)
Morning in the Burned House (1995)

NONFICTION

Survival: A Thematic Guide to Canadian Literature (1972)
Days of the Rebels 1815–1840 (1977)
Second Words: Selected Critical Prose 1960–1982 (1982)
Strange Things: The Malevolent North in Canadian Literature (1996)
Two Solicitudes: Conversations [with Victor-Lévy Beaulieu] (1998)
Negotiating with the Dead: A Writer on Writing (2000)
Moving Targets (2004)

FOR CHILDREN

Up in the Tree (1978)
Anna's Pet [with Joyce Barkhouse] (1980)
For the Birds (1990)
Princess Prunella and the Purple Peanut (1995)
Rude Ramsay and the Roaring Radishes (2003)
Bashful Bob and Doleful Dorinda (2004)

WRITING
with INTENT

Essays, Reviews, Personal Prose:
1983–2005

MARGARET ATWOOD

CARROLL & GRAF PUBLISHERS
NEW YORK

WRITING WITH INTENT
Essays, Reviews, Personal Prose: 1983–2005

Carroll & Graf Publishers
An Imprint of Avalon Publishing Group Inc.
245 West 17th Street
11th Floor
New York, NY 10011

AVALON
publishing group incorporated

Library of Congress Cataloging-in-Publication Data is available.

ISBN: 0-7867-1535-9

9 8 7 6 5 4 3 2 1

Interior design by Maria E. Torres

Printed in the United States of America
Distributed by Publishers Group West

For my family

CONTENTS

Introduction xiii

Part One: 1983–1989

1   Review: *The Witches of Eastwick* by John Updike 6

2   Laughter vs. Death 12

3   Review: *Difficult Loves* by Italo Calvino 19

4   That Certain Thing Called the Girlfriend 22

5   True North 31

6   Review: *Beloved* by Toni Morrison 46

7   Afterword: *A Jest of God* by Margaret Laurence 52

8   Great Aunts 56

9   Introduction: Reading Blind
     The Best American Short Stories 1989 68

10   Introduction: *Women Writers at Work: The Paris Review
     Interviews,* George Plimpton, editor 80

11   Review: *The Warrior Queens* by Antonia Fraser 89

12   Writing Utopia 92

Part Two: 1990–1999

13   Nine Beginnings 105

14   Review: *The General in His Labyrinth*
     by Gabriel García Márquez 111

15   Afterword: *Anne of Green Gables*
     by Lucy Maud Montgomery 115

16　Why I Love *The Night of the Hunter,*
　　a film by Charles Laughton　121

17　Spotty-Handed Villainesses: Problems of Female
　　Bad Behavior in the Creation of Literature　125

18　The Grunge Look　139

19　Review: *From the Beast to the Blonde:*
　　On Fairy Tales and Their Tellers by Marina Warner　147

20　Review: *Burning Your Boats: The Collected Short Stories*
　　by Angela Carter　151

21　Review: *An Experiment in Love* by Hilary Mantel　154

22　In Search of *Alias Grace*: On Writing Canadian Historical
　　Fiction　158

23　Review: *Trickster Makes This World: Mischief,*
　　Myth, and Art and *The Gift: Imagination and the Erotic*
　　Life of Property by Lewis Hyde　177

Part Three: 2000–2005

24　First Job, Waitressing　189

25　Eulogy: Mordecai Richler, 1931–2001:
　　Diogenes of Montréal　192

26　Review: *According to Queeney* by Beryl Bainbridge　194

27　Introduction: *She* by H. Rider Haggard　198

28　When Afghanistan Was at Peace　205

29　Review: *The Selected Letters of Dashiell Hammett, 1921–1960*
　　edited by Richard Layman with Julie M. Rivett; *Dashiell*
　　Hammet: A Daughter Remembers by Jo Hammett, edited by
　　Richard Layman with Julie M. Rivett; and *Dashiell Hammett:*
　　Crime Stories & Other Writings selected and edited by
　　Steven Marcus　208

30   Review: *Atanarjuat: The Fast Runner,*
     a film by Zacharias Kunuk   220

31   Review: *Life of Pi* by Yann Martel   224

32   Review: *Tishomingo Blues* by Elmore Leonard   227

33   Eulogy: Tiff and the Animals   237

34   *To the Lighthouse* by Virginia Woolf   240

35   Review: *The Birthday of the World and Other Stories*
     by Ursula K. Le Guin   243

36   Introduction: *Ground Works,* Christian Bök, editor   254

37   Introduction: *Doctor Glas* by Hjalmar Söderberg   260

38   Introduction: *High Latitudes* by Farley Mowat   265

39   Review: *Child of My Heart* by Alice McDermott   268

40   Napoleon's Two Biggest Mistakes   277

41   Letter to America   280

42   Writing *Oryx and Crake*   284

43   George Orwell: Some Personal Connections   287

44   Review: *Enough: Staying Human in an Engineered Age*
     by Bill McKibben   294

45   Foreword: *Victory Gardens: A Breath of Fresh Air*
     by Elise Houghton   305

46   Eulogy: Carol Shields, Who Died Last Week, Wrote Books
     That Were Full of Delights   313

47   Review: *Reading Lolita in Tehran: A Memoir in Books*
     by Azar Nafisi   317

48   Introduction: *The Complete Stories, Volume 4*
       by Morley Callaghan   322

49   Review: *Hope Dies Last: Keeping the Faith in Difficult Times*
       by Studs Terkel   331

50   Mortifications   343

51   Review: *A Story as Sharp as a Knife:*
       The Classical Haida Mythtellers and Their World
       by Robert Bringhurst   346

52   Review: *The Mays of Ventadorn* by W. S. Merwin   352

53   Review: *Snow* by Orhan Pamuk   356

54   Review: *From Eve to Dawn* by Marilyn French   360

55   To Beechy Island   365

56   Introduction: *Frozen in Time: The Fate of the Franklin*
       Expedition [revised edition] by Owen Beattie and
       John Geiger   375

57   Review: *Acquainted with the Night: Excursions Through the*
       World After Dark by Christopher Dewdney   382

58   Introduction: Ten Ways of Looking at *The Island of Doctor*
       Moreau by H. G. Wells   386

Acknowledgments   399

Bibliography   401

Index   407

About the Author   427

WRITING
with INTENT

INTRODUCTION

Writing with Intent is an assemblage of occasional pieces—that is, pieces written for specific occasions. Some of the occasions have been books written by other people, resulting in book reviews and articles; some of them have been political in nature, resulting in journalism of various kinds; some of them—increasingly, as time has moved on—have been the deaths of people I've known, often fellow writers, so I've been asked to write obituaries at short notice and in odd locations. The article on Carol Shields, for instance, was written on a moving train.

When you say the titles of your books out loud, people sometimes hear them wrong. I've seen *Bluebeard's Egg* become *Bluebird's Egg*, *The Handmaid's Tale* become *The Handmaiden's Tale*, *Oryx and Crake* become *Onyx and Crake*. When I told someone that this book was called *Writing with Intent*, she said, "*Writing within Tents?* How do you mean?" But this writing sometimes has been done in tents, or in their equivalent: provisional shelters with just enough light to see by, and just enough heat to make it possible to get on with the job.

Looking back at some of these essays—"essay" in the sense of "attempt"—I feel I might write them in another way if I were writing them today. But then, I'd be unlikely to write them today. Everything we do is embedded in time, and time changes not only us, but our point of view as well. Also, you find out *what happened.* One year's prophecy becomes the next year's certainty, and the year after that, it's history. How could I know, when visiting Afghanistan in 1978—six weeks before President Muhammad Daoud was assassinated, initiating the chain of events we're caught in today—that this beautiful, strange country would become unrecognizable over the next twenty-five years? We're always looking over our shoulders, wondering why we missed the clues that seem so obvious to us in retrospect.

I began writing occasional pieces in the 1950s, when I was sixteen: I was the designated reporter for my Toronto high school's Home and School Association meetings, and my accounts of these sometimes fraught events appeared in the mimeographed newsletter that was sent to the parents to keep them informed on such topics as the proper length of girls' skirts. By this age I had decided to be a dedicated novelist—a very dedicated one, with the resulting lung illnesses, unhappy affairs, alcoholism, and early death that would surely follow—but I knew I would have to have a day job in order to afford the squalid flat and the absinthe, and the Home and School Association newsletter was my first foray into the humiliating world of Grub Street hackwork. Did I learn anything from this experience? I ought to have learned that for every tale there is a teller but also a listener and that some jokes are not suitable for all occasions, but that particular lesson took a while to sink in.

Once at university, I took to producing book reviews and articles for the literary magazine—some of them under other names, since we liked to pretend, back then, that there were more people interested in the arts than there actually were. Like many young people I was demanding and intolerant, but I didn't let that show too much in the reviews, which were inclined to be amiably condescending. I continued with my reviewing while I was attending Harvard Graduate School in the 1960s, and then while I was holding down various low-paying jobs and publishing poetry and fiction in small magazines.

Eventually I found myself appearing in larger places such as the *New York Times* and the *Washington Post* and the *New York Review of Books* and the *Times* of London and the *Guardian*, but that took a while.

Looking back over this gathering of pages I see that my interests have remained fairly constant over the decades, although I like to believe their scope has broadened somewhat. Some of my earlier concerns—gender issues, environmental worries—were considered lunatic fringe when I first voiced them, but have since moved to the center of the opinion stage. I dislike advocacy writing—it's not fun, because the issues that generate it are not fun—but I feel compelled to do a certain amount of it anyway. The effects are not always pleasant, since what may be simple common sense to one person is annoying polemic to another.

Some of these pieces were originally lectures and speeches. I made my first speech at the age of ten; it was bad for me. I still have the stage fright in advance, during the writing of the speech. I'm haunted by a metaphor from Edith Wharton's story "The Pelican," in which a public lecturer's talk is compared to the trick by which a magician produces reams and reams of blank white paper out of his mouth. I still find book reviewing a problem: it's so much like homework, and it forces me to have opinions, instead of the Negative Capability that is so much more soothing to the digestion. I review anyway, because those who are reviewed must review in their turn or the principle of reciprocity fails. Where would blood banks be if none of us gave blood?

There's another reason, however: reviewing the work of others forces you to examine your own ethical and aesthetic tastes. What do we mean by "good" in a book? What qualities do we consider "bad," and why? Aren't there in fact two kinds of reviews, derived from two different ancestries? There's the newspaper review, which descends from gossip around the village well (loved her, hated him, and did you get a load of the shoes?). And then there's the "academic" review, which descends from Biblical exegesis and other traditions that involved the minute examination of sacred texts. This kind of analysis holds that some texts are more sacred than others, and that the application of a magnifying glass or lemon juice will reveal hidden meanings. I've written both.

Reviewers are either spankers, dealing out slaps for what they consider poor performance, or strokers, awarders of marshmallows for performances they consider admirable. I'm a stroker. I don't review books I don't like, although to do so would doubtless be amusing for the Ms. Hyde side of me and entertaining for the more malicious class of reader. But either the book is really bad, in which case no one should review it, or it's good but not my kind of thing, in which case someone else should review it. It's a great luxury not to be a professional full-time reviewer: I'm at liberty to close books that don't seize hold of me without having to savage them in print. Over the years, history—military history included—has become more interesting to me; so has biography. As for fiction, some of my less highfalutin reading preferences (crime writing, science fiction) have made their way out of the closet.

Speaking of these, it's as well to mention a pattern that recurs in these pages. As one early reader of this book pointed out, I have a habit of kicking off my discussion of a book or author or group of books by saying that I read it (or him, or her, or them) in the cellar when I was growing up; or that I came across them in the bookcase at home; or that I found them at the cottage; or that I took them out from the library. If these statements were metaphors I'd excise all of them except one, but they are simply snippets of my reading history. My justification for mentioning where and when I first read a book is that—as many other readers have observed—the impression a book makes on you is often tied to your age and circumstances at the time you read it, and your fondness for books you loved when young continues with you through your life.

I've divided *Writing with Intent* into three sections. Part One picks up from my 1983 collection of such pieces, *Second Words: Selected Critical Prose*, which covered the 1960s, 1970s, and early 1980s. This second collection continues through the rest of the 1980s—years during which I wrote and published a number of volumes of poetry and several novels, including *The Handmaid's Tale*, the book of mine that's most likely to turn up on college reading lists. This was the period during which I graduated from being world-famous in Canada—as Mordecai Richler used to say—to being world-famous, sort of, in the way that writers are. (We're not talking the Rolling Stones here.) It concludes with 1989, the year the Berlin Wall came down, thus ending the Cold War.

Part Two collects pieces from the nineties—a sort of lull, during which some folk proclaimed the end of history prematurely—culminating in the year 1999, when the twentieth century ended. Part Three runs from 2000, the year of the millennium, through 2001, when the unexpected September 11 explosions rocked the world, and thus to the present time. Not surprisingly, I found myself writing more about political issues during this last period than I had done for some time.

Back to the title: *Writing with Intent.* There's a legal echo here—"assault with intent to injure" comes to mind—and a tricky assumption, too, about the difference between this kind of writing and, say, fiction or poetry, which might thus be defined as writing without intent, thus free of instigated designs upon the reader. (They aren't, of course; insofar as they work toward an effect, they are just as intentional. They are simply more devious.)

But *intent* has other meanings. It can mean a state of mind or will, but it can also mean an inclination of spirit or soul. And, as a word, *intent* is joined at the hip with *intense.* "Eager," "keen," and "resolved" are also mentioned in its dictionary definition. "Having the mind strenuously bent upon something," says the *Shorter Oxford,* and that certainly describes the feeling you need to have—or that I need to have—when writing these kinds of pieces. Inertia is my constant companion, procrastination my household pet. If I'm not eager and keen and resolved and strenuously bent, I find it very difficult to write at all.

Part One
1983–1989

In the first years of the 1980s, the Cold War was still in process. The Soviet Union seemed firmly in place, and due to last for a long while yet. But it had already been sucked into a costly and debilitating war in Afghanistan—as is typical of empires, it had expanded its activities beyond its ability to sustain them financially—and in 1989 the Berlin Wall would come tumbling down. It's amazing how quickly certain kinds of power structures crumble once the cornerstone falls out. But in 1983, nobody foresaw this outcome.

I began the period quietly enough. I was trying, unsuccessfully and for the third time, to write the book that was later to become *Cat's Eye*, and I was ruminating about *The Handmaid's Tale*, although I was avoiding this second book as much as possible: it seemed too hopeless a task and too weird a concept.

Our family was living in Toronto's Chinatown, in a row house that had been modernized by the removal of many of its inner doors. I couldn't write there because it was too noisy, so I would bicycle westward to the Portuguese district, where I wrote on the third floor of another row house.

The second floor of this house was haunted, so I avoided it. Nonetheless, I felt strangely blocked, and so—as often happens—I began a third novel, one I wasn't destined to finish. All I can say for it is that it had some good chapter titles. I was, however, unable to come up with the good chapters that ought to have gone with them.

In the autumn of 1983 we went to England, where we rented a Norfolk manse also said to be haunted: by nuns in the parlor, a jolly cavalier in the dining room, and a headless woman in the kitchen. None of these was seen by us, though a jolly cavalier did stray in from the neighboring pub, looking for the washroom. The phone was a pay phone outside the house, in a booth also used for storing potatoes, and I would clamber over and through the potatoes to deal with the editing of—for instance—the Updike review that appears here. This was done by phone, for back then there were as yet no fax machines in general use, and e-mail was far in the future.

I wrote in a fisherman's cottage turned vacation home, where I struggled with the Aga heater as well as with the novel I'd started. I got my first case of chilblains doing this, but had to give up the novel when I found myself snarled up in the time sequence, with no escape visible.

Right after that we went to West Berlin, where, in 1984 and with no other prospects in sight, I began *The Handmaid's Tale*, on a rented typewriter with a German keyboard. The irony of the year was not lost on me: how could I be so corny as to start a dystopia in the year scheduled for George Orwell's? But the thing could no longer be avoided: it was that novel or none. We made some side visits, to Poland, East Germany, and Czechoslovakia, which doubtless contributed to the atmosphere of the book: totalitarian dictatorships, however different the costumes, share the same climate of fear and silence.

I finished the book in the spring of 1985, where I was a Visiting Chair at the University of Alabama in Tuscaloosa. It was the last book I wrote on an electric typewriter. I faxed the chapters as they were finished to my typist in Toronto, to be retyped properly—faxes could now be sent from copy stores—and I recall being amazed by the magic of instant transmission. The book came out in Canada in 1985 and in England and the United States in 1986; it won the *Los Angeles Times* fiction prize and was short-listed for the Booker Prize, among other forms of uproar.

We spent part of 1987 in Australia, where I was finally able to come to grips with *Cat's Eye*. The snowiest scenes in the book were written during balmy spring days in Sydney, with cuckaburras yelling for hamburger on the back porch. The book was published in 1988 in Canada and in the

United States and England in 1989, where it, too, was short-listed for the Booker Prize. It was at about this time that the fatwa was proclaimed against Salman Rushdie. Who knew that this was an early straw in what was to become not just a wind but a hurricane?

All this time *The Handmaid's Tale* had been making progress through the intestinal workings of the film industry. It finally emerged in finished form, scripted by Harold Pinter and directed by Volker Schlorndorff. The film premiered in the two Berlins in 1989, just as the Wall fell: you could buy pieces of it, with the colored ones being more expensive. I went there for the festivities. There were the same kinds of border guards who had been so cold in 1984, but now they were grinning and exchanging cigars with tourists. The East Berlin audience was the more receptive to the film. "This was our life," one woman told me quietly.

How euphoric we felt, for a short time, in 1989. How dazed by the spectacle of the impossible made real. No more Cold War! Now, surely, peace and prosperity could become possible for all. How wrong we were about the brave new world we were about to enter.

1

Review:

The Witches of Eastwick
by John Updike

*T*he Witches of Eastwick is John Updike's first novel since the much-celebrated *Rabbit Is Rich*, and a strange and marvelous organism it proves to be. Like his third novel, *The Centaur*, it is a departure from baroque realism. This time, too, Mr. Updike transposes mythology into the minor keys of small-town America, but this time he pulls it off, possibly because, like Shakespeare and Robert Louis Stevenson before him, he finds wickedness and mischief more engrossing as subjects than goodness and wisdom.

Mr. Updike's titles are often quite literal, and *The Witches of Eastwick* is just what it says. It's indeed about witches, real ones, who can fly through the air, levitate, hex people, and make love charms that work, and they live in a town called Eastwick. It's Eastwick rather than Westwick, since, as we all know, it's the east wind that blows no good. Eastwick purports to be in Rhode Island because, as the book itself points out, Rhode Island was the place of exile for Anne Hutchinson, the Puritan foremother who was kicked out of the Massachusetts Bay colony by the forefathers for female insubordination, a quality these witches have in surplus.

These are not 1980s Woman-power witches. They aren't at all interested in healing the earth, communing with the Great Goddess, or gaining power within (as opposed to power over). These are *bad* witches, and power within, as far as they are concerned, is no good at all unless you can zap somebody with it. They are spiritual descendants of the seventeenth-century New England strain and go in for sabbats, sticking pins in wax images, kissing the Devil's backside, and phallus worship; this latter, though—since it is Updike—is qualified worship. The Great Goddess is present only in the form of Nature itself, or, in this book, Nature herself, with which they, both as women and as witches, are supposed to have special affinities. Nature, however, is far from Wordsworth's big motherly breast. She, or it, is red in tooth, claw, and cancer cell, at best lovely and cruel, at worse merely cruel. "Nature kills constantly, and we call her beautiful."

How did these middle-class, small-town, otherwise ordinary women get their witchy powers? Simple. They became husbandless. All three are divorcées and embodiments of what American small-town society tends to think about divorcées. Whether you leave your husband or are left "doesn't make any difference," which will be news to many abandoned women stuck with full child support. Divorced, then, and with the images of their former husbands shrunk and dried and stored away in their minds and kitchens and cellars, they are free to be themselves, an activity Mr. Updike regards with some misgivings, as he regards most catchwords and psychofads.

Being yourself involves artistic activity, albeit of minor kinds. Lexa makes ceramic earthmothers, which are sold in the local crafts store, Jane plays the cello, and Sukie writes, badly, a gossip column for the weekly paper, her participles dangling like earrings. All three are dabblers, but their "creativity" is seen in the same light as that of other, more accomplished female artists. The townspeople of Eastwick, who act as a collective chorus, credit them with "a certain distinction, an inner boiling such as had in other cloistral towns produced Emily Dickinson's verses and Emily Brontë's inspired novel."

It's doubtful, however, that either of the Emilys went in for the sexual loop-the-loops indulged in by these three weird sisters. Sisters in more senses than one because the novel is cunningly set at a precise moment in America's recent history. The women's movement has been around just long enough for some of its phrases to have seeped from New York to the outer darkness of provincial towns such as Eastwick, and the witches toss around words such as "chauvinist" in light social repartee. In the public, male world, which is offstage, the Vietnam War goes on, watched by the witches' children on their television sets, and the antiwar activists are making bombs in cellars.

The witches don't busy themselves with "causes," however. At first they are merely restless and bored; they amuse themselves with spiteful gossip, playing mischievous tricks and seducing unhappily married men, which Eastwick supplies in strength; for if the witches are bad, the wives are worse, and the men are eviscerated. "Marriage," one of the husbands thinks, "is like two people locked up with one lesson to read, over and over, until the words become madness."

But enter the Devil, the world's best remedy for women's boredom, in the form of the dark, not very handsome, but definitely mysterious stranger Darryl Van Horne, who collects pop art and has an obvious name. Now mischief turns to *maleficio*, real evil occurs, and people die, because Van Horne's horn becomes a bone of contention—nothing like not enough men to go around to get the witches' cauldrons bubbling. And when Van Horne is snatched into marriage by a newcomer witchlet, the eye of newt comes out in earnest.

This may sound like an unpromising framework for a serious novelist. Has Mr. Updike entered second childhood and reverted to Rosemary's babyland? I don't think so. For one thing, *The Witches of Eastwick* is too well done. Like Van Horne, Mr. Updike has always wondered what it would be like to be a woman, and his witches give him a lot of scope for this fantasy. Lexa in particular, who is the oldest, the plumpest, the kindest, and the closest to Nature, is a fitting vehicle for some of his most breathtaking similes. In line of descent, he is perhaps closer than any other living American writer to the Puritan view of Nature as a lexicon written by God, but in hieroglyphs, so that unending translation is needed. Mr. Updike's prose, here more than ever, is a welter of suggestive metaphors and cross-references, which constantly point toward a meaning constantly evasive.

His version of witchcraft is closely tied to both carnality and mortality. Magic is hope in the face of inevitable decay. The houses and the furniture molder, and so do the people. The portrait of Felicia Gabriel, victim wife and degenerate afterimage of the onetime "peppy" American cheerleading sweetheart, is gruesomely convincing. Bodies are described in loving detail, down to the last tuft, wart, wrinkle, and bit of food stuck in the teeth. No one is better than Mr. Updike at conveying the sadness of the sexual, the melancholy of motel affairs—"amiable human awkwardness," Lexa calls it. This is a book that redefines magic realism.

There's room, too, for bravura writing. The widdershins' dance, portrayed as a tennis game in which the ball turns into a bat, followed by the sabbat as a hot-tub-and-pot session, is particularly fetching. Students of traditional Devil-lore will have as much fun with these transpositions as Mr. Updike had. Van Horne, for instance, is part Mephistopheles, offering Faustian pacts and lusting for souls, part alchemist-chemist, and part Miltonic Satan, hollow at the core; but he's also a shambling klutz whose favorite comic book is—what else?—Captain Marvel.

Much of *The Witches of Eastwick* is satire, some of it literary playfulness, and some plain bitchery. It could be that any attempt to analyze further would be like taking an elephant gun to a puff pastry: an Updike should not mean but be. But again, I don't think so. What a culture has to say about witchcraft, whether in jest or in earnest, has a lot to do with its views of sexuality and power, and especially with the apportioning of powers between the sexes. The witches were burned not because they were pitied but because they were feared.

Cotton Mather and Nathaniel Hawthorne aside, the great American witchcraft classic is *The Wizard of Oz*, and Mr. Updike's book reads like a rewrite. In the original, a good little girl and her familiar, accompanied by three amputated males, go seeking a wizard who turns out to be a charlatan. The witches in *Oz* really have superhuman powers, but the male figures do not. Mr. Updike's Land of Oz is the real America, but the men in it need a lot more than self-confidence; there's no Glinda the Good, and the Dorothy-like ingenue is a "wimp" who gets her comeuppance. It's the three witches of Eastwick who go back, in the end, to the equivalent of Kansas—marriage, flat and gray maybe, but at least known.

The Witches of Eastwick could be and probably will be interpreted as just another episode in the long-running American serial called "Blaming Mom." The Woman-as-Nature-as-magic-as-powerful-as-bad-Mom package has gone the rounds before, sometimes accompanied by the smell of burning. If prattle of witchcraft is heard in the land, can the hunt be far behind? Mr. Updike provides no blameless way of being female. Hackles will rise, the word *backlash* will be spoken; but anyone speaking it should look at the men in this book, who, while proclaiming their individual emptiness, are collectively, offstage, blowing up Vietnam. That's *male* magic. Men, say the witches more than once, are full of rage because they can't make babies, and even male babies have at their center "that aggressive vacuum." Shazam indeed!

A Martian might wonder at the American propensity for tossing the power football. Each sex hurls it at the other with amazing regularity, each crediting the other with more power than the other thinks it has, and the characters in this book join in the game with glee. The aim seems to be the avoidance of responsibility, the reversion to a childlike state of Huckleberry Finn–like "freedom." What the witches want from the Devil is to play without consequences. But all the Devil can really offer is temptation; hot-tubbery has its price, and the Devil must have his due; with the act of creation comes irreversibility, and guilt.

Mr. Updike takes "sisterhood is powerful" at its word and imagines it literally. What if sisterhood really is powerful? What will the sisters use their "powers" for? And what—given human nature, of which Mr. Updike takes not too bright a view—what then? Luckily these witches are only interested in the "personal" rather than the "political"; otherwise they might have done something unfrivolous, like inventing the hydrogen bomb.

The Witches of Eastwick is an excursion rather than a destination. Like its characters, it indulges in metamorphoses, reading at one moment like Kierkegaard, at the next like Swift's *Modest Proposal*, and at the next like Archie comics, with some John Keats thrown in. This quirkiness is part of its charm, for, despite everything, charming it is. As for the witches themselves, there's a strong suggestion that they are products of Eastwick's— read America's—own fantasy life. If so, it's as well to know about it. That's the serious reason for reading this book.

The other reasons have to do with the skill and inventiveness of the writing; the accuracy of the detail; the sheer energy of the witches; and, above all, the practicality of the charms. The ones for getting suitable husbands are particularly useful. You want a rich one for a change? First you sprinkle a tuxedo with your perfume and your precious bodily fluids and then . . .

2

Laughter vs. Death

W hen I was in Finland a few years ago for an international writers' conference, I had occasion to say a few paragraphs in public on the subject of pornography. The context was a discussion of political repression, and I was suggesting the possibility of a link between the two. The immediate result was that a male journalist took several large bites out of me. Prudery and pornography are two halves of the same coin, said he, and I was clearly a prude. What could you expect from an Anglo-Canadian? Afterward, a couple of pleasant Scandinavian men asked me what I had been so worked up about. All "pornography" means, they said, is graphic depictions of whores, and what was the harm in that?

Not until then did it strike me that the male journalist and I had two entirely different things in mind. By "pornography" he meant naked bodies and sex. I, on the other hand, had recently been doing the research for my novel *Bodily Harm*, and was still in a state of shock from some of the material I had seen, including the Ontario Board of Film Censors' "outtakes." By "pornography" I meant women getting their nipples snipped off with garden shears, having meat hooks stuck into their vaginas, being disemboweled; little girls being raped; men (yes, there are some men) being smashed to a pulp and forcibly sodomized. The cutting edge of pornography, as far as I could see, was no longer simple old copulation, hanging from the chandelier or otherwise: it was death, messy, explicit, and highly sadistic. I explained this to the nice Scandinavian men. "Oh, but that's just the United States," they said. "Everyone knows they're sick." In their country, they said, violent "pornography" of that kind was not permitted on television or in movies; indeed, excessive violence of any kind was not permitted. They had drawn a clear line between erotica, which earlier studies had shown did not incite men to more aggressive and brutal behavior toward women, and violence, which later studies indicated did.

Sometime after that I was in Saskatchewan, where, because of some of the scenes in *Bodily Harm,* I found myself on an open-line radio show answering questions about "pornography." Almost no one who phoned in was in favor of it, but again they weren't talking about the same stuff I was, because they hadn't seen it. Some of them were all set to stamp out bathing suits and negligees and, if possible, any depictions of the female body whatsoever. God, it was implied, did not approve of female bodies, and sex of any kind, including that practiced by bumblebees, should be shoved back into the dark, where it belonged. I had more than a suspicion that *Lady Chatterley's Lover,* Margaret Laurence's *The Diviners,* and indeed most books by most serious modern authors would have ended up as confetti if left in the hands of these callers.

For me, these two experiences illustrate the two poles of the emotionally heated debate that is now thundering around this issue. They also underline the desirability and even the necessity of defining the terms. "Pornography" is now one of those catchalls, like "Marxism" and "feminism," that have become so broad they can mean almost anything, ranging from certain verses in the Bible, ads for skin lotion, and sex texts for children to the contents of *Penthouse,* Naughty '90s postcards, and films with titles containing the word *Nazi* that show vicious scenes of torture and killing. It's easy to say that sensible people can tell the difference. Unfortunately, opinions on what constitutes a sensible person vary.

But even sensible people tend to lose their cool when they start talking about this subject. They soon stop talking and start yelling, and the name-calling begins. Those in favor of censorship (which may include groups not noticeably in agreement on other issues, such as some feminists and religious fundamentalists) accuse the others of exploiting women through the use of degrading images, contributing to the corruption of children, and adding to the general climate of violence and threat in which both women and children live in this society; or, though they may not give much of a hoot about actual women and children, they invoke moral standards and God's supposed aversion to "filth," "smut," and deviated *perversion*, which may mean ankles.

The camp in favor of total "freedom of expression" often comes out howling as loudly as the Romans would have if told they could no longer have innocent fun watching the lions eat up Christians. It, too, may include segments of the population who are not natural bedfellows: those who proclaim their God-given right to freedom—including the freedom to tote guns, drive when drunk, drool over chicken porn, and get off on videotapes of women being raped and beaten—may be waving the same anticensorship banner as responsible liberals who fear the return of Mrs. Grundy, or gay groups for whom sexual emancipation involves the concept of "sexual theater." *Whatever turns you on* is a handy motto, as is *A man's home is his castle* (and if it includes a dungeon with beautiful maidens strung up in chains and bleeding from every pore, that's his business).

Meanwhile, theoreticians theorize and speculators speculate. Is today's pornography yet another indication of the hatred of the body, the deep mind-body split, that is supposed to pervade Western Christian society? Is it a backlash against the women's movement by men who are threatened by uppity female behavior in real life, so like to fantasize about women done up like outsize parcels, being turned into hamburger, kneeling at their feet in slavelike adoration, or sucking off guns? Is it a sign of collective impotence, of a generation of men who can't relate to real women at all but have to make do with bits of celluloid and paper? Is the current flood just a result of smart marketing and aggressive promotion by the money men in what has now become a multibillion-dollar industry? If they were selling movies about men getting their testicles stuck full of knitting needles by women with swastikas on their sleeves, would they do as well, or is this penchant somehow peculiarly male? If so, why? Is pornography a power trip rather than a sex one? Some say that those ropes, chains, muzzles, and other restraining devices are an argument for the immense power female sexuality still wields in the male imagination: you don't put these things on dogs unless you're afraid of them. Others, more literary, wonder about the shift from the nineteenth-century magic woman or femme fatale image to the lollipop-licker, airhead, or turkey-carcass treatment of women in porn today. The proporners don't care much about theory; they merely demand product. The antiporners don't care about it in the final analysis either; there's dirt on the street, and they want it cleaned up, now.

It seems to me that this conversation, with its *You're-a-prude/You're a pervert* dialectic, will never get anywhere as long as we continue to think of this material as just "entertainment." Possibly we're deluded by the packaging, the format: magazine, book, movie, theatrical presentation. We're used to thinking of these things as part of the "entertainment industry," and we're used to thinking of ourselves as free adult people who ought to be able to see any kind of "entertainment" we want to. That was what the First Choice pay-TV debate was all about. After all, it's only entertainment, right? Entertainment means fun, and only a killjoy would be antifun. What's the harm?

This is obviously the central question: *What's the harm?* If there isn't any real harm to any real people, then the antiporners can tsk-tsk and/or throw up as much as they like, but they can't rightfully expect that the no-harm position is far from being proven.

(For instance, there's a clear-cut case for banning—as the Canadian government has proposed—movies, photos, and videos that depict children engaging in sex with adults: real children are used to make the movies, and hardly anybody thinks this is ethical. The possibilities for coercion are too great.)

To shift the viewpoint, I'd like to suggest three other models for looking at "pornography"—and here I mean the violent kind.

Hate literature Those who find the idea of regulating pornographic materials repugnant because they think it's fascist or Communist or otherwise not in accordance with the principles of an open democratic society should consider that Canada has made it illegal to disseminate material that may lead to hatred toward any group because of race or religion. I suggest that if pornography of the violent kind depicted these acts being done predominantly to Chinese, to blacks, or to Catholics, it would be off the market immediately under the present laws. Why is hate literature

15

illegal? Because whoever made the law thought that such material might incite real people to do really awful things to other real people. The human brain is to a certain extent a computer: garbage in, garbage out. We only hear about the extreme cases (like that of American multimur-derer Ted Bundy) in which pornography has contributed to the death and/or mutilation of women and/or men. Although pornography is not the only factor involved in the creation of such deviance, it certainly has upped the ante by suggesting both a variety of techniques and the social acceptability of such actions. Nobody knows yet what effect this stuff is having on the less psychotic.

Sex education Studies have shown that a large part of the market for all kinds of porn, soft and hard, is drawn from the sixteen-to-twenty-year-old population of young men. Boys used to learn about sex on the street; or (in Italy, according to Fellini movies) from friendly whores; or, in more genteel surroundings, from girls, their parents, or, once upon a time, in school, more or less. Now porn has been added, and sex education in the schools is rapidly being phased out. The buck has been passed, and boys are being taught that all women secretly like to be raped and that real men get high on scooping out women's digestive tracts.

Boys learn their concept of masculinity from other men; is this what most men want them to be learning? If word gets around that rapists are "normal" and even admirable men, will boys feel that to be normal, admirable, and masculine they will have to be rapists? Human beings are enormously flexible, and how they turn out depends a lot on how they're educated, by the society in which they're immersed as well as by their teachers. In a society that advertises and glorifies rape or even implicitly condones it, more women get raped. It becomes socially acceptable. And at a time when men and the traditional male role have taken a lot of flak and men are confused and casting around for an acceptable way of being male (and, in some cases, not getting much comfort from women on that score), this must be at times a pleasing thought.

It would be naive to think of violent pornography as just harmless entertainment. It's also an educational tool and a powerful propaganda device. What happens when boy educated on porn meets girl brought up on

16

Harlequin romances? The clash of expectations can be heard around the block. She wants him to get down on his knees with a ring; he wants her to get down on all fours with a ring in her nose. Can this marriage be saved?

Addiction Pornography has certain things in common with such addictive substances as alcohol and drugs: for some, though by no means for all, it induces chemical changes in the body, which the user finds exciting and pleasurable. It also appears to attract a "hard core" of habitual users and a penumbra of those who use it occasionally but aren't dependent on it in any way. There are also significant numbers of men who aren't much interested in it, not because they're undersexed but because real life is satisfying their needs, which may not require as many appliances as those of users.

For the "hard core," pornography may function as alcohol does for the alcoholic: tolerance develops, and a little is no longer enough. This may account for the short viewing time and fast turnover in porn theaters. Mary Brown, chairwoman of the Ontario Board of Film Censors, estimates that for every one mainstream movie requesting entrance to Ontario, there is one porno flick. Not only the quantity consumed but also the quality of explicitness must escalate, which may account for the growing violence: once the big deal was breasts, then it was genitals, then copulation, then that was no longer enough, and the hard users had to have more. The ultimate kick is death, and after that, as the Marquis de Sade so boringly demonstrated, multiple death.

The existence of alcoholism has not led us to ban social drinking. On the other hand, we do have laws about drinking and driving, excessive drunkenness, and other abuses of alcohol that may result in injury or death to others.

This leads us back to the key question: what's the harm? Nobody knows, but this society should find out fast, before the saturation point is reached. The Scandinavian studies that showed a connection between depictions of sexual violence and increased impulse toward it by male viewers would be a starting point, but many more questions remain to be raised as well as answered. What, for instance, is the crucial difference between men who are users and men who are not? Does using affect a man's relationship with actual women, and if so, adversely? Is there a clear line between erotica and violent pornography, or are they on an escalating continuum? Is this a "men versus women" issue, with all men secretly siding with the proporners and all women secretly siding against? (I think not; there *are* lots of men who don't think that running their true love through the Cuisinart is the best way they can think of to spend a Saturday night, and they're just as nauseated by films of someone else doing it as women are.) Is pornography merely an expression of the sexual confusion of this age or an active contributor to it?

Nobody wants to go back to the age of official repression, when even piano legs were referred to as "limbs" and had to wear pantaloons to be decent. Neither do we want to end up in George Orwell's *1984*, in which pornography is turned out by the state to keep the proles in a state of torpor, sex itself is considered dirty, and the approved practice it only for reproduction. But Rome under the emperors isn't such a good model either.

If all men and women respected each other, if sex were considered joyful and life-enhancing instead of a wallow in germ-filled glop, if everyone were in love all the time, if, in other words, many people's lives were more satisfactory for them than they appear to be now, pornography might just go away on its own. But since this is obviously not happening, we as a society are going to have to make some informed and responsible decisions about how to deal with it.

3

Review:

Difficult Loves
by Italo Calvino

*D*ifficult Loves is a beautifully translated collection of early stories by the highly regarded Italian writer Italo Calvino. Mr. Calvino is perhaps best known in North America for his antinovel *If on a Winter's Night a Traveler*, for his pseudo-geography *Invisible Cities*, and for *Italian Folk Tales*, which really are. What you think of the fictions of the mature Calvino will depend partly on whether you consider flirtation a delightful way of passing the time or a boring waste of it, and whether, after a magic show, you feel charmed or had. It's possible to get the sense you're being toyed with, that Mr. Calvino is fiddling with you and doesn't much care whether or not Rome is burning; that "reality" and "truth" are, for him, categories irrelevant to the hermetic world of art. There's something to be said for this stance: why should a rose—or Isak Dinesen, for that matter—have to demonstrate social relevance? Still, if you go too far into the palace of artifice you can turn into a rococo clock, a fate Mr. Calvino has so far been adroit enough to avoid.

All the more interesting, then, to open *Difficult Loves* expecting tricks with string, and to realize that instead you are watching a writer in the process of getting where he later got. These are very early stories indeed: the earliest were written in 1945, when Mr. Calvino was a damp-eared twenty-two, and the latest date from the 1950s, when he was in his early thirties.

Of the four sections in the book, the first, "Riviera Stories," is the most realistic in its inclinations. The stories are hardly stories at all but studies, carefully observed and detailed sketches of people in certain landscapes, social situations, and postures. Already Mr. Calvino is displaying a sensual delight in description—a painterliness, if you like—but these pieces are for the most part fragmentary, like Leonardo's studies of hands. Among them, two—"A Goatherd at Luncheon" and "Man in the Wasteland"—are less embryonic, but it is not until the second section, "Wartime Stories," that the fingerprints of a major talent begin to be visible. From the subject matter—peasants and partisans versus German soldiers and Italian Fascists— you might expect shrapnel and gore, death and squalor, and some is in fact provided. But the surprise is the freshness—the sweetness, even—that is present despite it. "Animal Woods," about a German soldier lost in a forest in which the peasants have hidden their animals, has the clear charm of a fairy tale, and "One of the Three Is Still Alive" manages to turn another German—a naked, harried one this time—into a sort of momentary Adam.

In the third section, "Postwar Stories," we find ourselves in an urban land-scape reminiscent of early Fellini films and populated with waifs and strays, eccentrics, fat and/or distorted prostitutes, and men given to bizarre excesses. The baroque blends with the grotesque in the sensuous gluttony of "Theft in a Pastry Shop." And "Desire in November" is every fur fetishist's dream come true.

Finally, in the fourth section, "Stories of Love and Loneliness," Mr. Calvino hits what was to become increasingly his stride. Of the eight sto-ries in this section, five explore the borderline that divides (or does it?) illu-sion from reality, the imagination from the outside world, art from its subject matter. The photographer who ends by being unable to photo-graph anything but other photographs and destroys his love affair in the process; the man who can't enjoy a real woman because he's too involved in reading about an imaginary one; the nearsighted man who must choose between seeing and being seen; and the poet for whom woman, nature, silence, and serenity form one set, while men, civilization, words, and suf-focation form another—these are early articulations of the illusionist's dilemma, of the complex relationship of the artist to a world he can't quite believe in as long as he views it as material for an art that is not quite believable either. It is the artist's love for the "real" world that drives him to transform it into an artifact, and, paradoxically—according to logic—to deny it. As the photographer says, the minute you start saying of something, "'Ah, how beautiful! We must photograph it!'" you are already close to the view of the person who thinks that everything that is not photographed is lost, as if it had never existed.

Difficult Loves has some of the fascination of a photo album (the author at twenty-two, the author at twenty-six, the author at thirty), but it has a lot more to offer than that. The quirkiness and grace of the writing, the originality of the imagination at work, the occasional incandescence of vision, and a certain lovable nuttiness make this collection well worth reading, and for more than archaeological reasons.

4

That Certain Thing Called
the Girlfriend

*And Ruth said, Entreat me not to leave thee, or to return from following after
thee: for whither thou goest, I will go; and where thou lodgest, I will lodge: thy
people shall be my people, and thy God my God: Where thou diest, will I die,
and there will I be buried: the Lord do so to me, and more also, if aught but
death part thee and me.*—Ruth 1:16–17

*Men are irrelevant. Women are happy or unhappy, fulfilled or unfulfilled, and
it has nothing to do with men.*—Fay Weldon, *Down Among the Women*

In recent years, much of the energy of women novelists—and they
have been energetic—has come from the sense that they were
opening forbidden doors, saying the hitherto unsayable, raising to
the level of art, or at least of the written word, material that was considered either too dirty or too abnormal or just too trivial to merit inclusion.
"Women's weeds" is a phrase that has stuck with me from high school
Shakespeare days: it suggests vacant lots rank with random and negligible
but tough and persistent flowers. Novels by women of the past fifteen
years have been full of women's weeds.

These writers have led us, with a certain relentless glee, through the
scrublands of domesticity, replete with porridge pots and soggy diapers and
the thorny jungles of heterosexual love, and through the architecture of
the family: mother-daughter, father-daughter, sibling-sibling. At no time

in literary history have women been examined, from toenails to neuroses, in such microscopic detail. But what lies beyond the last frontier? What turns out to be the latest on the list of unmentionables in female life now seen to deserve mention? Could it be . . . best girlfriends?

It seems so. In the last small while there has been a spate of novels by such leading writers as Toni Morrison, Joyce Carol Oates, Gail Godwin, and Alice Walker examining the relationships between women—not the sisters, the cousins and the aunts, the grannies and the mothers of books such as Joan Chase's *During the Reign of the Queen of Persia* and Marilynne Robinson's *Housekeeping*, not the lovers in the many novels featuring lesbians that have appeared since Radclyffe Hall's *Well of Loneliness* and Rita Mae Brown's *Rubyfruit Jungle*—but women bound together by ties more tenuous, though no less intense. Chums, as they used to be called; though in the hands of these writers, the term acquires a somewhat darker tone. Of course, best girlfriends are not new to the novel, or to novels of certain sorts.

We're familiar with them from books we read as girls. "I solemnly swear to be faithful to my bosom friend, Diana Barry, as long as the sun and moon shall endure," says Anne of Green Gables in her passionate prepubescent but also pre-Freudian way, recalling not only the Book of Ruth but also *Romeo and Juliet*. The original novelistic treatment of girls' boarding schools is perhaps the first section of *Jane Eyre*, which chronicles Jane's friendship with the dying Helen. But the English boarding-school novel is full of these highly charged worshipful duos, as epitomized by the works of the British children's author Enid Blyton, and by Antonia White's exemplary novel *Frost in May*. By and large, however, the novel's assumption has been that when you become a woman, you put away girlish things, and replace Diana with Gilbert Blythe, sickly Helen with sickly Mr. Rochester.

The nineteenth century was less queasy on this subject, both in literature and in life, than was the mid-twentieth, as witness Charlotte Brontë's *Shirley* and, recently, Doris Grumback's historical re-creation of a devoted—and much admired—pair in *The Ladies*. Queen Victoria's famous pronouncement that exempted women from antihomosexual laws because the queen didn't believe there were such things as lesbians reflected the contemporary belief that women's friendships of all kinds were beyond

23

sexual suspicion; and Carroll Smith-Rosenberg, in *Disorderly Conduct: Visions of Gender in Victorian America,* has chronicled the extent to which real-life women, faced with marriage to men from whom they felt distant because of their widely disparate upbringings and spheres of activity, relied on other women for intimacy and emotional intensity.

"The female friendship of the nineteenth century, the long-lived, intimate, loving friendship between two women, is an excellent example of the type of historical phenomena that most historians know something about, few have thought much about and virtually no one has written about," Mrs. Smith-Rosenberg writes. "It is one aspect of the female experience which, consciously or unconsciously, we have chosen to ignore. Yet an abundance of manuscript evidence suggests that eighteenth- and nineteenth-century women routinely formed emotional ties with other women. Such deeply felt same-sex friendships were casually accepted in American society. Indeed, from at least the late eighteenth through mid-nineteenth century, a female world of varied and yet highly structured relationships appears to have been an essential aspect of American society. These relationships ranged from the supportive love of sisters, through the enthusiasms of adolescent girls, to sensual avowals of love by mature women. It was a world in which men made but a shadowy appearance." What was true in America was true also in England, as many collections of letters testify.

Considering the prevalence of these friendships, "both sensual and platonic," as Carroll Smith-Rosenberg says, what's remarkable about the nineteenth-century novel, at least those that have come down to us, is that it doesn't deal with them more fully. Catherine Earnshaw in *Wuthering Heights* and Maggie Tulliver in *The Mill on the Floss* are splendid isolates; so is Jane Eyre after childhood. In *Middlemarch* George Eliot's Dorothea Brooke has a confidante in her sister, as do many of Jane Austen's heroines, but the main stories are about male-female courtship; friends are sidekicks. Isabel Archer, in Henry James's *Portrait of a Lady*, has one good friend, but this is a minor thread. Many female friendships in novels by men are seen as downright sinister: Amelia in Thackeray's *Vanity Fair*, for instance, is trifled with quite callously by Becky Sharpe, her schoolgirl friend; James's Milly Theale in *Wings of the Dove* is exploited and betrayed by her female friend, and in *Carmilla* by Sheridan Le Fanu the devoted and passionate female friend turns out to be, literally, a vampire. Adult women, so the novel in general had it, should concentrate their attentions on men, not only because that was where love and money were to be found, but also because women were either minor players, broken reeds, or snakes. The gap between life as it was lived by women, and life as portrayed in novels by both men and women, is of interest.

Possibly, Victorian novelists wrote so little about women's friendships because the perceived subject matter of the novel as a form—from Moll Flanders to Madame Bovary—was relentlessly heterosexual, though male-male friendships were frequently depicted. Perhaps it was female-audience demand: women's friendships were all real-life, romance was escape. Or perhaps it was connected to the fact that the publishing establishment was overwhelmingly male.

But that was the nineteenth century; what about the twentieth? When I was growing up in the 1950s, Ruth's eloquent pledge of loyalty to her mother-in-law Naomi (her mother-in-law!) had become a pop song, sung breathlessly by a woman and obviously directed to a man. As for mothers-in-law, they were jokes told by men. Serious literature was not Enid Blyton but Hemingway and Fitzgerald or, for the existentially minded, Sartre and Beckett. Female-female relationships were the cattiness of *The Women* by Clare Boothe Luce or Lillian Hellman's *Little Foxes*, and best girlfriends were for discussing the real business of life—boyfriends.

Freudianism had swept through same-sex relationships like the plague, and neither men nor women loaded these with too much intimacy or intensity on pain of being thought abnormal. Then years earlier there had been the Second World War, and although it had thrown women back on each other's company, it may have caused them to idealize the absent male even more than usual. Despite the Wonder Woman comic and its all-girl Amazon island, woman-woman friendship was considered something you did in your spare time, old-age old-maidishness with another old maid a thing to be dreaded.

That was the official version, but it was probably not the only real one. Mary McCarthy's 1963 novel *The Group*, a forerunner of the current crop of women-centered novels, suggests that even in the 1950s a substratum of women's friendships underlay all the surface heterosexual cheerleading.

Miss McCarthy examines this web of female relationships with irony and a by no means uncritical eye, but it's clear at least to the women in the book that part of the meaning of their lives comes not from their status in the world of men, but from their status in their own world, a world that persists beyond their college years far into their adult existence. That their queen bee and chief arbiter of taste turns out to be a lesbian is perhaps inevitable given the Freud-haunted times.

From England there was Fay Weldon's 1972 *Down Among the Women*, which follows a batch of women through domestic peregrinations and interactions with one another. Marilyn French's *Women's Room* came later, during the heat of some rediscoveries, among them the fact that women are important to one another. Both these books, however, are wide-ranging social-overview novels; they deal with many kinds of relationships. But they give those between women friends considerably more space than was customary in fiction. The latest batch includes novels less schematic than *The Group*, less homebound than *Down Among the Women*, less overtly political than *The Women's Room*, and they focus on single relationships rather than multiple ones. Perhaps for this reason, the female relationships seem deeper, more passionate and complex. Two recent novels by black women writers suggest their scope and central interests. In Alice Walker's *Color Purple*, for instance, the best, most loving, most enduring relationship in the life of the heroine, Celie, is that with her husband's onetime mistress Shug Avery, a relationship that includes sex but is by no means limited to it. And in Toni Morrison's dense and tragic novel *Sula* the emphasis is on the girlhood friendship between Nell and Sula, which passes through estrangement but returns to Nell's final realization, after Sula's death, of Nell's love for her:

> 'All that time, all that time, I thought I was missing Jude.' And the loss pressed down on her chest and came up into her throat. 'We was girls together,' she said as though explaining something. 'O Lord, Sula,' she cried, 'girl, girl, girlgirlgirl.'
>
> It was a fine cry—loud and long—but it had no bottom and no top, just circles and circles of sorrow.

In both these novels, one of each pair of women is more conventional, the other more exotic, flamboyant, and rebellious. In each case they share a man: Shug is Celie's husband's mistress, Sula seduces Nell's husband on a whim. But in both there is a sense that the friendship creates a synthesis, a completion, that is larger than each woman separately. "Never was no difference between you," Sula's grandmother says to Nell. "Just alike." These are not icing-sugar friendships, all sweetness and teacups. They are complex and important, and they include pain, anger, and feelings of betrayal, jealousy, and hatred, as well as love.

Sociologists might have something to say about why black women writers were among the first on this turf: they might cite the prevalence of households headed by women, the necessity of female support systems. Perhaps black women writers were less likely to accept the premises of the traditional novel because they were more interested in expressing truths about the life they saw around them, truths not available to them in white fiction. But meaningful friendships between women were not and are not exclusive to black society; there are even statistics on it, for what they are worth. In recent polls, 53 percent of the women questioned said that their closest friendships were with women, and women appeared to have closer friendships with women than men did with men. This may be self-evident to women who count themselves among the 53 percent; what is not self-evident is why it has taken so long for these friendships to appear as central plot lines in mainstream fiction.

But now they have. When such things turn up in successful television shows, such as *Cagney and Lacey* and *Kate and Allie*, you can assume someone is gambling on the possibility that large chunks of the female viewing audience must now be interested in—surprise!—other women. *And* when Bantam Books makes a bid for blockbuster status with a novel along the same lines, you can be sure of it. Iris Rainer Dart's *Beaches* (1985), a sort of young adult novel for adults, offers a not-unexpected pairing: conventional, repressed, somewhat wimpy Bertie playing adoring Amelia to Cee Cee Bloom's extroverted, clever, brash, and taboo-breaking Becky Sharp. Cee Cee is that figure so beloved in American popular mythology, the foulmouthed but good-hearted sequined floozy who comes through in a pinch, a sort of Mae West crossed with Bette Midler; Bertie, on the other hand, is *Good Housekeeping* crossed with *Mademoiselle*. After

27

many ups and downs, including estrangement over Cee Cee's presumed dabbling with Bertie's unbelievably awful husband (she's innocent, and Walt Disney has an option on the film), Bertie dies and Cee Cee is left with Bertie's daughter, who is a cross between the two of them. We are right back in the world described by Carroll Smith-Rosenberg, in which men have "but a shadowy appearance."

Men drop even more deeply into the shadows in novels about lesbians. Jane Rule's elegant and intricate 1970 novel *This Is Not for You* traces the interactions between two friends—Kate, the adorer, secretly lesbian, who eventually chooses solitude, and Esther, the adored one, a spiritual idealist who eventually chooses a silent order of nuns. Something like this is the underlying state of affairs in *The Magnificent Spinster* by May Sarton (1985), which is perhaps less novel than tribute. The adorer is the aptly named Ruth, once a student of the worshiped Jane Reid, who later becomes her lifelong but never fully accessible friend. Ruth, too, discovers her own lesbianism; Jane Reid, too, remains out of reach as a lover. Both novels are, in their different ways, meditations on spiritual virginity, on what saintliness and untouchability do to their devotees. It is the very admirability of the adored women, their childlike innocence, that sets them apart.

When the relationship is between an older woman and a younger one, the story often takes on unmistakably romantic overtones. That there is no overt sex only makes the comparison with novels about heterosexual romance more valid, since the hallmark of such novels—at least until recently—has been suppressed passion: witness *Gone with the Wind.* Just so, *The Finishing School* by Gail Godwin (1985) involves an intriguing older woman and a young girl's infatuation with her. Ursula de Vane not only has a pretentious name, she also has pretensions. She is forty-four and short of success, whereas Justin is fourteen and impressionable. Ursula takes on Justin as a sort of protégée; but this attempt to play Pygmalion, to make Justin her creature and shadow, is ultimately sinister because it is self-serving, and it has tragic consequences when Ursula's feet of clay are revealed and Justin cannot forgive the destruction of her own partially self-created illusion. Yet the two are kindred spirits, as Anne of Green Gables would have said, in spite of their betrayals of one another. "Despite everything that happened," Justin says later of Ursula, "I have absorbed you. As long as I live you live in me." At the end of the book she says, "Such possessions are rare now. I mean by another person." The "possession" has, finally, been educational for her, though possibly not for Ursula.

Finally, in an even darker vein, Joyce Carol Oates, in *Solstice* (1985), gives the theme yet another turn of the screw, as she is wont to do with themes. This is a shadowy, rich, suggestive book in which the word *possession* does not need quotation marks. If there's an echo of any nineteenth-century motif here, it's not from the devoted letter-writers collected by Carroll Smith-Rosenberg; rather it's from the vampire novel *Carmilla*, except that this time the vampirism is mutual. These two women have their psychic fangs sunk deeply into each other's necks.

Again, the pairing is complementary. The apparently weaker, more conventional, more insecure one is Monica, recently divorced and still shaky. The dominating eccentric is Sheila, a painter (watch out for those artists) with black eyes, "strong cheek bones," and a "long straight nose," who has dirty boots and who first appears riding up on a horse, just like the gothic hero she at first resembles. What she appears to hold for Monica is "a child-like offer of complicity, mutual recognition."

It doesn't take long for these two to get their hooks into each other. In a relationship that is erotic without being sensual or sexual—this is an eroticism of the psyche only—they slide into intimacy and then toward disaster. Each wants total territorial rights to the other, which each withholds. Sheila even goes so far as to hire a detective agency to keep an eye on Monica. To tease and torture Monica and keep her interested, Sheila hints at suicide, but Monica goes farther: she gets sick, refuses to call for help, and almost dies. Though all this is taking place ostensibly in Pennsylvania, not Transylvania, the inner landscape is one of moors, crags, and deserts—Brontë country, Bram Stoker country. Sheila has the last word: "We'll be friends for a long, long time," she says, "unless one of us dies." Considering what they've been through with each other, this is menacing rather than reassuring—a horror-house echo of Anne of Green Gables's pledge to little Diana.

Indeed, in this group of novels, the best-girlfriends motif turns out to be much less milk and water than you might have supposed back in 1955. The treatment runs the gamut from selfless idealism to pointy-toothed ego-devouring. What women may want in a friend is "that unconditional defender who always comes through," in the words of Iris Rainer Dart's promotional material; what they may get instead is something a good deal more problematical. Perhaps the reason it's taken women novelists so long to get around to dealing with women's friendships head on is that betrayal by a woman friend is the ultimate betrayal. In sexual love, betrayal is almost expected; if we don't allow for it, it's not for want of warning, because treacherous lovers are thoroughly built into popular mythology, from folk songs to pop songs to torch songs to Mom's advice. But who warns you about your best friend? Nell's clinching accusation to the dying Sula is, "We were friends." Because friendship is supposed to be unconditional, a free gift of the spirit, its violation is all the more unbearable.

Despite their late blooming, women's friendships are now firmly on the literary map as valid and multidimensional novelistic material.

5

True North

Land of the silver birch,
Home of the beaver,
Where still the mighty moose
Wanders at will,
Blue lake and rocky shore,
I will return once more;
Boom-diddy-boom-boom
Boom-biddy-boom-boom
Boo-OO-oo-oo-oom.
—Archaic Song

We sang this once, squatting around the papier-mâché magic mushroom in the Brownie pack, while pretending to be in Cub Scouts, or while watching marshmallows turn to melted Styrofoam on the ends of our sticks at some well-run, fairly safe summer camp in the wilds of Muskoka, Haliburton, or Algonquin Park. Then we grew up and found it corny. By that time we were into Jean-Paul Sartre and the lure of the nauseous. Finally, having reached the age of nostalgia, we rediscovered it on a cassette in The Children's Book Store, in a haunting version that invested it with all the emotional resonance we once thought it possessed, and bought it, under the pretense of giving our children a little ethnic musical background.

It brought tears to our eyes, not for simple reasons. Whales get to us that way, too, and whooping cranes, and other things hovering on the verge of extinction but still maintaining a tenuous foothold in the world of the actual. The beavers are doing all right—we know this because they just decimated our poplars—but the mighty moose is having a slimmer time of it. As for the blueness of the lakes, we worry about it: too blue and you've got acid rain.

Will we return once more, or will we go to Portugal instead? It depends, we have to admit, partly on the exchange rate, and this makes us feel disloyal. I am, rather quixotically, in Alabama, teaching, even more quixotically, a course in Canadian literature. Right now we're considering Marian Engel's novel *Bear.* Since everything in Canada, outside Toronto, begins with geography, I've unfolded a large map of Ontario and traced the heroine's route north; I've located the mythical house of the book somewhere on the actual shore of Georgian Bay, northern edge. I've superimposed a same-scale map of Alabama on this scheme, to give the students an idea of the distances. In the north, space is larger than you think, because the points of reference are farther apart.

"Are there any words you came across that puzzled you?" I ask.

Blackfly comes up. A large black fly is proposed. I explain blackflies, their smallness, their multitude, their evil habits. It gives me a certain kick to do this: I'm competing with the local water moccasins.

Mackinaw. A raincoat? Not quite.

Loon. Tamarack. Reindeer moss. Portage. Moose. Wendigo.

"Why does she make Lucy the old Indian woman talk so funny?" they ask. Lucy, I point out, is not merely Indian but a *French-speaking* Indian. This, to them, is a weird concept.

The north is another country. It's also another language. Or languages.

Where is the north, exactly? It's not only a place but also a direction, and as such its location is relative: to the Mexicans, the United States is the north, to Americans, Toronto is, even though it's on roughly the same latitude as Boston.

Wherever it is for us, there's a lot of it. You stand in Windsor and imagine a line going north, all the way to the pole. The same line going south would end up in South America. That's the sort of map we grew up with, at the front of the classroom in Mercator projection, which made it look even bigger than it was, all that pink stretching on forever, with a few cities sprinkled along the bottom edge. It's not only geographical space, it's also space related to body image. When we face south, as we often do, our conscious mind may be directed down there, toward crowds, bright lights, some Hollywood version of fame and fortune, but the north is at the back of our minds, always. There's something, not someone, looking over our shoulders; there's a chill at the nape of the neck.

The north focuses our anxieties. Turning to face north, face the north, we enter our own unconscious. Always, in retrospect, the journey north has the quality of dream.

Where does the north begin?

Every province, every city, has its own road north. From Toronto you go up the 400. Where you cross the border, from here to there, is a matter of opinion. Is it the Severn River, where the Laurentian Shield granite appears suddenly out of the earth? Is it the sign announcing that you're halfway between the equator and the North Pole? Is it the first gift shop shaped like a wigwam, the first town—there are several—that proclaims itself the Gateway to the North?

As we proceed, the farms become fewer, rockier, more desperate-looking, the trees change their ratios, coniferous moving in on deciduous. More lakes appear, their shorelines scraggier. Our eyes narrow and we look at the clouds: the weather is important again.

One of us used to spend summers in a cottage in Muskoka, before the road went in, when you took the train, when there were big cruise ships there, and matronly motor launches, and tea dances at the hotels, and men in white flannels on the lawns, which there may still be. This was not just a cottage but also a Muskoka cottage, with boathouse and maid's quarters. Rich people went north in the summers then, away from cities

and crowds; that was before the cure for polio, which has made a difference. In this sort of north, they tried to duplicate the south, or perhaps
some dream of country life in England. In the living room there were
armchairs, glass-fronted bookcases, family photos in silver frames, stuffed
birds under glass bells. The north, as I said, is relative.

For me, the north used to be completely in force by the Trout Creek
planing mill. Those stacks of fresh-cut lumber were the true gateway to
the north, and north of that was North Bay, which used to be, to be blunt,
a bit of an armpit. It was beef-sandwich-on-white-bread-with-gravy-and-
canned-peas country. But no more. North Bay now has shopping malls,
and baskets of flowers hanging from lampposts above paving-stone sidewalks downtown. It has a Granite Club. It has the new, swish, carpeted
buildings of Laurentian University. It has gourmet restaurants. And in the
airport, where southbound DC-9s dock side by side with northbound
Twin Otters, there's a book rack in the coffee shop that features Graham
Greene and Kierkegaard, hardly standard airport fare.
    The south is moving north.

We bypass North Bay, which now has a bypass, creeping southerliness, and
do not go, this time, to the Dionne Quints Museum, where five little sil-
houettes in black play forever beside an old log cabin, complete with the
basket where they were packed in cotton wool, the oven where they were
warmed, the five prams, the five Communion dresses.
    Beyond North Bay there is a brief flurry of eccentricity—lawns popu-
lated with whole flocks of wooden-goose windmills—and then we go for
miles and miles past nothing but trees, meeting nothing but the occasional
truck loaded with lumber. This area didn't used to be called anything. Now
it's the Near North Travel Area. You can see signs telling you that. Near
what? we wonder uneasily. We don't want to be near. We want to be far.
    At last we see the Ottawa River, which is the border. There's a dam
across it, two dams, and an island between them. If there were a customs house, it would be here. A sign faces us saying *Bievenue*; out the

back window there's one saying *Welcome*. This was my first lesson in points of view.

And there, across the border in Quebec, in Témiscaming, is an image straight from my childhood: a huge mountain made of sawdust. I always wanted to slide down this sawdust mountain until I finally did, and discovered it was not like sand, dry and slippery, but damp and sticky and hard to get out of your clothes. This was my first lesson in the nature of illusion.

Continue past the sawdust mountain, past the baseball diamond, up the hill, and you're in the center of town, which is remarkable for at least three things: a blocks-long public rock garden, still flourishing after more than forty-five years; a pair of statues, one a fountain, that look as if they came straight from Europe, which I think they did; and the excellent, amazingly low-priced hamburgers you can get at the Boulevard Restaurant, where the decor, featuring last year's cardboard Santa Claus and a stuffed twenty-three-pound pike, is decidedly northern. Ask the owner about the pike and he'll tell you about one twice as big—forty-five pounds, in fact—that a fellow showed him strapped to the tailgate of his van, and that long, too.

You can have this conversation in either French or English: Témiscaming is a border town and a northern one, and the distinctions made here are as likely to be north-south as French-English. Up in these parts you'll hear as much grumbling, or more, about Québec City as you will about Ottawa, which is, after all, closer. Spit in the river and it gets to Ottawa, eh?

For the north, Témiscaming is old, settled, tidy, even a little prosperous-looking. But it's had its crises. Témiscaming is the resource economy personified. Not long ago it was a company town, and when the company shut down the mill, which would have shut down the town, too, the workers took the unprecedented step of trying to buy it. With some help they succeeded, and the result was Tembec, still going strong. But Témiscaming is still a one-industry town, like many northern towns, and its existence is thus precarious.

Not so long ago, logging was a different sort of business. The men went into the woods in winter, across the ice, using horse-drawn sledges, and set up camp. (You still come across these logging camps now and then in your travels through the lakes, abandoned, already looking as ancient as Roman aqueducts; more ancient, since there's been no upkeep.) They'd cut selectively, tree by tree, using axes and saws and the skills that were necessary to avoid being squashed or hacked. They'd skid the trees to the ice; in the spring, after the ice went out, there would be a run down the nearest fast river to the nearest sawmill.

Now it's done with bulldozers and trucks, and the result is too often a blitzed shambles; cut everything, leave a wreck of dead and, incidentally, easily flammable branches behind. Time is money. Don't touch the shoreline, though; we need that for tourists. In some places, the forest is merely a scrim along the water. In behind it's been hollowed out.

Those who look on the positive side say it's good for the blueberries.

Sometimes we went the other way, across to Sudbury, the trees getting smaller and smaller and finally disappearing as you approached. Sudbury was another magic place of my childhood. It was like interplanetary travel, which we liked to imagine, which was still just imagination in those days. With its heaps of slag and its barren shoulders of stone, it looked like the moon. Back then, we tell the children, before there were washer-dryers and you used something called a wringer washer and hung the sheets out on something called a clothesline, when there weren't even colored sheets but all sheets were white, when Rinso white and its happy little washday song were an item, and "whiter than white" was a catchphrase and female status really did have something to do with your laundry, Sudbury was a housewife's nightmare. We knew people there; the windowsills in their houses were always gray.

Now the trees are beginning to come back because they built higher smokestacks. But where is all that stuff going now?

The Acid Rain Dinner, in Toronto's Sheraton Centre, in 1985. The first of these fund-raising events was fairly small. But the movement has grown, and this dinner is huge. The leaders of all three provincial parties are here. So is the minister of the environment from the federal government. So are several labor leaders, and several high-ranking capitalists, and representatives of numerous northerly chambers of commerce, summer residents' associations, tourist-camp runners, outfitters. Wishy-washy urban professionals who say "frankly" a lot bend elbows with huntin', shootin', fishin', and cussin' burnt-necks who wouldn't be caught dead saying "frankly." This is not a good place to be overheard saying that actually acid rain isn't such a bad thing because it gets rid of all that brown scum and leeches in the lake, or who cares because you can water-ski anyway. Teddy Kennedy, looking like a bulky sweater, is the guest speaker. Everyone wears a little gold pin in the shape of a raindrop. It looks like a tear.

Why has acid rain become the collective Canadian nightmare? Why is it—as a good cause—bigger than baby-seal-bashing? The reasons aren't just economic, although there are lots of those, as the fishing-camp people and foresters will tell you. It's more than that, and cognate with the outrage aroused by the uninvited voyage of the American icebreaker *Polar Sea* through the Northwest Passage, where almost none of us ever goes. It's territorial, partly; partly a felt violation of some area in us that we hardly ever think about unless it's invaded or tampered with. It's the neighbors throwing guck into our yard. It's our childhood dying.

On location, in summer and far from the glass and brass of the Sheraton Centre, we nervously check our lakes. Leeches still in place? Have the crayfish, among the first to go, gone yet? (We think in terms of "yet.") Are the loons reproducing? Have you seen any young? Any minnows? How about the lichen on the rocks? These inventories have now become routine, and that is why we're willing to fork out a hundred dollars a plate to support our acid-rain lobbyists in Washington. A summer without loons is unthinkable, but how do you tell that to people who don't know it because they've never had any to begin with?

We're driving through Glencoe, in the Highlands of Scotland. It's imposing, as a landscape: bleak, large, bald, apparently empty. We can see why the Scots took so well to Canada. Yet we know that the glens and crags round about are crawling with at least a thousand campers, rock climbers, and other seekers after nature; we also know that, at one end of this glen, the Campbells butchered the MacDonalds in the seventeenth century, thus propelling both of them into memorable history. Go walking here and you'll find things human—outlines of stone fences now overgrown, shards of abandoned crofts.

In Europe, every scrap of land has been claimed, owned, reowned, fought over, captured, bled on. The roads are the only no-man's-land. In northern Canada, the roads are civilization, owned by the collective human *we*. Off the road is *other*. Try walking in it, and you'll soon find out why all the early traffic here was by water. "Impenetrable wilderness" is not just verbal.

And suppose you get off the road. Suppose you get lost. Getting lost, elsewhere and closer to town, is not knowing exactly where you are. You can always ask, even in a foreign country. In the north, getting lost is not knowing how to get out.

You can get lost on a lake, of course, but getting lost in the forest is worse. It's tangly in there, and dim, and one tree does begin to look remarkably like another. The leaves and needles blot up sound, and you begin to feel watched—not by anyone, not by an animal even, or anything you can put a name to, just watched. You begin to feel judged. It's as if something is keeping an eye on you just to see what you will do.

What will you do? Which side of the tree does moss grow on, and here, where there are ferns and the earth is damp, or where it's dry as tinder, it seems that moss grows everywhere, or does not grow at all. Snippets of Boy Scout lore or truisms learned at summer camp come back to you, but scrambled. You tell yourself not to panic; you can always live off the land.

Easier said than done, you'd soon find. The Canadian Shield is a relatively foodless area, which is why even the Indians tended to pass through it, did not form large settlements except where there was arable land, and remained limited in numbers. This is not the Mekong Delta. If you had a gun you could shoot something, maybe, a red squirrel perhaps; but if you're lost you probably don't have a gun, or a fishing rod either. You could eat blueberries, or cattail stems, or crayfish, or other delicacies dimly remembered from stories about people who got lost in the woods and were found later in good health although somewhat thinner. You could cook some reindeer moss if you had matches.

Thus you pass on to fantasies about how to start a fire with a magnifying glass—you don't have one—or by rubbing two bits of stick together, a feat at which you suspect you would prove remarkably inept.

The fact is that not very many of us know how to survive in the north. Rumor has it that only one German prisoner of war ever made it out, although many made it out of the actual prisoner-of-war camps. The best piece of northern survival advice is: *Don't get lost.*

One way of looking at a landscape is to consider the typical ways of dying in it. Given the worst, what's the worst it could do? Will it be delirium from drinking salty water on the high seas, shriveling in the desert, snakebite in the jungle, tidal waves on a Pacific isle, volcanic fumes? In the north, there are several hazards. Although you're probably a lot safer there than you are on the highway at rush hour, given the odds, you still have to be a little wary.

Like most lessons of this sort, those about the north are taught by precept and example, but also, more enjoyably, by cautionary nasty tale. There is death by blackfly, the one about the fellow who didn't have his shirt cuffs tight enough in the spring and undressed at night only to find he was running with blood; the ones about the lost travelers who bloated up from too many bites and who, when found, were twice the size, unrecognizable, and dead. There is death from starvation, death by animal, death by forest fire; there is death from something called "exposure," which used to confuse me when I heard about men who exposed themselves: why would they intentionally do anything that fatal? There's death by thunderstorm, not to be sneered at: on the open lake, in one of the excessive northern midsummer thunderstorms, a canoe or a bush plane is a vulnerable target. The north is full of Struwwelpeter-like stories about people who didn't do as they were told and got struck by lightning. Above all, there are death by freezing and death by drowning. Your body's heat-loss rate in the water is twenty times that in air, and northern lakes are cold. Even in a life jacket, even holding on to the tipped canoe, you're at risk. Every summer the numbers pile up.

Every culture has its exemplary dead people, its hagiography of landscape martyrs, those unfortunates who, by their bad ends, seem to sum up
in one grisly episode what may be lurking behind the next rock for all of
us, all of us who enter the territory they once claimed as theirs. I'd say that
two of the top northern landscape martyrs are Tom Thomson, the painter
who was found mysteriously drowned near his overturned canoe with no
provable cause in sight, and the Mad Trapper of Rat River, also mysterious,
who became so thoroughly bushed that he killed a Mountie and shot two
others during an amazing wintertime chase before finally being mowed
down. In our retelling of these stories, mystery is a key element. So,
strangely enough, is a presumed oneness with the landscape in question.
The Mad Trapper knew his landscape so well he survived in it for weeks,
living off the land and his own bootlaces, eluding capture. One of the
hidden motifs in these stories is a warning: maybe it's not so good to get
too close to Nature.

I remember a documentary on Tom Thomson that ended, rather ominously, with the statement that the north had taken him to herself. This
was, of course, pathetic fallacy gone to seed, but it was also a comment on
our distrust of the natural world, a distrust that remains despite our
protests, our studies in the ethics of ecology, our elevation of "the environment" to a numinous noun, our save-the-tree campaigns. The question is,
would the trees save us, given the chance? Would the water, would the
birds, would the rocks? In the north, we have our doubts.

A bunch of us are sitting around the table, at what is now a summer cottage at Georgian Bay. Once it was a house, built by a local man for his
family, which finally totaled eleven children, after they'd outgrown this
particular house and moved to another. The original Findlay wood-burning
cookstove is still in the house, but so also are some electric lights and a
propane cooker, which have come since the end of the old days. In the old
days, this man somehow managed to scrape a living from the land: a little
of this, a little of that, some fishing here, some lumbering there, some
hunting in the fall. That was back when you shot to eat. "Scrape" is an
appropriate word: there's not much here between the topsoil and the rock.

We sit around the table and eat fish, among other things, caught by the children. Someone mentions the clams: there are still a lot of them, but who knows what's in them anymore? Mercury, lead, things like that. We pick at the fish. Someone tells me not to drink the tap water. I already have. "What will happen?" I ask. "Probably nothing," they reply. *Probably nothing* is a relatively recent phrase around here. In the old days, you ate what looked edible.

We are talking about the old days, as people often do once they're outside the cities. When exactly did the old days end? Because we know they did. The old days ended when the youngest of us was ten, fifteen, or twenty; the old days ended when the oldest of us was five, or twelve, or thirty. Plastic-hulled superboats are not old days, but ten-horsepower outboard motors, circa 1945, are. In the back porch there's an icebox, unused now, a simple utilitarian model from Eaton's, ice chamber in the top section, metal shelves in the bottom one. We all go and admire it. "I remember iceboxes," I say, and indeed I can dimly remember them; I must have been five. What bits of our daily junk—our toasters, our pocket computers—will soon become obsolete and therefore poignant? Who will stand around peering at them and admiring their design and the work that went into them, as we do with this icebox? "So this was a *toilet seat*," we think, rehearsing the future. "Ah! A *lightbulb*." The ancient syllables thick in our mouths.

The kids decided some time ago that all this chat is boring, and have asked if they can go swimming off the dock. They can, though they have to watch it, as this is a narrow place and speedboats tend to swoosh through, not always slowing down. Waste of gas, in the old days. Nobody then went anywhere just for pleasure; it was the war, and gas was rationed.

"Oh, *those* old days," says someone.

There goes a speedboat now, towing a man strapped in a kneeling position to some kind of board, looking as if he's had a terrible accident or is about to have one. This must be some newfangled variety of waterskiing.

"Remember Klim?" I say. The children come through, trailing towels. "What's Klim?" one asks, caught by the space-age sound of the word.

"Klim was 'milk' spelled backward," I say. "It was powdered milk."

"Yuk," they say.

"Not the same as now," I say. "It was whole milk, not skim; it wasn't instant. You had to beat it with an eggbeater." And even then some of it wouldn't dissolve. One of the treats of childhood was the little nodules of pure dry Klim that floated on top of your milk.

"There was also Pream," says someone. How revolutionary it seemed.

The children go down to take their chances in the risky motorized water. Maybe, much later, they will remember us sitting around the table, eating fish they themselves had caught, back when you could still (what? catch a fish? see a tree? What desolations lie in store, beyond the plasticized hulls and the knee-skiers?). By then we will be the old days, for them. We almost are already.

A different part of the north. We're sitting around the table, by lamp-light—it's still the old days here, no electricity—talking about bad hunters. Bad hunters, bad fishers, everyone has a story. You come upon a campsite, way in the back of beyond, no roads into the lake, they must have come in by float plane, and there it is, garbage all over the place, beer cans, blobs of human poop flagged by melting toilet paper, and twenty-two fine pickerel left rotting on a rock. Business executives who get themselves flown in during hunting season with their high-powered rifles, shoot a buck, cut off the head, fill their quota, see another one with a bigger spread of antlers, drop the first head, cut off the second. The woods are littered with discarded heads, and who cares about the bodies?

New way to shoot polar bear: you have the natives on the ground finding them for you, then they radio the location to the base camp, the base camp phones New York, fellow gets on the plane, gets himself flown in, they've got the rifle and the clothing all ready for him, fly him to the bear, he pulls the trigger from the plane, doesn't even get out of the g.d. *plane*, they fly him back, cut off the head, skin it, send the lot down to New York.

These are the horror stories of the north, one brand. They've replaced the ones in which you got pounced upon by a wolverine or had your arm chewed off by a she-bear with cubs or got chased into the lake by a moose in rut, or even the ones in which your dog got porcupine quills or rolled in poison ivy and gave it to you. In the new stories, the enemies and the victims of old have done a switch. Nature is no longer implacable, dangerous, ready to jump you; it is on the run, pursued by a number of unfair bullies with the latest technology.

One of the key nouns in these stories is "float plane." These outrages, this banditry, would not be possible without them, for the bad hunters are notoriously weak-muscled and are deemed incapable of portaging a canoe, much less paddling one. Among their other badnesses, they are sissies. Another key motif is money. What money buys these days, among other things, is the privilege of no-risk slaughter.

As for us, the ones telling the stories, tsk-tsking by lamplight, we are the good hunters, or so we think. We've given up saying we only kill to eat; Kraft dinner and freeze-dried food have put paid to that one. Really there's no excuse for us. However, we do have some virtues left. We can still cast a fly. We don't cut off heads and hang them stuffed on the wall. We would never buy an ocelot coat. We paddle our own canoes.

We're sitting on the dock at night, shivering despite our sweaters, in mid-August, watching the sky. There are a few shooting stars, as there always are at this time in August, as the earth passes through the Perseids. We pride ourselves on knowing a few things like that, about the sky; we find the Dipper, the North Star, Cassiopeia's Chair, and talk about consulting a star chart, which we know we won't actually do. But this is the only place you can really *see* the stars, we tell each other. Cities are hopeless.

Suddenly an odd light appears, going very fast. It spirals around like a newly dead firecracker and then bursts, leaving a cloud of luminous dust, caught perhaps in the light from the sun, still up there somewhere. What could this be? Several days later, we hear that it was part of an extinct Soviet satellite, or that's what they say. That's what they would say, wouldn't they? It strikes us that we don't really know very much about the night sky at all anymore. There's all kinds of junk up there: spy planes, old satellites, tin cans, man-made matter gone out of control. It also strikes us that we are totally dependent for knowledge of these things on a few people who don't tell us very much.

Once, we thought that if the balloon ever went up we'd head for the bush and hide out up there, living—we naively supposed—off the land. Now we know that if the two superpowers begin hurling things at each other through the sky, they're likely to do it across the Arctic, with big bangs and fallout all over the north. The wind blows everywhere. Survival gear and knowing which moss you can eat is not going to be a large help. The north is no longer a refuge.

Driving back toward Toronto from the Near North, a small reprise runs through my head:

> *Land of the septic tank,*
> *Home of the speedboat,*
> *Where still the four-wheel-drive*
> *Wanders at will,*
> *Blue lake and tacky shore,*
> *I will return once more:*
> *Vroom-diddy-vroom-vroom*
> *Vroom-diddy-vroom-vroom*
> *Vroo-OO-oo-oom.*

Somehow, just as the drive north inspires saga and tragedy, the drive south inspires parody. And here it comes: the gift shops shaped like teepees, the maple-syrup emporiums that get themselves up like olde-tyme sugaring-off huts; and, farther south, the restaurants that pretend to offer wholesome farm fare, the stores that pretend to be general stores, selling quilts, soap shaped like hearts, high-priced fancy conserves done up in frilly cloth caps, the way Grandma (whoever she might be) was fondly supposed to have made them.

And then come the housing developments, acres of prime farmland turning overnight into quality all-brick family homes; and then come the industrial parks; and there, in full antibloom, is the city itself, looming like a mirage or a chemical warfare zone on the horizon. A browny-gray scuzz hovers above it, and we think, as we always do when facing reentry, we're going into *that*? We're going to breathe *that*?

But we go forward, as we always do, into what is now to us the unknown. And once inside, we breathe the air, not much bad happens to us, we hardly notice. It's as if we've never been anywhere else. But that's what we think, too, when we're in the north.

6

Review:

Beloved
by Toni Morrison

eloved is Toni Morrison's fifth novel, and another triumph. Indeed, Ms. Morrison's versatility and technical and emotional range appear to know no bounds. If there were any doubts about her stature as a preeminent American novelist, of her own or any other generation, *Beloved* will put them to rest. In three words or less, it's a hair-raiser.

In *Beloved*, Ms. Morrison turns away from the contemporary scene that has been her concern of late. This new novel is set after the end of the Civil War, during the period of so-called Reconstruction, when a great deal of random violence was let loose upon blacks, both the slaves freed by Emancipation and others who had been given or had bought their freedom earlier. But there are flashbacks to a more distant period, when slavery was still a going concern in the South and the seeds for the bizarre and calamitous events of the novel were sown. The setting is similarly divided: the countryside near Cincinnati, where the central characters have ended up, and a slave-holding plantation in Kentucky, ironically named Sweet Home, from which they fled eighteen years before the novel opens.

There are many stories and voices in this novel, but the central one belongs to Sethe, a woman in her mid-thirties who is living in an Ohio farmhouse, with her daughter, Denver, and her mother-in-law, Baby Suggs. *Beloved* is such a unified novel that it's difficult to discuss it without giving away the plot, but it must be said at the outset that it is, among other things, a ghost story, for the farmhouse is also home to a sad, malicious, and angry ghost, the spirit of Sethe's baby daughter, who had her throat cut under appalling circumstances eighteen years before, when she was two. We never know this child's full name, but we—and Sethe—think of her as Beloved, because that is what is on her tombstone. Sethe wanted "Dearly Beloved," from the funeral service, but had only enough strength to pay for one word. Payment was ten minutes of sex with the tombstone engraver. This act, which is recounted early in the novel, is a keynote for the whole book: in the world of slavery and poverty, where human beings are merchandise, everything has its price, and price is tyrannical.

"Who would have thought that a little old baby could harbor so much rage?" Sethe thinks, but it does: breaking mirrors, making tiny handprints in cake icing, smashing dishes, and manifesting itself in pools of bloodred light. As the novel opens, the ghost is in full possession of the house, having driven away Sethe's two young sons. Old Baby Suggs, after a lifetime of slavery and a brief respite of freedom—purchased for her by the Sunday labor of her son Halle, Sethe's husband—has given up and died. Sethe lives with her memories, almost all of them bad. Denver, her teenage daughter, courts the baby ghost because, since her family has been ostracized by the neighbors, she doesn't have anyone else to play with.

The supernatural element is treated not in an *Amityville Horror*, watch-me-make-your-flesh-creep mode, but with magnificent practicality, like the ghost of Catherine Earnshaw in *Wuthering Heights*. All the main characters in the book believe in ghosts, so it's merely natural for this one to be there. As Baby Suggs says, "Not a house in the country ain't packed to its rafters with some dead Negro's grief. We lucky this ghost is a baby. My husband's spirit was to come back in here? or yours? Don't talk to me. You lucky." In fact, Sethe would rather have the ghost there than not there. It is, after all, her adored child, and any sign of it is better, for her, than nothing.

This grotesque domestic equilibrium is disturbed by the arrival of Paul D., one of the "Sweet Home men" from Sethe's past. The Sweet Home men were the male slaves of the establishment. Their owner, Mr. Garner, is no Simon Legree; instead, he's a best-case slaveholder, treating his "property" well, trusting them, allowing them choice in the running of his small plantation, and calling them "men" in defiance of the neighbors, who want all male blacks to be called "boys." But Mr. Garner dies, and weak, sickly Mrs. Garner brings in her handiest male relative, who is known as "the schoolteacher." This Goebbels-like paragon combines viciousness with intellectual pretensions; he's a sort of master-race proponent who measures the heads of the slaves and tabulates the results to demonstrate that they are more like animals than people. Accompanying him are his two sadistic and repulsive nephews. From there it's all downhill at Sweet Home, as the slaves try to escape, go crazy, or are murdered. Sethe, in a trek that makes the ice-floe scene in *Uncle Tom's Cabin* look like a stroll around the block, gets out, just barely; her husband, Halle, doesn't. Paul D. does, but has some very unpleasant adventures along the way, including a literally nauseating sojourn in a nineteenth-century Georgia chain gang.

Through the different voices and memories of the book, including that of Sethe's mother, a survivor of the infamous slave-ship crossing, we experience American slavery as it was lived by those who were its objects of exchange, both at its best—which wasn't very good—and at its worst, which was as bad as can be imagined. Above all, it is seen as one of the most viciously antifamily institutions human beings have ever devised. The slaves are motherless, fatherless, deprived of their mates, their children, their kin. It is a world in which people suddenly vanish and are never seen again, not through accident or covert operation or terrorism, but as a matter of everyday legal policy.

Slavery is also presented to us as a paradigm of how most people behave when they are given absolute power over other people. The first effect, of course, is that they start believing in their own superiority and justifying their actions by it. The second effect is that they make a cult of the inferiority of those they subjugate. It's no coincidence that the first of the deadly sins, from which all the others were supposed to stem, is pride, a sin of which Sethe is, incidentally, also accused.

In a novel that abounds in black bodies—headless, hanging from trees, frying to a crisp, locked in woodsheds for purposes of rape, or floating downstream drowned—it isn't surprising that the white people, especially the men, don't come off too well. Horrified black children see whites as men "without skin." Sethe thinks of them as having "mossy teeth" and is ready, if necessary, to bite off their faces, and worse, to avoid further mossy-toothed outrages. There are a few whites who behave with something approaching decency. There's Amy, the young runaway indentured servant who helps Sethe in childbirth during her flight to freedom, and inciden-tally reminds the reader that the nineteenth century, with its child labor, wage slavery, and widespread and accepted domestic violence, wasn't tough only for blacks, but for all but the most privileged whites as well. There are also the abolitionists who help Baby Suggs find a house and a job after she is freed. But even the decency of these "good" white people has a grudging side to it, and even they have trouble seeing the people they are helping as full-fledged people, though to show them as totally free of their xeno-phobia and sense of superiority might well have been anachronistic.

Toni Morrison is careful not to make all the whites awful and all the blacks wonderful. Sethe's black neighbors, for instance, have their own envy and scapegoating tendencies to answer for, and Paul D., though much kinder than, for instance, the woman-bashers of Alice Walker's novel *The Color Purple*, has his own limitations and flaws. But then, considering what he's been through, it's a wonder he isn't a mass murderer. If anything, he's a little too huggable, under the circumstances.

Back in the present tense, in chapter one, Paul D. and Sethe make an attempt to establish a "real" family, whereupon the baby ghost, feeling excluded, goes berserk, but is driven out by Paul D.'s stronger will. So it appears. But then along comes a strange, beautiful, real flesh-and-blood young woman, about twenty years old, who can't seem to remember where she comes from, who talks like a young child, who has an odd, raspy voice and no lines on her hands, who takes an intense, devouring interest in Sethe, and who says her name is Beloved.

Students of the supernatural will admire the way this twist is handled. Ms. Morrison blends a knowledge of folklore—for instance, in many tra-ditions, the dead cannot return from the grave unless called, and it's the passions of the living that keep them alive—with a highly original treat-ment. The reader is kept guessing; there's a lot more to Beloved than any one character can see, and she manages to be many things to several people. She is a catalyst for revelations as well as self-revelations; through her we come to know not only how, but also why, the original child Beloved was killed. And through her also Sethe achieves, finally, her own form of self-exorcism, her own self-accepting peace.

Beloved is written in an antiminimalist prose that is by turns rich, graceful, eccentric, rough, lyrical, sinuous, colloquial, and very much to the point. Here, for instance, is Sethe remembering Sweet Home:

> . . . suddenly there was Sweet Home rolling, rolling, rolling out before her eyes, and although there was not a leaf on that farm that did not want to make her scream, it rolled itself out before her in shameless beauty. It never looked as terrible as it was and it made her wonder if hell was a pretty place too. Fire and brimstone all right, but hidden in lacy groves. Boys hanging from the most beautiful sycamores in the world. It shamed her—remembering the wonderful soughing trees rather than the boys. Try as she might to make it otherwise, the sycamores beat out the children every time and she could not forgive her memory for that.

In this book, the other world exists and magic works, and the prose is up to it. If you can believe page one—and Ms. Morrison's verbal authority compels belief—you're hooked on the rest of the book.

The epigraph to *Beloved* is from the Bible, Romans 9:25: "I will call them my people, which were not my people; and her beloved, which was not beloved." Taken by itself, this might seem to favor doubt about, for instance, the extent to which Beloved was really loved, or the extent to which Sethe herself was rejected by her own community. But there is more to it than that. The passage is from a chapter in which the Apostle Paul ponders, Job-like, the ways of God toward humanity, in particular the evils and inequities visible everywhere on the earth. Paul goes on to talk about the fact that the Gentiles, hitherto despised and outcast, have now been redefined as acceptable. The passage proclaims not rejection, but reconciliation and hope. It continues, "And it shall come to pass, that in the place where it was said unto them, Ye are not my people; there shall they be called the children of the living God."

Toni Morrison is too smart, and too much of a writer, not to have intended this context. Here, if anywhere, is her own comment on the goings-on in her novel, her final response to the measuring and dividing and excluding "schoolteachers" of this world. An epigraph to a book is like a key signature in music, and *Beloved* is written in major.

7

A Jest of God
by Margaret Laurence

I still have my first copy of *A Jest of God*. It is, in fact, the first edition, with a medium-sized format, not very good quality paper, an unprepossessing jacket, maroon background, formal green border, no illustration. I got it for Christmas in 1966, from my parents, who had learned with some apprehension that I wanted to be a writer, and had done their best by giving me a book by one of the few Canadian writers they (or anyone else) knew about at the time. I was a graduate student in English literature at Harvard University. I read it in one sitting.

I had already read one other novel by Margaret Laurence, *The Stone Angel*, dropped into my hands by Jane Rule when I was living in Vancouver. It knocked me out, to put it mildly. So when I seized with eagerness on *A Jest of God*, it was in part to see if a hard act could be followed.

It could. But more of that shortly.

Four months later, I was notified by phone that I had won the Governor General's Award for Poetry for my first book, *The Circle Game*, which had been published in the fall. At first I thought this announcement was an error or a joke. When it turned out to be true, delight set in—I was very broke, and the money would go a long way—and then panic. My wardrobe at the time consisted of tweed skirts, dark-hued cardigans with woolly balls on them, and gray Hush Puppies, all appropriate for female graduate students but hardly suitable for the proposed formal dinner. What would I wear?

Worse, what would I say to Margaret Laurence, who had won the Governor General's Award for Fiction that year for *A Jest of God*? I had studied the handsome, austere photograph of her on the inside jacket flap, and had decided that nobody except Simone de Beauvoir would have such power to reduce me to quaking jelly. I was in awe of her talent, but also I was afraid of her hairdo. This was a serious person who would make judgments, unfavorable ones, about me. One zap from that intellect and I would be squashed like a bug.

My two Harvard roommates took me in hand. They did not know what the Governor General's Award was, but they did not want me to disgrace them. They went at me with big rollers and some hair-set and lent me a dress. I'd been adjusting to new contact lenses, and they were adamant about these: onto my eyes they must go on the gala evening; no tortoiseshell horn-rims allowed.

The ceremony and then the dinner went on longer than I had expected, and at the end of the first course I began to weep. It was the lenses: I had not yet developed the knack of removing them without a mirror. The two gentlemen from Québec who flanked me thought I was overcome with emotion, and were solicitous. I sat there in a frenzy of embarrassment, with the tears trickling from my eyes, wondering how soon I could decently make my escape. As soon as the presentation was concluded, I rushed to the washroom like Cinderella fleeing the ball.

Who should be in there but Margaret Laurence? She was in black and gold, but otherwise not at all as anticipated. Instead she was warm, friendly, and sympathetic. Also, she was more of a dithering nervous wreck than I was.

It was a moment worthy of Rachel Cameron, that avatar of social awkwardness and self-conscious embarrassment. Like Rachel, I had made an idiot of myself; like Rachel, too, I got my share of kindness from an unexpected source.

Much as I admire other books by Margaret Laurence, *A Jest of God* holds a special place for me, possibly because, when I read it, I was at the right age to appreciate the craft that lay behind its apparent artlessness. A few years earlier and I might have preferred the more obviously artistic, the more overtly experimental. I might have rejected its simplicity of an apple in favor of something more baroque, or—let's face it—more existential and French.

As it was, I found it an almost perfect book, in that it did what it set out to do, with no gaps and no excesses. Like a pool or a well, it covers a small area but goes deep. I once heard a Norwegian writer describe the work of another author as "an egg of a book." *A Jest of God*, too, is an egg of a book—plain, self-contained, elegant in form, holding within it the essentials of a life.

That life is Rachel Cameron's, who shares with several of Laurence's protagonists a Scottish last name and a biblical first name. Her namesake, however, is not the Rachel of the Jacob and Leah saga in *Genesis*, but that of Jeremiah 31:15: "Rachel weeping for her children refused to be comforted for her children, because they were not." Like several of Margaret Laurence's fictions, especially those concerned with the inhabitants of the town of Manawaka, Rachel's story is told as first-person narration, and is the story of a woman trapped in a prison partly of her own making. But the prison here is smaller and more tightly locked than any of the others. Hagar of *A Stone Angel* gets to Vancouver, as does Stacey of *The Fire-Dwellers*; Morag Gunn of *The Diviners* travels even farther afield, to Toronto and also England. But apart from her trip to the hospital, we never see Rachel anywhere but in her hometown: her break for freedom at the end of the book exists mostly in the future tense. Rachel's prison is so hard for her to get out of because it is made mostly from virtues gone sour: filial devotion, self-sacrifice, the concern for appearances advocated by St. Paul, a sense of duty, the desire to avoid hurting others, and the wish to be loved. It may be hard for us to remember, now, that Rachel is not some sort of aberration but merely the epitome of what nice girls were once educated to be. To go against such overwhelming social assumptions, to assert instead one's self, as Rachel finally does, takes more than a little courage and a good deal of desperation. Desperation and courage are the two magnetic poles of this book, which begins with the first and arrives at the second.

The desperation is conveyed by the texture of the prose, the accuracy of the physical details. Rachel's inner monologue is a little masterpiece in itself, rendered in a language by turns colloquial and flat as prairie speech, terse and ironic as jokes, self-mocking, charged with nervous irritability, and eloquent as psalms. Then there are the entirely believable, entirely minor, entirely horrifying domestic snippets from Rachel's claustrophobic life with her sweetly nagging hypochondriac of a mother, who plays guilt like a violin: the awfulness of the bridge-night asparagus sandwiches, the rotting, monstrous rubber douche bag Rachel unearths during her feverish brush with sex. Any novelist writing this kind of realism has to get such details right or the whole illusion falls apart. In *A Jest of God*, Laurence does not put a foot wrong.

Oddly, for a novel about what used to be called a spinster, *A Jest of God* is structured almost entirely around children, and the flow of time and emotion in and around them; and thus around mothers and mothering, fathers and fathering, and the relationships, often interchangeable, between those who mother and are mothered, those who give and receive nurturing and comfort. Rachel's false pregnancy is an ambiguous indication of the lesson she comes to learn: how to be a mother, to herself first of all, since true mothering has been denied her.

Rachel Cameron begins as a child, still stuck in the time of the little girls' skipping chant she hears through her open classroom window, still playing dutiful daughter to a mother who treats her as if she is only half grown. At the age of thirty-four, she arrives at gawky adolescence, agonizing over her appearance and sexuality, going through a painful and unrequited crush. But she ends as an adult, having realized the childishness of her own mother and thus her inability to offer emotional safety, having accepted the risks inherent in being alive, having taken her true place in time: "Beside me sleeps my elderly child. . . . What will happen? What will happen. It may be that my children will always be temporary, never to be held. But so are everyone's."

Rereading *A Jest of God* yet again, I was cheered by how little it has dated. Some of the social customs and sexual constraints may have vanished, but the kinds of expectations placed on women, although in different costume, are still around—perfect physical beauty, total self-confidence, angelic and selfless nurturing of one variety or another. What Rachel can offer us now as readers is something we still need to know: how to acknowledge our own human and necessary limitations, our own foolishness. How to say both No and Yes.

8

Great Aunts

Aunt J., who was my third and youngest aunt, took me to my first writers' conference. That was in Montréal, in 1958, when I was eighteen. I had already produced several impressive poems; at least I was impressed by them. They had decaying leaves, garbage cans, cigarette butts, and cups of coffee in them. I had been ambushed by T. S. Eliot several months previously, and had wrestled him to a standstill. I did not yet know that it was the done thing, by now, to refer to him as T. S. Idiot.

I didn't show my seedy poems to my mother, who was the oldest of the three sisters and therefore pragmatic, since it was she who had had to tend the others. She was the athlete of the family and was fond of horses and ice-skating and any other form of rapid motion that offered escapes from domestic duties. My mother had only written one poem in her life, when she was eight or nine; it began, "I had some wings, They were lovely things," and went on, typically for her, to describe the speed of the subsequent flight. I knew that if I forced her to read my butt-and-coffee-ground free verses, she would say they were very nice, this being her standard response to other puzzlements, such as my increasingly dour experiments with wardrobe. Clothing was not a priority of hers either.

But Aunt J. had written reams, according to my mother. She was a romantic figure, as she had once had pleurisy and had been in a san, where she had made flowery shellwork brooches; I had received several of these treasures for Christmas, as a child, in tiny magical boxes with cotton wool in them. Tiny boxes, cotton wool: these were not my mother's style. Aunt J. had to be careful of her health, an infirmity that seemed to go along with writing, from what I knew. She cried at the sad places in movies, as I did, and had flights of fantasy as a child in the Annapolis Valley of Nova Scotia, which was where they had all grown up. Her middle name was Carmen, and to punish what they thought to be her inordinate pride over this her two older sisters had named the pig Carmen.

Aunt J. was rounded in outline, myopic (as I was), and depicted herself as a sentimental pushover, though this was merely a useful fiction, part of the self-deprecating camouflage adopted by women, then, for various useful purposes. Underneath her facade of lavender-colored flutter she was tough-minded, like all three of those sisters. It was this blend of soft and hard that appealed to me.

So I showed my poems to Aunt J. She read them and did not laugh, or not in my presence; though knowing her I doubt that she laughed at all. She knew what it was to have ambitions as a writer, though hers had been delayed by Uncle M., who was a bank manager, and by their two children. Much later, she herself would be speaking at conferences, sitting on panels, appearing nervously on talk shows, having authored five books of her own. Meanwhile she wrote children's stories for the weekly Sunday school papers and bided her time.

She sent my gloomy poems to second cousin Lindsay, who was an English professor at Dalhousie University. He said I had promise. Aunt J. showed me his letter, beaming with pleasure. This was my first official encouragement.

The writers' conference Aunt J. took me to was put on by the Canadian Authors' Association, which at that time was the only writers' organization in Canada. I knew its reputation—it was the same tea-party outfit about which F. R. Scott had written, "Expansive puppets percolate self-unction/Beneath a portrait of the Prince of Wales." It was rumored to be full of elderly amateurs; I was unlikely to see anyone there sprouting a three-day beard or clad in a black turtleneck pullover, or looking anything like Samuel Beckett or Eugène Ionesco, who were more or less my idea of real writers. But Aunt J. and I were both so desperate for contact with anything that smacked of the world of letters that we were willing to take our chances with the C.A.A.

Once at the conference, we opted for a paper to be given by an expert on Fanny Burney. I goggled around the room: there were a lot of what I thought were middle-aged women in flowered dresses—not unlike Aunt J's own dress—and little suits, though there was no one who looked like my idea of a writer: pallid, unkempt, red-eyed. But this was Canada and not France, so what could I expect?

Up to this time I had seen only one Canadian writer in the flesh. His name was Wilson Macdonald, and he'd turned up in our high school auditorium, old and wispy and white-haired, where he'd recited several healthy-minded poems about skiing, from memory, and had imitated a crow. I had a fair idea what Jean-Paul Sartre would have thought of him, and was worried that I might end up that way myself: wheeled out for a bunch of spit-ball-throwing teenaged thugs, doing birdcalls. You could not be a real writer and a Canadian, too; that much was clear. As soon as I could, I was going to hit Paris and become incomprehensible.

Meanwhile, there I was in Montréal, waiting for the Fanny Burney expert with Aunt J. We were both nervous. We felt like spies of a sort, infiltrators; and so like infiltrators we began to eavesdrop. Right behind us was sitting a woman whose name we recognized because she frequently had poems about snow-covered spruce trees published in a daily Montréal newspaper. She was not discussing spruce trees now, but a hanging that had taken place the day before, at the prison. "It was so dreadful for him," she was saying. "He was so upset."

Our ears were flapping: had she known the condemned man personally? If so, how creepy. But as we listened on, we gathered that the upset man was not the hanged one; it was her husband, who was the prison chaplain.

Several gaps opened at my feet: the gap between the sentimentality of this woman's poems and the realities of her life, between the realities of her life and her perceptions of them; between the hangers and the hanged, and the consolers of the hanged, and the consolers of the hangers. This was one of my first intimations that, beneath its facade of teacups and outdoor pursuits and various kinds of trees, Canada—even this literary, genteel segment of Canada, for which I had such youthful contempt—was a good deal more problematic than I had thought.

But I should have known that already.

In the early part of my childhood, I had not known any of my relatives, because they lived in Nova Scotia, two thousand miles away. My parents had left Nova Scotia during the Depression because there were no jobs there. By the time I was born, the Second World War had begun, and nobody traveled great distances without official reasons and gas coupons. But although my aunts were not present in the flesh, they were very much present in the spirit. The three sisters wrote one another every week, and my mother read these letters out loud, to my father but by extension to myself and my brother, after dinner. They were called "letters from home." *Home*, for my mother, was always Nova Scotia, never wherever we might be living at the time, which gave me the vague idea that I was misplaced. Wherever I actually was living myself, *home* was not there.

So I was kept up on the doings of my aunts, and also of my cousins, my second cousins, and many other people who fitted in somewhere but were more distantly related. In Nova Scotia, it's not what you do or even who you know that is the most important thing about you. It's which town you're from and who you're related to. Any conversation between two Maritimers who've never met before will begin this way, and go on until both parties discover that they are in fact related to each other. I grew up in a huge extended family of invisible people.

It was not my invisible aunts in their present-day incarnation who made the most impression on me. It was my aunts in the past. There they were as children, in the impossible starched and frilled dresses and the floppy satin hairbows of the first decades of the century, or as teenagers, in black-and-white in the photograph album, wearing strange clothing— cloche hats, flapper coats up over the knee, standing beside antique motor-cars, or posed in front of rocks or the sea in striped bathing suits that came halfway down their legs. Sometimes their arms would be around one another. They had been given captions by my mother: "We Three," "Bathing Belles." Aunt J. was thin as a child, dark-eyed, intense. Aunt K., the middle sister, looked tailored and brisk. My mother, with huge pre-Raphaelite eyes and wavy hair and model's cheekbones, was the beauty, a notion she made light of: she was, and remained, notorious for her bad taste in clothes, a notion she cultivated so she wouldn't have to go shopping for them alone. But all three sisters had the same high-bridged noses—Roman noses, my mother said. I pored over these pictures, intrigued by the idea of the triplicate, identical noses. I did not have a sister myself, then, and the mystique of sisterhood was potent for me.

The photo album was one mode of existence for my invisible aunts. They were even more alive in my mother's stories, for, although she was no poet, my mother was a raconteur and deadly mimic. The characters in her stories about "home" became as familiar to me as characters in books; and, since we lived in isolated places and moved a lot, they were more familiar than most of the people I actually encountered.

The cast was constant. First came my strict, awe-inspiring grandfather, a country doctor who drove around the dirt roads in a horse and sleigh, through blizzards, delivering babies in the dead of night, and threatening to horse-whip his daughters—especially my mother—for real or imagined transgressions. I did not know what a horse whip was, so this punishment had the added attraction of the bizarre.

Then came my distracted, fun-loving grandmother, and my aunt K., a year younger than my mother but much more intellectual and firm of will, according to my mother. Then Aunt J., sentimental and apt to be left out. These three were "the girls." Then, somewhat later, "the boys," my two uncles, one of whom blew the stove lids off the country schoolhouse with some homemade explosive hidden in a log, the other who was sickly but frequently had everyone "in stitches." And the peripheral figures: hired girls who were driven away by the machinations of my mother and Aunt K., who did not like having them around, hired men who squirted them while milking the cows; the cows themselves; the pig; the horses. The horses were not really peripheral characters; although they had no lines, they had names and personalities and histories, and they were my mothers' partners in escapades. Dick and Nell were their names. Dick was my favorite; he had been given to my mother as a broken-down, ill-treated hack, and she had restored him to health and glossy beauty. This was the kind of happy ending I found satisfactory.

The stories about these people had everything that could be asked for: plot, action, suspense—although I knew how they would turn out, having heard them before—and fear, because there was always the danger of my grandfather's finding out and resorting to the horse-whip threat, although I don't believe he actually horse-whipped anyone.

What would he find out? Almost anything. There were many things he was not supposed to know, many things the girls were not supposed to know, but did. And what if he were to find out that they knew? A great deal turned, in these stories and in that family, on concealment; on what you did or did not tell; on what was said as distinct from what was meant. "If you can't say anything good, don't say anything at all," said my mother, saying a great deal. My mother's stories were my first lesson in reading between the lines.

My mother featured in these stories as physically brave, a walker of fences and also of barn ridge-poles, a sin of horse-whipping proportions— but shy. She was so shy that she would hide from visitors behind the barn, and she could not go to school until Aunt K. was old enough to take her. In addition to the bravery and the shyness, however, she had a violent temper. "Like Father's," she said. This was improbable to me, since I could not remember any examples. My mother losing her temper would have been a sight to behold, like the Queen standing on her head. But I accepted the idea on faith, along with the rest of her mythology.

Aunt K. was not shy. Although she was younger than my mother, you would never know it: "We were more like twins." She was a child of steely nerves, according to my mother. She was a ringleader, and thought up plots and plans, which she carried out with ruthless efficiency. My mother would be drawn into these, willy-nilly: she claimed she was too weak of will to resist.

"The girls" had to do household chores, more of them after they had driven away the hired girls, and Aunt K. was a hard worker and an exacting critic of the housework of others. Later in the story, Aunt K. and my mother had a double wedding; the night before this event they read their adolescent diaries out loud to one another and then burned them. "We cleaned the kitchen," said Aunt K.'s diary. "The others did not do an A-1 job." My mother and Aunt J. would always laugh when repeating this. It was, as Matthew Arnold would have had it, a touchstone line for them, about Aunt K.

But there was even more to Aunt K. She was a brilliant student, and had her M.A. in history from the University of Toronto. My grandfather thought my mother was a flighty, pleasure-bent flibbertigibbet until she saved her own money from schoolteaching and sent herself to college; but he was all set to finance Aunt K. for an advanced degree at Oxford. However, she turned this down in favor of marrying a local Annapolis Valley doctor and having six children. The reason, my mother implied, had something to do with Great-aunt Winnie, who also had an M.A., the first woman to receive one from Dalhousie, but who had never married. Aunt Winnie was condemned—it was thought of as a condemnation—to teach school forever, and turned up at family Christmases looking wistful. In those days, said my mother, if you did not get married by a certain age, it was unlikely that you ever would. "You didn't think about not marrying," said Aunt J. to me much later. "There wasn't any *choice* about it. It was just what you did."

Meanwhile, there was my aunt K. in the album, in a satin wedding gown and a veil identical to my mother's, and later, with all six children, dressed up as the Old Woman Who Lived in a Shoe in the Apple Blossom Festival Parade. Unlike the stories in books, my mother's stories did not have clear morals, and the moral of this one was less clear than most. Which was better? To be brilliant and go to Oxford, or to have six children? Why couldn't it be both?

When I was six or seven and my brother was eight or nine and the war was over, we began to visit Nova Scotia, every summer or every second summer. We had to: my grandfather had had something called a coronary—more than one of them, in fact—and he could die at any moment. Despite his strictness and what seemed, to me, to be acts of gross unfairness, he was loved and respected. Everyone agreed on that.

These visits were a strain. We reached Nova Scotia from Ontario by driving at breakneck speed and for a great many hours at a time over the postwar highways of Québec and Vermont and New Brunswick, so that we would arrive cranky and frazzled, usually in the middle of the night. During the visits we would have to be on whispering good behavior in my grandfather's large white house, and meet and be met by a great many relatives we hardly knew.

But the worst strain of all was fitting these real people—so much smaller and older and less vivid than they ought to have been—into the mythology in my possession. My grandfather was not galloping around the country-side, roaring threats and saving babies. Instead he carved little wooden fig-ures and had to have a nap every afternoon, and his greatest exertion was a stroll around the orchard or a game of chess with my brother. My grand-mother was not the harried although comical mother of five, but the care-taker of my grandfather. There were no cows anymore, and where were the beautiful horses Dick and Nell?

I felt defrauded. I did not want Aunt J. and Aunt K. to be the grown-up mothers of my cousins, snapping beans in the kitchen. I wanted them back the way they were supposed to be, in the bobbed haircuts and short skirts of the photo album, playing tricks on the hired girls, being squirted by the hired man, living under the threat of horse-whipping, failing to do an A-1 job.

Once I went on a literary outing with both my aunts.

It was in the early seventies, when I was over thirty and had published several books. Aunt J.'s husband had died, and she'd moved from Montréal back to Nova Scotia to take care of my aging grandmother. I was visiting, and the aunts and I decided to drive over to nearby Bridgetown, to pay a call on a writer named Ernest Buckler. Ernest Buckler had written a novel called *The Mountain and the Valley*, the mountain being North Mountain, the valley being Annapolis Valley. He'd had some success with it in the States—at that time, in Canada, a sure-fire ticket to hatred and envy—but because he was an eccentric recluse, the hatred and envy quotient was modified. But his success in the States had not been duplicated in Canada, because his Toronto publishers were United Church teetotalers, known for throwing launch parties at which they served fruit juice. (Modernization came finally, with the addition of sherry, doled out in a separate room, into which those who craved it could slink furtively.) These publishers had discovered that there were what my mother referred to as "goings-on" in Buckler's book, and had hidden it in the stockroom. If you wanted to actually buy one, it was like getting porn out of the Vatican.

I had read this book as a young adolescent because somebody had given it to my parents under the impression that they would like it because it was about Nova Scotia. My mother's comment was that it was not what things were like when she was growing up. I snuck this book up onto the garage roof, which was flat, where I swiftly located the goings-on and then read the rest of the book. It was probably the first novel for adults that I ever did read, with the exception of *Moby-Dick*.

So I remembered Ernest Buckler's book with fondness, and by the seventies I'd become involved in a correspondence with him. So over we went to see him in the flesh. My aunt J. was all agog, because Ernest Buckler was a real writer. My aunt K. drove. (My aunt J. never drove, having scraped the door handles off the car on one of her few attempts, according to her.)

Aunt K. knew the vicinity well, and pointed out the places of interest as we went by. She had a good memory. It was she who had told me something everyone else had forgotten, including myself: that I had announced, at the age of five, that I was going to be a writer.

During this drive, however, her mind was on other historical matters. "That's the tree where the man who lived in the white house hanged himself," she said. "That's where the barn got burned down. They know who did it but they can't prove a thing. The man in there blew his head off with a shotgun." These events may have taken place years, decades before, but they were still current in the area. It appeared that the Valley was more like *The Mountain and the Valley* than I had suspected.

Ernest Buckler lived in a house that could not have been changed for fifty years. It still had a horsehair sofa, antimacassars, a woodstove in the living room. Ernest himself was enormously likable and highly nervous, and anxious that we be pleased. He hopped around a lot, talking a mile a minute, and kept popping out to the kitchen, then popping in again. We talked mostly about books, and about his plans to scandalize the neighborhood by phoning me up at my grandmother's house, on the party line, and pretending we were having an affair. "That would give the old biddies something to talk about," he said. Everyone listened in, of course, whenever he had a call, but not just because he was a local celebrity. They listened in on everyone.

After we left, my aunt J. said, "That was something! He said you had a teeming brain!" (He had said this.) My aunt K.'s comment was, "That man was oiled." Of the three of us, she was the only one who had figured out why Mr. Buckler had made such frequent trips to the kitchen. But it was understandable that he should have been secretive about it: in the Valley, there were those who drank, and then there were decent people.

Also: there were those who wrote, and then there were decent people. A certain amount of writing was tolerated, but only within limits. Newspaper columns about children and the changing seasons were fine. Sex, swearing, and drinking were beyond the pale.

I myself, in certain Valley circles, was increasingly beyond the pale. As I became better known, I also became more widely read there, not because my writing was thought of as having any particular merit but because I was related. Aunt J. told me, with relish, how she'd hidden behind the parlor door during a neighbor's scandalized visit with my grandmother. The scandal was one of my own books: how, asked the outraged neighbor, could my grandmother have permitted her granddaughter to publish such immoral trash?

But blood is thicker than water in the Valley. My grandmother gazed serenely out the window and commented on the beautiful fall weather they were having, while my aunt J. gasped behind the door. My aunts and mother always found the spectacle of my grandmother preserving her dignity irresistible, probably because there was so much dignity to be preserved.

This was the neighbor, the very same one, who as a child had led my aunts astray, sometime during the First World War, inducing them to slide down a red clay bank in their little white lace-edged pantaloons. She had then pressed her nose up against the glass of the window to watch them getting spanked, not just for sliding but for lying about it. My grandmother had gone over and yanked the blind down then, and she was doing it now. Whatever her own thoughts about the goings-on in my fiction, she was keeping them to herself. Nor did she ever mention them to me.

For that I silently thanked her. I suppose any person, but especially any woman, who takes up writing has felt, especially at first, that she was doing it against a huge, largely unspoken pressure, the pressure of expectation and decorum. This pressure is most strongly felt, by women, from within the family, and more so when the family is a strong unit. There are things that should not be said. Don't tell. If you can't say anything nice, don't say anything at all. Was that counterbalanced adequately by that other saying of my mother's, "Do what you think is right, no matter what other people think"? And did those other people whose opinion did matter include the members of one's family?

With the publication of my first real book, I was dreading disapproval. I didn't worry much about my father and mother, who had gracefully survived several other eccentricities of mine—the skirts handprinted with trilobites and newts, the experiments with beer parlors, the beatnik boyfriends—although they had probably bitten their tongues a few times in the process. Anyway, they lived in Toronto, where goings-on of various kinds had now become more common; not in Nova Scotia, where, it was not quite said, things might be a bit more narrow. Instead, I worried about my aunts. I thought they might be scandalized, even Aunt J. Although she had been subjected to some of my early poems, coffee cups and rotting leaves were one thing, but there was more than dirty crockery and mulch in this book. As for Aunt K., so critical of the shoddy housework and drinking habits of others, what would she think?

To my surprise, my aunts came through with flying colors. Aunt J. thought it was wonderful—a real book! She said she was bursting with pride. Aunt K. said that there were certain things that were not done in her generation, but they could be done by mine, and more power to me for doing them.

This kind of acceptance meant more to me than it should have, to my single-minded, all-for-art, twenty-six-year-old self. (Surely I ought to be impervious to aunts.) However, like the morals of my mother's stories, what exactly it meant is far from clear to me. Perhaps it was a laying on of hands, a passing of something from one generation to another. What was being passed on was the story itself: what was known, and what could be told. What was between the lines. The permission to tell the story, wherever that might lead.

Or perhaps it meant that I, too, was being allowed into the magical, static but ever-continuing saga of the photo album. Instead of three different-looking young women with archaic clothes and identical Roman noses, standing with their arms around each other, there would now be four. I was being allowed into *home*.

9

Introduction:

Reading Blind
The Best American Short Stories 1989

Whenever I'm asked to talk about what constitutes a "good" story, or what makes one well-written story "better" than another, I begin to feel very uncomfortable. Once you start making lists or devising rules for stories, or for any other kind of writing, some writer will be sure to happen along and casually break every abstract rule you or anyone else has ever thought up, and take your breath away in the process. The word *should* is a dangerous one to use when speaking of writing. It's a kind of challenge to the deviousness and inventiveness and audacity and perversity of the creative spirit. Sooner or later, anyone who has been too free with it will be liable to end up wearing it like a dunce's cap. We don't judge good stories by the application to them of some set of external measurements, as we judge giant pumpkins at the fall fair. We judge them by the way they strike us. And that will depend on a great many subjective imponderables, which we lump together under the general heading of taste.

All of which may explain why, when I sat down to read through the large heap of stories from which I was to select for this collection, I did so with misgiving. There were so many stories to choose from, and all of them, as they say, publishable. I knew this because they had already been published. Over the course of the previous year, the indefatigable and devoted series editor, Shannon Ravenel, had read every short story in every known magazine, large or small, famous or obscure, in both the United

States and Canada—a total of more than 2,000 stories. Of these she had chosen 120, from which I was to pick 20. But how was I to do this? What would be my criteria, if any? How would I be able to tell the best from the merely better? How would I *know*?

I had elected to read these stories "blind," which meant that Shannon Ravenel had inked out the names of the authors. I had no idea, in advance, how these small black oblongs would transform the act of editing from a judicious task to a gleeful pleasure. Reading through these authorless manuscripts was like playing hooky: with 120 strokes of a black marker, I had been freed from the weight of authorial reputation. I didn't have to pay any attention to who ought to be in because of his or her general worthiness or previous critical hosannas. I didn't have to worry about who might feel slighted if not included. That weighing, measuring, calculating side of me—and even the most scrupulously disinterested editor has one—had been safely locked away, leaving me to wallow among the ownerless pages unencumbered. Picking up each new story was like a child's game of Fish. You never knew what you would get: it might be a piece of plastic or it might be something wonderful, a gift, a treasure.

In addition to remaining ignorant about authorial worth, I could disregard any considerations about territory. I had no way of knowing, for instance, whether a story with a female narrator was by a female author, whether one with a male narrator was by a man; whether a story about a Chinese immigrant was by a writer with a Chinese background, whether one about a nineteenth-century Canadian poet was by a Canadian. I've recently heard it argued that writers should tell stories only from a point of view that is their own, or that of a group to which they themselves belong. Writing from the point of view of someone "other" is a form of poaching, the appropriation of material you haven't earned and to which you have no right. Men, for instance, should not write as women, although it's less frequently said that women should not write as men.

This view is understandable but, in the end, self-defeating. Not only does it condemn as thieves and impostors such writers as George Eliot, James Joyce, Emily Brontë, and William Faulkner, and, incidentally, a number of the writers in this book; it is also inhibiting to the imagination in a fundamental way. It's only a short step from saying we can't write from the point of view of an "other" to saying we can't read that way either, and from there to the position that no one can really understand anyone else, so we might as well stop trying. Follow this line of reasoning to its logical conclusion and we would all be stuck with reading nothing but our own work, over and over, which would be my personal idea of hell. Surely the delight and the wonder come not from who tells the story but from what the story tells, and how.

Reading blind is an intriguing metaphor. When you read blind, you see everything but the author. He or she may be visible intermittently, as a trick of style, a locale about which nobody else is likely to write, a characteristic twist of the plot; but apart from such clues, he or she is incognito. You're stranded with the voice of the story.

The Voice of the Story, the Story as Voice

In the houses of the people who knew us we were asked to come in and sit, given cold water or lemonade; and while we sat there being refreshed, the people continued their conversations or went about their chores. Little by little we began to piece a story together, a secret, terrible, awful story.

—Toni Morrison, *The Bluest Eye*

It is only the story that can continue beyond the war and the warrior. . . . It is only the story . . . that saves our progeny from blundering like blind beggars into the spikes of the cactus fence. The story is our escort; without it, we are blind. Does the blind man own his escort? No, neither do we the story; rather it is the story that owns us.

—Chinua Achebe, *Anthills of the Savannah*

How do we learn our notions of what a story is? What sets "a story" apart from mere background noise, the wash of syllables that surrounds us and flows through us and is forgotten every day? What makes a good story a unified whole, something complete and satisfying in itself? What makes it significant speech? In other words, what qualities was I searching for, perhaps without knowing it, as I read diligently through my pile of tear sheets?

I've spoken of "the voice of the story," which has become a sort of catchall phrase; but by it I intend something more specific: a speaking voice, like the singing voice in music, that moves not across space, across the page, but through time. Surely every written story is, in the final analysis, a score for voice. Those little black marks on the page mean nothing without their retranslation into sound. Even when we read silently, we read with the ear, unless we are reading bank statements.

Perhaps, by abolishing the Victorian practice of family reading and by removing from our school curricula those old standbys, the set memory piece and the recitation, we've deprived both writers and readers of something essential to stories. We've led them to believe that prose comes in visual blocks, not in rhythms and cadences; that its texture should be flat because a page is flat; that written emotion should not be immediate, like a drumbeat, but more remote, like a painted landscape, something to be contemplated. But understatement can be overdone, plainsong can get too plain. When I asked a group of young writers, earlier this year, how many of them ever read their own work aloud, not one of them said she did.

I'm not arguing for the abolition of the eye, merely for the reinstatement of the voice, and for an appreciation of the way it carries the listener along with it at the pace of the story. (Incidentally, reading aloud disallows cheating; when you're reading aloud, you can't skip ahead.)

Our first stories come to us through the air. We hear voices.

Children in oral societies grow up within a web of stories; but so do all children. We listen before we can read. Some of our listening is more like listening in, to the calamitous or seductive voices of the adult world, on the radio or the television or in our daily lives. Often it's an overhearing of things we aren't supposed to hear, eavesdropping on scandalous gossip or family secrets. From all these scraps of voices, from the whispers and shouts that surround us, even from the ominous silences, the unfilled gaps in meaning, we patch together for ourselves an order of events, a plot or plots; these, then, are the things that happen, these are the people they happen to, this is the forbidden knowledge.

We have all been little pitchers with big ears, shooed out of the kitchen when the unspoken is being spoken, and we have probably all been tale-bearers, blurters at the dinner table, unwitting violators of adult rules of censorship. Perhaps this is what writers are: those who never kicked the habit. We remained tale-bearers. We learned to keep our eyes open, but not to keep our mouths shut.

If we're lucky, we may also be given stories meant for our ears, stories intended for us. These may be children's Bible stories, tidied up and simplified and with the vicious bits left out. They may be fairy tales, similarly sugared, although if we are very lucky it will be the straight stuff in both instances, with the slaughters, thunderbolts, and red-hot shoes left in. In any case, these tales will have deliberate, molded shapes, unlike the stories we have patched together for ourselves. They will contain mountains, deserts, talking donkeys, dragons; and, unlike the kitchen stories, they will have definite endings. We are likely to accept these stories as being on the same level of reality as the kitchen stories. It's only when we are older that we are taught to regard one kind of story as real and the other kind as mere invention. This is about the same time we're taught to believe that dentists are useful and writers are not.

Traditionally, both the kitchen gossips and the readers-out-loud have been mothers or grandmothers, native languages have been mother tongues, and the kinds of stories that are told to children have been called nursery tales or old wives' tales. It struck me as no great coincidence when I learned recently that when a great number of prominent writers were asked to write about the family member who had had the greatest influence on their literary careers, almost all of them, male as well as female, had picked their mothers. Perhaps this reflects the extent to which North American children have been deprived of their grandfathers, those other great repositories of story; perhaps it will come to change if men come to share in early child care, and we will have old husbands' tales. But as things are, language, including the language of our earliest-learned stories, is a verbal matrix, not a verbal patrix.

I used to wonder why—as seems to be the case—so many more male writers chose to write from a female point of view than the other way around. (In this collection, for instance, male authors with female narrators outnumber the reverse four to one.) But possibly the prevailing gender of the earliest storytelling voice has something to do with it.

Two kinds of stories we first encounter—the shaped tale, the overheard impromptu narrative we piece together—form our idea of what a story is and color the expectations we bring to stories later. Perhaps it's from the collisions between these two kinds of stories—what is often called "real life" (and which writers greedily think of as their "material") and what is sometimes dismissed as "mere literature" or "the kinds of things that happen only in stories"—that original and living writing is generated. A writer with nothing but a formal sense will produce dead work, but so will one whose only excuse for what is on the page is that it really happened. Anyone who has been trapped in a bus beside a nonstop talker graced with no narrative skill or sense of timing can testify to that. Or, as Raymond Chandler says in *The Simple Art of Murder*: All language begins with speech, and the speech of common men at that, but when it develops to the point of becoming a literary medium it only looks like speech. Expressing yourself is not nearly enough. You must express the story.

The Uncertainty Principle

All of which gets me no closer to an explanation of why I chose one story over another, twenty stories over the remaining hundred. The uncertainty principle, as it applies to writing, might be stated: *You can say why a story is bad, but it's much harder to say why it's good.* Determining quality in fiction may be as hard as determining the reason for the happiness in families, only in reverse. The old saying has it that happy families are all happy in the same way, but each unhappy family is unique. In fiction, however, excellence resides in divergence, or how else could we be surprised? Hence the trickiness of the formulations.

Here is what I did. I sat on the floor, spread out the stories, and read through them in no particular order. I put each completed story into a "yes" pile, a "no" pile, and a "maybe" pile. By the time I'd gone through them once, I had about twenty-five stories in yes, an equal number in "no," and the rest in "maybe."

Here things got harder. The first fourteen yes stories were instant choices: I knew I wouldn't change my mind about them. After that there were gradations, yeses shading to maybes, maybes that could easily be on the low end of yes. To make the final choices, I was forced to be more conscious and deliberate. I went back over my fourteen instant yes stories and tried to figure out what, if anything, they had in common.

They were widely different in content, in tone, in setting, in narrative strategy. Some were funny, others melancholy, others contemplative, others downright sad, yet others violent. Some went over ground that, Lord knows, had been gone over before: the breakdown, the breakup, love, and death. Collectively they did not represent any school of writing or propound any common philosophy. I was beginning to feel stupid and lacking in standards. Was I to be thrown back on that old crutch of the creative writing seminar, *It worked for me*?

Perhaps, I thought, my criteria are very simple-minded. Perhaps all I want from a good story is what children want when they listen to tales both told and overheard—which turns out to be a good deal.

They want their attention held, and so do I. I always read to the end, out of some puritanical, and adult, sense of duty owed; but if I start to fidget and skip pages, and wonder if conscience demands I go back and read the middle, it's a sign that the story has lost me, or I have lost it.

They want to feel they are in safe hands, that they can trust the teller. With children this may mean simply that they know the speaker will not betray them by closing the book in the middle, or mixing up the heroes and the villains. With adult readers it's more complicated than that, and involves many dimensions, but there's the same element of keeping faith. Faith must be kept with the language—even if the story is funny, its language must be taken seriously—with the concrete details of locale, mannerism, clothing; with the shape of the story itself. A good story may tease, as long as this activity is foreplay and not used as an end in itself. If there's a promise held out, it must be honored. Whatever is hidden behind the curtain must be revealed at last, and it must be at one and the same time completely unexpected and inevitable. It's in this last respect that the story (as distinct from the novel) comes closest to resembling two of its oral predecessors, the riddle and the joke. Both, or all three, require the same mystifying buildup, the same surprising twist, the same impeccable sense of timing. If we guess the riddle at once, or if we can't guess it because the answer makes no sense—if we see the joke coming, or if the point is lost because the teller gets it muddled—there is failure. Stories can fail in the same way.

But anyone who has ever told, or tried to tell, a story to children will know that there is one thing without which none of the rest is any good. Young children have little sense of dutifulness or of delaying anticipation. They are longing to hear a story, but only if you are longing to tell one. They will not put up with your lassitude or boredom: if you want their full attention, you must give them yours. You must hold them with your glittering eye or suffer the pinches and whispering. You need the Ancient Mariner element, the Scheherazade element: a sense of urgency. *This is the story I must tell; this is the story you must hear.*

Urgency does not mean frenzy. The story can be a quiet story, a story about dismay or missed chances or a wordless revelation. But it must be urgently told. It must be told with as much intentness as if the teller's life depended on it. And, if you are a writer, so it does, because your life as the writer of each particular story is only as long, and as good, as the story itself. Most of those who hear it or read it will never know you, but they will know the story. Their act of listening is its reincarnation.

Is all this too much to ask? Not really; because many stories, many of these stories, do it superbly.

Down to Specifics

But they do it in a multiplicity of ways. When I was reading through the stories, someone asked me, "Is there a trend?" There is no trend. There are only twenty strong, exciting, and unique stories.

I didn't think anyone could ever write a story about taking drugs in the sixties that would hold my attention for more than five minutes, but Michael Cunningham does it brilliantly in "White Angel"— because the narrator is a young boy, "the most criminally advanced nine-year-old in my fourth-grade class," who is being initiated into almost everything by his adored sixteen-year-old brother. The sensual richness of this story is impressive; so is the way it shifts from out-of-control feverishness and hilarity, as the two brothers scramble their brains with acid against a background of Leave-It-to-Beaver Cleveland domesticity ("We slipped the tabs into our mouths at breakfast, while our mother paused over the bacon"), to the nearly unbearable poignancy of its tragic ending.

Another story that blindsided me by taking an unlikely subject and turning it inside out was "The Flowers of Boredom." Who could hope to write with any conviction or panache about working as a paper-shuffler for a defense contractor? But Rick DeMarinis does. The visionary glimpse of cosmic horror at the end is come by honestly, step by step, through dailiness and small disgusts. This story is one of those truly original collisions between delicately handled form and banal but alarming content that leaves you aghast and slightly battered.

"Hell lay about them in their infancy," Graham Greene remarks in *The Lawless Roads*, and this is the tone of Barbara Gowdy's "Disneyland." If "The Flowers of Boredom" views the military enterprise as a giant, superhuman pattern, "Disneyland" squints at it through Groucho Marx glasses gone rotten. The controlling figure is a domineering father obsessed with his early-sixties fallout shelter. He and his mania would be ludicrous, almost a parody, viewed from a safe distance; but the distance is not safe. This man is seen from beneath by his children, who are forced to play platoon to his drill sergeant in the smelly, dark, tyrannical, and terrifying hell in which he has imprisoned them. The senses of claustrophobia and entrapment are intense.

There are several other fine stories that concern themselves with the terrors, and sometimes the delights, of childhood and with the powerlessness of children caught under the gigantic, heedless feet of the adult world. Mark Richard's "Strays," with its two poor-white boys abandoned by their runaway mother and rescued, after a fashion, by their rogue gambler of an uncle, is one fine example. Its deadpan delivery of the squalid and the grotesque reminds us that everything that happens to children is accepted as normal by them; or if not exactly normal, unalterable. For them, reality and enchantment are the same thing, and they are held in thrall.

Dale Ray Phillips's "What Men Love For" contains another child who is under a spell, that cast by his fragile, manic-depressive mother. Against the various rituals she uses to keep herself stuck together, and those the boy himself is in the process of inventing for his own preservation, there's the magic of his father—a magic of luck, risk, hope, and chance embodied in the motorcycle he drives too fast.

"The Boy on the Train," by Arthur Robinson, is a wonderful, warped memoir of sorts. Instead of being about one childhood, it's really about two. Two children grow up to be fathers, two fathers misunderstand their sons, and two sons bedevil their fathers in niggling, embarrassing, or nauseating ways designed to get right under their skin: "In prepubescence, Edward gazed at his face in the mirror a great deal and studied the effects he could get with it. Once he discovered that a strip of toothpaste artfully placed just below a nostril produced an effect that could easily turn his father's queasy stomach. The result was more than he could have hoped for." The beautiful way this story turns around on itself, loops back, plays variations on three generations, is a delight to follow.

Two of these stories have an almost fablelike simplicity and structure. One of them is M. T. Sharif's "The Letter Writer," whose hapless protagonist, Haji, is arrested during the Iranian revolution because he is suspected of being the brother of a supposed spy and can't prove he isn't. But the authorities can't prove he is, and since he won't confess and they can't convict him, he is given a make-work job: covering up the bare arms, legs, heads, and necks of women pictured in Western magazines by drawing clothes on them with pen and ink. Earlier, a passing dervish had prophesied that Haji would end up living in a palace, attended by concubines and servants. The manner in which this fate is actually fulfilled is reminiscent of both Kafka and the tradition of the ironic Eastern tale.

Harriet Doerr's "Edie: A Life" has the plain charm of a sampler. It violates almost every rule I have ever heard about the construction of short stories. It doesn't concentrate, for instance, on an in-depth study of character, or on a short period of time, a single incident that focuses a life. Instead it gives the entire life—in miniature, as it were—complete and rounded and unexplained as an apple.

Other stories persuade us and move us in other ways. Larry Brown, in "Kubuku Rides (This Is It)," gives his sad story of an alcoholic wife its edge and drive through the immediacy and vigor of his language, as does Blanche McCrary Boyd in her uneasily uproarious "The Black Hand Girl." (The hand, which is a man's, gets black by being sprained in a panty girdle. Read on.) Douglas Glover, in "Why I Decide to Kill Myself and Other Jokes," also draws on the mordant, self-deprecating humor of women. There's a murder with a hammer, a rescue from the snow, an attempted rescue with a skillet. There's a Chinese woman, in David Wong Louie's

"Displacement," who is trying to make the best of America, and a native Indian woman, in Linda Hogan's "Aunt Moon's Young Man," who is also trying to make the best of it. There's a left-wing mother whose son rebels by taking up religion. But these are just hints. To get the real story, you have to read the story, as always.

I must admit that although I was reading blind, I did guess the identities of three of the authors. Bharati Mukherjee's "The Management of Grief" wasn't even a guess, as I had read it before and it had stayed with me. It's a finely tuned, acutely felt story about an Indian immigrant wife's reactions when the plane carrying her husband and sons is blown up over the Irish Sea by terrorists. The sleepwalking intensity with which she gropes her way through the emotional debris scattered by these senseless deaths and eventually makes a mystic sense out of them for herself is sparely but unsparingly rendered.

When I read "The Concert Party," I guessed that it was either by Mavis Gallant or by a male writer doing a very good imitation of her. Who else would, or could, write so convincingly and with such interest about a hopeless nerd from Saskatchewan bungling around loose in France in the early fifties? The story did turn out to be by Mavis Gallant, leaving me to admire once again her deftness with a full canvas, her skill at interweaving the fates of her characters, her sharp eye for the details of small pomposities, and her camerawork, if it may be called that. Watch the way she shifts, at the end, from close-up to long shot:

> Remembering Edie at the split second when she came to a decision, I can find it in me to envy them. The rest of us were born knowing better, which means we were stuck. When I finally looked away from her it was at another pool of candlelight, and the glowing, blooming children. I wonder now if there was anything about us for the children to remember, if they ever later on reminded one another: There was that long table of English-speaking people, still in bud.

I think I would recognize an Alice Munro story in Braille, even though I don't read Braille. The strength and distinctiveness of her voice will always give her away. "Meneseteung" is, for my money, one of Alice Munro's best and, in the manner of its telling, quirkiest stories yet. It purports to be about a minor sentimental "poetess"—the word, here, is appropriate—living in a small, raw, cowpat-strewn, treeless nineteenth-century town, which is as far a cry from our idyllic notions of a golden past as the poet's sugary verses are from real life. Our sweet picture of bygone days is destroyed, and, in the process, our conceptions of how a story should proceed. Similarly, the poet herself disintegrates in the harsh and multiple presence of the vivid life that surrounds her and that finally proves too huge and real for her. Or does it? Does she disintegrate or integrate? Does crossing the borders of convention lead toward insanity or sanity? "She doesn't mistake that for reality, and neither does she mistake anything else for reality," we are told when the crocheted roses on the tablecloth began to float, "and that is how she knows that she is sane."

The last word is not the poet's, however, but the nameless narrator's, the "I" who has been searching for the poet, or scraps of her, through time. These last words could be an epigraph for this collection of stories, or for the act of writing itself:

> People are curious. A few people are. They will be driven to find things out, even trivial things. They will put things together, knowing all along that they may be mistaken. You see them going around with notebooks, scraping the dirt off gravestones, reading microfilm, just in the hope of seeing this trickle in time, making a connection, rescuing one thing from the rubbish.

I thank all the authors in this book for the pleasure their stories have given me, and for what they added to my own sense of what a story is, and can be.

From listening to the stories of others, we learn to tell our own.

10

Introduction:

Women Writers at Work: The Paris Review Interviews, George Plimpton, editor

What is it about interviews that attracts us? Specifically, what is it about interviews with writers? Why should we pry? If a writer is august enough to be subject to interviews, we already have the books to read; shouldn't that be enough for us? (And the books must be books we like, because if we didn't, we presumably wouldn't be much interested in knowing anything about the person who has written them.)

Some of us are wary; even if we admire a book, we avoid an interview with its author. The writer is just the raw material, after all, and we prefer things cooked. Or perhaps we have a superstition about peeking: why ruin the memory of a night of magic by sneaking a look backstage, where the magician is wiping off the grimy makeup and the rabbits are born in hutches instead of, miraculously, out of silk hats? As Dorothy discovered in *The Wizard of Oz,* the fire that burns yet is not consumed may turn out to be—much to our disappointment—just a trick pulled by some wizened old fraud from Kansas. Some people may not be able to tell the dancer from the dance, but we think we can, and we prefer the dance.

Sometimes, on the other hand, we're greedy to know more. More of what? More of everything; more of anything; more of how and why, more of how-to. We would like to stand behind the interviewer and dictate the questions: What road did you travel on, and whom did you meet on the way, and who helped you across the river where the water was deepest? What other writers did you learn from, and does it matter what age, color, gender, or nationality they where? (P. L. Travers's Mary Poppins as an avatar of the Great Mother in her Kali incarnation? Alarming, but just barely possible. Simone de Beauvoir influenced by *The Mill on the Floss*? After the first shock it fits. . . .) Once upon a time you, too, were young, untried, unpublished; so how did you manage, against all odds—or against some odds, at least—to accomplish as much as you have? Do you think that what you do makes any difference, to your individual readers or to the world in general? Where did the books come from—what part of your life? Does the writing always flow, or do you struggle? Do you have to suffer to be an artist, and if so, how much, and what kind of suffering would you recommend? Should you use—*do* you use—a pencil, or a pen, or your finger dipped in blood? Are there any special foods? What kind of chair?

It is our illusion that by knowing the answers to these questions we will know the central, the hidden, the necessary thing; that a writer's power is to be found in the sum of such answers. It isn't, of course. An interview is also a performance, and although a performance can reveal much, its revelations are selective, and its omissions and concealments are often as instructive as its grand pronouncements. (In this collection, for instance, it's an education to watch Elizabeth Bishop evading the issues.) Sometimes a writer doesn't want to tell; sometimes a writer doesn't know; sometimes a writer has forgotten. But why should a writer tell all? Why should anyone? How can anyone? *All* is a giant subject. In the interview, we must largely settle for conversation instead.

Your next-door neighbor might give you some of the very same answers as the ones you'll find in this collection—with a pencil, on a bed, with a glass of sherry, and yes to the suffering—but that is the mystery; or, if you prefer, the lack of mystery. Writers are human beings; they, too, inhabit bodies, had childhoods, get through the day somehow, experience joy and fear and boredom, confront death. The rabbits they produce are only common rabbits, after all; it's the hat that's magic. And yet it is only a hat. This is what fuels our curiosity: the mix of the familiar, even the banal, and the radically inexplicable.

This volume is a revised version of the 1988 collection *Women Writers at Work*, which was part of the *Paris Review*'s highly praised series of inter-views with writers. Both that book and this one are a departure from the norm. Previous *Paris Review* collections mixed men and women, but *Women Writers at Work*, as its title suggests, is unisexual. That the editors have chosen to bring together fifteen writers as diverse as Dorothy Parker and Nadine Gordimer, P. L. Travers and Maya Angelou, Marianne Moore and Simone de Beauvoir, Toni Morrison and Katherine Anne Porter, over what, in some cases, would be their dead bodies, merely because they share a double-X chromosome, was the result of readers' requests. Why not a gathering of women writers? the editors were asked. Which is not quite the same thing as *why*.

To some, the answer is self-evident: women writers belong together because they are different from men, and the writing they do is different as well and cannot be read with the same eyeglasses as those used for the reading of male writers. Nor can writing by women be read in the same way by men as it can by women, and vice versa. For many women, Heath-cliff is a romantic hero; for many men, he's a posturing oaf they'd like to punch in the nose. *Paradise Lost* reads differently when viewed by the daughters of Eve, and with Milton's browbeaten secretarial daughters in mind; and so on down through the canon.

Such gender-polarized interpretations can reach beyond subject matter and point of view to encompass matters of structure and style: Are women really more subjective? Do their novels really end with questions? Gender-linked analysis may seek to explore attitudes toward language itself. Is there a distinct female *écriture?* Does the mother tongue really belong to mothers, or is it yet one more male-shaped institution bent, like foot-binding, on the deformation and hobbling of women? I have had it sug-gested to me, in all seriousness, that women ought not to write at all, since to do so is to dip one's hand, like Shakespeare's dyre, into a medium both sullied and sullying. (This suggestion was not made telepathically, but in spoken sentences, since, for polemicists as for writers themselves, the alter-native to language is silence.)

Some years ago I was on a panel—that polygonal form of discourse so beloved of the democratic twentieth century—consisting entirely of

women, including Jan Morris, who used to be James Morris, and Nayantara Sahgal of India. From the audience came the question "How do you
feel about being on a panel of women?" We all prevaricated. Some of us
protested that we had been on lots of panels that included men; others said
that most panels were male, with a woman dotted here and there for dec-
orative effect, like parsley. Jan Morris said that she was in the process of
transcending gender and was aiming at becoming a horse, to which Nayantara Sahgal replied that she hoped it was an English horse, since in some
other, poorer, countries, horses were not treated very well. Which underlined, for all of us, that there are categories other than male or female
worth considering.

I suppose we all should have said, "Why not?" Still, I was intrigued by
our collective uneasiness. No woman writer wants to be overlooked and
undervalued for being a woman; but few, it seems, wish to be defined
solely by gender, or constrained by loyalties to it alone—an attitude that
may puzzle, hurt, or enrage those whose political priorities cause them to
view writing as a tool, a means to an end, rather than as a vocation subject
to a Muse who will desert you if you break trust with your calling. In the
interview that begins this collection, Dorothy Parker articulates the
dilemma:

> I'm a feminist and God knows I'm loyal to my sex, and you must
> remember that from my very early days, when this city was scarcely
> safe from buffaloes, I was in the struggle for equal rights for women.
> But when we paraded through the catcalls of men and when we
> chained ourselves to lamp posts to try to get our equality—dear
> child, we didn't foresee those female writers.

Male writers may suffer strains on their single-minded dedication to their
art for reasons of class or race or nationality, but so far no male writer is
likely to be asked to sit on a panel addressing itself to the special problems
of a male writer, or be expected to support another writer simply because
he happens to be a man. Such things are asked of women writers all the
time, and it makes them jumpy.

Virginia Woolf may have been right about the androgynous nature of

the artist, but she was right also about the differences in social situation
these androgynous artists are certain to encounter. We may agree with
Nadine Gordimer when she says, "By and large, I don't think it matters a
damn what sex a writer is, so long as the work is that of a real writer," if
what she means is that it *shouldn't* matter, in any true assessment of talent
or accomplishment; but unfortunately it often has mattered, to other
people. When Joyce Carol Oates is asked the "woman" question, phrased
in her case as "What are the advantages of being a woman writer?" she
makes a virtue of necessity:

> Advantages! Too many to enumerate, probably. Since, being a
> woman, I can't be taken altogether seriously by the sort of male
> critics who rank writers 1, 2, 3 in the public press, I am free, I sup-
> pose, to do as I like.

Joan Didion is asked the same question in its negative form—"disadvan-
tages" instead of "advantages"—and also focuses on social differences,
social acceptance, and role:

> When I was starting to write—in the late fifties, early sixties—there
> was a kind of social tradition in which male novelists could operate.
> Hard drinkers, bad livers. Wives, wars, big fish, Africa, Paris, no
> second acts. A man who wrote novels had a role in the world, and
> he could play that role and do whatever he wanted behind it. A
> woman who wrote novels had no particular role. Women who wrote
> novels were quite often perceived as invalids. Carson McCullers,
> Jane Bowles. Flannery O'Connor, of course. Novels by women
> tended to be described, even by their publishers, as sensitive. I'm not
> sure this is so true anymore, but it certainly was at the time, and I
> didn't much like it. I dealt with it the same way I deal with every-
> thing. I just tended my own garden, didn't pay much attention,
> behaved—I suppose—deviously.

I think of Marianne Moore, living decorously with her mother and her
"dark" furniture, her height of social rebellion the courageous ignoring of

the need for chaperons at Greenwich Village literary parties, and wonder how many male writers could have lived such a circumscribed life and survived the image.

Not the least among perceived social differences is the difficulty women writers have experienced in being taken "altogether seriously" as legitimate artists. Ezra Pound, writing in the second decade of this century, spoke for many male authors and critics before and since: "I distrust the 'female artist'. . . . Not wildly antifeminist we are yet to be convinced that any woman ever invented anything in the arts." Cognate with this view of writing as a male preserve has been the image of women writers as lightweight puffballs, neurotic freaks suffering from what Edna O'Brien has called "a double dose of masochism: the masochism of the woman and that of the artist," or, if approved of, as honorary men. Femininity and excellence, it seemed, were mutually exclusive. Thus Katherine Anne Porter:

> If there is such a thing as a man's mind and a woman's mind—and I'm sure there is—it isn't what most critics mean when they talk about the two. If I show wisdom, they say I have a masculine mind. If I am silly and irrelevant—and Edmund Wilson says I often am— why then, they say I have a typically feminine mind! . . . But I haven't ever found it unnatural to be a woman.

The interviewer responds with a question that is asked, in one form or another, not only of almost every woman included in this book but also of almost every woman writer ever interviewed: "But haven't you found that being a woman presented to you, as an artist, certain special problems?"

Katherine Anne Porter's reply—"I think that's very true and very right"—is by no means the only one possible. Some, such as Mary McCarthy, are clearly impatient with the question itself. McCarthy accepts some version of the "masculine" versus the "feminine" sensibility, but aligns herself firmly with the former.

> INTERVIEWER: What do you think of women writers, or do you think the category "woman writer" should not be made?

MCCARTHY: Some women writers make it. I mean, there's a certain kind of Woman writer who's a capital W, capital W. Virginia Woolf certainly was one, and Katherine Mansfield was one, and Elizabeth Bowen is one. Katherine Anne Porter? Don't think she really is—I mean, her writing is certainly very feminine, but I would say that there wasn't this "WW" business in Katherine Anne Porter. Who else? There's Eudora Welty, who's certainly not a "Woman Writer," though she's become one lately.

INTERVIEWER: What is it that happens to make this change?

MCCARTHY: I think they become interested in decor. You notice the change in Elizabeth Bowen. Her early work is much more masculine. Her later work has much more drapery in it. . . . I was going to write a piece at some point about this called "Sense and Sensibility," dividing women writers into these two. I am for the ones who represent sense.

There is, still, a sort of trained-dog fascination with the idea of women writers—not that the thing is done well, but that it is done at all, by a creature that is not supposed to possess such capabilities. And so a biographer may well focus on the woman, on gossip and sexual detail and domestic arrangements and political involvement, to the exclusion of the artist. However, what these writers have in common is not their diverse responses to the category "woman writer," but their shared passion toward the category "writer."

This is true as well when that other "special" category, race, is tacked on. Neither the white women writers nor the black women writers in this book feel that they have to deny anything about themselves to gain entry into the category of writer; but none of them feel, either, that their other attributes should be allowed to obscure what they are focused on, what it is they have been called to do. For them, writing is not an offshoot; it is the one thing that includes all the other aspects of their lives. Thus Maya Angelou:

When I am writing, I am trying to find out who I am, who we are, what we're capable of, how we feel, how we lose and stand up, and go on from darkness into darkness. I'm trying for that. But I'm also trying for the language. I'm trying to see how it can really sound. I really love language. I love it for what it does for us, how it allows us to explain the pain and the glory, the nuances and delicacies of our existence. And then it allows us to laugh, allows us to show wit. Real wit is shown in language. We need language.

Reading through these interviews, I was struck again and again by the intensity of the writers' dedication: their commitment to craft, the informed admiration for the work of other writers from whom they have learned, the insistence on the importance of what has been done, and what can be done, through the art itself. Thus Toni Morrison:

It is not possible for me to be unaware of the incredible violence, the willful ignorance, the hunger for other people's pain. . . . What makes me feel I belong here, out in this world, is not the teacher, not the mother, not the lover but what goes on in my mind when I am writing. Then I belong here, and then all of the things that are disparate and irreconcilable can be useful. I can do the traditional things that writers always say they do, which is to make order out of chaos.

In no other art is the relationship of creation to creator so complex and personal and thus so potentially damaging to self-esteem; if you fail, you fail alone. The dancer realizes someone else's dance, the writer her own. The relationship of any writer toward a vocation so exacting in its specificity, so demanding of love and energy and time, so resistant to all efforts to define its essence or to categorize its best effects, is bound to be an edgy one, and in these conversations the edginess shows through. Some disclaim ego, remarkable in a collection of such strong, assertive, individual voices; others keep secrets; others fence with their considerable intelligence; others have recourse to mysticism; others protect themselves with wit. It would be a brave person who would try to stuff these wonderful

and various talents into one tidy box labeled "WW," and accept that des-
ignation to be definitive. Despite the title of this book, the label should
probably read, "WWAAW," Writers Who Are Also Women.

To write is a solitary and singular act; to do it superbly, as all of these
writers have done, is a blessing. Despite everything that gets said about the
suffering and panic and horror of being a writer, the final impression left
by these remarkable voices is one of thankfulness, of humility in the face
of what has been given. From Joyce Carol Oates, one of the youngest
writers in this group:

> I take seriously Flaubert's statement that we must love one another
> in our art as the mystics love one another in God. By honoring one
> another's creation we honor something that deeply connects us all,
> and goes beyond us.

And from Dorothy Parker, one of the oldest:

> I want so much to write well, though I know I don't. . . . But during
> and at the end of my life, I will adore those who have.

11

Review:

The Warrior Queens
by Antonia Fraser

*T*he *Warrior Queens*, Antonia Fraser's most recent historical book, is lore-packed, quirky in its approach, and fascinating to read. If nonfiction books can be thought of as detailed answers to unvoiced questions, then the questions answered by this one are: How have female political and military leaders gotten away with it? How have they managed to fob themselves off on those hardest-to-convince soldiers and other politicians—those quintessentially male devisers and players of boys' games—as worthy leaders of the charge or captains of the ship of state, although long of hair and bulgy of breast? Such women have been few enough in number so that the exceptions have very much proven the rule. But what about those exceptions? What was their strategy, their sleight-of-hand? What was their secret?

In pursuit of answers, Fraser has assembled a remarkable group of women for our contemplation. She begins with Boadicea herself, that famed but shadowy first-century British tribal queen who led a revolt against the occupying and oppressive Romans, massacred a lot of them, and was said to have committed suicide when her forces were massacred in return. Fraser provides as faithful an account of the events as is possible, given that information is scarce and reports vary. But she is just as interested in Boadicea's metamorphoses in historical and literary accounts through the ages—from pious patriot and martyr, mother of her people, to unwomanly, bloodthirsty shrew, to symbol of heroic British imperialism, ironic in view of the fact that her own revolt was against an earlier imperialism. The accounts of her have varied according to what men considered proper womanly behavior, and to what the British considered proper British behavior; thus Boadicea has been both slut and saint. Very early on, the myth detached itself from the real woman in question, and has been floating around ever since, ready to stick itself like a leech to any woman hardy enough to brandish a spear or declare for office.

Fraser follows up with a varied assortment of women from many centuries and civilizations who have held, however briefly, the reins of power: Zenobia, the third-century queen of Palmyra who also challenged Roman rule; Empress Maud, of the twelfth-century English wars of succession; Queen Tamara of Georgia, "The Lion of the Caucasus"; Elizabeth I, inspiring her troops to battle the Spanish Armada; Isabella of Spain; the engaging Queen Jinga of Angola, who successfully defied the Portuguese colonists; Catherine the Great of Russia; the Vietnamese heroines Trung Trac and Trung Nhi; the amazing Rani of Jhansi, who fought the British in India; Indira Gandhi, Golda Meir, and a good many more, concluding with that handy bookend to Boadicea, Margaret Thatcher. Their childhoods, their paths to leadership, and their styles vary enormously, but they have one thing in common: all were instantly mythologized. Male military leaders, taken for all in all, have been men, and that has been enough; but female ones cannot be mere women. They are aberrations, and as such are thought to partake of the supernatural or the monstrous: angels or devils, paragons of chastity or demons of lust, Whores of Babylon or Iron Maidens. Sometimes they have profited from the female saints or goddesses available to them through their cultures, sometimes they have had to work against such images. Their femininity has been both shackle and banner.

As leaders, they have had to be, like female doctors a decade ago, better than men. They have shamed their male followers by displaying superior courage; they have shamed their male adversaries by inflicting defeat on them at the hands of a mere woman. They have outmaneuvered, outtalked, outblustered, and in some cases outshot and outridden the cream of the male crop. Altogether they are an impressive lot, and Fraser is to be congratulated for rescuing them from their own myths and for giving them their due as individuals, the lesser-known among them as well as the household names.

But although they have been trotted out like a roll call by many advocates for the equality of women, and presented in many guises—from turn-of-the-century pageants to Judy Chicago's "Dinner Party"—these women have seldom allied themselves with women in general, or with movements for the improvement of their lot. More typically, they have distanced themselves from women, like Elizabeth I, who was against female rule but saw herself as a divinely placed exception, or like Catherine the Great, who spoke of the "weak, frivolous, whining species of women." Many have preferred the status of honorary males. If you're playing boys' games, you need to be one of the boys.

This book should be required reading for any woman going into politics, truck driving, or the army; indeed, for any woman going into anything, unless her chosen field is uniquely feminine. Public women are put through different tests of nerve, attract different kinds of criticism, and are subject to different sorts of mythologizing than are men, and *The Warrior Queens* indicates what kinds.

Those of us for whom politics is a spectator sport will find it useful, too. It goes a long way toward explaining the various media transformations of, for instance, Margaret Thatcher, from her Attila-the-Hen period through her Iron Maiden–Falkland War phase to her incarnation as an editorial-cartoon Boadicea, complete with whip and chariot, triumphant on election day and dragging a clutch of pygmy men in her wake. Women leaders, it seems, find it difficult to be life-size. For good or ill, they are gigantic.

12

Writing Utopia

ow did *The Handmaid's Tale* get written? The answer could be, partly on a rented electric typewriter with a German keyboard in a walk-up flat in West Berlin, and partly in a small house in Tuscaloosa, Alabama—which, it was announced to me with a certain pride, is the per capita murder capital of the United States. "Gosh," I said. "Maybe I shouldn't be here." "Aw, don't y'all worry," they replied. "They only shoots family." But although these two places provided, shall we say, a certain atmosphere, there is more to the story than that.

The Handmaid's Tale, I must explain for the benefit of the one person in the audience who may not have read it yet—out in paperback, and a bargain of creepy thrills for only $4.95—is set in the future. This conned some people into believing it is science fiction, which, to my mind, it is not. I define science fiction as fiction in which things happen that are not possible today—that depend, for instance, on advanced space travel, time travel, the discovery of green monsters on other planets or galaxies, or that contain various technologies we have not yet developed. But in *The Handmaid's Tale*, nothing happens that the human race has not already done at some time in the past, or that it is not doing now, perhaps in other countries, or for which it has not yet developed the technology. We've done it, or we're doing it, or we could start doing it tomorrow. Nothing inconceivable takes place, and the projected trends on which my future society is based are already in motion. So I think of *The Handmaid's Tale* not as science fiction but as speculative fiction; and, more particularly, as that negative form of Utopian fiction that has come to be known as the Dystopia.

A Utopia is usually thought of as a fictional perfect society, but in fact the word does not mean "perfect society." It means "nowhere," and was used sardonically by Sir Thomas More as the title of his own sixteenth-century fictional discourse on government. Perhaps he meant to indicate that although his Utopia made more rational sense than the England of his day, it was unlikely to be found anywhere outside a book.

Both the Utopia and the Dystopia concern themselves with the designing of societies—good societies for the Utopias, bad ones for the Dystopias. There is some of the same pleasure in this, for the writer, that we used to get as children when we built sand cities, or dinosaur jungles from Plasticine or drew entire wardrobes for paper dolls. But in a Utopia, you get to plan everything—the cities, the legal system, the customs, even facets of the language. The Dystopian bad design is the Utopian good design in reverse—that is, we the readers are supposed to deduce what a good society is by seeing, in detail, what it isn't.

The Utopia-Dystopia as a form tends to be produced only by cultures based on monotheism—or, like Plato's system, on a single idea of the Good—and that postulate also a single goal-oriented timeline. Cultures based on polytheism and the circularity of time don't seem to produce them. Why bother to try to improve society, or even to visualize it improved, when you know it's all going to go around again, like clothes in the wash? And how can you define a "good" society as opposed to a "bad" one if you see good and bad as aspects of the same thing? But Judeo-Christianity, being a linear monotheism—one God and one plotline, from Genesis to Revelation—has generated many fictional Utopias, and a good many attempts to create the real thing right here on earth, the venture of the Pilgrim Fathers being one of them—"We shall be as a city upon a hill, a light to all nations"—and Marxism being another. In Marxism, history replaces God as a determinant, and the classless society replaces the New Jerusalem, but change through time, heading in the direction of perfection, is similarly postulated. In the background of every modern Utopia lurk Plato's Republic and the Book of Revelation, and modern Dystopias have not been uninfluenced by various literary versions of Hell, especially those of Dante and Milton, which in their turn go right back to the Bible, that indispensable sourcebook of Western literature.

Sir Thomas More's original *Utopia* has a long list of descendants, many of which I read as I hacked my way through high school, through college, and later through graduate school. This list includes Swift's *Gulliver's Travels*, and, in the nineteenth century, William Morris's *News from Nowhere*, in which the ideal society is a kind of artists' colony; H. G. Wells's *Time Machine*, in which the lower classes actually eat the upper; Butler's *Erewhon*, in which crime is a sickness and sickness is a crime; and W. H. Hudson's *A Crystal Age*. In our own century, the classics are Huxley's *Brave New World*; Bellamy's *Looking Backward*; and, of course, *1984*, to mention a few. Utopias by women are also of note, though not as numerous. There are, for instance, *Herland* by Charlotte Perkins Gilman, and *Woman on the Edge of Time* by Marge Piercey.

Utopias are often satirical, the satire being directed at whatever society the writer is currently living in—that is, the superior arrangements of the Utopians reflect badly on *us*. Dystopias are often more like dire warnings than satires, dark shadows cast by the present into the future. They are what will happen to us if we don't pull up our socks.

What aspects of this life interest such writers? To no one's surprise, their concerns turn out to be much the same as those of society. There are, of course, the superficial matters of clothing and cuisine, partial nudity and vegetarianism making regular appearances. But the main problems are the distribution of wealth; labor relations; power structures; the protection of the powerless, if any; relations between the sexes; population control; urban planning, often in the form of an interest in drains and sewers; the rearing of children; illness and its ethics; insanity ditto, the censorship of artists and suchlike riffraff and antisocial elements; individual privacy and its invasion; the redefinition of language; and the administration of justice— if, that is, any such administration is needed. It is a characteristic of the extreme Utopia, at one end, and the extreme Dystopia, at the other, that neither contains any lawyers. Extreme Utopias are communities of spirit, in which there cannot be any real disagreements among members because all are of like and right mind; extreme Dystopias are absolute tyrannies, in which contention is not a possibility. In Utopia, then, no lawyers are needed; in Dystopia, no lawyers are allowed.

In between, however, is where most Utopias-Dystopias as well as most human societies fall, and here the composers of these fictions have shown remarkable fecundity. Relations between the sexes exhibit perhaps the widest range. Some Utopias go for a sort of healthy-minded communal sex; others, such as W. H. Hudson's *Crystal Age*, for an antlike arrangement in which most citizens are sexually neutral and only one pair per large country mansion actually breed, which is how they cut down on the birth rate. Still others, such as Marge Piercey's, allow men to participate almost equally in childrearing by allowing them to breast-feed via hormone injections, an option that may not rejoice your hearts but at least has the virtue of novelty. Then there are Huxley's ritualistic group sex and bottle babies, Skinner's boxes, and various minor science fictions—written by men, I hasten to add—in which women devour their mates or paralyze them and lay eggs on them, à la spiders. Sexual relations in extreme Dystopias usually exhibit some form of slavery or, as in Orwell, extreme sexual repression.

The details, then, vary, but the Utopia-Dystopia as a form is a way of trying things out on paper first to see whether we might like them, should we ever have the chance to put them into actual practice. In addition, it challenges us to reexamine what we understand by the word *human*, and above all what we intend by the word *freedom*. For neither the Utopia nor the Dystopia is open-ended. Utopia is an extreme example of the impulse to order; it's the word *should* run rampant. Dystopia, its nightmare mirror image, is the desire to squash dissent taken to inhuman and lunatic lengths. Neither are what you'd call tolerant, but both are necessary to the imagination: if we can't visualize the good, the ideal, if we can't formulate what we want, we'll get what we don't want, in spades. It's a sad commentary on our age that we find Dystopias a lot easier to believe in than Utopias: Utopias we can only imagine; Dystopias we've already had. But should we try too hard to enforce Utopia, Dystopia rapidly follows; because if enough people disagree with us we'll have to eliminate or suppress or terrorize or manipulate them, and then we've got *1984*. As a rule, Utopia is only safe when it remains true to its name and stays nowhere. It's a nice place to visit, but do we really want to live there? Which may be the ultimate moral of such stories.

All this was by way of background, to let you know that I'd done the required reading long before launching myself into *The Handmaid's Tale*. There are two other lots of required reading I would like to mention. The first had to do with the literature of the Second World War—I read Winston Churchill's memoirs when I was in high school, not to mention a biography of Rommel, the Desert Fox, and many another tome of military history. I read these books partly because I was an omnivorous reader and they were there; my father was a history buff, and these things were just lying around. By extension, I read various books on totalitarian regimes, of the present and the past; the one that sticks out was called *Darkness at Noon*, by Arthur Koestler. (This was not my only reading when I was in high school; I was also reading Jane Austen and Emily Brontë and a particularly lurid book of sci-fi called *Donovan's Brain*. I would read anything, and still will; when all else is lacking, I read airline in-flight magazines, and I have to say, I am getting tired of those articles on billionaire businessmen. Don't you think it's time for some other kinds of fiction?)

This "political" area of my reading was reinforced later by travel to various countries where, to put it mildly, certain things we consider freedoms are not universally in force, and by conversations with many people; I remember in particular meeting a woman who had been in the French Resistance during the war, and a man who had escaped from Poland at the same time.

The other lot of required reading has to do with the history of the seventeenth-century Puritans, especially those who ended up in the United States. At the front of *The Handmaid's Tale* there are two dedications. One is to Perry Miller, who was a professor of mine at the dreaded Harvard Graduate School, and who almost single-handedly was responsible for resurrecting the American Puritans as a field for literary investigation. I had to take a lot of this stuff, and I needed to "fill my gap" to pass my comprehensives, and this was one area I had not studied as an undergraduate. Perry Miller pointed out that contrary to what I had been taught earlier, the American Puritans did not come to North America in search of religious toleration, or not what we mean by it. They wanted the freedom to practice *their* religion, but they were not particularly keen on anyone else practicing his or hers. Among their noteworthy achievements were the banishing of so-called heretics, the hanging of Quakers, and the well-known witchcraft trials. I get to say these bad things about them because they were my ancestors—in a way, *The Handmaid's Tale* is my book about my ancestors—and the second dedication, to Mary Webster, is indeed to one of these very same ancestors. Mary was a well-known witch, or at least she was tried for witchcraft and hanged. But it was before they had invented the drop, which breaks your neck—they merely strung her up and let her dangle, and when they came to cut her down the next morning, she was still alive. Under the law of double jeopardy, you couldn't execute a person twice for the same crime, so she lived for another fourteen years. I felt that if I was going to stick my neck out by writing this book, I'd better dedicate it to someone with a very tough neck.

Puritan New England was a theocracy, not a democracy; and the future society proposed in *The Handmaid's Tale* has the form of a theocracy, too, on the principle that no society every strays completely far from its roots. Stalinist Russia would have been unthinkable without Czarist Russia to precede it, and so forth. Also, the most potent forms of dictatorship have always been those that have imposed tyranny in the name of religion; and even folk such as the French Revolutionaries and Hitler have striven to give a religious force and sanction to their ideas. What is needed for a really good tyranny is an unquestionable idea or authority. Political disagreement is political disagreement; but political disagreement with a *theocracy* is heresy, and a good deal of gloating self-righteousness can be brought to bear on the extermination of heretics, as history has demonstrated, through the Crusades, the forcible conversions to Islam, the Spanish Inquisition, the burnings at the stake under the English queen Bloody Mary, and so on through the years. It was in the light of history that the American constitutionalists in the eighteenth century separated church from state. It is also in the light of history that my leaders in *The Handmaid's Tale* recombine them.

All fictions begin with the question *What if . . . ?* The What if? varies from book to book: What if John loves Mary? What if John doesn't love Mary? What if Mary gets eaten by an enormous shark? What if the Martians invade? What if you find a treasure map, and so forth—but there is always a *What if . . . ?* to which the novel is the answer. The *what if* for

97

The Handmaid's Tale could be formulated: What if it *can* happen here? What kind of "it" would it be? (I have never believed any fictions about the Russians taking over. If they can't get their refrigerators to work, they quite frankly wouldn't stand much of a chance. So that, for me, is not a plausible "it.")

Or *what if* you wanted to take over the United States and set up a totalitarian government, the lust for power being what it is? How would you go about it? What conditions would favor you, and what slogan would you propose, what flag would you fly that would attract the necessary 20 percent of the population, without which no totalitarianism can stay in power? If you proposed communism, you'd be unlikely to get many takers. A dictatorship of liberal democrats would be seen even by the slightly dull-witted as a contradiction in terms. Although many dubious acts have been committed, let's face it, in the name of the great god democracy, they've usually been done in secret, or with a good deal of verbal embroidery covering them up. In this country you'd be more likely to try some version of Puritan Fatherhood if you wanted a takeover. That would definitely be your best plan.

But true dictatorships do not come *in* in good times. They come in in bad times, when people are ready to give up some of their freedoms to someone—anyone—who can take control and promise them better times. The bad times that made Hitler and Mussolini possible were economic, with some extra frills such as a shortage of men in proportion to women, due to the high death rates during the First World War. To make my future society possible, I proposed something a little more complex. Bad economic times, yes, due to a shrinking area of global control, which would mean shrinking markets and fewer sources of cheap raw materials. But also a period of widespread environmental catastrophe, which has had several results: a higher infertility and sterility rate due to chemical and radiation damage (this, by the way, is happening already) and a higher birth-defect rate, which is also happening. The ability to conceive and bear a healthy child would become rare, and thus valued; and we all know who gets most—in any society—of things that are rare and valued. Those at the top. Hence my proposed future society, which, like many human societies before it, assigns more than one woman to its favored male members.

There are lots of precedents for this practice, but my society, being derived from Puritanism, would, of course, need biblical sanction. Luckily for them, Old Testament patriarchs were notoriously polygamous; the text they chose as their cornerstone is the story of Rachel and Leah, the two wives of Jacob, and their baby competition. When they themselves ran out of babies, they pressed their handmaids into service and counted the babies as their own, thus providing a biblical justification for surrogate motherhood, should anyone need one. Among these five people—not two—the twelve tribes of Israel were produced.

Woman's place, in the Republic of Gilead—so named for the mountain where Jacob promised to his father-in-law, Laban, that he would protect his two daughters—woman's place is strictly in the home. My problem as a writer was, given that my society has stuffed all women back into their homes, how did they go about it? How do you *get* women back into the home, now that they are running around *outside* the home, having jobs and generally flinging themselves around? Simple. You just close your eyes and take several giant steps back, into the not-so-very-distant past—the nineteenth century, to be exact—deprive them of the right to vote, own property, or hold jobs, and prohibit public prostitution in the bargain, to keep them from hanging out on street corners, and presto, there they are, back in the home. To stop them from using their gold Amex cards to make quick airplane escapes, I have their credit frozen overnight; after all, if everyone is on computers and cash is obsolete—which is where we're heading—how simple to single out any one group—all those over sixty, all those with green hair, all women. Of the many scary features of my future society, this one seems to have gotten to the most people. That their beloved, friendly, well-trained credit cards could rise up against them! It is the stuff of nightmares.

This, then, is part of the core of what I hope you will think is relentless logic running like a spine through *The Handmaid's Tale*. While I was writing it, and for some time after, I kept a scrapbook with clippings from newspapers referring to all sorts of material that fitted in with the premises on which the book was based—everything from articles on the high level of PCBs found in polar bears, to the biological mothers assigned to SS troops by Hitler, in addition to their legal wives, for purposes of child production, to conditions in prisons around the world, to computer technology, to underground polygamy in the state of Utah. There is, as I have said, nothing in the book without a precedent. But this material in itself would not constitute a novel. A novel is always the story of an individual, or several individuals; never the story of a generalized mass. So the real problems in the writing of *The Handmaid's Tale* were the same as the problems involved in the writing of any novel: how to make the story real at a human and individual level. The pitfalls that Utopian writing so frequently stumbles into are the pitfalls of disquisition. The author gets too enthusiastic about sewage systems or conveyor belts, and the story grinds to a halt while the beauties of these are explained. I wanted the factual and logical background to my tale to remain background; I did not want it usurping the foreground.

Part Two
1990–1999

The year 1990 was supposed to be the first year of a brand-new era. The Soviet Union was disintegrating. Germany was reunifying, a thing we thought we'd never witness in this lifetime. The West, and that body of practices and values attached to something called "capitalism" or "the free-market economy," seemed triumphant. It was not yet foreseen that with the disappearance of its enemy, the Western moral balloon would lose helium: it's great to champion freedom in the absence of it, but hard to feel hand-on-heart noble about shopping malls and parking lots and the right to kill yourself through overeating. We approached the last decade before that artificial times-change hinge, the millennium, in a strange state of disorientation. But as Roberto Calasso has pointed out, heroes have a need for monsters, though monsters can do very well without heroes; and, unknown to us, the monster-producing energies were gathering themselves together throughout the decade.

Things were quieter on the writing front, mine at least. In 1991 I published *Wilderness Tips*, a collection of stories written during the late 1980s. In the same year we went to France in search of writing time. We could not rent one house for the whole period, so we rented three successive houses—one for fall, one for winter, one for spring—in and around the town of Lourmarin, in Provence. It was in these three houses that I began writing my novel *The Robber Bride*, the occasion for the essay in this volume called "Spotty-Handed Villainesses." I also put together a selection of very short fiction called *Good Bones*, a companion to the 1983 *Murder in the Dark*. It was published in 1992, with a cover design I'd pasted together out of issues of French *Vogue* magazine. (The books were done for a small press, and author collage saves money.)

We returned to Canada in time for the summer of 1992. I completed *The Robber Bride* in January 1993, on a train going across Canada. My father had died earlier that month, right after I myself had been seriously ill with scarlet fever, and it was an effort of will for me to finish.

A book of poetry, *Morning in the Burned House*, came out in 1995. Also in that year I published a series of four lectures I'd given at Oxford University on the subject of Canadian literature and the north. The title was *Strange Things*, after the first two words in the Robert Service poem "The Cremation of Sam McGee." That poem goes on to talk about the men who moil for gold. It was a moiling decade.

I began the novel *Alias Grace* while I was on a book tour in Europe—in Switzerland, a suitably Freudian/Jungian locale. The process is described in the essay "In Search of *Alias Grace*." What I didn't put in is that right after finishing the book we went to a small village in western Ireland, and I had to edit the book by FedEx—I did not yet have e-mail—which meant that I had to hang a tea towel on the hedge so the deliveryman would know where we were.

A year with three nines in it—one that, in addition, was the last in a thousand-year sequence—this ought to have been potent. The fact that nothing much happened underlines the arbitrariness of numbers, and of the division of time into neat slices such as this one. Nonetheless, it was a satisfying number to write on the left-hand sides of letters. *1999*. How far away it seems, already.

13

Nine Beginings

1. *Why do you write?*
I've begun this piece nine times. I've junked each beginning.

I hate writing about my writing. I almost never do it. Why am I doing it now? Because I said I would. I got a letter. I wrote back *no*. Then I was at a party and the same person was there. It's harder to refuse in person. Saying *yes* had something to do with being nice, as women are taught to be, and something to do with being helpful, which we are also taught. Being helpful to women, giving a pint of blood. With not claiming the sacred prerogatives, the touch-me-not self-protectiveness of the artist, with not being selfish. With conciliation, with doing your bit, with appeasement. I was well brought up. I have trouble ignoring social obligations. Saying you'll write about your writing is a social obligation. It's not an obligation to the writing.

2. *Why do you write?*
I've junked each of nine beginnings. They seemed beside the point. Too assertive, too pedagogical, too frivolous or belligerent, too falsely wise. As if I had some special self-revelation that would encourage others, or some special knowledge to impart, some pithy saying that would act like a talisman for the driven, the obsessed. But I have no such talismans. If I did, I would not continue, myself, to be so driven and obsessed.

3. Why do you write?

I hate writing about my writing because I have nothing to say about it. I have nothing to say about it because I can't remember what goes on when I'm doing it. That time is like small pieces cut out of my brain. It's not time I myself have lived. I can remember the details of the rooms and places where I've written, the circumstances, the other things I did before and after, but not the process itself. Writing about writing requires self-consciousness; writing itself requires the abdication of it.

4. Why do you write?

There are a lot of things that can be said about what goes on around the edges of writing. Certain ideas you may have, certain motivations, grand designs that don't get carried out. I can talk about bad reviews, about sexist reactions to my writing, about making an idiot of myself on television shows. I can talk about books that failed, that never got finished, and about why they failed. The one that had too many characters, the one that had too many layers of time, red herrings that diverted me when what I really wanted to get at was something else, a certain corner of the visual world, a certain voice, an inarticulate landscape.

I can talk about the difficulties that women encounter as writers. For instance, if you're a woman writer, sometime, somewhere, you will be asked: *Do you think of yourself as a writer first, or as a woman first?* Look out. Whoever asks this hates and fears both writing and women.

Many of us, in my generation at least, ran into teachers or male writers or other defensive jerks who told us women could not really write because they couldn't be truck drivers or Marines and therefore didn't understand the seamier side of life, which included sex with women. We were told we wrote like housewives, or else we were treated like honorary men, as if to be a good writer was to suppress the female.

Such pronouncements used to be made as if they were the simple truth. Now they're questioned. Some things have changed for the better, but not all. There's a lack of self-confidence that gets instilled very early in many young girls, before writing is even seen as a possibility. You need a certain amount of nerve to be a writer, an almost physical nerve, the kind you need to walk a log across a river. The horse throws you and you get back on the horse. I learned to swim by being dropped into the water. You need to know you can sink, and survive it. Girls should be allowed to play in the mud. They should be released from the obligations of perfection. Some of your writing, at least, should be as evanescent as play.

A ratio of failures is built into the process of writing. The wastebasket has evolved for a reason. Think of it as the altar of the Muse Oblivion, to whom you sacrifice your botched first drafts, the tokens of your human imperfection. She is the tenth Muse, the one without whom none of the others can function. The gift she offers you is the freedom of the second chance. Or as many chances as you'll take.

5. *Why do you write?*
In the mid-eighties I began a sporadic journal. Today I went back through it, looking for something I could dig out and fob off as pertinent instead of writing this piece about writing. But it was useless. There was nothing in it about the actual composition of anything I've written over the past six years. Instead there are exhortations to myself—to get up earlier, to walk more, to resist lures and distractions. *Drink more water,* I find. *Go to bed earlier.* There were lists of how many pages I'd written per day, how many I'd retyped, how many yet to go. Other than that, there was nothing but descriptions of rooms, accounts of what we'd cooked and/or eaten and with whom, letters written and received, notable sayings of children, birds and animals seen, the weather. What came up in the garden. Illnesses, my own and those of others. Deaths, births. Nothing about writing.

January 1, 1984. Blakeny, England. As of today, I have about 130 pp. of the novel done and it's just beginning to take shape & reach the point at which I feel that it exists and can be finished and may be worth it. I work in the bedroom of the big house, and here, in the sitting room, with the wood fire in the fireplace and the coke fire in the dilapidated Roeburn in the kitchen. As usual I'm too cold, which is better than being too hot—today is gray, warm for the time of year, damp. If I got up earlier maybe I would work more, but I might just spend more time procrastinating—as now.

And so on.

6. *Why do you write?*

You learn to write by reading and writing, writing and reading. As a craft it's acquired through the apprentice system, but you choose your own teachers. Sometimes they're alive, sometimes dead.

As a vocation, it involves the laying on of hands. You receive your vocation and in your turn you must pass it on. Perhaps you will do this only through your work, perhaps in other ways. Either way, you're part of a community, the community of writers, the community of storytellers that stretches back through time to the beginning of human society.

As for the particular human society to which you yourself belong—sometimes you'll feel you're speaking for it, sometimes—when it's taken an unjust form—against it, or for that other community, the community of the oppressed, the exploited, the voiceless. Either way, the pressures on you will be intense; in other countries, perhaps fatal. But even here—speak "for women," or for any other group that is feeling the boot, and there will be many at hand, both for and against, to tell you to shut up, or to say what they want you to say, or to say it a different way. Or to save them. The bill-board awaits you, but if you succumb to its temptations you'll end up two-dimensional.

Tell what is yours to tell. Let others tell what is theirs.

7. *Why do you write?*

Why are we so addicted to causality? *Why do* you *write?* (Treatise by child psychologist, mapping your formative traumas. Conversely: palm-reading, astrology and genetic studies, pointing to the stars, fate, heredity.) *Why do you write?* (That is, why not do something useful instead?) If you were a doctor, you could tell some acceptable moral tale about how you put Band-Aids on your cats as a child, how you've always longed to cure suffering. No one can argue with that: But writing? What is it *for?*

Some possible answers: *Why does the sun shine? In the face of the absurdity of modern society, why do anything else? Because I'm a writer. Because I want to discover the patterns in the chaos of time. Because I must. Because someone has to bear witness. Why do you read?* (This last is tricky: maybe they don't.) *Because I wish to forge in the smithy of my soul the uncreated conscience of my race. Because I wish to make an ax to break the frozen sea within.* (These have been used, but they're good.)

If at a loss, perfect the shrug. Or say: *It's better than working in a bank.* Or say: *For fun.* If you say this, you won't be believed, or else you'll be dismissed as trivial. Either way, you'll have avoided the question.

8. *Why do you write?*

Not long ago, in the course of clearing some of the excess paper out of my workroom, I opened a filing cabinet drawer I hadn't looked into for years. In it was a bundle of loose sheets, folded, creased, and grubby, tied up with leftover string. It consisted of things I'd written in the late fifties, in high school and the early years of university. There were scrawled, inky poems, about snow, despair, and the Hungarian Revolution. There were short stories dealing with girls who'd had to get married, and dispirited, mousy-haired high-school English teachers—to end up as either was at that time my vision of Hell—typed finger-by-finger on an ancient machine that made all the letters half red.

There I am, then, back in grade twelve, going through the writers' magazines after I'd finished my French composition homework, typing out my lugubrious poems and my grit-filled stories. (I was big on grit. I had an eye for lawn litter and dog turds on sidewalks. In these stories it was usually snowing damply, or raining; at the very least there was slush. If it was summer, the heat and humidity were always wiltingly high and my characters had sweat marks under their arms; if it was spring, wet clay stuck to their feet. Though some would say all this was just normal Toronto weather.)

In the top right-hand corners of some of these, my hopeful seventeen-year-old self had typed, "First North American Rights Only." I was not sure what "First North American Rights" were; I put it in because the writing magazines said you should. I was at that time an aficionado of writing magazines, having no one else to turn to for professional advice.

If I were an archaeologist, digging through the layers of old paper that mark the eras in my life as a writer, I'd have found, at the lowest or Stone Age level—say, around ages five to seven—a few poems and stories, unremarkable precursors of all my frenetic later scribbling. (Many children write at that age, just as many children draw. The strange thing is that so few of them go on to become writers or painters.) After that there's a great blank. For eight years I simply didn't write. Then, suddenly, and with no missing links in between, there's a wad of manuscripts. One week I wasn't a writer, the next I was.

Who did I think I was, to be able to get away with this? What did I think I was doing? How did I get that way? To these questions I still have no answers.

9. *Why do you write?*

There's the blank page, and the thing that obsesses you. There's the story that wants to take you over and there's your resistance to it. There's your longing to get out of this, this servitude, to play hooky, to do anything else: wash the laundry, see a movie. There are words and their inertias, their biases, their insufficiencies, their glories. There are the risks you take and your loss of nerve, and the help that comes when you're least expecting it. There's the laborious revision, the scrawled-over, crumpled-up pages that drift across the floor like spilled litter. There's the one sentence you know you will save.

Next day there's the blank page. You give yourself up to it like a sleep-walker. Something goes on that you can't remember afterward. You look at what you've done. It's hopeless.

You begin again. It never gets any easier.

14

Review:

The General in His Labyrinth
by Gabriel García Márquez

The general of the title of Gabriel García Márquez's new novel is Simón Bolívar, "The Liberator," who in the years 1811 to 1824 led the revolutionary armies of South America in a brilliant and grueling series of campaigns that swept the Spaniards from their former colonies. In the process, many rich and long-established cities were devastated; vast wealth was captured and squandered; whole populations were laid waste through slaughter, famine, and disease; and, in the aftermath, the unified South America Bolívar so fervently desired—a country that would have balanced, and challenged, the United States—fell apart in a series of jealous bickerings, intrigues, assassinations, secessions, local feuds, and military coups.

Had Bolívar not existed, Mr. García Márquez would have had to invent him. Seldom has there been a more fitting match between author and subject. Mr. García Márquez wades into his flamboyant, often improbable, and ultimately tragic material with enormous gusto, heaping detail upon sensuous detail, alternating grace with horror, perfume with the stench of corruption, the elegant language of public ceremony with the vulgarity of private moments, the rationalistic clarity of Bolívar's thought with the malarial intensity of his emotions, but tracing always the main compulsion that drives his protagonist: the longing for an independent and unified South America. This, according to Bolívar himself, is the clue to all his contradictions.

Just now, when empires are disintegrating and the political map is being radically redrawn, the subject of *The General in His Labyrinth* is a most timely one. It is noteworthy that Mr. García Márquez has chosen to depict his hero not in the days of his astonishing triumphs, but in his last months of bitterness and frustration. One feels that, for the author, the tale of Bolívar is exemplary, not just for his own turbulent age but for ours as well. Revolutions have a long history of eating their progenitors.

Each book by Mr. García Márquez is a major literary event. Each has also been quite different from its predecessors, and the new novel, ably translated by Edith Grossman, is no exception. It is set in the past, but to call it a historical novel would be to do it an injustice. Nor is it one of those fictions—such as, for instance, *A Maggot* by John Fowles—in which a few real personages are mingled with the imagined ones. In this book the element of the real is front and center: most of the people in it actually lived; all of the events and most of the incidents actually took place, and the rest have their foundation in voluminous research: if someone eats a guava, then guavas existed, in that place and at that season.

But Mr. García Márquez avoids a chronological narrative (although, very helpfully, the linear sequence of events is provided in a note at the end). Instead he begins his book at the point at which General Bolívar, an old man at age forty-six, literally shrunken by the unspecified illness that will soon kill him, is rejected as president of the new government he himself has helped to create. Cold-shouldered by the elite, jeered by the rabble, he leaves the Colombian city of Bogotá for a meandering journey by barge down the Magdalena River with the stated intention of sailing to Europe.

He never makes it. Thwarted by the oppressive and calamitous weather, by the machinations of his enemies—in particular his fellow revolutionary and archrival Francisco de Paula Santander—by the political ambitions of his friends, by his illness, and above all by his own reluctance to leave the scene of his former glories, he wanders from city to city, house to house, refuge to refuge, dragging his increasingly baffled and restless entourage in his wake. In some places he is treated with scorn, in others with veneration; he endures endless celebrations in his honor, pleas for his intercession, fiestas and official receptions, punctuated by the brutal interventions of

112

nature—floods, heat waves, epidemics—and by fresh episodes in the decay of his own body.

Always he is dogged by a question he refuses to answer: will he recapture the presidency to suppress the anarchy and civil war that are threatening to tear the continent apart? In other words, is he willing to purchase unity at the expense of a rudimentary democracy, and at the price of a dictatorship headed by himself? Possibly he is waiting for the right moment to make a comeback; but this moment never arrives. "The headlong race between his misfortunes and his dreams" is won by the misfortunes, and the monster at the center of his "labyrinth" gets him in the end.

The structure of the book is itself labyrinthine, turning the narrative back on itself, twisting and confusing the thread of time until not only the general but also the reader cannot tell exactly where or when he is. Woven into the present, as memory, reveries, dream, or feverish hallucination, are many scenes from the general's earlier life: near catastrophes in war, splendid triumphs, superhuman feats of endurance, nights of orgiastic celebration, portentous turns of fate and romantic encounters with beautiful women, of which there seem to have been a large number. There is the deeply suppressed image of his young wife, dead after eight months of marriage; there is his devoted, cigar-smoking Amazonian mistress, Manuela Sáenz, who once saved him from assassination. But there were also—according to his faithful valet, José Palacios, who plays Leporello to Bolívar's Don Juan—thirty-five other serious affairs, "not counting the one-night birds, of course."

Of course: because Bolívar is not only a prime exponent of the well-known Latin American machismo but also a true child of the Romantic age. His political imagination was formed by the French Revolution; his heroes were Napoleon and Rousseau. Like Byron, he was a romantic ironist, a skeptic in religion, a flouter of social norms, a philanderer—a man capable of great self-sacrifice in the pursuit of large and glorious goals, but otherwise a worshiper at the altar of his own ego. He approached each new woman as a challenge; "once satisfied, he [would] . . . send them extravagant gifts to protect himself from oblivion, but, with an emotion that resembled vanity more than love, he would not commit the least part of his life to them."

On the subject of politics, Mr. García Márquez's Bolívar is little short of prophetic. Just before his death, he proclaims that South America "is ungovernable, the man who serves a revolution plows the sea, this nation will fall inevitably into the hands of the unruly mob and then will pass into the hands of almost indistinguishable petty tyrants." He foresees the perils of debt: "I warned Santander that whatever good we had done for the nation would be worthless if we took on debt because we would go on paying interest till the end of time. Now it's clear: debt will destroy us in the end." He has something to say, as well, about the role of the United States in Latin American affairs: inviting the United States to the Congress of Panama is "like inviting the cat to the mice's fiesta." "Don't go . . . to the United States," he warns a colleague. "It's omnipotent and terrible, and its tale of liberty will end in a plague of miseries for us all." As Carlos Fuentes has remarked, the patterns of Latin American politics, and of United States intervention in them, have not changed much in 160 years.

In addition to being a fascinating literary tour de force and a moving tribute to an extraordinary man, *The General in His Labyrinth* is a sad commentary on the ruthlessness of the political process. Bolívar changed history, but not as much as he would have liked. There are statues of "The Liberator" all over Latin America, but in his own eyes he died defeated.

15

Afterword:

Anne of Green Gables
by Lucy Maud Montgomery

*A*nne of Green Gables is one of those books you feel almost guilty liking, because so many other people seem to like it as well. If it's that popular, you feel, it can't possibly be good, or good for you. Like many others, I read this book as a child, and absorbed it so thoroughly that I can't even remember when. I read it to my own daughter when she was eight, and she read it again to herself later, and acquired all the sequels—which she, like everyone else, including the author, realized were not on quite the same level as the original. I saw the television series, too, and, despite rewrites and excisions, the central story was as strong and as appealing as ever.

And several summers ago, when my family and I were spending some time on Prince Edward Island, I even saw the musical. The theater gift store was offering *Anne* dolls, an *Anne* cookbook, and *Anne* paraphernalia of all kinds. The theater itself was large but crowded; in front of us was a long row of Japanese tourists. During one especially culture-specific moment—a dance in which a horde of people leapt around holding eggs glued to spoons clenched between their teeth—I wondered what the Japanese tourists could possibly be making of it. Then I took to wondering what they could be making of the whole phenomenon. What did they make of the *Anne* dolls, the *Anne* knickknacks, the *Anne* books themselves? Why was Anne Shirley, the talkative, red-haired orphan, so astonishingly popular among them?

Possibly it was the red hair: that must be exotic, I thought. Or possibly Japanese women and girls found Anne encouraging: in danger of rejection because she is not the desired and valued boy, she manages to win over the hearts of her adoptive parents and to end the book with a great deal of social approval. But she triumphs without sacrificing her sense of herself: she will not tolerate insult, she defends herself, she even loses her temper and gets away with it. She breaks taboos. On a more conventional level, she studies hard at school and wins a scholarship, she respects her elders, or at least some of them, and she has a great love of Nature (although it is Nature in its more subdued aspect; hers is a pastoral world of gardens and blossoming trees, not mountains and hurricanes).

It was helpful for me to try looking at *Anne's* virtues through other eyes, because for a Canadian woman—once a Canadian girl—*Anne* is a truism. Readers of my generation, and of several generations before and since, do not think of *Anne* as "written." It has simply always been there. It is difficult not to take the book for granted, and almost impossible to see it fresh, to realize what an impact it must have had when it first appeared.

It is tempting to think of *Anne* as just a very good "girls' book," about—and intended for—preadolescents. And on one level, it is just that. Anne's intense friendship with the ever-faithful Diana Barry, the hatefulness of Josie Pye, the schoolroom politics, the tempest-in-a-teapot "scrapes," Anne's overdone vanity and her consciousness of fashion in clothes and bookmarks—all are familiar to us, both from our own observation and experience and from other "girls' books."

But *Anne* draws on a darker and, some would say, a more respectable literary lineage. Anne Shirley is, after all, an orphan, and the opening chapters of *Jane Eyre* and *Oliver Twist* and *Great Expectations,* and, later and closer to Anne, the bad-tempered, unhappy, sallow-faced little Mary of *The Secret Garden,* have all contributed both to Anne Shirley's formation as orphan-heroine and to the reader's understanding of the perils of orphanhood in the nineteenth and early twentieth centuries. Unless she had been allowed to stay at Green Gables, Anne's fate would have been to be passed around as a cheap drudge from one set of uncaring adults to another. In the real world, as opposed to the literary one, she would have been in great danger of ending up pregnant and disgraced, raped—like many of the Barnardo Homes female orphans—by the men in the families in which they had been "placed." We have forgotten, by now, that orphans were once despised, exploited, and feared, considered to be the offspring of criminals or the products of immoral sex. Rachel Lynde, in her tales of orphans who have poisoned and set fire to the families who have taken them in, is merely voicing received opinion. No wonder Anne cries so much when she thinks she will be "returned," and no wonder Marilla and Matthew are considered "odd" for keeping her!

But Anne partakes of another "orphan" tradition as well: the folk-tale orphan who wins despite everything, the magic child who appears, as it seems, from nowhere—like King Arthur—and proves to have qualities far superior to anyone around her.

Such literary echoes may form the structural underpinnings of Anne's tale, but the texture is relentlessly local. L. M. Montgomery stays within the parameters of the conventions available to her: nobody goes to the bathroom in this book, and although we are in the country, no pigs are visibly slaughtered. But, that said, she remains faithful to her own aesthetic credo, as set forth by Anne's beloved schoolteacher Miss Stacy, who "won't let us write anything but what might happen in Avonlea in our own lives." Part of the current interest in "Avonlea" is that it appears to be a "jollier," more innocent world, long gone and very different from our own; but for Montgomery, "Avonlea" was simply reality edited. She was determined to write from what she knew: not the whole truth, perhaps, but not a total romanticization either. Rooms and clothes and malicious gossip are described much as they were, and people talk in the vernacular, minus the swear words—but then, the people we hear speaking are mostly "respectable" women, who would not have sworn anyway. This world was familiar to me through the stories told to me by my Maritime parents and aunts: the sense of community and "family," the horror of being "talked about," the smug rectitude, the distrust of outsiders, the sharp division between what was "respectable" and what was not, as well as the pride in hard work and the respect for achievement, all are faithfully depicted by Montgomery. Marilla's speech to Anne—"I believe in a girl being fitted to earn her own living whether ever she has to or not"—may sound like radical feminism to some, but in fact it is just a sample of Maritime self-reliance. My mother was brought up like that; consequently, so was I.

Montgomery wrote from her own experience in another and more profound way as well. Knowing what we now know about her life, we realize that Anne's story was a mirror image of her own, and gathers much of its force and poignancy from thwarted wish fulfillment. Montgomery, too, was virtually an orphan, abandoned by her father after her mother's death to a set of strict, judgmental grandparents, but she never gained the love she grants so lavishly to Anne. Anne's experience of exclusion was undoubtedly hers; the longing for acceptance must have been hers as well. So was the lyricism; so was the sense of injustice; so was the rebellious rage.

Children identify with Anne because she is what they often feel themselves to be—powerless and scorned and misunderstood. She revolts as they would like to revolt, she gets what they would like to have, and she is cherished as they themselves would like to be. When I was a child, I thought—as all children do—that Anne was the center of the book. I cheered her on, and applauded her victories over the adults, her thwartings of their wills. But there is another perspective.

Although *Anne* is about childhood, it is also very much centered on the difficult and sometimes heartbreaking relationship between children and adults. Anne seems to have no power, but in reality she has the vast though unconscious power of a beloved child. Although she changes in the book—she grows up—her main transformation is physical. Like the Ugly Duckling, she becomes a swan; but the inner Anne—her moral essence—remains much what it has always been. Matthew, too, begins as he means to go on: he is one of those shy, childlike men who delight Montgomery's heart (like Cousin Jimmy in the *Emily* books); he loves Anne from the moment he sees her, and he takes her part in every way and on every occasion.

The only character who goes though any sort of essential transformation is Marilla. *Anne of Green Gables* is not about Anne becoming a good little girl; it is about Marilla Cuthbert becoming a good—and more complete—woman. At the book's beginning, she is hardly even alive; as Rachel Lynde, the commonsense voice of the community, puts it, Marilla is not *living*, just *staying*. Marilla takes Anne on not out of love, as Matthew does, but out of a cold sense of duty. It is only in the course of the book that we realize there is a strong family resemblance between the two. Matthew, as we have always known, is a "kindred spirit" for Anne, but the kinship with Marilla goes deeper: Marilla, too, has been "odd," ugly, unloved. She, too, has been a victim of fate and injustice.

Anne without Marilla would—admit it—be sadly one-dimensional, an overtalkative child whose precocious cuteness might very easily pall. Marilla adds the saving touch of lemon juice. On the other hand, Anne acts out a great many of Marilla's concealed wishes, thoughts, and desires, which is the key to their relationship. And, in her battles of will with Anne, Marilla is forced to confront herself, and to regain what she has lost or repressed: her capacity to love, the full range of her emotions. Underneath her painful cleanliness and practicality, she is a passionate woman, as her outpouring of grief at Matthew's death testifies. The most moving declaration of love in the book has nothing to do with Gilbert Blythe: it is Marilla's wrenching confession in the penultimate chapter:

> Oh, Anne, I know I've been kind of strict and harsh with you maybe—but you mustn't think I didn't love you as well as Matthew did, for all that. I want to tell you now when I can. It's never been easy for me to say things out of my heart, but at times like this it's easier. I love you as dear as if you were my own flesh and blood and you've been my joy and comfort ever since you came to Green Gables.

The Marilla we first meet could never have laid herself bare like this. Only when she has recovered—painfully enough, awkwardly enough—her capacity to feel and express, can she become what Anne herself has lost long ago, and truly wants: a mother. But to love is to become vulnerable. At the beginning of the book, Marilla is all-powerful, but by the end, the structure has been reversed, and Anne has much more to offer Marilla than the other way around.

It may be the ludicrous escapades of Anne that render the book so attractive to children, but it is the struggles of Marilla that give it resonance for adults. Anne may be the orphan in all of us, but then, so is Marilla.

Anne is the fairy-tale wish-fulfillment version, what Montgomery longed for. Marilla is, more likely, what she feared she might become: joyless, bereft, trapped, hopeless, unloved. Each of them saves the other. It is the neatness of their psychological fit—as well as the invention, humor, and fidelity of the writing—that make *Anne* such a satisfying and enduring fable.

16

Why I Love
The Night of the Hunter,
a film by Charles Laughton

I'm incapable of choosing my single favorite anything, so I picked *The Night of the Hunter* for other reasons. First, it's among those films that made an indelible impression on me when it came out. That was in 1955, when I was a teenager and the theaters were blue with smoke: your boyfriend held his cigarette in one hand and attempted to sneak the other into your Peter Pan bra. What was on the screen was the secondary action, and it's a tribute to *The Night of the Hunter* that I can't remember which boyfriend I saw it with. So gripping was it that it warped my young brain, and several of its images have haunted me ever since. The underwater Shelley Winters, for instance, in her aspect of wrecked mermaid, has made several disguised appearances in my own writing.

My second reason was that The Word [a London literary festival] is an English event, and this film has an English connection. It was directed by Charles Laughton, who had a noteworthy stage career in London and made many English films before joining the European exiles who illuminated Hollywood from the thirties to the fifties. A bleak romantic trapped in an odd body, he often played monsters, which doubtless informed his direction of *The Night of the Hunter*—as did his interest in art and his wide literary and biblical background. Surely it's his sympathy with the material that enabled him to extract such extraordinary performances from the cast—Robert Mitchum, Shelley Winters, and Lillian Gish in particular.

The film came out in the same year as *The Blackboard Jungle* and *Rebel*

Without a Cause, so did not have the impact it deserved, although it has gathered a serious following since. European critics in particular have delved into its filmic influences, supplied Freudian analyses (frail mothers, sons and their torn loyalties to fathers, whether dead, fake, or ideal—vide the portrait of Abraham Lincoln tucked into the trial scene), and made Bettelheimian references to its fairy-tale depth psychology, not to mention the depth psychology of Laughton himself.

This film and its director appear made for each other—paradoxical, because *The Night of the Hunter* is such a profoundly American film. It is also a writers' film, another reason I chose it for a literary festival. For many films, the scenario serves only as a skeleton upon which the director hangs his own ideas and effects, but almost every image in this film—every rabbit, owl, and so forth—was thoroughly described in the scenario. A script like this probably wouldn't get to first base in Hollywood today; it would be considered too wordy.

The film was adapted from a novel by Davis Grubb and was written by James Agee, the author of *Let Us Now Praise Famous Men* and *A Death in the Family*, and of the film *The African Queen*. Both Grubb and Agee grew up in the Ohio River Valley during the Depression, which is where and when the film is set. Both were part of a general movement that turned away from the cosmopolitanism of the twenties to focus on the dark, poverty-stricken heartland of America. But Agee and Grubb, although they remembered the thirties, were not writing then. By their time, they would have had the benefit of a generation of literary scholars dedicated to the unraveling of the twisted, gothic skeins of American Puritanism, through such earlier writers as Hawthorne, Poe, Melville, and Twain. It shows.

The film has a double framework. It opens with Rachel—an older woman whom we later meet as a rescuer of stray children—invoking the world of bedtime stories and dreams. (One might say that if this is her idea of a restful tale for kiddies, she's a sadistic bitch, because this dream is a nightmare; but then, folktales have always been nightmares. Her job as narrator is to render the nightmare at least partially safe.) The next framework is a social one: the Depression, cause of the desperation that drives the film's initial robbery.

Within this double frame is the folkloric tale itself, with its ogre (played by Mitchum). His name is Harry, as in "Old Harry," vernacular for the Devil. Cross Richard III with Milton's Satan and enclose him in a Southern psychopath posing as a preacher, and this character is what you'd get. He cannot be explained by the Depression—he is simply radical evil—but, in Laughton's hands, he's a complex figure as well, one of those fast-talking con men who recur throughout American art, embraced by society, then torn apart by it. He's a monster, but finally a sacrificial one.

On one level the plot is simplicity itself: Dad has done a stickup and stashed the money in a doll. This Mammonish idol, a Venus of Willendorf with its tummy stuffed with cash, becomes the desired treasure in the struggle between evil and innocence. The robber's two children—a girl and an older boy—have been sworn not to tell the doll's secret to anybody, especially not to their mother, the fleshly and therefore willful Willa. Wolfish fellow prisoner Harry knows about the money, but not where it's hidden; so after Dad is hanged he puts on his sheep's clothing and goes off to romance the widow, oozing sexual power from every pore but especially from his lower eyelids. Willa falls for it and marries him, but Harry's not interested in her body. He cuts her throat and sinks her in the river, then claims she's run off, as demonish women do.

Now he can get his hands on the kids. He forces the secret of the doll, but the children make their escape in a boat and go down the Ohio River, with the enraged preacher hunting them. It's a quintessential American image—the two floating innocents recall Huckleberry Finn and Jim, and, behind them, that favorite American biblical image, the Ark riding the deluge with its saving remnant—in this case, the deluge that has over- whelmed the children's mother. That this particular deluge is all mixed up with adult sexuality, and also with the repression of it, is quintessentially American as well—it being the nature of Puritanism to produce a world that repudiates sexuality but is also thoroughly sexualized.

The children are sheltered by Rachel (who's a good woman, since she's well past sex), and stalked by their pursuer. Finally there's a standoff, a cap- ture, and a trial, and the villain is dead. But we can't breathe easily: the metaphysics are too unsettling. The film is punctuated by images of hands: toward the beginning, the preacher makes a puppet show with his knuckles, which have LOVE and HATE tattooed on them. Will love win over hate? If so, what kind of love? Does God himself love you or hate you, and if you place yourself in his hands, what is the nature of those hands?

The hands return at the end, when there's a duet sung by Harry the monster and Rachel the savior—incidentally, perhaps the only time Jesus has appeared in the guise of a sweet little old lady with a gun. They sing the hymn "Leaning on the Everlasting Arms"—they both sing it, but each is referring to a different arm; and at the end of every arm there's a hand, and for every right hand there's also a left.

But for every Song of Experience there's a Song of Innocence, and it's the child's-eye view that gives this film its translucence and candor. Its crucial perspective is that of the young boy, John Harper, poised between innocence and experience. He alone distrusts the preacher from the beginning, he alone realizes what's become of his mother; but, tellingly, he refuses to testify against her murderer. Son of a hanged killer and a butchered mother, stepson of a maniac, he has strong reason to distrust the adult world, but Rachel's house can shelter him only while he remains a child. Perhaps he will grow up to become a robber. Or perhaps, as his name suggests, a singer of blood-spattered sagas and the author of apocalyptic revelations?

There's a happy ending complete with Christmas presents, but we don't credit it and neither should John. He knows too much. In other words, if it's the night of the hunter, what will it be the day of, once that morning sun comes up?

17

Spotty-Handed Villainesses:
Problems of Female Bad Behavior
in the Creation of Literature

My title is "Spotty-Handed Villainesses"; my subtitle is "Problems of Female Bad Behavior in the Creation of Literature." I should probably have said "in the creation of novels, plays, and epic poems." Female bad behavior occurs in lyric poems, of course, but not at sufficient length.

I began to think about this subject at a very early age. There was a children's rhyme that went:

> *There was a little girl*
> *Who had a little curl*
> *Right in the middle of her forehead;*
> *When she was good, she was very, very good,*
> *And when she was bad, she was horrid!*

No doubt this is a remnant of the angel/whore split so popular among the Victorians, but at age five I did not know that. I took this to be a poem of personal significance—I did, after all, have curls—and it brought home to me the deeply Jungian possibilities of a Dr. Jekyll–Mr. Hyde double life for women. My older brother used this verse to tease me, or so he thought. He did manage to make "very, very good" sound almost worse than "horrid," which remains an accurate analysis for the novelist. Create a flawless character and you create an insufferable one, which may be why I am interested in spots.

Some of you may wonder whether the spotty-handedness in my title refers to age spots. Was my lecture perhaps going to center on that once-forbidden but now red-hot topic, The Menopause, without which any collection of female-obilia would be incomplete? I hasten to point out that my title is not age-related; it refers neither to age spots nor to youth spots. Instead it recalls that most famous of spots, the invisible but indelible one on the hand of wicked Lady Macbeth. Spot as in guilt, spot as in blood, spot as in "out, damned." Lady Macbeth was spotted, Ophelia unspotted; both came to sticky ends, but there's a world of difference.

But is it not, today—well, somehow *unfeminist* to depict a woman behaving badly? Isn't bad behavior supposed to be the monopoly of men? Isn't that what we are expected—in defiance of real life—to somehow believe now? When bad women get into literature, what are they doing there? Are they permissible? And what, if anything, do we need them for?

We do need something like them, by which I mean something disruptive to static order. When my daughter was five, she and her friend Heather announced that they were putting on a play. We were conscripted as the audience. We took our seats, expecting to see something of note. The play opened with two characters having breakfast. This was promising—an Ibsenian play, perhaps, or something by G. B. Shaw? Shakespeare is not big on breakfast openings, but other playwrights of talent have not disdained them.

The play progressed. The two characters had more breakfast. Then they had more. They passed each other the jam, the cornflakes, the toast. Each asked if the other would like a cup of tea. What was going on? Was this Pinter, perhaps, or Ionesco, or maybe Andy Warhol? The audience grew restless. "Are you going to do anything except have breakfast?" we said. "No," they said. "Then it isn't a play," we said. "Something else has to happen."

And there you have it, the difference between literature—at least literature as embodied in plays and novels—and life. *Something else has to happen.* In life we may ask for nothing more than a kind of eternal breakfast—it happens to be my favorite meal, and certainly it is the most hopeful one, since we don't yet know what atrocities the day may choose to visit upon us—but if we are going to sit still for two or three hours in a theater, or wade through two or three hundred pages of a book, we certainly expect something more than breakfast.

What kind of something? It can be an earthquake, a tempest, an attack by Martians, the discovery that your spouse is having an affair; or, if the author is hyperactive, all of these at once. Or it can be the revelation of the spottiness of a spotty woman. I'll get around to these disreputable folks shortly, but first let me go over some essentials that may be insulting to your intelligence but that are comforting to mine, because they help me to focus on what I'm doing as a creator of fictions. If you think I'm flogging a few dead horses—horses that have been put out of their pain long ago— let me assure you that this is because the horses are not in fact dead, but are out there in the world, galloping around as vigorously as ever.

How do I know this? I read my mail. Also, I listen to the questions people ask me, both in interviews and after public readings. The kinds of questions I'm talking about have to do with how the characters in novels ought to behave. Unfortunately, there is a widespread tendency to judge such characters as if they were job applicants, or public servants, or prospective roommates, or somebody you're considering marrying. For instance, I sometimes get a question—almost always, these days, from women—that goes something like, "Why don't you make the men stronger?" I feel that this is a matter that should more properly be taken up with God. It was not, after all, I who created Adam so subject to temptation that he sacrificed eternal life for an apple; which leads me to believe that God—who is, among other things, an author—is just as enamored of character flaws and dire plots as we human writers are. The characters in the average novel are not usually folks you would want to get involved with at a personal or business level. How then should we go about responding to such creations? Or, from my side of the page, which is blank when I begin—how should I go about creating them?

What is a novel, anyway? Only a very foolish person would attempt to give a definitive answer to that, beyond stating the more or less obvious facts that it is a literary narrative of some length that purports, on the reverse of the title page, not to be true, but seeks nevertheless to convince its readers that it is. It's typical of the cynicism of our age that if you write a novel, everyone assumes it's about real people, thinly disguised; but if you write an autobiography everyone assumes you're lying your head off. Part of this is right, because every artist is, among other things, a con artist.

We con artists do tell the truth, in a way; but as Emily Dickinson said, we tell it slant. By indirection we find direction out—so here, for easy reference, is an elimination-dance list of what novels are not.

- Novels are not sociological textbooks, although they may contain social comment and criticism.

- Novels are not political tracts, although "politics"—in the sense of human power structures—is inevitably one of their subjects. But if the author's main design on us is to convert us to something—whether that something be Christianity, capitalism, a belief in marriage as the only answer to a maiden's prayer, or feminism—we are likely to sniff it out, and to rebel. As André Gide once remarked, "It is with noble sentiments that bad literature gets written."

- Novels are not how-to books; they will not show you *how to* conduct a successful life, although some of them may be read this way. Is *Pride and Prejudice* about how a sensible middle-class nineteenth-century woman can snare an appropriate man with a good income, which is the best she can hope for out of life, given the limitations of her situation? Partly. But not completely.

- Novels are not, primarily, moral tracts. Their characters are not all models of good behavior—or, if they are, we probably won't read them. But they are linked with notions of morality, because they are about human beings, and human beings divide behavior into good and bad. The characters judge each other, and the reader judges the characters. However, the success of a novel does not depend on a not-guilty verdict from the reader. As Keats said, Shakespeare took as much delight in creating Iago—that archvillain—as he did in creating the virtuous Imogen. I would say probably more, and the proof of it is that I'd bet you're more likely to know which play Iago is in.

- But although a novel is not a political tract, a how-to book, a sociology textbook, or a pattern of correct morality, it is also not merely a piece of Art for Art's Sake, divorced from real life. It cannot do without a conception of form and a structure, true, but its roots are in the mud; its flowers, if any, come out of the rawness of its raw materials.

- In short, novels are ambiguous and multifaceted, not because they're perverse, but because they attempt to grapple with what was once referred to as the human condition, and they do so using a medium that is notoriously slippery—language itself.

Now let's get back to the notion that in a novel, something else has to happen—other than breakfast, that is. What will that "something else" be, and how does the novelist go about choosing it? Usually it's backward to what you were taught in school, where you probably got the idea that the novelist had an overall scheme or idea and then went about coloring it in with characters and words, sort of like paint by numbers. But in reality the process is much more like wrestling a greased pig in the dark.

Literary critics start with a nice, clean, already-written text. They then address questions to this text, which they attempt to answer, "What does it mean?" being both the most basic and the most difficult. Novelists, on the other hand, start with the blank page, to which they similarly address questions. But the questions are different. Instead of asking, first of all, "What does it mean?" they work at the widget level; they ask, "Is this the right word?" "What does it mean" can only come when there is an "it" to mean something. Novelists have to get some actual words down before they can fiddle with the theology. Or to put it another way, God started with chaos—dark, without form, and void—and so does the novelist. Then God made one detail at a time. So does the novelist. On the seventh day, God took a break to consider what he'd done. So does the novelist. But the critic starts on day seven.

The critic, looking at plot, asks, "What's happening here?" The novelist, creating plot, asks, "What happens next?" The critic asks, "Is this believable?" The novelist, "How can I get them to believe this?" The novelist, echoing Marshall McLuhan's famous dictum that art is what you can get away with, says, "How can I pull this off?"—as if the novel itself were a kind of bank robbery. Whereas the critic is liable to exclaim, in the mode of the policeman making the arrest, "Aha! You can't get away with that!"

In short, the novelist's concerns are more practical than those of the critic; more concerned with "how to," less concerned with metaphysics. Any novelist—whatever his or her theoretical interests—has to contend with the following how-to questions:

What kind of story shall I choose to tell? Is it, for instance, comic or tragic or melodramatic, or all? How shall I tell it? Who will be at the center of it, and will this person be (a) admirable or (b) not? And—more important than it may sound—will it have a happy ending or not? No matter what you are writing—what genre and in what style, whether cheap formula or high-minded experiment—you will still have to answer—in the course of your writing—these essential questions. Any story you tell must have a conflict of some sort, and it must have suspense. In other words: something other than breakfast.

Let's put a woman at the center of the something other than breakfast and see what happens. Now there is a whole new set of questions. Will the conflict be supplied by the natural world? Is our female protagonist lost in the jungle, caught in a hurricane, pursued by sharks? If so, the story will be an adventure story and her job is to run away, or else to combat the sharks, displaying courage and fortitude, or else cowardice and stupidity. If there is a man in the story as well, the plot will alter in other directions: he will be a rescuer, an enemy, a companion in struggle, a sex bomb, or someone rescued by the woman. Once upon a time, the first would have been more probable—that is, more believable to the reader; but times have changed and art is what you can get away with, and the other possibilities have now entered the picture.

Stories about space invasions are similar, in that the threat comes from outside and the goal for the character, whether achieved or not, is survival. War stories, per se—ditto, in that the main threat is external. Vampire and werewolf stories are more complicated, as are ghost stories; in these, the threat is from outside, true, but the threatening thing may also conceal a split-off part of the character's own psyche. Henry James's *The Turn of the*

Screw and Bram Stoker's *Dracula* are in large part animated by such hidden agendas; and both revolve around notions of female sexuality. Once all werewolves were male, and female vampires were usually mere sidekicks; but there are now female werewolves, and women are moving in on the star bloodsucking roles as well. Whether this is good or bad news I hesitate to say.

Detective and espionage stories may combine many elements, but would not be what they are without a crime, a criminal, a tracking-down, and a revelation at the end; again, all sleuths were once male, but sleuthesses are now prominent, for which I hope they lay a votive ball of wool from time to time upon the tomb of the sainted Miss Marple. We live in an age not only of gender crossover but also of *genre* crossover, so you can throw all of the above into the cauldron and stir.

Then there are stories classed as "serious" literature, which center not on external threats—although some of these may exist—but on relationships among the characters. To avoid the eternal breakfast, some of the characters must cause problems for some of the others. This is where the questions really get difficult. As I've said, the novel has its roots in the mud, and part of the mud is history; and part of the history we've had recently is the history of the women's movement, and the women's movement has influenced how people read, and therefore what you can get away with in art.

Some of this influence has been beneficial. Whole areas of human life that were once considered nonliterary or subliterary—such as the problematical nature of homemaking, the hidden depths of motherhood, and of daughterhood as well, the once-forbidden realms of incest and child abuse—have been brought inside the circle that demarcates the writeable from the nonwriteable. Other things, such as the Cinderella happy ending—the Prince Charming one—have been called into question. (As one lesbian writer remarked to me, the only happy ending she found believable anymore was the one in which girl meets girl and ends up with girl; but that was fifteen years ago, and the bloom is off even that romantic rose.)

To keep you from being too depressed, let me emphasize that none of this means that you, personally, cannot find happiness with a good man, a good woman, or a good pet canary; just as the creation of a bad female character doesn't mean that women should lose the vote. If bad male characters meant that, for men, all men would be disenfranchised immediately.

We are talking about what you can get away with in art; that is, what you can make believable. When Shakespeare wrote his sonnets to his dark-haired mistress, he wasn't saying that blondes were ugly, he was merely pushing against the notion that only blondes were beautiful. The tendency of innovative literature is to include the hitherto excluded, which often has the effect of rendering ludicrous the conventions that have just preceded the innovation. So the form of the ending, whether happy or not, does not have to do with how people live their lives—there is a great deal of variety in that department (and, after all, in life every story ends with death, which is not true of novels). Instead it's connected with what literary conventions the writer is following or pulling apart at the moment. Happy endings of the Cinderella kind do exist in stories, of course, but they have been relegated largely to genre fiction, such as Harlequin romances.

To summarize some of the benefits to literature of the women's movement —the expansion of the territory available to writers, both in character and in language; a sharp-eyed examination of the way power works in gender relations, and the exposure of much of this as socially constructed; a vigorous exploration of many hitherto-concealed areas of experience. But as with any political movement that comes out of real oppression—and I do emphasize the word *real*—there was also, in the first decade at least of the present movement, a tendency to cookie-cut: that is, to write to a pattern and to oversugar on one side. Some writers tended to polarize morality by gender—that is, women were intrinsically good and men bad; to divide along allegiance lines—that is, women who slept with men were sleeping with the enemy; to judge by tribal markings—that is, women who wore high heels and makeup were instantly suspect, those in overalls were acceptable; and to make hopeful excuses—that is, defects in women were ascribable to the patriarchal system and would cure themselves once that system was abolished. Such oversimplifications may be necessary to some phases of political movements. But they are usually problematical for novelists unless the novelist has a secret desire to be in billboard advertising.

If a novelist writing at that time was also a feminist, she felt her choices restricted. Were all heroines to be essentially spotless of soul—struggling against, fleeing from, or done in by male oppression? Was the only plot to be that of *The Perils of Pauline*, with a lot of mustache-twirling villains but minus the rescuing hero? Did suffering prove you were good? (If so—think hard about this—wasn't it all for the best that women did so much of it?) Did we face a situation in which women could do no wrong, but could only have wrong done to them? Were women being confined yet again to that alabaster pedestal so beloved of the Victorian age, when woman as better than man gave men a license to be gleefully and enjoyably worse than women, while all the while proclaiming that they couldn't help it because it was their nature? Were women to be condemned to virtue for life, slaves in the salt mines of goodness? How intolerable.

Of course, the feminist analysis made some kinds of behavior available to female characters, which, under the old dispensation—the prefeminist one—would have been considered bad, but under the new one were praiseworthy. A female character could rebel against social strictures without then having to throw herself in front of a train like Anna Karenina; she could think the unthinkable and say the unsayable; she could flout authority. She could do new bad-good things, such as leaving her husband and even deserting her children. Such activities and emotions, however, were—according to the new moral thermometer of the times—not really bad at all; they were good, and the women who did them were praiseworthy. I'm not against such plots. I just don't think they are the only ones.

And there were certain new no-nos. For instance: was it at all permissible, anymore, to talk about women's will to power, because weren't women supposed by nature to be communal egalitarians? Could one depict the scurvy behavior often practiced by women against one another, or by little girls against other little girls? Could one examine the Seven Deadly Sins in their female versions—to remind you, Pride, Anger, Lust, Envy, Avarice, Greed and Sloth—without being considered antifeminist? Or was a mere mention of such things tantamount to aiding and abetting the enemy, namely the male power structure? Were we to have a warning hand clapped over our mouths, yet once again, to prevent us from saying the unsayable—though the unsayable had changed? Were we to listen to our mothers, yet once again, as they intoned, "If you can't say anything nice, don't say anything at all?" Hadn't men been giving women a bad reputation for centuries? Shouldn't we form a wall of silence around the badness of women, or at best explain it away by saying it was the fault of Big Daddy, or—permissible, too, it seems—of Big Mom? Big Mom, that agent of the patriarchy, that pronatalist, got it in the neck from certain seventies feminists; though mothers were admitted into the fold again once some of these women turned into them. Briefly: were women to be homogenized— one woman is the same as another—and deprived of free will—as in, *The patriarchy made her do it?*

Or, again briefly: were men to get all the juicy parts? Literature cannot do without bad behavior, but was all the bad behavior to be reserved for men? Was it to be all Iago and Mephistopheles, and were Jezebel and Medea and Medusa and Delilah and Regan and Goneril and spotty-handed Lady Macbeth and Rider Haggard's powerful superfemme fatale in *She*, and Toni Morrison's mean Sula, to be banished from view? I hope not. Women characters, arise! Take back the night! In particular, take back The Queen of the Night, from Mozart's *Magic Flute*. It's a great part, and due for revision.

I have always known that there were spellbinding evil parts for women. For one thing, I was taken at an early age to see *Snow White and the Seven Dwarfs*. Never mind the Protestant work ethic of the dwarfs. Never mind the tedious housework-is-virtuous motif. Never mind the fact that Snow White is a vampire—anyone who lies in a glass coffin without decaying and then comes to life again must be. The truth is that I was paralyzed by the scene in which the evil queen drinks the magic potion and changes her shape. What power, what untold possibilities!

Also, I was exposed to the complete, unexpurgated Grimms' fairy tales at an impressionable age. Fairy tales had a bad reputation among feminists for a while—partly because they'd been cleaned up, on the erroneous supposition that little children don't like gruesome gore, and partly because they'd been selected to fit the fifties Prince Charming Is Your Goal ethos. So Cinderella and the Sleeping Beauty were okay, though The Youth Who Set Out to Learn What Fear Was, which featured a good many rotting corpses, plus a woman who was smarter than her husband, were not. But many of these tales were originally told and retold by women, and these unknown women left their mark. There is a wide range of heroines in these tales; passive good girls, yes, but adventurous, resourceful women as well, and proud ones, and slothful ones, and foolish ones, and envious and greedy ones, and also many wise women and a variety of evil witches, both in disguise and not, and bad stepmothers and wicked, ugly sisters and false brides as well. The stories, and the figures themselves, have immense vitality, partly because no punches are pulled—in the versions I read, the barrels of nails and the red-hot shoes were left intact—and also because no emotion is unrepresented. Singly, the female characters are limited and two-dimensional. But put all together, they form a rich, five-dimensional picture.

Female characters who behave badly can, of course, be used as sticks to beat other women—though so can female characters who behave well: witness the cult of the Virgin Mary, better than you'll ever be, and the legends of the female saints and martyrs—just cut on the dotted line, and, minus one body part, there's your saint, and the only really good woman is a dead woman, so if you're so good, why aren't you dead?

But female bad characters can also act as keys to doors we need to open, and as mirrors in which we can see more than just a pretty face. They can be explorations of moral freedom—because everyone's choices are limited, and women's choices have been more limited than men's, but that doesn't mean women can't make choices. Such characters can pose the question of responsibility, because if you want power you have to accept responsibility, and actions produce consequences. I'm not suggesting an agenda here, just some possibilities; nor am I prescribing, just wondering. If there's a closed-off road, the curious speculate about why it's closed off, and where it might lead if followed; and evil women have been—for a while, recently—a somewhat closed-off road, at least for fiction writers.

While pondering these matters, I thought back over the numerous bad female literary characters I have known, and tried to sort them into categories. If you were doing this on a blackboard, you might set up a kind of grid: bad women who do bad things for bad reasons, good women who do good things for good reasons, good women who do bad things for good reasons, bad women who do bad things for good reasons, and so forth. But a grid would just be a beginning, because there are so many factors involved: for instance, what the character thinks is bad, what the reader thinks is bad, and what the author thinks is bad, may all be different. But let me define a thoroughly evil person as one who intends to do evil, and for purely selfish reasons. The queen in Snow White would fit that.

So would Regan and Goneril, Lear's evil daughters; very little can be said in their defense, except that they seem to have been against the patriarchy. Lady MacBeth, however, did her wicked murder for a conventionally acceptable reason, one that would win approval for her in corporate business circles—she was furthering her husband's career. She pays the corporate-wife price, too—she subdues her own nature, and has a nervous breakdown as a result. Similarly, Jezebel was merely trying to please a sulky husband; he refused to eat his dinner until he got ahold of Naboth's vineyard, so Jezebel had its owner bumped off. Wifely devotion, as I say. The amount of sexual baggage that has accumulated around this figure is astounding, since she doesn't do anything remotely sexual in the original story, except put on makeup.

The story of Medea, whose husband, Jason, married a new princess, and who then poisoned the bride and murdered her own two children, has been interpreted in various ways. In some versions Medea is a witch and commits infanticide out of revenge; but the play by Euripides is surprisingly neofeminist. There's quite a lot about how tough it is to be a woman, and Medea's motivation is commendable—she doesn't want her children to fall into hostile hands and be cruelly abused—which is also the situation of the child-killing mother in Toni Morrison's *Beloved*. A good woman, then, who does a bad thing for a good reason. Hardy's *Tess of the D'Urbervilles* kills her nasty lover due to sexual complications; here, too, we are in the realm of female-as-victim, doing a bad thing for a good reason. (Which, I suppose, places such stories right beside the front page, along with women who kill their abusive husbands. According to a recent *Time* story, the average jail sentence in the United States for men who kill their wives is four years, but for women who kill their husbands—no matter what the provocation—it's twenty. For those who think equality is already with us, I leave the statistics to speak for themselves.)

These women characters are all murderers. Then there are the seducers; here again, the motive varies. I have to say, too, that with the change in sexual mores, the mere seduction of a man no longer rates very high on the sin scale. But try asking a number of women what the worst thing is that a woman friend could possibly do to them. Chances are the answer will involve the theft of a sexual partner.

Some famous seductresses have really been patriotic espionage agents. Delilah, for instance, was an early Mata Hari, working for the Philistines, trading sex for military information. Judith, who all but seduced the enemy general Holofernes and then cut off his head and brought it home in a sack, was treated as a heroine, although she has troubled men's imaginations through the centuries—witness the number of male painters who have depicted her—because she combines sex with violence in a way they aren't accustomed to and don't much like. Then there are figures like Hawthorne's adulterous Hester Prynne, she of *The Scarlet Letter*, who becomes a kind of sex saint through suffering—we assume she did what she did through love, and thus she becomes a good woman who did a bad thing for a good reason—and Madame Bovary, who not only indulged her romantic temperament and voluptuous sensual appetites but spent too much of her husband's money doing it, which was her downfall. A good course in double-entry bookkeeping would have saved the day. I suppose she is a foolish woman who did a stupid thing for an insufficient reason, since the men in question were dolts. Neither the modern reader nor the author consider her very evil, though many contemporaries did, as you can see if you read the transcript of the court case in which the forces of moral rectitude tried to get the book censored.

One of my favorite bad women is Becky Sharpe, of Thackeray's *Vanity Fair*. She makes no pretensions to goodness. She is wicked, she enjoys being wicked, and she does it out of vanity and for her own profit, tricking and deluding English society in the process—which, the author implies, deserves to be tricked and deluded, since it is hypocritical and selfish to the core. Becky, like Undine Spragg in Edith Wharton's *The Custom of the Country*, is an adventuress; she lives by her wits and uses men as ambulatory bank accounts. Many literary adventurers are male—consider Thomas Mann's *Felix Krull, Confidence Man*—but it does make a difference if you change the gender. For one thing, the nature of the loot changes. For a male adventurer, the loot is money and women; but for a female one, the loot is money and men.

Becky Sharpe is a bad mother, too, and that's a whole other subject—bad mothers and wicked stepmothers and oppressive aunts, like the one in

Jane Eyre, and nasty female teachers, and depraved governesses, and evil grannies. The possibilities are many.

But I think that's enough reprehensible female behavior for you today. Life is short, art is long, motives are complex, and human nature is endlessly fascinating. Many doors stand ajar; others beg to be unlocked. What is in the forbidden room? Something different for everyone, but something you need to know and will never find out unless you step across the threshold. If you are a man, the bad female character in a novel may be—in Jungian terms—your anima; but if you're a woman, the bad female character is your shadow; and as we know from the Offenbach opera *Tales of Hoffman,* she who loses her shadow also loses her soul.

Evil women are necessary in story traditions for two much more obvious reasons, of course. First, they exist in life, so why shouldn't they exist in literature? Second—which may be another way of saying the same thing—women have more to them than virtue. They are fully dimensional human beings; they, too, have subterranean depths; why shouldn't their many-dimensionality be given literary expression? And when it is, female readers do not automatically recoil in horror. In Aldous Huxley's novel *Point Counter Point,* Lucy Tantamount, the man-destroying vamp, is preferred by the other female characters to the earnest, sniveling woman whose man she has reduced to a wet bath sponge. As one of them says, "Lucy's obviously a force. You may not like that kind of force. But you can't help admiring the force in itself. It's like Niagara." In other words, awesome. Or, as one Englishwoman said to me recently, "Women are tired of being *good* all the time."

I will leave you with a final quotation. It's from Dame Rebecca West, speaking in 1912—"Ladies of Great Britain . . . we have not enough evil in us." Note where she locates the desired evil. In *us.*

18

The Grunge Look

I first went to Europe on May 13, 1964. I had been told I was going to do this five months earlier by a male psychic working out of a Toronto tea shop. "You will be going to Europe in May," he said.

"No, I won't," I said.

"Yes, you will," he said, smugly reshuffling his cards.

I did.

Fleeing a personal life of Gordian complexity, and leaving behind a poetry manuscript rejected by all, and a first novel ditto, I scraped together what was left after a winter of living in a Charles Street rooming house and writing tours de force of undiscovered genius while working by day at a market research company, borrowed six hundred dollars from my parents, who were understandably somewhat nervous about my choice of the literary life by then, and climbed onto a plane. In the fall I would be teaching grammar to engineering students at eight-thirty in the morning in a Quonset hut at the University of British Columbia, so I had about three months. In this period of time I intended to become—what? I wasn't sure exactly, but I had some notion that the viewing of various significant pieces of architecture would improve my soul—would fill in a few potholes in it, get rid of a few cultural hangnails, as it were. Here, I had been studying English literature for six years—I even had an M.A., which had gotten me rejected for employment by the Bell Telephone Company on the grounds of overqualification—and I had never even seen . . . well, things.

Stonehenge, for instance. A visit to Stonehenge would surely improve my understanding of Thomas Hardy. Or someone. Anyway, a lot of my friends from college had already run to England, intending to be actors and the like. So England was my first stop.

The truth is that I didn't have much idea of what I was really doing. Certainly, I had almost no idea at all of where I was really going, and how much it had changed since I'd last checked in via the pages of Charles Dickens. Everything was so much smaller and shabbier than I had imagined. I was like the sort of Englishman who arrives in Canada expecting to find a grizzly bear on every street corner. "Why are there so many *trucks?*" I thought. There were no trucks in Dickens. There weren't even any in T. S. Eliot. "I did not know Death had undone so many," I murmured hopefully, as I made my way across Trafalgar Square. But the people there somehow refused to be as hollow-cheeked and plangent as I'd expected. They appeared to be mostly tourists, like myself, and were busy taking pictures of one another with pigeons on their heads.

My goal, of course, was Canada House, the first stop of every jet-stunned, impecunious young Canadian traveler in those days. But before I go on, let me say a few words about those days. What sort of year was 1964?

It was the year after 1963, in which John Kennedy had been so notably shot. It was the year before the first (to my knowledge) anti-Vietnam peace march; it was roughly four years before the great hippie explosion, and five years before the onset of the early-seventies wave of feminism. Miniskirts had not yet arrived; panty hose were approaching, but I don't believe they had as yet squeezed out the indigenous population of garter belts and stockings. In hair, something called the bubble cut was favored: women rolled their hair in big, bristle-filled rollers to achieve a smoothly swollen look, as if someone had inserted a tube into one of their ears and blown up their heads like balloons. I indulged in this practice, too, though with mixed results, since my hair was ferociously curly. At best it resembled a field of weeds gone over with a lawn roller—still squiggly, though somewhat mashed. At worst it looked as if I'd stuck my finger in a light socket. This silhouette was later to become stylish, but was not so yet. As a result I went in for head scarves, of the Queen Elizabeth at Balmoral type. Paired

140

with the slanty-eyed, horn-rimmed glasses I wore in an attempt to take myself seriously, they were not at all flattering.

Come to think of it, neither was anything in my suitcase. (Hitchhiking backpackers had not yet overrun Europe, so it was, still, a suitcase.) Fashionwise, 1964 was not really my year. Beatniks had faded, and I hadn't discovered the romantic raggle-taggle gypsy mode; but then, neither had anyone else. Jeans had not yet swept all before them, and for ventures to such places as churches and museums, skirts were still required; gray flannel jumpers with Peter Pan–collared blouses were my uniform of choice. High heels were the norm for most occasions, and about the only thing you could actually walk in were some rubber-soled suede items known as Hush Puppies.

Lugging my suitcase, then, I Hush-Puppied my way up the imposing steps of Canada House. At that time it offered—among other things, such as a full shelf of geological surveys—a reading room with newspapers in it. I riffled anxiously through the Rooms to Let, since I had no place to stay that night. By pay telephone, I rented the cheapest thing available, which was located in a suburb called Willesden Green. This turned out to be about as far away from everything as you could get, via the London Underground, which I promptly took (here at last, I thought, looking at my intermittently bathed, cadaverous, and/or dentally challenged fellow passengers, were a few people Death had in fact undone, or was about to). The rooming house furnishings smelled of old, sad cigarette smoke, and were of such hideous dinginess that I felt I'd landed in a Graham Greene novel; and the sheets, when I finally slid between them, were not just cold and damp, they were wet. ("North Americans like that kind of thing," an Englishwoman said to me much later. "Unless they freeze in the bathroom they think they've been cheated of the English experience.")

The next day I set out on what appears to me in retrospect a dauntingly ambitious quest for cultural trophies. My progress through the accumulated bric-a-brac of centuries was marked by the purchase of dozens of brochures and postcards, which I collected to remind myself that I'd actually been wherever it was I'd been. At breakneck speed I gawped my way through Westminster Abbey, the Houses of Parliament, St. Paul's Cathedral, the Tower of London, the Victoria and Albert Museum, the National

Portrait Gallery, the Tate, the house of Samuel Johnson, Buckingham Palace, and the Albert Memorial. At some point I fell off a double-decker bus and sprained my foot, but even this, although it slowed me down, did not stop me in my headlong and reckless pursuit. After a week of this, my eyes were rolling around like loose change, and my head, although several sizes larger, was actually a good deal emptier than it had been before. This was a mystery to me.

Another mystery was why so many men tried to pick me up. It was hardly as if I was, in my little gray-flannel jumpers, dressed to kill. Museums were the usual locale, and I suppose there was something about a woman standing still with her head tilted at a ninety-degree angle that made solicitation more possible. None of these men was particularly rude. "American?" they would ask, and when I said Canadian, they would look either puzzled or disappointed, and would proceed only tentatively to the next question. When they got no for an answer, they simply moved along to the next upstretched neck. Possibly they hung around tourist lodestones on the theory that female travelers traveled for the same kinds of sexual adventure reasons they would have traveled, had they been traveling themselves. But in this there was—and possibly still is—a gender difference. Ulysses was a sailor, Circe was a stay-at-home with commodious outbuildings.

When not injecting myself with culture, I was looking for something to eat. In England in 1964, this was quite difficult, especially if you didn't have much money. I made the mistake of trying a hamburger and a milkshake, but the English didn't yet have the concept: the former was fried in rancid lamb fat, the latter fortified with what tasted like ground-up chalk. The best places were the fish-and-chip shops, or, barring that, the cafés, where you could get eggs, sausages, chips, and peas, in any combination. Finally I ran into some fellow Canadians who'd been in England longer than I had and who put me onto a Greek place in Soho, which actually had salads, a few reliable pubs, and the Lyons' Corner House on Trafalgar Square, which had a roast beef all-you-can-eat for a set price. A mistake, as the Canadian journalists would starve themselves for a week, then hit the Lyons' Corner House like a swarm of locusts. (The Lyons' Corner House did not survive.)

It must have been through these expatriates that I hooked up with Alison

Cunningham, whom I'd known at university and who was now in London, studying modern dance and sharing a second-floor flat in South Kensington with two other young women. Into this flat, Alison—when she heard of my wet-sheeted Willesden Green circumstances—generously offered to smuggle me. "Smuggle" is appropriate; the flat was owned by aristocratic twins called Lord Cork and Lady Hoare, but as they were ninety and in nursing homes, it was actually run by a suspicious dragon of a housekeeper; so for purposes of being in the flat I had to pretend I didn't exist.

In Alison's flat I learned some culturally useful things that have stuck with me through the years: how to tell a good kipper from a bad one, for instance; how to use an English plate-drying rack; and how to make coffee in a pot when you don't have any other device. I continued with my tourist program—stuffing in Cheyne Walk, several lesser-known churches, and the Inns of Court—and Alison practiced a dance, which was a reinterpretation of *The Seagull*, set to several of the Goldberg Variations as played by Glenn Gould. I can never hear that piece of music without seeing Alison, in a black leotard and wearing the severe smile of a Greek caryatid of the Archaic period, bending herself into a semipretzel on that South Kensington sitting-room floor. Meanwhile, I was not shirking in the salt mines of art. Already, my notebook contained several new protogems, none of which, oddly, busied itself with the age-old masterworks of Europe. Instead, they were about rocks.

When things got too close for comfort with the dragon housekeeper, I would have to skip town for a few days. This I did by cashing in some miles on the rail pass I had purchased in Canada—one of the few sensible preparations for my trip I had managed to make. (Why no Pepto-Bismol? I ask myself: Why no acetaminophen with codeine? Why no Gravol? I would never think of leaving the house without them now.) On this rail pass you could go anywhere the railways went, using up miles as you did so. My first journeys were quite ambitious. I went to the Lake District, overshooting it and getting as far north as Carlisle before I had to double back; whereupon I took a bus tour of the Lakes, viewing them through fumes of cigar smoke and nausea, and, although surprised by their smallness, was reassured to hear that people still drowned in them every year. Then I went to Glastonbury, where, after seeing the cathedral, I was waylaid by an elderly lady

who got five pounds out of me to help save King Arthur's Well, which—
she said—was in her backyard and would be ruined by a brewery unless I
contributed to the cause. I made it to Cardiff with its genuine-ersatz castle,
and to Nottingham and the ancestral home of the Byrons, and to York, and
to the Brontë manse, where I was astonished to learn, from the size of their
tiny boots and gloves, that the Brontës had been scarcely bigger than children. As a writer of less than Olympian stature, I found this encouraging.

But as my rail pass dwindled, my trips became shorter. Why did I go to
Colchester? To the Cheddar Gorge? To Ripon? My motives escape me, but
I went to these places; I have the postcards to prove it. Julius Caesar visited
Colchester, too, so there must have been something to it; but I was driven
by frugality rather than by the historicist imperative: I didn't want any of
my rail pass miles to go to waste.

Around about July, Alison decided that France would be even more
improving for me than England had been, so in the company of a male
friend of mine from Harvard, in full retreat from a Southern girlfriend who
had brought several ball gowns to a student archaeological graveyard excavation, we took the night boat-train. It was an average Channel crossing,
during which we all turned gently green. Alison bravely continued to discourse on intellectual matters but finally turned her head and, with a
dancer's casual grace, threw up over her left shoulder. These are the
moments one remembers.

By the time we'd been two days in Paris, where we subsisted on a diet of
baguettes, café au lait, oranges, pieces of cheese, and the occasional bean-
heavy bistro meal, I was in an advanced state of dysentery. We were
shunting around from cheap pension to cheap pension; the rooms were
always up gloomy flights of stairs, with lights that went off when you
were halfway up and cockroaches that rustled and crackled underfoot.
None of these establishments allowed you to stay in them during the day;
so I lay moaning softly on hard French park benches, in gravelly French
parks, while Alison, with a sense of duty Florence Nightingale would have
envied, read me long, improving passages from Doris Lessing's *The
Golden Notebook*. Every fifteen minutes a policeman would come by and

tell me I had to sit up, since lying on the park benches was forbidden; and every half hour I would make a dash for the nearest establishment with a toilet, which featured not the modern plumbing that has taken over today but a hole in the ground and two footrests, and many previous visitors with imperfect aims.

A diet of bread and water, and some potent French emulsion, administered by Alison, improved my condition, and I dutifully hiked around to Notre Dame, the Eiffel Tower, and the Louvre. In Paris, the men bent on pickups didn't bother to wait until you had stopped and were craning your neck; they approached at all times, even when you were crossing the street. *"Américaine?"* they would ask hopefully. They were polite—some of them even used the subjunctive, as in *"Voudriez-vous coucher avec moi?"*—and, when refused, would turn away with a beaglelike melancholy which I chose to find both existential and Gallic.

When we had only a week and a half left, the three of us pooled our resources and rented a car, with which we toured the châteaus of the Loire, viewing a great many eighteenth-century gilded chairs, staying in youth hostels, and living on more cheese. By this time I was supersaturated with culture; waterlogged, so to speak. If someone had stepped on my head, a stream of dissolved brochures would have poured forth.

Then, for some reason now lost in the mists of history, I decided to go to Luxembourg. On the way there, a middle-aged conductor chased me around the train compartment; when I explained that I was not in fact American, as he had supposed, he shrugged and said "Ah," as if that explained my reluctance. By this time I was getting somewhat fed up with the excess of dog-and-fire-hydrant male attention, and I let my irritation spill over onto the cultural agenda; when I finally got to Luxembourg, I did not go to visit a single church. Instead, I saw *Some Like It Hot*, with subtitles in Flemish, French, and German, where I was the only person in the theater who laughed in the right places.

This seemed an appropriate point of reentry to North America. Culture is as culture does, I thought as I returned to England, steered myself and my Hush Puppies toward the plane, and prepared for decompression.

At that moment my trip in retrospect felt a lot like stumbling around in the dark, bumping into heavy, expensive pieces of furniture while being mistaken for someone else. But distance adds perspective, and in the months that followed, I tried hard for it. Had my soul been improved? Possibly, but not in the ways I'd anticipated. What I took back with me was not so much the churches and museums and the postcards of them I'd collected, but various conversations, in buses, on trains, and with the pickup men at the museums. I remembered especially the general bafflement when it turned out that I was not what I appeared to be—an American. For the Europeans, there was a flag-shaped blank where my nationality should have been. What was visible to me was invisible to them; nor could I help them out by falling back on any internationally famous architectural constructs. About all I had to offer as a referent was a troop of horsy policemen, which hardly seemed enough.

But one person's void is another person's scope, and that was where the new poems I'd brought back squashed at the bottom of my suitcase would come in, or so I thought. Speaking of which, my gray-flannel wardrobe— I could see it now—definitely had to go. As a deterrent to stray men it was inadequate, as a disguise irrelevant, as a poetic manifesto incoherent. I did not look serious in it, merely earnest, and also—by now—somewhat grubby. I had picked up a brown suede vest, on sale at Liberty's, which, with the addition of a lot of black and some innovation with the hair, would transform me into something a lot more formidable, or so I intended.

I did get to Stonehenge, incidentally. I felt at home with it. It was pre-rational, and pre-British, and geological. Nobody knew how it had arrived where it was, or why, or why it had continued to exist; but there it sat, challenging gravity, defying analysis. In fact, it was sort of Canadian. "Stonehenge," I would say to the next mournful-looking European man who tried to pick me up. That would do the trick.

19

Review:

From the Beast to the Blonde: On Fairy Tales and Their Tellers
by Marina Warner

The accomplished British novelist Marina Warner is also the author of several intriguing works of nonfiction, including *Alone of All Her Sex*, an examination of the Virgin Mary cult, and *Monuments and Maidens*, an analysis of female allegorical figures. Her new book inhabits roughly the same territory—the widespread icon, the popular image, the much-told tale—but is even more ambitious in scope.

From the Beast to the Blonde is what its subtitle proclaims: a book about fairy tales and also about those who have told them. As befits its subject, it is a thing of splendor—marvelous, bizarre, exotic—but at the same time familiar as porridge. It's crammed full of goodies—stick your thumb into it anywhere, and out comes a plum—and profusely illustrated. It is also simply essential reading for anyone concerned not only with fairy tales, myth, and legends, but also with how stories of all kinds get told.

Like many children, I devoured fairy tales. Having cut my milk teeth on the unexpurgated Grimms—despite my parents' fears that the red-hot shoes and poked-out eyeballs might be too much for a six-year-old—I went on to the Andrew Lang collections, the *Arabian Nights*, and anything else I could get my hands on—if eerily illustrated by Arthur Rackham or Edmund Dulac, so much the better. By the time I hit college I was well prepared for the more Jungian of my professors, who, in those myth-oriented days of the late fifties, referred casually to such fairy-tale denizens as WOMs (Wise Old Men) and WOWs (Wise Old Women).

Fairy tales were said to contain universal archetypes, and to teach deep and timeless psychic lessons. Of course, a WOM could just as easily be a Wandering Old Molester and a WOW, a Wicked Old Witch, and if encountered in the forest, or, say, the corner drugstore, a girl was hard-pressed to know whether to give them her crust of bread or a very wide berth. Still, there was a definite mystique.

Then fairy tales fell on hard times. Despite such thoughtful studies as Bruno Bettelheim's *The Uses of Enchantment*, they were prettied up and weeded—adventurous heroines as well as grisly doings were downplayed, and the prone or Sleeping Beauty position was favored. After that, the tales were—understandably—attacked by feminists as brainwashing devices aimed at turning women into beautiful, dutiful automatons, at extolling the phallic power of sword-sporting princes, and at slandering nonbiological parental units and the chronologically enhanced. Like corsets, they were designed to confine, and as such were reprehensibly outmoded.

But now Marina Warner rides to the rescue. Fiddle-dee-dee, says she, in true Wise Woman fashion, as she rolls up her sleeves and sets to work salvaging things from the closet of discards. Look! Not musty old straw at all, she proclaims. Real gold! You just have to know how to spin it. And quicker than you can say Rumpelstiltskin backward, out the window goes the theory of timeless archetypes, as well as the Volkish idea that these stories were authentic, indigenous, preliterate, out-of-the-soul-of-the-soil emanations. (Her impressive collection of sources and variants puts paid to that.)

Away, too, goes the recent school of disparagement. If you want a feminist heroine, she suggests, how about Mother Goose? Reconsider the beaky nose, the funny bonnet, and the nursery pinafore. Mother Goose dresses like a featherbrain for the same reason that female "tourists" are favored as espionage couriers: both disarm suspicion. But underneath, what surprises! Disguise! Ambiguity! Subversion!

Warner's theory of narrative, once put forth, is eminently sensible: for any tale told, there is a teller, but also a tellee. Also a social context, which changes over time: "historical realism" is a term she favors. Even when the narrative events themselves remain constant, the moral spin put on them may not, for both the tellers and the tellees have their own fluctuating agendas.

Is it a coincidence that "old wives' tales" about the advisability of being nice to elderly women were once told by elderly women, who needed all the help they could get? Or that Bluebeard stories about young girls being married off to murderous husbands should have peaked during a reaction against made-for-money forced nuptials? Or that the beastliness of the fur-bearing Beast, he of Beauty-and-the, should once have been held against him, but in these green times is seen as a plus? (This book surely contains the definitive in-depth analysis of the Disney film of the tale, if "in-depth" here is not oxymoronic.)

The first section of Warner's book is about the tellers. It deals engagingly with those who collected, rewrote, and concocted such stories, from Marie-Jeanne L'Heritier to Perrault to the studious Grimm brothers and the melancholy Hans Andersen. But also, even more entertainingly, it considers the imagined teller of tales, she (and it is mostly a "she") from whom story itself was perceived to flow. Who would have suspected that the Mother Goose whose comical portrait adorned so many early collections had such an ancient and august lineage? The cackly voiced bird-woman, it appears, goes all the way back to the feather-bodied sirens. The sibyl figures in her genealogy, too, as does the Queen of Sheba, who was thought by medieval artists to have a bird's foot. So do such disparate figures as the hard-pressed but cool Scheherazade, the pious and instructive St. Anne, and a bevy of raucous crones, who, like Juliet's nurse, are vulgar in their speech and erotic in their interests.

But the more women as a group were misprized by society, the greater the level of disguise required by any who dared to break silence. In times of oppression, wisdom of certain kinds can safely be spoken only through the mouths of those playing the fool. Thus the goose face.

The second part of the book deals with the tales themselves—not only in their verbal forms but also as they feature in plays, operas, films, and pictures. Warner focuses on stories with female protagonists—beanstalk Jack and his bravely bladed brethren get short shrift, while maiden-devouring ogres, demon lovers, and incest-inclined fathers are bathed in the lurid spotlight—but then, this book does not pretend to be an encyclopedia. Nor are all the girls in it goody-goodies: unpleasant females such as ugly sisters, bad fairies, and wicked stepmothers get a thorough going-over, with the caveat that stepmothers in our changed socioeconomic times need no longer be wicked. (I was relieved to hear that, being one.)

Why so many dead mothers? Why so many blond heroines? Why indeed a chapter called, enticingly, "The Language of Hair"? From which Rapunzel-like German hair-water ad did the Dadaists pinch their name? Only list, Dear Reader—Warner herself is a dab hand at lists—and you shall know all. Or if not all, at least a good deal more than you did when you came in.

At times you may feel you're at risk of falling into a charmed sleep, having pricked your finger on one spinster too many, but that just means you've been reading too fast. This is a complex tapestry woven of many yarns, and you shouldn't try to unravel all of its threads at once.

Although Warner is entranced by the vitality and metamorphic properties of the fairy tale as form, she does not try to make a case for it as at all times politically appropriate. She recognizes "the contrary directions of the genre," which pull it "toward acquiescence on one hand and rebellion on the other." Because a story—any story, but especially one that exists in such a vernacular domain—is a negotiation between teller and audience, the listeners are accomplices. The aim of the tale may well be to instruct, but if it does not also delight, it will play to empty houses. As Warner says, "Fairystorytellers know that a tale, if it is to enthrall, must move the listeners to pleasure, laughter or tears. . . . The sultan is always there, half asleep, but quite awake enough to rouse himself and remember that death sentence he threatened."

We the audience are the collective sultan. If we want insipid heroines, that's what we'll get, and ditto for bigotries and prejudices and superheated shoes. But not forever. As Warner also says, "What is applauded and who sets the terms of the recognition and acceptance are always in question." We need not content ourselves with limp compliance or sullen revenge: the creative retelling, the utopian dream, the mischievous reversal, the rightly chosen wish, and the renewed sense of wonder may instead be ours.

This is a happy ending—and Warner knows her genre far too well not to give us one—but it is also a challenge. The uses of enchantment, it seems, are in our hands.

20

Review:

Burning Your Boats:
The Collected Short Stories
by Angela Carter

The British writer Angela Carter died too early, at age fifty-three. Her career spanned four decades and produced several acclaimed novels and much astute criticism. It also produced four collections of the extravagant, baroque, and disconcertingly down-to-earth short pieces—such as "The Company of Wolves"—that have become her trademark; so much so that publishers are now sending out requests for fabulist fiction "in the manner of Angela Carter." Ironically, she's become more widely appreciated since her death than she ever was before and is now the most frequently studied author in British universities. She's even become that rarest of creatures, an unabashed feminist it's okay for the guys to like. Maybe it's because her feminism is not of a very puritanical sort. She's a rowdy girl rather than a goody-two-shoes: she can say *tits and bum* with the best of them, and does so quite frequently. If she were a character in a work of fiction in the style of Angela Carter, she'd now, in spirit form, be guffawing raucously down the chimney. "In the manner of," indeed! Who would dare?

Burning Your Boats is a collection of her short fictional pieces, including some very early ones and some that were unpublished at the time of her death. It's an amazing plum pudding. If Carter were a color she'd be purple; if a flower, a cross between a wild rose with lots of thorns and a Venus fly-trap; if an animal, a cunning fox with gryphon claws; if a bird or other air-borne device, hybrid lyrebird-cum-Siren, with a bit of jackdaw thrown in—for all things bright and beautiful, as well as all things gnarled and macabre, appeal to her, and she filches them with abandon, picks them apart, sticks them together again in a new order, and adds them to her deliberately cluttered verbal nest. Not for her Hemingway's clean, well-lighted place, or Orwell's clear prose like a pane of glass. She prefers instead a dirty, badly lit place, with gnawed bones in the corner and dusty mirrors you'd best not consult. Prose like glass, yes—but it's stained glass. Many of her best effects are achieved by overloading. She piles the adjectives up into a towering chocolate-and-cherries mound, then pulls the tablecloth out from under it so the whole edifice comes crashing delightfully down. She loves blowing bubbles, and she also loves bursting them.

If you were writing her literary *naissance* in the manner of Angela Carter, you'd have to provide a troupe of ghostly godpersons gathered round her typewriter. Oscar Wilde would be there, whispering "Nothing succeeds like excess" and bestowing the gift of the inversion of truisms; Sylvia Townsend Warner, with her clutch of ruthless fairies; Edgar Allan Poe, the subject of one of her more spectacular stories, although Carter wears her Rue Morgue with a difference. And Bram Stoker, and Perrault, and Sheridan Le Fanu, and George MacDonald, and Mary Shelley, and perhaps even Carson McCullers, and a whole gaggle of disreputable tale-telling old grannies. Although like every child she had ancestors, like every child she was unique; though Carter, it must be said, was more unique than most. (I know: *more unique* is a contradiction; but I said this was *in the manner of*.)

Burning Your Boats is an apt title: it's what you do when you're fighting on perilous ground and choose to cut off your own retreat. At the outset Carter was obstinately unfashionable, both in manner and in matter, but she didn't give a toss. She became herself almost immediately and never looked back: "A Very, Very Great Lady and Her Son at Home," one of her first stories, is about the deadening grip of dominating mothers on their children, and so is one of her last: "Ashputtle or The Mother's Ghost." "A Victorian Fable (with Glossary)" is an early piece written in Victorian thieves' cant, and illustrates both Carter's penchant for combining scholarship with little bits of junk picked up in curio shops, and the lifelong delight she took in the gaudiness, multiplicity, and untidiness of language itself.

Sows' ears into silk purses, and vice versa; the smart-as-a-whip intellectual essay blending into the sensual narrative mode, and vice versa: what concerned her was the magical act of transformation. She knew no bounds, and also no boundaries.

She's best known for her haunted European forests, replete with wolves and werewolves, but England is here, too—the polymorphous-perverse pantomime, and a wonderful country-house kitchen, and Shakespeare's enchanted woods. So is America—the mythological America, that is. Carter redoes John Ford's Jacobean shocker "'Tis Pity She's a Whore" as a Western movie directed by the *other* John Ford, and provides two renderings of Lizzie Borden, and a bravura piece in which she transmutes *Der Freischütz* into a Mexican-border melodrama, and an Indian captivity narrative in which the captured white heroine prefers the Indians, as they frequently did in real life.

But the attempt to summarize is hopeless. Suffice to say that you should not miss this book, nor should you try to read it all at once, as, like a pound of Turkish delight, it's too rich for a single mouthful. There's a warm and perceptive introduction by Carter's old friend Salman Rushdie, in which he pays tribute both to the woman—"sharp, foulmouthed, passionate"—and to her work. As he says, "She hadn't finished. . . . The stories in this volume are the measure of our loss. But they are also our treasure, to savour and to hoard."

21

Review:

An Experiment in Love
by Hilary Mantel

Hilary Mantel's seventh novel, *An Experiment in Love*, is only the second to be published in the United States. This is a shame, because Ms. Mantel is an exceptionally good writer. Her book's title, however, is somewhat misleading. *Experiment* suggests clinical detachment; but if experiments are going on, they're more like what Dr. Frankenstein got up to with the body parts: intense, unholy, and messy. As for *Love*, the inaccuracy is that it's singular: there are many kinds of love in this book, almost all contaminated. *Enter the Dragonness* might be a more likely title, for this is a story about emotional kung fu, female style—except that by the end, although all are wounded or worse, there's no clear winner.

The playing field is England, with its bafflingly complex and minutely calibrated systems of class and status, of region and religion; the players are little girls; larger girls; young women; and, looming huge over all, mothers. The weapons are clothing, schools, intelligence, friendships, insults, accents, trophy boyfriends, material possessions, and food. The battle cry is *"Sauve qui peut!"*

The narrator is Carmel McBain, who—having somehow survived to adulthood—kicks off the action with a Proustian time-warp experience, triggered by a newspaper photograph of her former roommate. Back she goes, sucked through the plug hole of memory into her dire childhood. One of her quirks is that she's dogged by lines from the poems she's learned at school, "The Rime of the Ancient Mariner" among them. Carmel is both the Mariner, doomed to relate, and the Wedding Guest, doomed to listen; and we, too, are held enthralled while she unwraps her own personal albatross and tells us how she got sadder but wiser.

"I wanted to separate myself from the common fate of girls who are called Carmel," she tells us, "and identify myself with girls with casual names, names which their parents didn't think about too hard." Carmel is the name of the mountain where the prophet Elijah slaughtered the priests of Baal: it's not quite like being called Linda. Indeed, Carmel is sometimes less a person than a geographic site, where embattled forces play themselves out despite her.

It's her mother who saddled her with this weighty name: a formidable north of England working-class mother, of wrathful temperament and Irish Catholic descent, who covers her daughter with her own elaborate embroidery, crams her with homework, and launches her like a missile at the social establishment she both despises and envies. Carmel's mother expects her to climb the heights: "The task in life that she set for me was to build my own mountain, build a step-by-step success: the kind didn't matter as long as it was high and it shone. And as she had told me that it is ruthless people who rise highest in this life, I would slash through the ropes of anyone who tried to climb after me . . . and jump about on the summit alone."

Carmel's forced climb leads from the grim 1950s Catholic primary school of her small, decrepit mill town to the Holy Redeemer, a superior establishment run by sarcastic nuns. There she wears a uniform that includes both a tie and a girdle, and is "stuffed with education," though other nutrients are scarce. The aim is to turn women into "little chappies with breasts." "Women were forced to imitate men, and bound not to succeed at it." Nevertheless, Carmel achieves a meager scholarship and a bed in Tonbridge Hall, a neo-Brontëan women's residence at London University. Among other things, this novel is a *Bildungsroman,* and one of the issues raised is the form of education appropriate for women.

All along the way, Carmel has a fellow climber, her doppelgänger and nemesis, the stolid and implacable Karina. Karina's parents are immigrants. They have undergone the war—cattle cars are mentioned—although they

155

are not Jewish. Out of compunction, Carmel's mother insists on a friend-ship between the girls; thereafter Karina is linked to Carmel, and where Carmel goes, Karina follows. Like Carmel's mother, she, too, envies and despises, but the object of these emotions is Carmel herself. Whatever Carmel has, Karina takes or else destroys, though it is not a one-sided war. Carmel gets her licks in, too, and may even have started it all in kinder-garten by kicking Karina's baby doll: an early recognition, perhaps, that all was not well in the world of mums and tots. Over the years, Karina is Carmel's enemy, but also—when the girls enter the alien territory of upmarket nuns and middle-class southerners—her oldest friend and grudging ally. "I never thought she was dangerous, except to me," thinks Carmel—wrongly, as it turns out.

They are a Jack Spratt-and-his-wife couple: Carmel thin and childish, not even allowed to help burn the sparse family dinner; Karina rotund and prematurely competent, a little housewife at age twelve. Carmel is cold and hungry and watery, and dreams of drowning; Karina is warm and wool-covered, associated with Catherine wheels and fire. Above all, Karina is the protégée and voice of the mothers, especially Carmel's mother: angry, self-righteous, annihilating.

Although she is acquiescent and browbeaten, Carmel has ways of rebelling. At school she practices "dumb insolence," and her first act on reaching the university is to chop off her hair, which, via the torturing use of curl rags, has been one of the instruments of maternal control. But she also takes over her mother's role. Her mother has deprived her not only of affection and approval but also of actual nourishment, and now Carmel begins to deprive herself. Karina, on the other hand, is gorging herself to blimplike proportions. As one character comments, "More and more of Karina. Less and less of Carmel."

We are warned against considering this a story about anorexia; too middle-class. Rather, claims the narrator, it is a story about "appetite." Well, perhaps. This portion of the book is set in 1970, at the precise time when anorexia was becoming common but was not yet common knowl-edge; any later and Carmel could not have been so unself-conscious about her plight. In any case, the dwindling of Carmel has complex causes. There is the nuns' connection of eating with sin and their emphasis on self-denial—but how much self can you do without and still remain alive? There's also Carmel's poverty, and the dreadful food of Tonbridge Hall. But the difficulty for Carmel goes well beyond the pinched pennies and the underdone vegetables: How much of life does she dare to eat? How much enjoy? The pleasure principle has not been exactly fostered.

The pleasures of the novel, however, are many. The women's-residence portions of *An Experiment in Love* are as harshly delicious as those in *The Group*; the childhood sections are immediate and vivid, funny and bleak, and the intricate love and love-hate relationships among the women, which, as the narrator says, have nothing to do with sex, are right on target. This is Carmel's story, but it is that of her generation as well: girls at the end of the sixties, caught between two sets of values, who had the Pill but still ironed their boyfriends' shirts.

Moral confusion reigns, and moral questions also: What makes bad people bad? Even more mysteriously, what makes good people good? Why Karina, and why the heartbreakingly kind Lynette, Karina's affluent roommate, rebuffed by her at every turn? Carmel's weak father, who has retreated into jigsaw puzzles, can't find the missing part of Judas, and neither can Carmel.

"Descriptions are your strong point," Carmel is told, and they are Ms. Mantel's as well. Never have dripping tights hung over a radiator or the smell of a child's wooden ruler been so meticulously rendered. The similes and metaphors glint brightly: the sheets in the dormitory are "tucked strap-tight into the bed's frame, as if to harness a lunatic"; the residence soup is "an uncleaned aquarium, where vegetable matter swam." Much of this verbal dexterity is exercised on food, but as a narrator, Carmel is like her mother: she does a little embroidery on everything.

If there's any complaint, it's that we want to know more; like Carmel herself, the book could have been a little fatter. What happened to Karina and Carmel after the horrifying denouement? But perhaps that's the point: it's what you'll never know that haunts you; and with all its brilliance, its sharpness, and its clear-eyed wit, *An Experiment in Love* is a haunting book.

22

In Search of *Alias Grace*:
On Writing Canadian Historical Fiction

What I am going to talk about this evening has to do with the Canadian novel, and more particularly, the Canadian historical novel. I will address the nature of this genre insofar as it has to do with the mysteries of time and memory; I will meditate on why so many of this kind of novel have been written by English-speaking Canadian authors lately; and after that I'll talk a little about my own recent attempt to write such a novel. At the end I'll attempt some sort of meaning-of-it-all nugget or philosophical summation, as such a thing is implicitly called for in the list of ingredients on the cookie box.

Fiction is where individual memory and experience and collective memory and experience come together, in greater or lesser proportions. The closer the fiction is to us, the more we recognize and claim it as individual rather than collective. Margaret Laurence used to say that her English readers thought *The Stone Angel* was about old age, the Americans thought it was about some old woman they knew, and the Canadians thought it was about their grandmothers. Each character in fiction has an individual life, replete with personal detail—the eating of meals, the flossing of teeth, the making of love, the birthing of children, the attending of funerals, and so forth—but each also exists within a context, a fictional world comprised of geology, weather, economic forces, social classes, cultural references, and wars and plagues and such big public events; you'll note that, being Canadian, I put the geology first. This fictional world so lovingly delineated by the writer may bear a more obvious or a less obvious relation to the world we actually live in, but bearing no relation to it at all is not an option. We have to write out of who and where and when we are, whether we like it or not, and disguise it how we may. As Robertson Davies has remarked, ". . . we all belong to our own time, and there is nothing whatever that we can do to escape from it. Whatever we write will be contemporary, even if we attempt a novel set in a past age. . . ."[1] We can't help but be modern, just as the Victorian writers—whenever they set their books—couldn't help but be Victorian. Like all beings alive on Middle Earth, we're trapped by time and circumstance.

What I've said about fictional characters is, of course, also true of every real human being. For example: here I am, giving this Bronfman Lecture in Ottawa; and it was in Ottawa that I was born, fifty-seven years, three days, and several hours ago. The place was the Ottawa General Hospital; the date, November 18, 1939. About the exact hour, my mother—to the despair of many astrologers since—is a little vague, that being a period when women were routinely conked out with ether. I do know that I was born after the end of the Grey Cup Football Game. The doctors thanked my mother for waiting; they'd all been following the game on the radio. In those days most doctors were men, which may explain their sportive attitude.

"In those days"—there I am, you see, being born in *those* days, which are not the same as these days; no ether now, and many a woman doctor. As for Ottawa, I wouldn't have been there at all if it hadn't been for the Great Depression: my parents were economic refugees from Nova Scotia—there's your economic force—from which they were then cut off by the Second World War—there's your big public event.

We lived—here's your personal detail—in a long, dark, railroad-car-shaped second-story apartment on Patterson Avenue, near the Rideau Canal—there's your geology, more or less—an apartment in which my mother once caused a flood by rinsing the diapers in the toilet, where they got stuck—in *those* days there were no disposable diapers, and not even any diaper services. In *those* days, as I'm sure some of you believe you remember, there was much more snow—there's your weather—and it was much whiter and more beautiful than any snow they ever come up with nowadays. As a child I helped to build snow forts that were much bigger than the Parliament Buildings, and even more labyrinthine—there's your cultural reference. I remember this very clearly, so it must be true, and there's your individual memory.

What's my point? It's out of such individual particulars that fiction is constructed; and so is autobiography, including the kind of autobiography we are each always writing but haven't yet gotten around to writing down; and so, too, is history. History may intend to provide us with grand patterns and overall schemes, but without its brick-by-brick, life-by-life, day-by-day foundations, it would collapse. Whoever tells you that history is not about individuals, only about large trends and movements, is lying. The shot heard 'round the world was fired on a certain date, under certain weather conditions, out of a certain rather inefficient type of gun. After the Rebellion of 1837, William Lyon Mackenzie escaped to the United States dressed in women's clothing; I know the year, so I can guess the style of his dress. When I lived in the rural Ontario countryside north of Toronto, a local man said, "There's the barn where we hid the women and children, that time the Fenians invaded." An individual barn; individual women and children. The man who told me about the barn was born some sixty years after the Fenian attack, but he said *we*, not *they*: he was remembering as a personal experience and event at which he had not been present in the flesh, and I believe we have all done that. It's at such points that memory, history, and story all intersect; it would take only one step more to bring all of them into the realm of fiction.

We live in a period in which memory of all kinds, including the sort of larger memory we call history, is being called into question. For history as for the individual, forgetting can be just as convenient as remembering, and remembering what was once forgotten can be distinctly uncomfortable. As a rule, we tend to remember the awful things done to us and to forget the awful things we did. The Blitz is still remembered; the firebombing of Dresden—well, not so much, or not by us. To challenge an accepted version of history—what we've decided it's proper to remember— by dredging up things that society has decided are better forgotten, can cause cries of anguish and outrage, as the makers of a recent documentary about the Second World War could testify. Remembrance Day, like

Mother's Day, is a highly ritualized occasion; for instance, we are not allowed, on Mother's Day, to commemorate *bad* mothers, and even to acknowledge that such persons exist would be considered—on that date— to be in shoddy taste.

Here is the conundrum, for history and individual memory alike, and therefore for fiction also: How do we *know* we know what we think we know? And if we find that, after all, we don't know what it is that we once thought we knew, how do we know we are who we think we are, or thought we were yesterday, or thought we were—for instance—a hundred years ago? These are the questions one asks oneself, at my age, whenever one says, *Whatever happened to old what's-his-name?* They are also the questions that arise in connection with Canadian history, or indeed with any other kind of history. They are also the questions that arise in any contemplation of what used to be called "character"; they are thus central to any conception of the novel. For the novel concerns itself, above all, with time. Any plot is a *this* followed by a *that;* there must be change in a novel, and change can only take place over time, and this change can only have significance if either the character in the book, or, at the very least, the reader, can remember what came before. As Henry James's biographer Leon Edel has said, if there's a clock in it, you know it's a novel.

Thus there can be no history, and no novel either, without memory of some sort; but when it comes right down to it, how reliable is memory itself—our individual memory, or our collective memory as a society? Once, memory was a given. You could lose it and you could recover it, but the thing lost and then recovered was as solid and all-of-a-piece, was as much a *thing,* as a gold coin. "Now it all comes back to me," or some version of it, was a staple of the recovering-from-amnesia scenes in Victorian melodramas—indeed, even so late as the recovering-from-amnesia scene in Graham Greene's *The Ministry of Fear*; and there was an *it,* there was an *all.* If the seventeenth century revolved around faith—that is, what you believed—and the eighteenth around knowledge—that is, what you could prove—the nineteenth could be said to have revolved around memory. You can't have Tennyson's *Tears, idle tears . . . Oh death in life, the days that used to be,* unless you can remember those days that used to be and are no more. Nostalgia for what once was, guilt for what you once did, revenge for what someone else once did to you, regret for what you once might have done but didn't do—how central they all are to the previous century, and how dependent each one of them is on the idea of memory itself. Without memory, and the belief that it can be recovered whole, like treasure fished out of a swamp, Proust's famous *madeleine* is reduced to a casual snack. The nineteenth-century novel would be unimaginable without a belief in the integrity of memory; for what is the self without a more or less continuous memory of itself, and what is the novel without the self? Or so they would have argued back then.

As for the twentieth century, at least in Europe, it has been on the whole more interested in forgetting—forgetting as an organic process, and sometimes as a willed act. Dali's famous painting *The Persistence of Memory* features a melting clock and a parade of destructive ants; Beckett's famous play *Krapp's Last Tape* is relentless in its depiction of how we erase and rewrite ourselves over time; Milan Kundera's novel *The Book of Laughter and Forgetting* has a touchstone twentieth-century title; the horrifying film *Night and Fog* is only one of many twentieth-century statements about how we industriously and systematically obliterate history to suit our own vile purposes; and in Orwell's *1984*, the place where documents are sent to be destroyed is called, ironically, the Memory Hole. The twentieth century's most prominent theories of the psyche—those that evolved from Freud—taught us that we were not so much the sum of what we could remember, as the sum of what we had forgotten;[2] we were controlled by the Unconscious, where unsavory repressed memories were stored in our heads like rotten apples in a barrel, festering away but essentially unknowable, except for the suspicious smell. Furthermore, twentieth-century European art as a whole gradually lost faith in the reliability of time itself. No longer an evenly flowing river, it became a collage of freeze-frames, jumbled fragments, and jump cuts.[3]

The hero of Spanish writer Javier Marias's 1989 novel *All Souls* represents a host of twentieth-century European spiritual relatives when he says, ". . . I must speak of myself and of my time in the city of Oxford, even though the person speaking is not the same person who was there. He seems to be, but he is not. If I call myself 'I,' or use a name which has accompanied me since birth and by which some will remember me . . . it is simply because I prefer to speak in the first person and not because I believe that the faculty of memory alone is any guarantee that a person remains the same in different times and different places. The person recounting here and now what he saw and what happened to him then is not the same person who saw those things and to whom those things happened; neither is he a prolongation of that person, his shadow, his heir or his usurper."[4]

Fine and dandy, we say, with our streetwise postmodern consciousness. However, problems do arise. If the I of now has nothing to do with the I of then, where did the I of now come from? Nothing is made from nothing, or so we used to believe. And, to get back to Canadian studies—why is it that it's now—within the past fifteen or twenty years, and so near the end of the fragmenting and memory-denying twentieth century—that the Canadian historical novel has become so popular, with writers and readers alike?

But what exactly do we mean by "historical novel"? All novels are in a sense "historical" novels; they can't help it, insofar as they have to, they *must*, make reference to a time that is not the time in which the reader is reading the book. (A reference to science fiction novels will not save us here, as the writer has, of course, written the book in a time that is already past to the reader.) But there is the past tense—yesterday and yesterday and yesterday, full of tooth flossing and putting the antifreeze into the car, a yesterday not so long ago—and then there is The Past, capital T and P.

Charles Dickens's Scrooge timorously asks the Ghost of Christmas Past whether the past they are about to visit is "long past" and is told, "No— *your* past." For a considerable period it was only "your past"—the personal past of the writer, and, by extension, that of the reader—that was at issue in the Canadian novel. I don't recall any serious writer in the sixties writing what we think of as historical romances proper—that is, the full-dress petticoat-and-farthingale kind, which were associated with subjects such as Mary, Queen of Scots. Perhaps it was thought that Canada lacked the appropriate clothing for such works; perhaps the genre itself was regarded as a form of trash writing, such as bodice rippers—which, like any other genre, it either is or it isn't, depending on how it's done.

Once, we as a society were not so squeamish. Major Richardson's hugely popular nineteenth-century novel *Wacousta* was, among other things, a historical novel along the lines of Sir Walter Scott, granddaddy of the form, and Fenimore Cooper, his even more prolix descendant. These were nineteenth-century novelists, and the nineteenth century loved the historic novel. *Vanity Fair, Middlemarch, A Tale of Two Cities, Ivanhoe, Treasure Island*—all are historic novels of one kind or another, and these are only a few. Perhaps the question to be asked is not why we're writing historic novels now, but why we didn't do it before.

In any case, by the 1960s it was as if we'd forgotten that on this continent, and especially north of the forty-ninth parallel, there was ever a bodice to be ripped or a weak-minded lady to be rendered hysterical by the experience. We were instead taken up by the momentous discovery that we actually existed, in what was then the here and now, and we were busily exploring the implications of that.

Our generation of English-speaking Canadians—those of us who were children in the forties and adolescents in the fifties—grew up with the illusion that there was not then and never had been a Canadian literature. I say "illusion" because there had in fact been one; it's just that we weren't told about it. The collapse of old-style English colonial imperialism had abolished the old-style school reader—the kind that used to contain excerpts from English literature mingled with bits from our native singers and songstresses, usually so termed. Thus you could go through twelve years of schooling, back then, and come out with the impression that there had only ever been one Canadian writer, and that was Stephen Leacock.

The fifties came right after the forties and the thirties; and the double whammy of the Depression followed by the war had wiped out what in the teens and twenties had been a burgeoning indigenous publishing industry, complete with best sellers. (Remember Mazo De La Roche? We didn't. We were told nothing about her.) Add to that the weight of the paperback book industry—completely controlled, back then, from the United States—and the advent of television, most of which came from south of the border, and you get the picture. There was radio, of course. There was the CBC. There were Wayne and Schuster and *Our Pet, Juliet*. But it wasn't much of a counterbalance.

When we hit university in the late fifties and encountered intellectual magazines, we found ourselves being fed large doses of anxiety and contempt, brewed by our very own pundits and even by some of our very own poets and fiction writers, concerning our own inauthenticity, our feebleness from the cultural point of view, our lack of a real literature, and the absence of anything you could dignify by the name of history—by which was meant interesting and copious bloodshed on our own turf. In Québec, people were more certain of their own existence, and especially of their own persistence, although they had lots of Parisian-oriented voices to tell them how substandard they were. In "Angloland," Earle Birney's famous poem concludes "It's only by the lack of ghosts we're haunted," which sums up the prevailing attitude of the time.

Well, we young writers charged ahead anyway. We thought we were pretty daring to be setting our poems and stories in Toronto and Vancouver and Montréal, and even Ottawa, rather than in London or Paris or New York. We were, however, relentlessly contemporary: history, for us, either didn't exist; or it had happened elsewhere; or if ours, it was boring.

This is often the attitude among the young, but it was especially true of us, because of the way we'd encountered our own history. Québec has always had its own version of history, with heroes and villains, and struggle, and heartbreak, and God; God was a main feature until recently. But those of us in English Canada who went to high school when I did weren't dosed with any such strong medicine. Instead we were handed a particularly anemic view of our past, insofar as we were given one at all. For others on more troubled shores the epic battles, the heroes, the stirring speeches, the do-or-die last stands, the freezing to death during the retreat from Moscow. For us the statistics on wheat and the soothing assurances that all was well in the land of the cow and potato, not to mention— although they *were* mentioned—the vein of metallic ore and the stack of lumber. We looked at these things and saw that they were good, if tedious, but we didn't really examine how they'd been obtained or who was profiting by them, or who did the actual work, or how much they got paid for it. Nor was much said about who inhabited this space before white Europeans arrived, bearing gifts of firearms and smallpox, because weren't we nice people? You bet we were, and nice people do not dwell on morbid subjects. I myself would have been much more interested in Canadian history if I'd known that our dull prime minister, Mackenzie King, had believed that the spirit of his mother was inhabiting his dog, which he always consulted on public policy—it explains so much—but nobody knew about such things back then.

The main idea behind the way we were taught Canadian history seemed to be reassurance: as a country, we'd had our little differences, and a few embarrassing moments—the Rebellion of '37, the hanging of Louis Riel, and so forth—but these had just been unseemly burps in one long gentle after-dinner nap. We were always being told that Canada had come of age. This was even a textbook title: *Canada Comes of Age.* I'm not sure what it was supposed to mean—that we could vote and drink and shave and fornicate, perhaps; or that we had come into our inheritance and could now manage our own affairs.

Our inheritance. Ah, yes—the mysterious sealed box handed over by the family solicitor when young master comes into his majority. But what was inside it? Many things we weren't told about in school, and this is where the interest in historical writing comes in. For it's the very things that *aren't* mentioned that inspire the most curiosity in us. *Why* aren't they mentioned? The lure of the Canadian past, for the writers of my generation, has been partly the lure of the unmentionable—the mysterious, the buried, the forgotten, the discarded, the taboo.

This digging up of buried things began perhaps in poetry; for instance, E. J. Pratt's narrative poems on subjects such as the sinking of the *Titanic* and the life of the French Jesuit missionary Brébeuf. Pratt was followed by certain younger writers; I think of Gwendolyn MacEwen's midsixties verse play *Terror and Erebus,* about the failure of the Franklin expedition. I blush to mention Margaret Atwood's *The Journals of Susanna Moodie* of 1970, but since I'll need to mention it later anyway, I'll get the blushing over with now. Other poets—Doug Jones and Al Purdy in particular, but there were more—used historic events as subjects for individual poems. James Reaney was a pioneer in the use of local history—he was writing the Donnelly trilogy in the late sixties, although the plays were not produced until later. There were other plays in the 1970s, too—Rick Salutin's *The Farmers' Rebellion,* about the Upper Canadian Rebellion, springs to mind.

Then came the novels. These weren't historical romances of the bodice-ripping kind; instead they were what we should probably term "novels set in the historic past," to distinguish them from the kind of thing you find in drugstores that have cloaks on them and raised silver scrollwork titles. When is the past old enough to be considered historic? Well, roughly, I suppose you could say it's anything before the time at which the novel-writer came to consciousness; that seems fair enough.

In the novel, then, we had Anne Hébert's excellent *Kamouraska*, as early as 1970. It was written in French, but it was translated, and many English-speaking writers read it. As far back as Margaret Laurence's *The Diviners* in 1974 and Marian Engel's *Bear* in 1976, figures from the Canadian past were used as points of reference for the Canadian present—Catherine Parr Traill by Laurence, an obscure and probably invented nineteenth-century English emigrant by Engel. Rudy Wiebe's *The Temptations of Big Bear* in 1973 and *The Scorched Wood People* in 1977 are usually thought of as being enclosed by the parentheses *Native People*, but they are, of course, set entirely in the past. Then there's Timothy Findley's *The Wars* in 1977.

In the 1980s and 1990s, the trend intensified. Graeme Gibson's *Perpetual Motion* was published in 1982. After that their names are legion. Robertson Davies's *Murther and Walking Spirits* is a historical novel. So—using my definition of historic—are Michael Ondaatje's *In the Skin of a Lion* and *The English Patient*, and Brian Moore's *Blackrobe*. So are Alice Munro's two stories "Meneseteung" and "A Wilderness Station." So are George Bowering's *Burning Waters* and Daphne Marlatt's *Ana Historic*, and Jane Urquhart's *The Whirlpool* and *Away*; so is Carol Shields's *The Stone Diaries*; so is Timothy Findley's *The Piano Man's Daughter*. In this year alone, we have Findley's *You Went Away*, Anne Marie Macdonald's *Fall on Your Knees*, Katherine Govier's *Angel Walk*, Anne Michaels's *Fugitive Pieces*, Gail Anderson-Dargatz's *The Cure for Death by Lightning*, and Guy Vanderhaeghe's *The Englishman's Boy*.

All of these are set in the past—Dickens's *long* past—but not all use the past for the same purposes. Of course not; the authors of them are individuals, and each novel has its own preoccupations. Some attempt to give more or less faithful accounts of actual events, in answer perhaps to such questions as "Where did we come from?" and "How did we get here?" Some attempt restitution of a sort, or at least an acknowledgment of past wrongs—I'd put the Rudy Wiebe novels and Guy Vanderhaeghe's book in this category, dealing as they do with the deplorable North American record on the treatment of native peoples. Others, such as Graeme Gibson's, look at what we have killed and destroyed in our obsessive search for the pot of gold. Others delve into class structure and political struggles— Ondaatje's *In The Skin of a Lion*, for instance. Yet others unearth a past as it was lived by women, under conditions a good deal more stringent than our own; yet others use the past as background to family sagas—tales of betrayal and tragedy and even madness. "The past is another country," begins the English novel *The Go-Between*;[5] "they do things differently there." Yes, they do, and these books point that out; but they also do quite a few things the same, and these books point that out as well.

Why then has there been such a spate of historical novels in the past twenty years, and especially in the past decade? Earlier, I gave some possible reasons as to why this trend didn't occur earlier. But why is it happening now?

Some might say that we're more confident about ourselves—that we're now allowed to find ourselves more interesting than we once did; and I think they would be right. In this, we're part of a worldwide movement that has found writers and readers, especially in ex-colonies, turning back toward their own roots, while not rejecting developments in the imperial centers. London and Paris are still wonderful places, but they are no longer seen as the only homes of the good, the true, and the beautiful, as well as of those more typical twentieth-century tastes, the bad, the false, and the ugly. You want squalor, lies, and corruption? Hell, we've got 'em homegrown, and not only that, we always have had, and there's where the past comes in.

Some might say that, on the other hand, the past is safer; that at a time when our country feels very much under threat—the threat of splitting apart, and the threat of having its established institutions and its social fabric and its sense of itself literally torn apart—it feels comforting to escape backward, to a time when these things were not the problems. With the past, at least we know what happened: while visiting there, we suffer from no uncertainties about the future, or at least the part of it that comes between them and us; we've read about it. The *Titanic* may be sinking, but we're not on it. Watching it subside, we're diverted for a short time from the leaking lifeboat we're actually in right now.

Of course, the past was not really safer. As a local museum custodian has commented, "Nostalgia is the past without the pain,"[6] and for those living in it, the past was their present, and just as painful as our present is to us—and perhaps more so, considering the incurable diseases and the absence of anesthesia, central heating, and indoor plumbing back then, to mention a few of the drawbacks. Those who long for a return to the supposed values of the nineteenth century should turn away from the frilly-pillow magazines devoted to that era and take a good, hard look at what was really going on. So although coziness may be an attraction, it's also an illusion; and not many of the Canadian historical novels I've mentioned depict the past as a very soothing place.

There's also the lure of time travel, which appeals to the little cultural anthropologist in each of us. It's such fun to snoop, as it were; to peek in the windows. What did they eat back then? What did they wear, how did they wash their clothes, or treat their sick, or bury their dead? What did they think about? What lies did they tell, and why? Who were they, really? The questions, once they begin, are endless. It's like questioning your dead great-grandparents—does any of what they did or thought live on in us?

I think there's another reason for the appeal, and it has to do with the age we are now. Nothing is more boring to a fifteen-year-old than Aunt Agatha's ramblings about the family tree; but often, nothing is more intriguing to a fifty-year-old. It's not the individual authors who are now fifty—some of them are a good deal younger than that. I think it's the culture.

I once took a graduate course titled "The Literature of the American Revolution," which began with the professor saying that there actually *was* no literature of the American Revolution, because everyone was too busy being too revolting during that period to write any, so we were going to study the literature just before it, and the literature just after it. What came after it was a lot of hand-wringing and soul-searching by the American artistic community, such as it was. Now that we've had the Revolution, they fretted, where is the great American genius that ought to burst forth? What should the wondrous novel or poem or painting be like to be truly American? Why can't we have an American fashion industry? And so on. When *Moby-Dick* and Walt Whitman finally did appear, most right-thinking people wiped their feet on them; but such is life.

However, it was out of this questioning and assessing climate—where did we come from, how did we get from there to here, where are we going, who are we now?—that Nathaniel Hawthorne wrote *The Scarlet Letter*, a historic novel set in seventeenth-century New England. The eighteenth century had mostly been embarrassed by the Puritans, and especially by their crazed zeal during the Salem witchcraft trials, and had tried to forget about them; but Hawthorne dug them up again, and took a long, hard look at them. *The Scarlet Letter* is not, of course, seventeenth-century in any way the Puritans would have recognized; in good nineteenth-century style, it's far too admiring and respectful of that adulterous baggage, Hester Prynne. Instead it's a novel that uses a seventeenth-century English Colonial setting for the purposes of a newly forged nineteenth-century American republic. And I think that's part of the interest for writers and readers of Canadian historical fiction, now: by taking a long, hard look backward, we place ourselves.

Having more or less delivered two of the three main things I promised you, I'll now turn to the third: my own attempt to write a piece of fiction set in the past. I didn't plan to do it, but I somehow ended up doing it anyway, which is how my novels generally occur. Nor was I conscious of any of the motives I've just outlined. I think novelists begin with hints and images and scenes and voices rather than with theories and grand schemes. It's individual characters interacting with and acted upon by the world that surrounds them that the novel has to do; with the details, not the large pattern; although a large pattern may then, of course, emerge.

The book in question is *Alias Grace*, and here is how it came about. In the sixties, for reasons that can't be rationally explained, I found myself writing a sequence of poems called *The Journals of Susanna Moodie*, which was about an English emigrant who came to what is now Ontario in the 1830s and had a truly awful time in a swamp north of Peterborough, and wrote about her experiences in a book called *Roughing It in the Bush*, which warned English gentlefolk not to do the same. Canada, in her opinion, was a land suited only to horny-handed peasants, otherwise known as honest sons of toil. After she escaped from the woods she wrote *Life in the Clearings*, which contains her version of the Grace Marks story.

Susanna Moodie describes her meeting with Grace in the Kingston Penitentiary in 1851; she then retells the double murder in which Grace was involved. The motive, according to Moodie, was Grace's passion for her employer, the gentleman Thomas Kinnear, and her demented jealousy of Nancy Montgomery, Kinnear's housekeeper and mistress. Moodie portrays Grace as the driving engine of the affair—a scowling, sullen, teenage temptress—with the comurderer, the manservant James McDermott, shown as a mere dupe, driven by his own lust for Grace as well as by her taunts and blandishments.

Thomas Kinnear and Nancy Montgomery ended up dead in the cellar, and Grace and McDermott made it across Lake Ontario to the States with a wagonful of stolen goods. They were caught and brought back, and tried for the murder of Thomas Kinnear; the murder of Nancy was never tried, as both were convicted and condemned to death. McDermott was hanged. Grace was sentenced as an accessory, but as a result of petitions by her well-wishers, and in consideration of her feebler sex and extreme youth—she was barely sixteen—her sentence was commuted to life.

Moodie saw Grace again, this time in the violent ward of the newly built lunatic asylum in Toronto; and there her account ends, with a pious hope that perhaps the poor girl was deranged all along, which would explain her shocking behavior and also afford her forgiveness in the afterlife. That was the first version of the story I came across, and being young, and still believing that "nonfiction" meant "true," I did not question it.

Time passed. Then, in the seventies, I was asked by CBC producer George Jonas to write a script for television. My script was about Grace Marks, using Moodie's version, which was already highly dramatic in form. In it, Grace is brooding and obsessive, and McDermott is putty in her hands. I did leave out Moodie's detail about Grace and McDermott cutting Nancy up into four pieces before hiding her under a washtub. I thought it would be hard to film, and anyway, why would they have bothered?

I then received an invitation to turn my television script into a theater piece. I did give this a try. I hoped to use a multilevel stage, so the main floor, the upstairs, and the cellar could all be seen at once. I wanted to open it in the penitentiary and close it in the lunatic asylum, and I had some idea of having the spirit of Susanna Moodie flown in on wires, in a black silk dress, like a cross between Peter Pan and a bat; but it was all too much for me, and I gave it up, and then forgot about it.

More time passed. Soon enough it was the early 1990s, and I was on a book tour, and sitting in a hotel room in Zurich. A scene came to me vividly, in the way that scenes often do. I wrote it down on a piece of hotel writing paper, lacking any other kind; it was much the same as the opening scene of the book as it now exists. I recognized the locale: it was the cellar of the Kinnear house, and the female figure in it was Grace Marks. Not immediately, but after a while, I continued with the novel. This time, however, I did what neither Moodie nor I had done before: I went back to the past.

The past is made of paper; sometimes, now, it's made of microfilm and CD-ROMs, but ultimately they, too, are made of paper. Sometimes there's a building or a picture or a grave, but mostly it's paper. Paper must be taken care of; archivists and librarians are the guardian angels of paper: without them there would be a lot less of the past than there is, and I and many other writers owe them a huge debt of thanks.

What's on the paper? The same things that are on paper now. Records, documents, newspaper stories, eyewitness reports, gossip and rumor and opinion and contradiction. There is—as I increasingly came to discover— no more reason to trust something written down on paper then than there is now. After all, the writers-down were, and are, human beings, and are subject to error, intentional or not, and to the very human desire to magnify a scandal, and to their own biases. I was often deeply frustrated as well, not by what those past recorders had written down, but by what they'd left out. History is more than willing to tell you who won the Battle of Trafalgar and which world leader signed this or that treaty, but it's more reluctant about the now obscure details of daily life. Nobody wrote these things down, because everybody knew them, and considered them too mundane and unimportant to record. Thus I found myself wrestling not only with who said what about Grace, but also with how to clean a chamber pot, what footgear would have been worn in winter, the origins of quilt pattern names, and how to store parsnips. If you're after the truth, the whole and detailed truth, and nothing but the truth, you're going to have a thin time of it if you trust to paper; but with the past, it's almost all you've got.

Susanna Moodie said at the outset of her account that she was writing the story from memory, and as it turns out, her memory was no better than most. She got the location wrong, and the names of some of the participants, just for starters. Not only that, the story was much more problematic, although less neatly dramatic, than the one Moodie had told. For one thing, the witnesses—even eyewitnesses, even at the trial itself—could often not agree; but then, how is this different from most trials? For instance, one says the Kinnear house was left in great disarray by the criminals; another says it was tidy, and it was not realized at first that anything had been taken. Confronted with such discrepancies, I tried to deduce which account was the most plausible.

Then there was the matter of the central figure, about whom opinion was very divided indeed. All commentators agreed that Grace was uncommonly good-looking, but they could not agree on her height or the color of her hair. Some said Grace was jealous of Nancy, others that Nancy was, on the contrary, jealous of Grace. Some viewed Grace as a cunning female demon; others considered her a simple-minded and terrorized victim who had only run away with McDermott out of fear for her own life.

I discovered as I read that the newspapers of the time had their own political agendas. Canada West was still reeling from the effects of the 1837 Rebellion, and this influenced both Grace's life before the murders and her treatment at the hands of the press. A large percentage of the population—some say up to a third—left the country after the Rebellion; the poorer and more radical third, we may assume, which may account for the Tory flavor of those who remained. The exodus meant a shortage of servants, which in turn meant that Grace could change jobs more frequently than her counterparts in England. In 1843—the year of the murder—editorials were still being written about the badness or worthiness of William Lyon Mackenzie; and as a rule, the Tory newspapers that vilified him also vilified Grace—she had, after all, been involved in the murder of her Tory employer, an act of grave insubordination; but the Reform newspapers that praised Mackenzie were also inclined to clemency toward Grace. This split in opinion continued through later writers on the case, right up to the end of the nineteenth century.

I felt that, to be fair, I had to represent all points of view. I devised the following set of guidelines for myself: When there was a solid fact, I could not alter it; long as I might to have Grace witness McDermott's execution, it could not be done, because, worse luck, she was already in the penitentiary on that day. Also, every major element in the book had to be suggested by something in the writing about Grace and her times, however dubious such writing might be; but in the gaps left unfilled, I was free to invent. Since there were a lot of gaps, there is a lot of invention. *Alias Grace* is very much a novel rather than a documentary.

As I wrote, I found myself considering the number and variety of the stories that had been told: Grace's own versions—there were several—as reported in the newspapers and in her "Confession"; McDermott's versions, also multiple; Moodie's version; and those of the later commentators. For each story, there was a teller, but—as is true of all stories—there was also an audience; both were influenced by received climates of opinion, about politics, but also about criminality and its proper treatment, about the nature of women—their weakness and seductive qualities, for instance—and about insanity; in fact, about everything that had a bearing on the case.

In my fiction, Grace, too—whatever else she is—is a storyteller, with strong motives to narrate, but also strong motives to withhold; the only power left to her as a convicted and imprisoned criminal comes from a blend of these two motives. What is told by her to her audience of one, Dr. Simon Jordan—who is not only a more educated person than she is, but also a man, which gave him an automatic edge in the nineteenth century, and a man with the potential to be of help to her—is selective, of course. It's dependent on what she remembers; or is it what she says she remembers, which can be quite a different thing? And how can her audience tell the difference? Here we are, right back at the end of the twentieth century, with our own uneasiness about the trustworthiness of memory, the reliability of story, and the continuity of time. In a Victorian novel, Grace would say "Now it all comes back to me"; but as *Alias Grace* is not a Victorian novel, she does not say that; and if she did, would we—any longer—believe her?

These are the sorts of questions that my own fictional excursion into the nevertheless real Canadian past left me asking. Nor did it escape me that a different writer, with access to exactly the same historical records, could have—and without doubt would have—written a very different sort of novel. I'm not one of those who believes there is no truth to be known; but I have to conclude that although there undoubtedly was a truth— somebody did kill Nancy Montgomery—truth is sometimes unknowable, at least by us.

What does the past tell us? In and of itself, it tells us nothing. We have to be listening first, before it will say a word; and even so, listening means telling, and then retelling. It's we ourselves who must do such telling about the past, if anything is to be said about it; and our audience is one another. After we in our turn have become the past, others will tell stories about us, and about our times; or not, as the case may be. Unlikely as it seems, it's possible we may not interest them.

But meanwhile, while we still have the chance, what should we ourselves tell? Or rather, what *do* we tell? Individual memory, history, and the novel, are all selective: no one remembers everything, each historian picks out the facts he or she chooses to find significant, and every novel, whether historical or not, must limit its own scope. No one can tell all the stories there are. As for novelists, it's best if they confine themselves to the Ancient Mariner stories—that is, the stories that seize hold of them and torment them until they've grabbed a batch of unsuspecting Wedding-Guests with their skinny hands and held them with their glittering eyes or else their glittering prose, and told them a tale they cannot choose but hear.

Such stories are not about this or that slice of the past, or this or that political or social event, or this or that city or country or nationality, although, of course, these may enter into it, and often do. They are about human nature, which usually means they are about pride, envy, avarice, lust, sloth, gluttony, and anger. They are about truth and lies, and disguises and revelations; they are about crime and punishment; they are about love and forgiveness and long-suffering and charity; they are about sin and retribution and sometimes even redemption.

In the recent film *Il Postino*, the great poet Pablo Neruda upbraids his friend, a lowly postman, for having filched one of Neruda's poems to use in his courtship of a local girl. "But," replies the postman, "poems do not belong to those who write them. Poems belong to those who need them." And so it is with stories about the past. The past no longer belongs only to those who lived in it; the past belongs to those who claim it, and are willing to explore it, and to infuse it with meaning for those alive today. The past belongs to us because we are the ones who need it.

Notes

1. Robertson Davies, *The Merry Heart* (Toronto: McClelland & Stewart, 1996), p. 358.
2. See, for instance, Ian Hacking, *Rewriting the Soul* (Princeton, N.J.: Princeton University Press, 1995).
3. See, for instance, Paul Fussell's *The Great War and Modern Memory* (Oxford University Press, 1975).
4. Javier Marias, *All Souls* (London: Harvill Press, 1995).
5. *The Go-Between.*
6. *Lost in Time,* CBC show about Canadian museums, summer 1996.

23

Review:

Trickster Makes This World: Mischief, Myth, and Art and The Gift: Imagination and the Erotic Life of Property
by Lewis Hyde

*T*rickster Makes This World: Mischief, Myth, and Art is Lewis Hyde's second masterpiece of—well, of what? Of wondering, of pertinent storytelling, pondering. Of making connections that seem both absolutely true and absolutely obvious once Hyde has made them but that we've somehow never noticed before. He's one of those quirky, eccentric Wise Children the United States sometimes throws up—a sort of Thoreau-cum-anthropologist-cum-seer, an asker of naive questions that turn out to be the reverse of naive, fascinated by why we behave the way we do, and why our right hand is often so blind to what our left hand is up to, and why it matters, especially to that elusive entity we've named the soul. Robert Bly calls Hyde a mythologist, which sort of fits, but perhaps he could also be called an illuminationist. In short, he casts light.

It's hard to discuss *Trickster Makes This World* apart from Hyde's first such syncretic masterpiece, *The Gift: Imagination and the Erotic Life of Property.* The classification on *The Gift*'s back cover reads, "Literary Criticism/Sociology," but I expect many distraught bookstore workers have attempted to jam it also into "Anthropology," "Economics," "Theology," or "Philosophy." *The Gift* was first published in 1979 and has been in print ever since. It passes from hand to hand, primarily the hands of those in any way connected with the arts but also the hands of all who are interested in the sometimes arbitrary values placed on the material goods of this world.

The primary question it poses is simple: Why is a poet, in our society, unlikely ever to be rich? Or, in another form: What is it about a series of romance novels designed entirely through market research that leads us to believe none of them will ever be a work of art? Or else: What is Keats's "Ode to a Nightingale" worth in dollar terms? In the course of explaining why the answer is both "nothing" and "it's priceless," Hyde stitches together not only folk tale and impressive erudition but also biographical anecdote, personal observation, and anything else he finds useful, and on this flying patchwork he covers an immense amount of essential human ground.

By the pressures of the market economy we live in, he says, we've been fooled into believing that there is only one way in which things are exchanged: through money transactions, or buying and selling. Yet on some level we know there's another economy at work in human societies: the gift economy, which has quite different rules and consequences. It's the relation between the two economies that *The Gift* explores. In the course of reading it, we discover how "Indian givers" got their undeserved name, why usury developed the way it did, why you don't normally charge for donating a kidney to your brother, why women were traditionally "given" in marriage and sons were "given" by mothers in war, and why the Welsh passed free meals over the coffins of their dead.

Money transactions create no bonds of love or gratitude and imply no obligations. Gifts, on the other hand, are reciprocal and also emotionally loaded. Market exchanges move through the bank account, gifts through the heart. Where the gift circulates, spiritual life flourishes. All societies exist in both economies, says Hyde, but each tends to value one economy over the other. Our own society has overemphasized the market and denied the gift, and the result is stagnant wealth on the one hand and spiritual death and material poverty on the other.

The artist belongs primarily to the gift economy; without that element of creation that arrives uncommanded and cannot be bought, the work is unlikely to be alive. *The Gift* is the best book I know of for the aspiring young, for talented but unacknowledged creators, or even for those who have achieved material success and are worried that this means they've sold out. It gets to the core of their dilemma: how to maintain yourself alive in the world of money when the essential part of what you do cannot be bought or sold. All literary and theatrical and film agents should read this book; they may be surprised to learn what a mythological role they play as guardians of the threshold that separates gift from dollar transaction but that must somehow be crossed if the artist is to eat. *The Gift* should also be read by every patron, every legislator, and every diehard opponent of arts funding. It lights up the dark corners.

Trickster Makes This World picks up a motif from *The Gift* in which the god Hermes, or Mercury, makes an appearance as that part of the human imagination that governs quick changes, as well as quick money exchanges. If you pray to Hermes, Hyde notes, you'll get action, but it will be action with no moral strings attached and no guarantees: Hermes goes in for one-night stands. (He's also the patron of thieves, liars, crossroads, footloose wandering, and the guide for souls on their way to the underworld. In his role as messenger to the gods, he used to appear on the cover of our telephone book, with his midsection modestly wreathed in trunk line cables.)

As Hyde points out, Hermes has many brothers in cultures worldwide. Coyote and Raven in North America; Eshu and Legba in Africa; the Monkey King in China; Krishna in India; not to mention Br'er Rabbit of the American South: these are a few of the trickster figures whose devious ways Hyde explores. (Why are they all male? That would be telling. Read on!) In every culture that has a trickster god, it's the other gods who have made the various forms of perfection, but it's the trickster who's responsible for the changes—the mistakes, if you like—that have brought about the sometimes deplorable mess and the sometimes joyful muddle of this world as it is.

And what an ambiguous creature trickster is! He's cunning personified, a sleight-of-hand artist and a cheat, yet through his overweening curiosity and his tendency to meddle in things about which he lacks true knowledge, he often makes a fool of himself. He steals fire and burns his fingers. He lives by his wits, yet he falls into traps. He's subversive in that he disrupts conventions and transgressive because he crosses forbidden boundaries, yet he displays no overtly high and solemn purpose in these activities. He's a god, but a god of dirt and mixture and of shameless, unsanctioned sex. He's a teller of lies, but of lies without malice. He lies to cover up his thefts—thefts made from the motive of simple appetite or simply for the fun of stealing—or merely to fool people or to concoct stories or to stir things up. "Trickster," says Hyde, "feels no anxiety when he deceives. . . . He . . . can tell his lies with creative abandon, charm, playfulness, and by that affirm the pleasures of fabulation." As Hyde says, "Almost everything that can be said about psychopaths can also be said about tricksters," although the reverse is not the case. "Trickster is among other things the gatekeeper who opens the door into the next world; those who mistake him for a psychopath never even know such a door exists."

What is "the next world"? It might be the underworld, or the world of the imagination, or—in real-life terms—the unobtainable, the denied, the forbidden: other cultures, other nations, other forms of sexuality, other classes and races. Hyde illustrates his theme not only with tales of the ancient gods and heroes but also with the work of present-day creators such as Maxine Hong Kingston and Allen Ginsberg—crossers of boundaries themselves and explorers of the crossing—and with the real people in whom the spirit of trickster has been incarnate. Foremost among these is Frederick Douglass, who in the nineteenth century crossed the perilous line dividing black from white, slave from free man, and in doing so turned the assumptions that governed such divisions upside down. Such figures remind us that it's Odysseus the trickster who tells a lie good enough to get his men alive out of the monster Cyclops's cave, and Prometheus the trickster who steals fire from the gods and makes a gift of it to man. Through his daring and wiliness, trickster, too, can be a hero.

The pleasures of fabulation, the charming and playful lie—this line of thought leads Hyde to the last link in his subtitle, the connection of the trickster to art. Hyde reminds us that the wall between the artist and that American favorite son, the con artist, can be a thin one indeed; that craft and crafty rub shoulders; and that the words *artifice, artifact, articulation,* and *art* all come from the same ancient root, a word meaning "to join," "to fit," and "to make." If it's a seamless whole you want, pray to Apollo, who sets the limits within which such a work can exist. Tricksters, however, stand where the door swings open on its hinges and the horizon expands; they operate where things are joined together and thus also can come apart.

At the end of James Joyce's *A Portrait of the Artist as a Young Man*, cunning is one of the virtues invoked, and it's Daedalus, maker of mazes, to whom Stephen Dedalus addresses his invocation: "Old father, old artificer, stand me now and ever in good stead"; we can guess by this that Joyce has crafty disruption on his mind. Tricksters aren't the only kind of artists who exist, but there's a healthy population of trickster artists. Picasso and Marcel Duchamp—he of the urinal as found art—are just a couple of those on Hyde's list. Such artists can be mere lightweight playful brats, but they can also be those who come along when a tradition has become too set in its ways, too orderly, too Apollonian, and shake it out of its rut. And artists of whatever sort need trickster's help from time to time: When you're blocked or stuck, take an aimless walk and let your mind off its leash and call on trickster. He's the opener of dreams, of roads, and of possibilities. Like T. S. Eliot and Walt Whitman, both apple-cart upsetters in their day, he can tell you there are diamonds in the mud.

I've suggested just a few of the reasons why *Trickster Makes This World* will be as widely read by those in the arts as *The Gift* has been, but there are lots of other reasons, and lots of reasons, too, why *Trickster Makes This World* should be read by anyone interested in the grand and squalid matter of all things human. Hyde's book is a glorious grab bag stuffed with necessary loot, a joyful plum pudding rich in treasures. Once more, we are indebted to him.

Part Three
2000–2005

On New Year's Eve 2000, the millennium was ushered in. Our computers were supposed to go into meltdown, but they didn't. It was also rumored that a terrorist had been intercepted on his way to blow up the midnight celebrations in San Francisco.

My mother was by this time very old and nearly blind, but she could still see bright lights. We arranged some fireworks outside her picture window so she could participate, and my sister accidentally set fire to the back yard. That's my image of the grand event—my sister jumping up and down in the dry weeds, attempting to stamp out the conflagration.

On my journal page that began the year 2000, I scribbled: *The fireworks were very good on TV except for the fatuous commentary. Nothing leaked. The church bells rang. It was quite warm. There was a half moon. The angels did not arrive, or at least none visible to the naked eye. No bombs fell. No snow. No terrorists around here.*

Famous last words.

I completed *The Blind Assassin* after several false starts, one of them in Canada, one of them in a curious rented-by-Internet flat in London. The breakthrough came in France, where I was writing on the assemblage of end tables that served as a desk. I finished the novel in late 1999 and did the editing in February 2000 in Madrid, where I was also finishing the six lectures I gave that spring at Cambridge University on the subject of writers and writing. (These were later published as *Negotiating with the Dead*.) So during the early months of that first year of the twenty-first century, it was bright blue skies and sunlight and the eating of *churros* for me, followed by the Cambridge gardens in full bloom, and bluebells in the woods, and mist.

The Blind Assassin came out in the fall of 2000. It was the fourth of my novels to be short-listed for the Booker Prize. To my surprise the book committed what Oscar Wilde would have called an unpardonable solecism of style by actually winning.

In the first part 2001 I was still on a book tour for *The Blind Assassin*. I'd gotten as far as New Zealand and Australia and was taking a break in Queensland to do some bird-watching with friends when I unaccountably found myself beginning another novel—a process described in the short piece "Writing *Oryx and Crake*."

I continued with this novel back in Canada. I wrote part of it on an island in Lake Erie, where my novel-writing was sadly interrupted by the untimely death of Mordecai Richler. Several other friends and fellow writers also died during this period, and I wrote about some of them.

I composed several chapters of *Oryx and Crake* on a boat in the Arctic, a good location for writing, as nobody can phone. In September 2001 I was in the Toronto airport waiting for a plane to New York for the paperback launch of *The Blind Assassin* when the 9/11 catastrophe took place.

One of the pieces in this section is connected with that event. I happened to be working on an introduction to Rider Haggard's peculiar novel *She*; the editor on this quixotic project was a young man named Benjamin Dreyer, and it was from him that I was able to learn—via e-mail, during that time of blocked phone lines—that my friends and colleagues in New York were safe.

In times of crisis, the temptation is to throw everything into defense mode, to believe that the best defense is offense—which can lead, in the human body, to death from your own immune response—and to jettison the very values you thought you were defending in the first place. Too often, the operation can be a success, but the patient dies. Urgers of moderation and multilateralism are seen as wimps, and chest-thumping becomes the order of the day. My "Letter to America" was written because I'd made a promise to Victor Navasky, the editor of *The Nation*, to write such a thing, back in the summer of 2002, before the invasion of Iraq was even mentioned. "Letter" appeared just before that invasion began. It was widely reprinted and generated a great deal of response from around the world. The essay on Napoleon's mistakes came from my reading of history and my sense of caution.

I seem to have done more occasional writing per square foot of time in the past five years than in any other period. Possibly that's because there have been more occasions. Human history is a lot like a game of chess: for a long time, things happen slowly. Then there's a sudden flurry of activity, and the whole game shifts momentously. We are surely living through such a period right now.

It may, too, be a function of age. Wisdom is thought to accumulate on a person with age, like moss. It doesn't feel like that from the inside, but one's mossiness does generate more requests from editors to write things.

In fact, this part of the book might well be called "A Fistful of Editors," in tribute to the many editors I have worked with over the years. In occasional writing it's usually the editors who come up with the occasions. Then they cajole you into writing about them, hold your hand while you're doing it, and attempt to save you from your more embarrassing mistakes. There have been magazine editors, newspaper editors, editors of anthologies, and editors in charge of introductions and afterwords. They've all been wonderful. Some new editors came into my life at this period—Erica Wagner of the *Sunday Times* of London, Robert Silvers of the *New York Review of Books*. Mr. Silvers is the only editor I know who seems to be at his most elegant and charming—at least on the subject of semicolons—over the phone and in the middle of the night. That is probably why he always gets his way. Ms. Wagner is the only editor I know who has a brush cut and tattoos, and started life as an eight-year-old, answering the fan mail of Kermit the Frog.

Whenever I resolve to write less and do something healthful instead, such as ice dancing, some honey-tongued editor is sure to call me up and make me an offer I can't refuse. So in some ways this book is simply the result of an underdeveloped ability to say no.

But few succumb to temptations they find unattractive. What is it, this compulsion to scrawl things on blank pages? Why this boundless out-flowing of words? What drives us to it? Is writing some sort of disease? Or rather—being speech in visual form—is it simply a manifestation of being human? I choose the latter.

24

First Job,
Waitressing

I'll pass over the minijobs of adolescence—the summer camp stints that were more like getting paid for having fun. I'll pass over, too, the self-created pin-money generators—the puppet shows put on for kids at office Christmas parties, the serigraph posters turned out on the Ping-Pong table—and turn to my first real job. By "real job" I mean one that had nothing to do with friends of my parents or parents of my friends, but was obtained in the adult manner, by looking through the ads in newspapers and going in to be interviewed—one for which I was entirely unsuited, and that I wouldn't have done except for the money. I was surprised when I got it, underpaid while doing it, and frustrated in the performance of it, and these qualities have remained linked, for me, to the ominous word "job."

The year was 1962, the place was Toronto. It was summer, and I was faced with the necessity of earning the difference between my scholarship for the next year and what it would cost me to live. The job was in the coffee shop of a small hotel on Avenue Road; the coffee shop is now in the process of being torn down, but at that time it was a clean, well-lighted place, with booths along one side and a counter—possibly marble—down the other. The booths were served by a waitressing pro who lipsticked outside the lines and who thought I was a mutant. My job would be serving things at the counter—coffee I would pour, toast I would create from bread, milkshakes I would whip up in the obstetrical stainless-steel device

provided. ("Easy as pie," I was told.) I would also be running the customers' money through the cash register—an opaque machine with buttons to be pushed, little drawers that shot in and out, and a neurotic system
of locks.

I said I had never worked a cash register before. This delighted the
manager, a plump, unctuous character out of some novel I hadn't yet read.
He said the cash register, too, was easy as pie, and I would catch on to it
in no time, as I was a smart girl with an M.A. He said I should go and get
myself a white dress.

I didn't know what he meant by "white dress." I bought the first on-sale
one I could find, a nylon afternoon number with daisies appliquéd onto
the bodice. The waitress told me this would not do: I needed a dress like
hers, a *uniform*. ("How dense can you be?" I overheard her saying.) I got the
uniform, but I had to go through the first day in my nylon daisies.

This first humiliation set the tone. The coffee was easy enough—I just
had to keep the Bunn filled—and the milkshakes were possible; few people
wanted them anyway. The sandwiches and deep-fried shrimp were cooked
at the back: all I had to do was order them over the intercom and bin the
leftovers.

But the cash register was perverse. Its drawers would pop open for no
reason, or it would ring eerily when I swore I was nowhere near it; or it
would lock itself shut, and the queue of customers waiting to pay would
lengthen and scowl as I wrestled and sweated. I kept expecting to be fired
for incompetence, but the manager chortled at me more than ever. Occasionally he would bring some other man in a suit to view me. "She's got an
M.A.," he would say in a proud but pitying voice, and the two of them
would stare at me and shake their heads.

An ex-boyfriend discovered my place of employment, and would also
come to stare and shake his head, ordering a single coffee, taking an hour
to drink it, leaving me a sardonic nickel tip. The Greek short-order cook
decided I would be the perfect up-front woman for the restaurant he
wanted to open: he would marry me and do the cooking, I would speak
English to the clientele, and work—was he mad?—the cash register. He
divulged his bank balance, and demanded to meet my father so the two of
them could close the deal. When I declined, he took to phoning me over

the intercom to whisper blandishments, and to plying me with deep-fried shrimps. A girl as scrawny as myself, he pointed out, was unlikely to get such a good offer again.

Then the Shriners hit town, took over the hotel, and began calling for buckets of ice, or for doctors because they'd had heart attacks: too much tricycle-riding in the hot sun was felling them in herds. I couldn't handle the responsibility, the cash register had betrayed me once too often, and the short-order cook was beginning to sing Frank Sinatra songs to me. I gave notice.

Only when I'd quit did the manager reveal his true stratagem: they'd wanted someone as inept as me because they suspected their real cashier of skimming the accounts, a procedure I was obviously too ignorant to ever figure out. "Too stunned," as the waitress put it. She was on the cashier's side, and had me fingered as a stoolie all along.

25

Mordecai Richler, 1931–2001: Diogenes of Montréal

ordecai Richler is gone, and a major light has been snuffed out. But what sort of light? No athlete's torch, no angel's halo. Picture instead the lantern of grumpy, scathing, barrel-dwelling Diogenes, who walked around in daylight searching for an honest man.

Mordecai was the searcher and the honest man both, and equally dis-trustful of fine feathers. Tarted up for grand events, he somehow gave the impression that he'd be happier in the barrel. Rumpled, tie askew, glass of Scotch at his elbow, thin cigar in mouth, his sad bloodhound's gaze fixed on the bogusness of the passing scene, while in one hand he held the pen that was both lance (as in chivalry, as in boil) and balloon-puncturing pin—this is the image of him beloved by his public and perfected by his friend Aislin, the celebrated cartoonist. Mordecai seemed so permanent, so substantial, so on top of things, so much to be depended on when each new hot-air blimp loomed into view, that it's difficult to believe in his mortality.

But—as with all fine writers—mortality was his subject. Human nature, in all its nakedness, paltriness, silliness, avariciousness, crassness, meanness, and downright evil—he knew it inside out, having had a ring-side view as he came of age in a poor Jewish area of Montréal during the Depression and then witnessed not only the atrocities but also the hypocrisies of the Second World War, followed—for him—by the hard scrabbling of the literary life in London, as seen from the bottom.

He'd paid—as we say—his dues. His bullshit radar was acute, his hopes for the innate goodness of the human species not very high, and in this he was a satirist, a true child of Jonathan Swift. When he went after separatism in Québec, he rubbed fur the wrong way; but all of his fur-rubbing was deliberate—he would have been horrified to have wounded the innocent unintentionally. Québec was hardly alone: anyone was fair game, as long as the target had committed the ultimate sin in his eyes, which was— or so I'd guess—pomposity.

His propensity for skewering the inflated, coupled with a wonderful sense of mischief, produced some of the most hilarious moments in Canadian literature. The pretentious "art" film of a bar mitzvah in *The Apprenticeship of Duddy Kravitz*, the travesty of the Franklin expedition in *Solomon Gursky Was Here*, in which the heroic sailors dress up in ladies' frillies—this is Mordecai at his most inventively outrageous. But every satirist cherishes an alternative to the vices and follies he depicts, and so did Mordecai. His alternative was not so far from that of Charles Dickens— the warmhearted, sane, and decent human being—and this side of him comes to the fore in his novels, most particularly in his tragicomic meditation on fallibility, *Barney's Version*. Behind the formidable public persona was a shy and generous man who gave his time to efforts he believed in— most recently, the "best book only" Giller Prize, for which he served as an architect and first-year juror.

He was a consummate professional with high standards and no time for fools, but he was also a dear man who was loved by everyone who knew him well, respected by his fellow writers, and trusted by his many devoted readers to tell it straight. For my generation, he was a trailblazer who went on to create and occupy a unique place in our national life and literature, and we will miss him very much.

26

Review:

According to Queeney
by Beryl Bainbridge

According to Queeney is Beryl Bainbridge's sixteenth novel. Like its recent predecessors, it is a stellar literary event.

Bainbridge herself is an original. Cigarette end smoldering in mouth corner, stuffed water buffalo in front hall, she is an English national treasure. The list of her books is long, but the books themselves are short and pungent, dense with necessary detail, written with panache and an enviable economy. Five have been short-listed for the Booker, and Bainbridge has won both the Whitbread and the W. H. Smith Literary Award; she has also been recognized with a Damehood. Not that any of this has softened her edges: Dame Beryl is likely to greet her fellow novelists by saying, with blunt cheeriness, "Sorry I haven't read your book, but I only ever read books written before 1940."

Before 1940 is increasingly her fictional territory. Her earlier novels—*The Bottle Factory Outing, Sweet William*—were set in her own time, but then she began to move backward and to focus on well-known historic events. *The Birthday Boys* deals with Scott's Antarctic fiasco, *Every Man for Himself* with the *Titanic* disaster; both take place in the twentieth century, but just barely. After these, Bainbridge leaped back more than a century: the protaganist of *Master Georgie* ends his sexually tangled career during the Crimean War.

Now Bainbridge has taken the biggest risk of her literary life, for the central subject of *According to Queeney* is none other than Dr. Johnson, he of the eighteenth century, the famous *Dictionary,* of *The Lives of English Poets* and Boswell's engaging biography. Surely there can be few men about whom more has been written! What could possibly be created by a novelist out of the vast mound of factoids and verbiage that already exists, heaped high on the grave of the celebrated, eccentric, smelly, largehearted, self-centered, gluttonous, guilt-ridden, and intermittently batty Doctor?

Bainbridge strides into her material with an ease of manner that belies the difficulties even she must have faced: *According to Queeney* is very much a novel, not a research paper. It opens with a prologue in which the poor Doctor is found in the very state he dreaded most: dead, and being carted off to be coldly anatomized. Thereafter, the chapters are given single-word titles, followed by their definitions as provided in his *Dictionary* by Dr. Johnson himself.

In the first chapter, "Crisis"—"The point of time at which any affair comes to its height"—he is discovered in middle age, an established celebrity, his horrible childhood behind him, most of his major works completed, his beloved wife dead. He has established a household of misfits like himself, whom he pities and shelters—two women, one blind, who adore him, oversee his establishment, and squabble incessantly; a drunken medical doctor who is disliked by both; and a mulatto orphan who acts as page. He is subject to deep melancholy, riddled with guilty thoughts and nervous tics, and afraid of the dark.

Lured to dinner with a promise of good food, Johnson meets the Thrales, a wealthy brewer and his attractive but supposedly light-minded and flighty wife, to whom Johnson is immediately drawn. Mrs. Thrale can see the advantages of having a literary lion at her table, and woos the notoriously crotchety Dr. Johnson by flattering and coddling him; and here begins one of the book's basic conflicts, for his interest in her—disguise it from himself as he may, and does—is sexual, and hers in him is not. Or not exactly, for she is an accomplished tease, and not above drinking chocolate in his room in her bed gown.

The third person in the triangle is not Mr. Thrale, who isn't in love with his wife no matter how often he impregnates her, but their first daughter, Queeney. Queeney, too, loves Mrs. Thrale; she, too, feels that her love is unrequited. Dr. Johnson takes a fatherly interest in Queeney, teaching her

Latin, writing charming notes to her, and presenting her with a curio cabinet in which are kept exotic monstrosities such as he feels himself to be. But he is also resented by Queeney as a rival, for he steals too much of Mrs. Thrale's perennially wandering attention.

The story unfolds partly through the eyes of Queeney at various stages of her life—as an infant, as a young girl, and also as a grown woman sending evasive and disingenuous letters to a pushy acquaintance who wants to write yet another book about Dr. Johnson and his circle. But there are other viewpoints, too: Dr. Johnson has his spot-lit moments, as do Mrs. Thrale and the jealous housekeeper, Mrs. Desmoulins. None sees the whole picture; all are deceived, not only by appearances but also by their own desires, angers, and fears.

It is these inner forces that propel the action through the well-known phases of Dr. Johnson's relationship with the Thrale family—his depressive "madness" and his "cure" at the hands of Mrs. Thrale, who uses manacles to this end; the deaths of the children Mrs. Thrale drops like puppies, whips at the slightest excuse, and inadvertently polishes off with a tin pill; the family's accident-prone trip to Italy with a neurotic Johnson in tow; the death of Mr. Thrale and Johnson's misplaced hopes of taking his place; the ironic denouement as Mrs. Thrale elopes with a music teacher, much to the enraged horror of Dr. Johnson and Queeney both. The players in this drama dine socially, talk wonderfully and at odds, behave unwisely, strike sparks, reach accords, have moments of joy, mistake one another's meanings, spurn one another, and are spurned.

Perhaps the most interesting twosome is composed of Dr. Johnson and Queeney, who meet when she is only a year old.

" 'Sweeting,' he had said, and bowed.

" 'Da-da,' she had crowed, and crawled onwards on hands and knees."

Her phrase is well chosen, for this Beauty and this Beast have a lot in common.

Both of them feel like captive bears with chains around their necks. Both are balked by Mrs. Thrale; both are sulkers. Both are twirlers: Queeney twirls out of youthful high spirits, Dr. Johnson compulsively.

This circular or spiral motion, as of winds and clouds, is one of the key images in the novel. How to seize the evanescent moment? Are the workings of the mind as aimless as Dr. Johnson fears? Should a chance at happiness cancel out duty?

How to grasp the essence of life, which is always slipping away through your fingers?

Bainbridge handles her material as Paganini was said to play the violin—with masterful attack and virtuoso dexterity, and a hint of sinister forces at work.

She is not a writer for readers inclined to the pinkly romantic, and she serves notice of that in the first pages: Johnson is laid out on the anatomy table like a fleshly memento mori, exposed not only warts and all but also gonads and all.

Hers is a dark, often hilarious, and deeply human vision: no burp or bad odor or freakishness or moment of squalor or pathos is spared, nor any impulse toward generosity, however subverted by frailty and chance.

In Dr. Johnson, soul in torment, genius and grotesque dancing bear, Beryl Bainbridge has found a subject perfectly suited to her curious and splendid talents. *According to Queeney* is a vastly enjoyable book and a major literary accomplishment.

27

Introduction:

She
by H. Rider Haggard

When I first read Rider Haggard's highly famous novel *She*, I didn't know it was highly famous. I was a teenager, it was the 1950s, and *She* was just one of the many books in the cellar. My father unwittingly shared with Jorge Luis Borges a liking for nineteenth-century yarns with touches of the uncanny coupled with rip-roaring plots; and so, in the cellar, where I was supposed to be doing my homework, I read my way through Rudyard Kipling and Conan Doyle, and *Dracula* and *Frankenstein*, and Robert Louis Stevenson and H. G. Wells, and also Henry Rider Haggard. I read *King Solomon's Mines* first, with its adventures and tunnels and lost treasure, and then *Allan Quatermain*, with its adventures and tunnels and lost civilization. And then I read *She*.

I had no sociocultural context for these books then—the British Empire was the pink part of the map, "imperialism and colonialism" had not yet acquired their special negative charge, and the accusation "sexist" was far in the future. Nor did I make any distinctions between great literature and any other kind. I just liked reading. Any book that began with some mysterious inscriptions on a very old broken pot was fine with me, and that is how *She* begins. There was even a picture at the front of my edition—not a drawing of the pot, but a *photograph* of it, to make the yarn really convincing. (The pot was made to order by Haggard's sister-in-law; he intended it to function like the pirate map at the beginning of *Treasure Island*—a book the popularity of which he hoped to rival, and it did.)

Most outrageous tales state at the very beginning that what follows is so incredible the reader will have trouble believing it, which is both a come-on and a challenge. The messages on the pot stretch credulity, but having deciphered them, the two heroes of *She*—the gorgeous but none too bright Leo Vincey and the ugly but intelligent Horace Holly—are off to Africa to hunt up the beautiful, undying sorceress who is supposed to have killed Leo's distant ancestor. Curiosity is their driving force, vengeance is their goal. Many a hardship later, and after having narrowly escaped death at the hands of the savage and matrilineal tribe of the Amahagger, they find not only the ruins of a vast and once-powerful civilization and the numerous mummified bodies of the same, but also, dwelling among the tombs, the selfsame undying sorceress, ten times lovelier, wiser, and more ruthless than they had dared to imagine.

As Queen of the Amahagger, "She-who-must-be-obeyed" wafts around wrapped up like a corpse, in order to inspire fear; but once tantalizingly peeled, under those gauzy wrappings is a stunner, and—what's more—a virgin. "She," it turns out, is two thousand years old. Her real name is Ayesha. She claims she was once a priestess of the Egyptian nature goddess Isis. She's been saving herself for two millennia, waiting for the man she loves: one Kallikrates, a very good-looking priest of Isis and the ancestor of Leo Vincey. This man broke his vows and ran off with Leo's ancestress, whereupon Ayesha slew him in a fit of jealous rage. For two thousand years she's been waiting for him to be reincarnated; she's even got his preserved corpse enshrined in a side room, where she laments over it every night. A point-by-point comparison reveals—what a surprise!—that Kallikrates and Leo Vincey are identical.

Having brought Leo to his knees with her knockout charms, and having polished off Ustane, a more normal sort of woman with whom Leo has formed a sexual pair bond, and who just happens to be a reincarnation of Ayesha's ancient Kallikrates-stealing enemy, She now demands that Leo accompany her into the depths of a nearby mountain. There, She says, is where the secret of extremely long and more abundant life is to be found. Not only that, She and Leo can't be One until he is as powerful as She— the union might otherwise kill him (as it does, in the sequel *Ayesha: The Vengeance of She*). So off to the mountain they go, via the ruins of the ancient, once-imperial city of Kôr. To get the renewed life, all one has to do—after the usual Haggard adventures and tunnels—is to traverse some caverns measureless to man, step into a very noisy rolling pillar of fire, and then make one's getaway across a bottomless chasm.

This is how She acquired her powers two thousand years before, and to show a hesitating Leo how easy it is, She does it again. Alas, this time the thing works backward, and in a few instants Ayesha shrivels up into a very elderly bald monkey and then crumbles into dust. Leo and Holly, both hopelessly in love with She and both devastated, totter back to civilization, trusting in Her promise that She will return.

As a good read in the cellar, this was all very satisfactory, despite the overblown way in which She tended to express herself. *She* was an odd book in that it placed a preternaturally powerful woman at the center of things: the only other such woman I'd run into so far had been the Wonder Woman of the comics, with her sparkly lasso and star-spangled panties. Both Ayesha and Wonder Woman went all weak-kneed when it came to the man they loved—Wonder Woman lost her magic powers when kissed by her boyfriend, Steve Trevor; Ayesha couldn't focus on conquering the world unless Leo Vincey would join her in that dubious enterprise—and I was callow enough, at fifteen, to find this part of it not only soppily romantic but also pretty hilarious. Then I graduated from high school and discovered good taste, and forgot for a while about *She.*

For a while, but not forever. In the early sixties I found myself in graduate school, in Cambridge, Massachusetts. There I was exposed to the Widener Library, a much larger and more organized version of the cellar; that is, it contained many sorts of books, not all of which bore the Great Literature Seal of Approval. Once I was let loose in the stacks, my penchant for not doing my homework soon reasserted itself, and it wasn't long before I was snuffling around in Rider Haggard and his ilk once more.

This time, however, I had some excuse. My field of specialization was the nineteenth century, I was busying myself with Victorian quasi-goddesses, and no one could accuse Haggard of not being Victorian. Like his age, which practically invented archaeology, he was an amateur of vanished civilizations; also like his age, he was fascinated by the exploration of unmapped territories and encounters with "undiscovered" native peoples. As an individual, he was such a cookie-cutter county gentleman—albeit with some African traveling in his past—that it was hard to fathom where his overheated imagination had come from, though it may have been this by-the-book-English-establishment quality that allowed him to bypass intellectual analysis completely. He could sink a core-sampling drill straight down into the great English Victorian unconscious, where fears and desires—especially male fears and desires—swarmed in the darkness like blind fish. Or so claimed Henry Miller, among others.

Where did it all come from? In particular, where did the figure of She come from—old-young, powerful-powerless, beautiful-hideous, dweller among tombs, obsessed with an undying love, deeply in touch with the forces of Nature and thus of Life and Death? Haggard and his siblings were said to have been terrorized by an ugly rag doll that lived in a dark cupboard and was named "She-who-must-be-obeyed," but there is more to it than that. *She* was published in 1887, and thus came at the height of the fashion for sinister but seductive women. It looked back also on a long tradition of the same. Ayesha's literary ancestresses include the young-but-old supernatural women in George MacDonald's "Curdie" fantasies, but also various Victorian femmes fatales: Tennyson's Vivien in *The Idylls of the King*, bent on stealing Merlin's magic; the Pre-Raphaelite temptresses created in both poem and picture by Rossetti and William Morris; Swinburne's dominatrices; Wagner's nasty pieces of female work, including the very old but still toothsome Kundry of *Parsifal*; and, most especially, the Mona Lisa of Walter Pater's famous prose poem, older than the rocks upon which she sits, yet young and lovely, and mysterious, and filled to the brim with experiences of a distinctly suspect nature.

As Sandra Gilbert and Susan Gubar pointed out in their 1989 book *No Man's Land*, the ascendency in the arts of these potent but dangerous female figures is by no means unconnected with the rise of "Woman" in the nineteenth century, and with the hotly debated issues of her "true nature" and her "rights," and also with the anxieties and fantasies these controversies generated. If women ever came to wield political power—to which they were surely, by their natures, unsuited—what would they do with it? And if they were beautiful and desirable women, capable of attacking on the sexual as well as the political front, wouldn't they drink men's blood, sap their vitality, and reduce them to groveling serfs? As the century opened, Wordsworth's Mother Nature was benign, and "never would betray/The heart that loved her"; but by the end of the century, Nature and the women so firmly linked to her were much more likely to be red in tooth and claw—Darwinian goddesses rather than Wordsworthian ones. When, in *She*, Ayesha appropriates the fiery phallic pillar at the heart of Nature for the second time, it's just as well that it works backward. Otherwise men could kiss their own phallic pillars good-bye.

"You are a whale at parables and allegories and one thing reflecting another," wrote Rudyard Kipling in a letter to Rider Haggard, and there appear to be various hints and verbal signposts scattered over the landscape of *She*. For instance, the Amahagger, the tribe ruled by She, bear a name that not only encapsulates *hag* but also conflates the Latin root for *love* with the name of Abraham's banished wilderness-dwelling concubine Hagar, and thus brings to mind a story of two women competing for one man. The ancient city of Kôr is named perhaps for *core*, cognate with the French *coeur*, but suggesting also *corps*, for body, and thus *corpse*, for dead body; for She is in part Nightmare Life-in-Death. Her horrid end is reminiscent of Darwinian evolution played backward—woman into monkey— but also of vampires after the stake-into-the-heart maneuver. (Bram Stoker's *Dracula* appeared after *She*, but Sheridan Le Fanu's "Carmilla" predates it, as does many another vampire story.) These associations and more point toward some central significance that Haggard himself could never fully explicate, though he chalked up a sequel and a couple of prequels trying. "*She*," he said, was "some gigantic allegory of which I could not catch the meaning."

Haggard claimed to have written *She* "at white heat," in six weeks. "It came," he said, "faster than my poor aching hand could set it down," which would suggest hypnotic trance or possession. In the heyday of Freudian and Jungian analysis, *She* was much explored and admired, by Freudians for its womb-and-phallus images, by Jungians for its anima figures and thresholds. Northrop Frye, proponent of the theory of archetypes in literature, says this of *She* in his 1975 book *The Secular Scripture: A Study of the Structure of Romance:*

> In the theme of the apparently dead and buried heroine who comes to life again, one of the themes of Shakespeare's *Cymbeline*, we seem to be getting a more undisplaced glimpse of the earth-mother at the bottom of the world. In later romance there is another glimpse of such a figure in Rider Haggard's *She*, a beautiful and sinister female ruler, buried in the depths of a dark continent, who is much involved with archetypes of death and rebirth. . . . Embalmed mummies suggest Egypt, which is preeminently the land of death and burial, and, largely because of its Biblical role, of descent to a lower world.

Whatever *She* may have been thought to signify, its impact upon publication was tremendous. *Everyone* read it, especially men; a whole generation was influenced by it, and the generation after that. A dozen or so films have been based on it, and a huge amount of the pulp-magazine fiction churned out in the teens, twenties, and thirties of the twentieth century bears its impress. Every time a young but possibly old and/or dead woman turns up, especially if she's ruling a lost tribe in a wilderness and is a hypnotic seductress, you're looking at a descendant of She.

Literary writers, too, felt Her foot on their necks. Conrad's *Heart of Darkness* owes a lot to Her, as Gilbert and Gubar have indicated. James Hilton's Shangri-la, with its ancient, beautiful, and eventually crumbling heroine, is an obvious relative. C. S. Lewis felt Her power, fond as he was of creating sweet-talking, good-looking evil queens; and in Tolkien's *The Lord of the Rings*, She splits into two: Galadriel, powerful but good, who's got exactly the same water-mirror as the one possessed by She; and a very ancient cave-dwelling, man-devouring spider-creature named, tellingly, Shelob.

Would it be out of the question to connect the destructive Female Will, so feared by D. H. Lawrence and others, with the malign aspect of She? For Ayesha is a supremely transgressive female who challenges male power;

though her shoe size is tiny and her fingernails are pink, she's a rebel at heart. If only she hadn't been hobbled by love, she would have used her formidable energies to overthrow the established civilized order. That the established civilized order was white and male and European goes without saying; thus She's power was not only female—of the heart, of the body— but also barbaric, and "dark."

By the time we find John Mortimer's Rumpole of the Bailey referring to his dumpy, kitchen-cleanser-conscious wife as "she who must be obeyed," the once-potent figure has been secularized and demythologized, and has dwindled into the combination of joke and rag doll that it may have been in its origins. Nevertheless, we must not forget one of Ayesha's preeminent powers—the ability to reincarnate herself. Like the vampire dust at the end of Christopher Lee movies, blowing away only to reassemble itself at the outset of the next film, She could come back. And back. And back.

No doubt this is because She is in some ways a permanent feature of the human imagination. She's one of the giants of the nursery, a threatening but compelling figure, bigger and better than life. Also worse, of course. And therein lies Her attraction.

Sources

Atwood, Margaret. "Superwoman Drawn and Quartered: The Early Forms of *She*." *Alphabet* 10 (July 1965).

Frye, Northrop. *The Secular Scripture: A Study of the Structure of Romance*. Cambridge, Mass.: Harvard University Press, 1976.

Gilbert, Sandra M., and Susan Gubar. *No Man's Land: The Place of the Woman Writer in the Twentieth Century*. Vol. 2, *Sexchanges*. New Haven, Conn.: Yale University Press, 1989.

Karlin, Daniel. Introduction. In H. Rider Haggard, *She*. Oxford: Oxford University Press, 1991.

28

When Afghanistan
Was at Peace

I n February 1978, almost twenty-three years ago, I visited
Afghanistan with my spouse, Graeme Gibson, and our eighteen-
month-old daughter. We went there almost by chance: we were on
our way to the Adelaide literary festival in Australia. Pausing at intervals,
we felt, would surely be easier on a child's time clock. (Wrong, as it turned
out.) We thought Afghanistan would make a fascinating two-week
stopover. Its military history impressed us—neither Alexander the Great
nor the British in the nineteenth century had stayed in the country long
because of the ferocity of its warriors.

"Don't go to Afghanistan," my father said when told of our plans.
"There's going to be a war there." He was fond of reading history books. "As
Alexander the Great said, Afghanistan is easy to march into but hard to
march out of." But we hadn't heard any other rumors of war, so off we went.

We were among the last to see Afghanistan in its days of relative
peace—relative, because even then there were tribal disputes and superpowers in play. The three biggest buildings in Kabul were the Chinese
embassy, the Soviet embassy, and the U.S. embassy, and the head of the
country was reportedly playing the three against one another.

The houses of Kabul were carved wood, and the streets were like a
living *Book of Hours*: people in flowing robes, camels, donkeys, carts with
huge wooden wheels being pushed and pulled by men at either end. There
were few motorized vehicles. Among them were buses covered with ornate

Arabic script, with eyes painted on the front so the buses could see where they were going.

We managed to hire a car to see the terrain of the famous and disastrous British retreat from Kabul to Jalalabad. The scenery was breathtaking: jagged mountains and the *Arabian Nights* dwellings in the valleys—part houses, part fortresses—reflected in the enchanted blue-green of the rivers. Our driver took the switchback road at breakneck speed since we had to be back before sundown because of bandits.

The men we encountered were friendly and fond of children: our curly-headed, fair-haired child got a lot of attention. The winter coat I wore had a large hood so that I was sufficiently covered and did not attract undue notice. Many wanted to talk; some knew English, while others spoke through our driver. But they all addressed Graeme exclusively. To have spoken to me would have been impolite. And yet when our interpreter negotiated our entry into an all-male teahouse, I received nothing worse than uneasy glances. The law of hospitality toward visitors ranked higher than the no-women-in-the-teahouse custom. In the hotel, those who served meals and cleaned rooms were men, tall men with scars either from dueling or from the national sport, played on horseback, in which gaining possession of a headless calf is the aim.

Girls and women we glimpsed on the street wore the chador, the long, pleated garment with a crocheted grill for the eyes that is more comprehensive than any other Muslim cover-up. At that time, you often saw chic boots and shoes peeking out from the hem. The chador wasn't obligatory back then; Hindu women didn't wear it. It was a cultural custom, and since I had grown up hearing that you weren't decently dressed without a girdle and white gloves, I thought I could understand such a thing. I also knew that clothing is a symbol, that all symbols are ambiguous, and that this one might signify a fear of women or a desire to protect them from the gaze of strangers. But it could also mean more negative things, just as the color red can mean love, blood, life, royalty, good luck—or sin.

I bought a chador in the market. A jovial crowd of men gathered around, amused by the spectacle of a Western woman picking out such a non-Western item. They offered advice about color and quality. Purple was better than light green or blue, they said. (I bought the purple.) Every writer wants the Cloak of Invisibility—the power to see without being seen—or so I was thinking as I donned the chador. But once I had put it on, I had an odd sense of having been turned into negative space, a blank in the visual field, a sort of antimatter—both there and not there. Such a space has power of a sort, but it is a passive power, the power of taboo.

Several weeks after we left Afghanistan, the war broke out. My father was right, after all. Over the next years, we often remembered the people we met and their courtesy and curiosity. How many of them are now dead, through no fault of their own?

Six years after our trip, I wrote *The Handmaid's Tale*, a speculative fiction about an American theocracy. The women in that book wear outfits derived in part from nuns' costumes, partly from girls' schools' hemlines, and partly—I must admit—from the faceless woman on the Old Dutch Cleanser box, but also partly from the chador I acquired in Afghanistan and its conflicting associations. As one character says, there is freedom to and freedom from. But how much of the first should you have to give up to assure the second? All cultures have had to grapple with that, and our own—as we are now seeing—is no exception. Would I have written the book if I never visited Afghanistan? Possibly. Would it have been the same? Unlikely.

29

Review:

The Selected Letters of Dashiell Hammett, 1921–1960 edited by Richard Layman with Julie M. Rivett

Dashiell Hammett: A Daughter Remembers by Jo Hammett, edited by Richard Layman with Julie M. Rivett

Dashiell Hammett: Crime Stories & Other Writings selected and edited by Steven Marcus

When I was a preadolescent spending summers in northern Canada, I read a lot of old detective fiction because it was there. When I'd got through the pile I read some of it over again, there being no library where I could go and get more. I didn't reread Erle Stanley Gardner or Ellery Queen; I found them dry. But I did reread Dashiell Hammett.

What was it about these books that intrigued me as an avid but ignorant child reader? Their world was fast-paced, sharp-edged, and filled with zippy dialogue and words I'd never heard pronounced—slang words such as "gunsel," fancy words such as "punctilious." This was not the Agatha Christie sort of story—there were fewer clues, and these were more likely to be lies people told than cuff buttons they'd left strewn around. There were more corpses, with less importance bestowed on each: a new character would appear, only to be gunned down by a fire-spitting revolver. In a "clues" novel, everything depended on who was where; in a Hammett one, it was more likely to be who was who, given to disguises and false names as these folk were. The action was dispersed, not sealed up as in a nobody-leaves-this-house puzzle: dark, mean streets were prowled, cars were driven at speed, people blew in from elsewhere and hid out and skipped town. Oddly enough, clothing was described in more detail than in many country-house murders—a feature I appreciated. There was a lot of drinking, of substances I had never heard of, and a great deal of smoking. As an eleven-year-old I found this world very, very sophisticated.

It's odd to think that in July 1951, while I was trying to figure out why a man would turn a strange shade of yellow, with bloodshot eyes, while telling a woman that maybe he loved her and maybe she loved him but he wasn't going to play the sap for her, the author of the books that so fascinated me was about to be jailed. The McCarthy Red scare was at its height, and Hammett had been called into U.S. district court as a representative of the Civil Rights Congress Bail Fund, to be questioned about four fugitives. Notoriously, he refused to testify. He wouldn't even give his name. The man whose books had been legends in their time had now become a legend of a different kind: exemplary, not only of a certain kind of American fiction, but also of a certain kind of American life.

Forty years after his death, Dashiell Hammett continues to intrigue. While he was still alive, Raymond Chandler wrote his famous 1944 tribute to him, "The Simple Art of Murder." After his death, his companion of many years and literary executrix, Lillian Hellman, served him up as a dreamlife portrait in her 1973 memoir *Pentimento*. Attempting to control the legend, Hellman then authorized a biography;[1] there have been several unauthorized biographies as well. In 2001 there were three new additions to works by and about Hammett: *The Selected Letters of*

Dashiell Hammett, 1921–1960, edited by Richard Layman with Hammett's granddaughter Julie M. Rivett; *Dashiell Hammett: A Daughter Remembers,* a personal memoir by Hammett's second daughter, Josephine, who also supplied a foreword for the *Letters;* and *Dashiell Hammett: Crime Stories & Other Writings,* selected and edited by Steven Marcus.

The man who created and solved so many mysteries left quite a few of his own behind him, it seems: many have been the attempts to explicate him. Where did his talent come from? Why the extreme drinking, the reckless spending? Why the communism, in such a patriotic American? Why the sudden creative silence, and then that other silence, the one that landed him in jail? Did Lillian Hellman exhaust him, or was she, on the contrary, his right-hand gal and kindly keeper? These are the sorts of questions that have raised themselves over time.

Those who have read even a little about Hammett know the main outlines of the plot. It's laid before us in condensed form at the end of *Dashiell Hammett: Crime Stories & Other Writings,* and again in the excellent summaries dividing the periods of his life in the *Selected Letters,* and yet again, in a different mode, in Jo Hammett's memoir.

This last is exactly what the jacket says it is: a reminiscence presented in "straightforward prose, with unaffected charm." It contains a lot of photos, and some new, suggestive information about Hammett's family background. It also tells the story of how the photos came to light—one of those proverbial stashes of old cardboard boxes in the garage that turn out to be a treasure trove. Jo Hammett writes concisely, with much personal anecdote and wry observation. She sees her father from a necessarily intimate angle, and though she adored him, she also naturally resented his treatment of the family—of her mother, Jose, her older sister Mary, and herself. Hammett wasn't evil or violent, and he tried to send sufficient money; he gave the daughters lavish treats; he wrote them loving, funny letters; but he was seldom there.

Jo Hammett saves the largest part of her resentment for Lillian Hellman, who seems to have deserved it. Ms. Hammett tries her best to acknowledge Hellman's virtues—she was smart, she had good taste, she took care of Hammett during his last, broke decade—but it costs her a lot of teeth-grinding to do so. Hellman, it seems, was close to being a mythomaniac, and a ruthless power player; gaining control of Hammett's copyrights was one of her milder gambits. No Other Woman would have come out well from the daughter's point of view, but this portrait of Hellman does raise a question: what did Hammett see in her? As his daughter says, he appreciated people who went too far, as he often did himself; and his admiration for attractive women who lied outrageously—so evident in *The Maltese Falcon* and elsewhere—predates Hellman. It's another of Hammett's enigmas, for otherwise he set great store by speaking honestly.

Samuel Dashiell Hammett was born in rural Maryland in 1894. As a boy he wanted to read all the books in the Baltimore public library, but he had to quit high school at age fourteen to help out with the shaky family finances. (His father, whom he didn't like, was a spendthrift, drinker, sharp dresser, and womanizer; but unlike Hammett, who resembled him in all these respects, he was mean and stingy.) At twenty-one, Hammett got a job as a Pinkerton's detective agency operative, which he left in 1918 to join the army. He suffered the first of many severe respiratory illnesses then. During one recuperation he married a nurse he met at the infirmary; then he signed on at Pinkerton's once more, but his health broke down. It was then that he began writing crime stories for the pulps. [2]

Once Hammett had teamed up with the magazine *Black Mask*, an astonishing burst of creativity followed. He turned out stories at an amazing rate, followed by five highly successful novels, including *Red Harvest, The Dain Curse, The Glass Key,* and *The Maltese Falcon,* this last perhaps the best-known American crime novel of all time. By that time he was famous and rich, but he was also drinking and spending money, both at a prodigal rate. Then followed the liaison with Lillian Hellman and his silence as a writer. Later in the thirties he became involved in the activities of the Communist Party of America, as did many who were appalled by the rise of fascism. That he had been a witness to violent union-busting during his Pinkerton days may also have played a part. [3] After serving in the army during World War II—he edited an army paper in the Aleutians—he was caught in the Red scare dragnet and jailed for contempt of court. His books and the radio shows based on them were blacklisted, and the IRS went after him for back taxes. He came out of prison minus his health and his money, neither of which he ever regained. He died in 1961, at age sixty-six.

The *Selected Letters* was made possible by the same lucky garage find that enabled Jo Hammett to piece together her memoir. All of the letters are by Hammett: the answers to them have disappeared. Most of the letters are to women—his wife, his daughters, Lillian Hellman, other mistresses, and women friends—either because women saved the letters, or because Hammett felt more comfortable writing to women than to men. Reading them is like reading the letters of anyone you don't know—first names you can't place, books you've never heard of, private jokes you don't get—but then some bon mot or caustic remark will liven things up again. ("Bruce Lockwood, who has been borrowing money from me, sent me a dozen of his wife's horrible watercolors, from which I'm supposed to select a couple to be gifted with.") Many letters are ornamented with drawings or stuck with newspaper clippings; some are whimsical pieces of wordplay. They're the letters of a man who loved to write, to flirt, and to amuse others. It's plain to see why women liked him.

The letters have been meticulously edited, and among them are some documents that will be very helpful to anyone studying, for instance, American intellectual and political life of the thirties and forties. The letters to Hammett's first daughter, Mary, in which he tries to answer her questions about the chief issues of the day—Why support the Republican side in the Spanish Civil War? What's the scoop on Hitler?—are particularly sober and thoughtful. The letters to Lillian Hellman show that the two of them had—whatever their respective failings—a deep-rooted, enduring, and often frisky relationship, though it's somewhat unnerving to come across the tough and ambitious Hellman being addressed as "my little cabbage."

The letters begin in 1921, with a series to Josephine Dolan, soon to become Hammett's wife. Anyone who was around in the first half of the twentieth century will recognize the young-man-to-girlfriend style. He teases her and sweet-talks, and brags about how much hell he's been raising. Presumably she scolded him about his health and teased him in return. It's a sweet beginning.

Another sweet beginning is his letters to the editor of *Black Mask*. Already, in 1923, he's making fun of himself: Creda Dexter in *The Tenth Clew* is described as looking like a kitten, but Hammett confesses to the *Black Mask* editor that her original looked "exactly like a young white-faced bull pup." Then, he claims, his nerve failed him: " 'Nobody will believe you if you write a thing like that,' I told myself. 'They'll think you're trying to spoof them.' So, for the sake of plausibility, I lied about her."

But such gentle ridicule of the genre alternates with earnestness: in a 1928 letter to his book publisher, he says he wants to try adapting the "stream-of-consciousness method" to the detective story. "I'm one of the few—if there are any more—people moderately literate who take the detective story seriously," he says. "I don't mean that I necessarily take my own or anybody else's seriously—but the detective story as a form. Someday somebody's going to make 'literature' out of it . . . and I'm selfish enough to have my hopes."

Dashiell Hammett: Crime Stories & Other Writings contains the foundation for those hopes. The "other writings" are two small and admired nonfiction pieces, "From the Memoirs of a Private Detective" and "Suggestions to Detective Story Writers." The first is a string of anecdotes about human stupidity and bits of cynical, tongue-in-cheek wisdom reminiscent of Ambrose Bierce: "Pocket-picking is the easiest to master of all the criminal trades. Anyone who is not crippled can become an adept in a day." The second—the "Suggestions"—displays the practical seriousness with which Hammett viewed his craft, while at the same time it's hilariously scathing at the expense of other, sloppier detective story writers. "A pistol, to be a revolver, must have something on it that revolves," he remarks. " 'Youse' is the plural of 'you.' " "A trained detective shadowing a subject does not ordinarily leap from doorway to doorway."

This approach brings to mind that other American Samuel, Sam Clemens (Mark Twain), who so famously took the stuffing out of Fenimore Cooper's standards of accuracy. Indeed, the two Samuels[4] have a lot in common: the combination of steely-eyed observation of the dirty underbelly of America and the idealistic wish that it would live up to its founding principles, the deadpan humor, and above all the dedication to language. This last, in both, took the form of an attempt to capture the tone and cadence of the American vernacular in literature, of which *Huckleberry Finn* is surely the first fully triumphant example.

Seen in this light, Hammett, with his word-collecting and ear for slang dialects,[5] is part of the project of American linguistic self-definition that began with Noah Webster's 1783 *The American Spelling Book* and his later dictionary. The effort was continued through Fenimore Cooper's Natty Bumppo of the *Leatherstocking Tales*, and gathered speed with various dialect and regional writers of the nineteenth century, as well as Whitman and his barbaric yawp. Owen Wister and his creation of the Western—its *ur*-plot, its tall tales and talk—belongs here, too, and Bret Harte, and many after them. The hard-boiled detective story lent itself to this sort of exploration, criminal slang being not only colorful but also often indigenous.

If this is Hammett's literary ancestry, or part of it, his subsequent family tree is equally noteworthy. He was an admirer of Sherwood Anderson, who wrote concisely about hitherto overlooked corners of small-town life. He respected Faulkner as one might respect a very bright but weird second cousin.[6] He found Hemingway irritating, like a brother who is also a rival, and took little pokes at him—in "The Main Death" he has a particularly vacuous rich girl reading *The Sun Also Rises*. He must have found it gratifying to be called "better than Hemingway" in the 1930 publisher's ad for *The Maltese Falcon.*

Like Wister's *Virginian*, the granddaddy of all Westerns, Hammett's work had incalculable influence. He was one of those writers whom everyone of a certain age read as a matter of course. He himself said, "I've been as bad an influence on American literature as anyone I can think of." Raymond Chandler is the younger brother: he inherited the battered office furniture and the type of the romantic-loner detective, though Philip Marlowe is more of an intellectual than Sam Spade, and more fascinated with upholstery. Nathanael West was arguably a melancholy cousin. Elmore Leonard—who, like Hammett, began in magazines—has Hammett's pace, descriptive eye, and dead-on ear for dialogue. Carl Hiassen has the outrageousness, the taste for the hilariously bizarre, and the manic inventiveness.[7]

The Hammett prize for experimenting with language in a criminal set-ting must surely go to Jonathan Lethem's beguiling *Motherless Brooklyn*, in which the sleuth has Tourette's syndrome. And there are many, many more. Even the pratfalling body pileups were inherited by an unlikely third cousin: read Hammett's "Dead Yellow Women" or "The Big Knockover," then the riot-in-the-bar sequence in the first chapter of Thomas Pynchon's *V*, just for fun. The most recent addition is the fine Spanish thriller writer Pérez-Reverte, who pays direct homage to *The Maltese Falcon*.

Dashiell Hammett: Crime Stories & Other Writings takes us back to the beginning of the line. Twenty-four of the early magazine stories have been selected. In addition, there's the manuscript of *The Thin Man*, much shorter and almost completely different from the published book. (No Nick and Nora Charles tossing back the booze in their chic apartment, no Asta the dog.) The stories give us a good look at the young Hammett staking out his territory. They're best read one at a time, with pauses between, since too much at once dulls the edge. They are very much of their period and genre—"hard-boiled" was the term used of this kind of side-of-the-mouth crime fiction. (Hard-boiled eggs were what blue-collar workers had in their lunch boxes.) But despite their adherence to formulas, it's easy to see from the stories why Hammett rose so rapidly.

Low life and high life are his interests: each set is motivated largely by money, power, and sex, and each behaves badly, though the highlifes are less likely to have poor complexions, perhaps because they don't eat at grease joints—about the only places in Hammett stories where people consume food. The cozy middle-class Norman Rockwell front-porch folks do not concern him; when their representatives appear, they are likely to be thugs in disguise, like the "affectionate old couple" with their twinkling eyes in "The House in Turk Street" who are fronting for a mob, or the entire population of the town of Izzard, in "Nightmare Town," including the jolly banker and the kindly doctor, who are all part of a huge criminal conspiracy. [8]

"Realism" is a word often used to describe Hammett's writing, but the sto-ries are realistic only in their settings and details—the pimples on nasty youths, the dingy office furniture of the cheap private eyes—and in their forthright use of the vernacular. The dialogue was influenced by its period, when the wisecrack and the vaudeville one-liner were valued and a smart mouth like Dorothy Parker's was an asset. The plots are Jacobean in their doubled and redoubled vengeance, and also in their carnage: they resemble multiple car crashes. This was the age of the Keystone Kops, when mayhem was first being portrayed on the screen,[9] and surely some of the brawls and corpsefests in Hammett were intended to be funny in this quasi-slapstick way. The exuberance of language, the relish with which seediness is described, the playing with aphorisms, the joy of bizarre invention—it's a pleasure to imagine the young Hammett cutting loose with whatever rascally high jinks he could cook up and put over. The aim was not realism, but to make things seem real—"real as a dime," as one narrator says of a farfetched yarn he's been reading.

For the pulp adventure-crime stories of this era are not real realism. Instead they're romances in the Northrop Frye sense, with knights-errant disguised as detectives, and treasures with criminal-mastermind ogres guarding them. There are trolls in the guise of goons with huge chins, pasty faces, dead eyes, or other physical distortions, and threatened maidens who sometimes really are maidens—innocent heiresses transgressing social boundaries—but most likely, instead, femmes fatales with silver eyes or other enchantments. These latter turn into clawing cats or foul-mouthed banshees when the hero calls their bluff. Quite often the spell-breaking words are "You are a liar," or words to that effect; for like Sam Spade after him, the hero always resists female blandishments in pursuit of his higher mission. This mission is not exactly justice; it's more like professionalism. The hero has a job to do and is good at his job. He's a working man, and this kind of thoroughness gets Hammett's respect. Also this kind of toughness, for toughness was a cardinal virtue for him.[10]

The hero who most frequently appears in these stories, and the one that made Hammett so popular with his readers, is a man without a name. He's known as the Continental Op—an operative working for the Continental Detective Agency. The Op reports to the Old Man—surely the original of James Bond's M, George Smiley's Control, and Charlie of *Charlie's Angels.* This hero makes a point of avoiding heroics, as his aim is not to get himself killed but to catch the criminals. He's short and fat and down-to-earth, playing a grouchy Sancho Panza to the thin, idealistic tilter at windmills who was lurking inside Hammett and would make such a decisive appearance in the courtroom in his later life.

Fatness and thinness are distinguishing markers in the stories and novels, but they're also recurring motifs in the letters. Time and again Hammett tells his correspondents that he's eating again, that he's gaining weight, or—when illness or drink have gotten the better of him—that he hasn't been able to eat at all. In the light of this constant struggle with his thinness—at bottom a struggle to remain alive—the title of Hammett's last novel, *The Thin Man*, may have been a wry joke, the subject of which was Hammett himself. The thin man in the book is a mad genius who's dead before the book begins. He appears to be alive only because other people say he is; in reality, he's so thin he isn't there at all. "Count me out," Hammett may have been saying. "I've run out of energy, I'm gone." And he was gone—from the writing scene, at least.

Which brings us to the two silences: the literary silence, and the dramatic, public one in federal court. Of the literary one—the absence of any new books after the midthirties—Jo Hammett makes short work. "He didn't stop writing. Not until the very last. What he stopped was finishing." And indeed the letters are sprinkled with references to books he was beginning or continuing, and to possibilities for having the free time and the space in which to write.[11] This part of the story makes painful reading for anyone who's trying to write books, since the moves—the setting out with optimism, the evasion, the fading away of purpose—are so familiar.

None of the attempts came to anything. Drink has been suggested as the reason, and illness, and other activities that interfered, though it was Hammett's choice to let them. Then there were ambition and high standards: Hammett wanted to go "mainstream"—to get outside what he felt was the limiting circle of crime writing—and that was a big leap. Perhaps, however, his fundamental problem was with language. "I stopped writing because I was repeating myself," he said in 1956. "It is the beginning of the end when you discover you have style." And he did have style, or rather a style—a mannered implement he'd worked up and polished, but an implement very much of its time. Possibly he could no longer settle on a language equal to the occasion; or rather, the occasion itself had passed by. By the forties and fifties the scene had changed radically, and he must have felt out of his element. He couldn't go to town on the language anymore, because that kind of town no longer existed.

Then there's the other silence, the one in court. The virtues of silence as a stratagem had occurred to Hammett early. "It doesn't matter how shrewd a man is, or how good a liar," the Op says in the 1924 story "ZigZags of Treachery": "If he'll talk to you and you play your cards right, you can hook him—can make him help you convict him. But if he won't talk you can't do a thing with him."

Also, if Hammett kept silent, he wouldn't implicate anyone else: only he would suffer. Strangely enough, there's a literary precedent even for that. The young boy who'd wanted to read all the books in the Baltimore public library can hardly have escaped Longfellow, then the most revered of American poets. Longfellow's poem "The Children's Hour"[12] was chosen by Hammett as the title of the play attributed to Lillian Hellman, though Hammett had provided the story for it and did much of the work. So Hammett more than likely knew Longfellow's verse drama, *Giles Corey of the Salem Farms*.

Giles Corey was the man who refused to plead either guilty or not guilty during the Salem witchcraft episode. If he pled, he'd have been tried, and if tried, he'd have been found guilty—all those accused were. His property would then have been confiscated by the state, and his family deprived. He took his stand on principle, but also out of consideration for others, as Hammett himself did. The penalty for failure to plead was "pressing"—stones were piled on top of you until you either pled or died. Giles Corey did the latter.[13] If Hammett considered the Salem trials as a paradigm for the McCarthy "witch hunt," he was not alone. Many used that metaphor, including Arthur Miller in his play *The Crucible*.

In Longfellow's play, the last words spoken about Corey before his death are "I wonder now/If the old man will die, and will not speak? He's obstinate enough and tough enough/For anything on earth." Silence equals toughness. Could it be that this verbal equation was first planted in young Hammett's head by the author of *Evangeline*?

Well, it's one more clue.

Notes

1. Diane Johnson, *Dashiell Hammett: A Life* (New York: Random House, 1983).

2. The term "pulp" didn't refer to the sleaziness of the writing, but to the quality of the paper: the "pulps" were printed on uncoated paper, as opposed to the more upmarket "slicks." But many good writers got their start in the pulps, and they were a source of income if you could write quickly.

3. As he was already a star by then, he evidently didn't have to suffer the mind-bending and humiliation dished out to lesser CPUSA members, such as Richard Wright.

4. The third Samuel in the trio is Sam Spade. Hammett was very conscious of names, and would have given his own to this character quite deliberately.

5. As Jo Hammett remarks, "Papa loved all kinds of word play: thieves' cant, convict argot, Yiddish expressions, restaurant and cowboy talk, Cockney rhyming slang, gangster-lowlife speak."

6. In 1931 he was reading *Sanctuary*, which—with its twisted Popeye and its socialite who plays with the toughs—is probably Faulkner's most Hammett-like book. Hammett didn't think highly of it, but revised his opinion of Faulkner upward in later years.

7. Hiassen's amazing "Velcro-Face" of *Skin Tight* and his road-kill-eating ex-governor exist on a continuum that leads from Hammett's squinty or big-chinned grotesques through Faulkner's twisted Popeye through *Dick Tracy* of the comics, with its gargoyle thugs such as "Anyface," who looked like Swiss cheese.

8. This strain—awfulness behind the apple-pie facade—runs through Hawthorne's "Young Goodman Brown," in which the wholesome townsfolk are in league with the Devil, through Hammett, through Ray Bradbury's *Martian Chronicles*, where the town conceals murderous Martians, through the film *The Stepford Wives*, in which robot wife doubles have replaced real wives, to the television show *Twin Peaks* and certain episodes of *The X Files*. In real life it has played itself out in versions of Satanic cults, as well as its *ur*-form, the infamous Salem witch-craft trials.

9. Hammett was a moviegoer. It's endearing to find him giving his opinion of the relative merits of *Pinocchio* versus *Snow White*. Needless to say, he liked *Pinocchio* better.

10. Jo Hammett describes all the kinds of toughness Hammett admired: tough men, tough women, tough sports. It was a quality of character as well as a physical quality. "Toughness," she says, "would take him through the last bad years."

11. There were three main attempts: *My Brother Felix*, which was "going to be pretty good for both magazines and movies"; *The Valley Sheep Are Fatter*, a title that comes from one of Thomas Love Peacock's novels; and *Tulip*, this last about a writer who can no longer write.

12. Thought of as a piece of syrupy kitsch by those who haven't read it closely. But Hammett was a good reader, and must have seen it for the creepy poem it is.

13. The only words Corey is said to have uttered were "Put on more stones," but Longfellow has the pressing take place offstage and so does not use them.

30

Review:

Atanarjuat: The Fast Runner,
a film by Zacharias Kunuk

tanarjuat: The Fast Runner is the first feature film ever to be made in Inuktitut. It's also the first to be made almost entirely by Inuit—*made* in many ways, for the clothing; the artifacts, such as spears and kayaks; and the dwellings were all painstakingly researched and then handmade by artisans to re-create the world of almost a thousand years ago, long before the coming of Europeans. For the people of the community out of which this film emerged, it will be what they have lacked for so many years: a validation of their roots.

The danger might have been that such a film would have only a curio value, but nothing could be farther from the truth. *Atanarjuat* won the Camera d'Or at Cannes for best first feature and then went on to collect six Genie Awards, and no wonder. It's already being called a masterpiece. This film is a knockout.

I've seen it, or parts of it, on three occasions. I'll talk about them in reverse order.

The film was viewable in England before its release in Canada, so I saw it in its entirety in London, at the Institute of Contemporary Art. We went to the matinee, but even so we were lucky to get in; the place was packed. During the screening, my English pal and I—supposed mistresses of sang-froid, both of us—did a lot of arm-clutching, and, at the end, some unseemly sniveling. As we staggered out of the theater, red-eyed and wobbly-kneed, she said, "My God! What a film!" Speechlessness is the best tribute.

I'd known *Atanarjuat* was going to be on in London because, while I'd been in Paris doing my bad imitation of a person who can speak French, we'd happened to turn on the BBC, and the film was being reviewed, complete with excerpts. I don't think I've ever heard an English film critic indulging in this kind of breathless rhapsody. "If Homer had been given a video camera, this is what he would have done," said he, and there's something to that.

Which bit of Homer? The story of the House of Atreus would be my guess, for this is a generational saga with many Homeric elements—love, jealousy, rivalry between young contenders, extraordinary feats of strength, resentments passed from fathers to sons, and crimes that beget consequences years later. The world of Greek myth is one in which gods interact with human beings, dreams have significance, grudges are held, vengeance is exacted, the ways of Fate are dark, food can cast a spell, and animals aren't always what they seem; and if you substitute the word "spirits" for the word "gods," these things are true as well of *Atanarjuat*.

It helps going into the film to know a couple of things. First, this is not a "made-up" story, any more than Homer would have said *The Iliad* was made up. It's based on oral tradition—on a series of events said to have really happened, in real places. (You can follow the travels of the characters on the film's Web site.) So it would be beside the point to fault someone called "the author" for something you don't like about "the plot."

Second, a newborn child was thought to be a reincarnation of someone who'd died. Thus, when the grandmother addresses a young woman as "little mother"—which throws you the first time you hear it—it's not just that the girl is named after the old woman's mother; she is that mother.

Third, spirits are all around. They can confer extra strength, and they can enter into people and make them behave badly (like the demons cast out by Christ). But they can be mastered to some extent by shamans, who can also call on the dead for help. So, as in Homer, this story isn't just about conflict between human rivals. It's a battle between one lot of spirits and another, kicked off when an evil spirit arrives and sows discord among the members of a hunting group, and enters into one of them.

Fourth, it was forbidden for a woman to speak to or even look at her brother-in-law. That's why the bad sex scene between the wayward second wife of the hero and the hero's brother isn't just any old roll in the fur. It's really bad.

Fifth, there are various kinds of strength. There's the strength conferred by the position of leadership—keep your eye on the teeth-and-tusk necklace, the equivalent of the crown in *Richard III*—and this position is always held by a man, because the group is a hunting group and it's the men who hunt. There's the strength conferred by shamanistic power, which can be used for good or ill; but it helps to know that both the woman (later the grandmother) who gives a talismanic rabbit's foot to her brother, and the brother himself, possess this power.

And finally, there's moral authority. This can be earned or lost. (Watch out for the moment when, in any Western genre film, the hero—his enemies finally at his mercy—would blow them to bits. This doesn't happen. Instead, Atanarjuat says, "The killing stops here," thus gaining moral authority. We could use a little of that right now.) But the ultimate moral authority resides with the elders, who wield it sparingly, though to crushing effect. Keep your eye on the grandmother.

These were things I would have liked to have known the first time I saw this film. It was the summer before it was to preview at the Toronto International Film Festival (on September 12, 2001: the preview was canceled). I was on an icebreaker in the Arctic, with a tour group called Adventure Canada. They'd asked me to come along and give a couple of talks, a small price to pay for the experience of seeing places I'd only ever dreamed about. Everything about this voyage was magic; the Arctic light effects alone—the mirages, the Fats Morgana, the "glories"—were worth the trip. At one point we all got out and stood on an ice pan, looking forebodingly like a David Blackwood lithograph.

If we'd taken off all our clothes and leapt from floe to floe, we might have resembled instead—from a distance—the spectacular scene in which the hero of *Atanarjuat* runs stark naked across miles and miles of broken pan ice. I didn't get as far as this during my first viewing. It wasn't that the film was being shown in episodes on a TV set and it was hard to read the subtitles. But Pakkak Innukshuk—the man who plays the Strong One, the hero's older brother—was on the ship with us. He was a man of few but cogent words, a hunter from much farther north, and in the film he was much as he seemed in life: more brusque, but recognizable. So I watched up to the place where Pakkak was sleeping in a skin tent along with his brother and the three murderous rivals were sneaking up on them. I knew Pakkak was about to be horribly speared, and I didn't think I could go through with it. (It was okay to watch Pakkak being speared in London. I hadn't just had pancakes with him.)

There's a permeable boundary between reality and art. We know there's a connection, we know there's a difference, but there's no stone wall. When I think of *Atanarjuat*, of course I will always think of Pakkak. While we were scrambling around on the Arctic landscape one day, I recalled with some embarrassment having been told that a native band, lacking a word for "northern tourism," had come up with an expression that means "white men playing in the woods." So there we were, mostly white people playing on the rocks, and there was Pakkak, standing on a cliff where he had a good view.

He had a large bear gun. He was watching out for animals. As he, and all the men of whom (says the lore) he is an incarnation, have been doing for thousands of years.

31

Review:

Life of Pi
by Yann Martel

Yann Martel's third work of fiction, *Life of Pi*, is a terrific book. It's fresh, original, smart, devious, and crammed with absorbing lore. But that said, caveat emptor. *Life of Pi* is not just a readable and engaging novel, it's also a finely twisted length of yarn—*yarn* implying a farfetched story you can't quite swallow whole, but can't dismiss outright. Most yarns have been—over the millennia—travelers' tales, point being that the traveler was there and you weren't, so how can you question his eye-witness report? Even Herodotus—dubbed both the father of history and the father of lies—told more of the truth, it now appears, than was once supposed.

Life of Pi is in this tradition—a story of uncertain veracity, made credible by the art of the yarn spinner. Like its noteworthy ancestors, among which I take to be *Robinson Crusoe, Gulliver's Travels, The Ancient Mariner, Moby-Dick,* and *Pincher Martin,* it's a tale of disaster at sea coupled with miraculous survival—a boys' adventure for grown-ups. The hero is a sixteen-year-old castaway; the other hero is a ferocious tiger. How will the first outwit the second, given that both are stuck on a lifeboat in the shark-infested Pacific Ocean?

Yann Martel is no dummy. He knows that if he's to get the hook in, he has to do it right at the beginning. The Old Master Yarners knew how to frame the fabulous—*Dr. Jekyll and Mr. Hyde* has a dry-as-dust narrator, *The Turn of the Screw* begins with a bunch of solid chaps exchanging views.

Yann Martel's plausible frame is himself. In the preliminary author's note he recounts how, as a novelist whose second book has croaked at the box office—true enough—he went to India to write a third. The attempt failed. Then he just kind of stumbled across the incredible but true narrative he's about to relate. In Pondicherry he met an elderly man who said, "I have a story that will make you believe in God." Martel, the candid fellow, lets us know he's just as skeptical about that as the reader is.

And we're off.

The story is the story of Pi Patel, whom the author tracks to Scarborough, one of the plainer and more unvarnished burbs of Toronto. "I love Canada," says Pi. "It is a great country much too cold for good sense, inhabited by compassionate, intelligent people with bad hairdos." He, too, is a candid fellow.

Pi Patel was named after a swimming pool, the Piscine Molitar. His name has caused him much grief, as it invites the mocking nickname "Pissing"; so he manages to rename himself Pi, "that elusive, irrational number with which scientists try to understand the universe." Thus he becomes—like many heroes—one of the twice-born. It's a better name two ways; he's now free from jeers, and his world—until now so small-scale and domestic—is about to take a major turn toward the elusive and the irrational. He joins all three of the faiths available to him—the Hindu, the Muslim, and the Christian—and so is well equipped spiritually for the ordeal to come.

His father owns a zoo in Pondicherry, but after giving his children some blood-curdling lessons about the wildness of wild animals, he sells up. Pi and his family and the zoo animals embark on a rat trap of a ship, bound for North America and a new life. The ship sinks. All perish but Pi, a zebra, a hyena, an orangutan, and a Bengal tiger named Richard Parker.

The tiger burns bright. He is everything Blake would want in a tiger, and more. He growls, he glows with life-force energy, he roars, he's divinely beautiful, he rips things apart. Which of his fellow passengers on the Noah's Ark from Hell will be his dinner first, and how will Pi avoid this fate, and the other fates in store—dying of thirst and exposure, starving to death, giving up in despair? Here the story turns both lyrical and—literally—visceral. This book has guts. But Pi is an ingenious and practical boy, and he makes use of the materials on hand. Suffice it to say that if you ever need to know how to train a tiger using the whistle from a life jacket, this is the book for you.

Then comes the mysterious floating island inhabited by meerkats, and the blind cannibal, and then . . . but it would be wrong to divulge any more of the plot. Suffice it to say that there's a knot at the end of the yarn, and it's a knot that leaves the reader pondering the ways of tales and their tellers, and their metaphysical import, and the power of belief over skepticism. For Pi—it turns out—can tell not only one story about the shipwreck, but two. One has a tiger in it, the other does not. But the one with the tiger is a better story.

Scientists, we are led to suspect, will never be able to understand the universe using numbers, unless those are numbers like Pi—elusive—because the universe is not rational. As Pi himself says, things can be going along normally, but then "normal" sinks. Our customary picture of life is torn apart, and through the rent in the canvas we see the real world. And it's a world of wonders, and there are tigers in it.

32

Review:

Tishomingo Blues
by Elmore Leonard

*T*ishomingo Blues is Elmore Leonard's thirty-seventh novel. At that number you'd think he'd be flagging, but no, the maestro is in top form. If, like Graham Greene, he were in the habit of dividing his books into "novels" and "entertainments"—with, for instance, *Pagan Babies* and *Cuba Libre* in the former list, and *Glitz*, *Get Shorty*, and *Be Cool* in the latter—this one might fall on the "entertainment" side; but, as with Greene, those that might be consigned to the "entertainment" section are not necessarily of poorer quality.

Those offended by what my grandmother called "language," and by what used to be termed, in adventure stories, "fearful oaths," and by the derogatory epithets and salacious jokes that used to pass from mouth to ear in the smoking cars of trains and now whiz to and fro over the Internet, should avoid *Tishomingo Blues*. But Leonard is often and justly praised for his mastery of the demotic, and the demotic would not be itself without this kind of thing. Anyway, it's pretty much always apt: each character speaks in character. Here's one of the more villainous heavies:

No mention of the smoke or the two greasers—Newton thinking of the one he'd asked that time where the nigger was and the one said he'd gone to fuck your wife. It had set him off, sure, even knowing it wasn't true. One, Myrna wasn't ever home, she played bingo every night of her life. And two, not even a smoke'd want to fuck her,

Myrna going four hundred pounds on the hoof. Try and find the
wet spot on her.

This is an object lesson in economy worthy of a short essay in *Maladicta*,
the defunct scholarly journal devoted to foul language (still available on the
Internet): three racial slurs, two F-words, misogyny combined with
lookism, and a sneer at bingo players, all wrapped up in five terse lines. The
man who speaks this will surely die. ("Good" characters in Leonard swear
differently from the way "bad" characters do.)

As to what Leonard is up to beyond the texture of his prose, it's what
he's been up to for some time. A good deal of any Leonard novel—or those
of, say, the past twenty years—consists of deadpan social observation. John
le Carré has maintained that, for the late twentieth century at least, the spy
novel is the central fictional form, because it alone tackles the implemen-
tation of the hidden agendas that—we suspect, and as the evening news
tends to confirm—surround us on all sides.[1] Similarly, Elmore Leonard
might argue—if he were given to argument, which he is not—that a novel
without some sort of crime or scam in it can hardly claim to be an accurate representation of today's reality. He might add that this is especially
true when that reality is situated in America, home of Enron and of the
world's largest privately held arsenal, where casual murders are so common
that most aren't reported, and where the CIA encourages the growing and
trading of narcotics to finance its foreign adventures.

Not only that—Leonard might continue, and it's a point he's copiously
illustrated—the line between the law and the lawbreakers is, in his native
land, at any rate, not a firm one. (One of the nasties in this book is an ex-
sheriff's deputy, an employment category about which few have a good
word to say.) In fact, the uncertainties about this division—law enforcers
vs. lawbreakers, with coins tossed over who the villains are to be—goes far
back, and is firmly embedded in American folklore. The Revolutionaries
of 1776 were in essence rebels against the established government of their
time, and ever since then there has been some question about who is enti-
tled to impose what sort of legal code upon whom, and by what means.

The Klan vigilantes and the lynch mob have been—as Leonard reminds us in this book—two of the less pleasant historical responses.

There are righteous causes in aid of which breaking the law is surely the moral thing to do, but who is to decide what those causes are? It's a series of short steps from the rude bridge that spanned the flood, where the embattled and incidentally lawbreaking Concord farmers stood, to John Brown's celebrated abolitionist and also homicidal Body, to Thoreau's classic "Civil Disobedience," to Darlin' Corrie of the well-known folk song, who has to wake up and get her shotgun because the Revenooers are a-comin' to tear her still-house down.

Like all writers who concern themselves with crimes and punishments, Leonard is interested in moral issues, but these issues are for him by no means clear-cut. Having been born in 1925, he entered the scene as a conscious observer during the half century when this tendency—the questioning of law, the admiration of its breakers—was at its peak. It was the thirties, and the Depression was causing much real desperation. No wonder that many followed the exploits of the James brothers and Bonnie and Clyde with a great deal of interest—young Leonard, by his own account, among them. For if oppression is economic, and the bank has grabbed your farm and turfed out your family, isn't it at least slightly heroic to stick your hand in the till? The father who hangs in connection with such a crime in Davis Grubb's thirties-era novel *The Night of the Hunter* is not a bad guy: he's a good guy, and it's the system that hangs him that bears the moral taint.

But the James brothers and Bonnie and Clyde were not Robin Hoods, even in mythologized retellings. The American version of the robber as folk hero is very potent, but it doesn't include giving to the poor: that would be sappy, and perhaps Communist as well. The best thing to do with the poor is to remove yourself from their number by any means at your disposal, and this is largely what Leonard's crooks set out to accomplish. Thus, quite often in Leonard's books you don't get a choice between good noncriminals and bad criminals; instead, you get a choice between good guys and bad guys, period. There are many factors that determine whether a guy is good or bad—more specifically, whether he is an asshole, a pompous blowhard, a coward, a condescending jerk, a moron, or a man a man can respect—but which side of the legal line he happens to be on is not among them.

As every child who has ever played cops and robbers knows, it was more fun being a robber, because you could fool people and get away with forbidden behavior, and there was more risk. In *Tishomingo Blues*, fun, risk, forbidden behavior, and fooling people go together. There are two main characters. The first is not a criminal. Instead he's an edge dweller and risk taker of another sort. He's a professional high diver named Dennis Lenahan, who makes a living at amusement parks going off an eighty-foot tower into a tank that looks, from above, to be the size of a fifty-cent piece. He does this, as far as we can tell, for three reasons: it gives him a rush, it helps him to pick up girls, and he has no other marketable skills. When we enter his picture he's beginning to worry about how much longer he'll be able to keep up the performances without breaking his neck. (Or rupturing his anus and ruining his genitalia, two other hazards of high diving about which we are duly informed on the first page.) Dennis is not someone who's ever given a thought to stock options or gated retirement communities—his first marriage failed because he was "too young," and, although nearing forty, he's still too young—so these are new and depressing thoughts for the likable lad.

Dennis soothes his anxieties by wafting into bed with nice women who never turn him down—well, he's very fit—and this is the one matter that may give the female reader thoughtful pause. Leonard is precise about physicality in other respects. His characters piss, take dumps, fart, have bad breath, and much else. Unlike some fictional characters, they eat and drink, and they do this accurately, brand names and all. (Early Times, Pepsis, and Lean Cuisines are featured.) But Dennis floats into the sack with nary a question and nary a precaution: no thoughts of STDs trouble his enthusiastic head. Maybe this is accurate, too—probably it is, or there wouldn't be so many cases of herpes, not to mention AIDS. But you want to whisper—especially when Dennis is tumbling around with the disaffected wife of a morally disgusting man who's done hard time in an unsanitary prison—"Dennis honey, don't you know who's been in there before you?" Dennis, we fear, will wake up one morning with a dose of something he can't get rid of. But such dismal futures lie outside the margins of the book, and to dwell too long on them would be like anticipating Cin-derella's wedding night, when she will pop out of her trance and realize that Prince Charming is a shoe fetishist.

The second main character has a lot more bulbs in his chandelier. The name he's going by is Robert Taylor—we assume it's assumed[2]—and he's definitely a criminal element. He's handsome, slick, personable, cool, well dressed, Jaguar-driving, and from Detroit. (He also carries an attaché case with a gun in it, but this is a part of the country—Tunica, Mississippi—where people have guns the way most people have noses, so it elicits scant surprise.) In addition to all of the above, Robert is black. Add in the set-ting and an upcoming historical reenactment of a Civil War battle, and you've got the nitroglycerin for the dynamite.

When I started reading about Tunica, Mississippi, as described by Elmore Leonard, it seemed so extravagantly over the top—even just architecturally—that I thought I'd stumbled upon a made-up place, like the Emerald City of Oz, which it somewhat resembles. (Oz, too, is a city of illusions con-trolled by a scam artist who deceives people and holds out false promises.) But I should have known better, because Leonard doesn't make up this sort of stuff. He doesn't need to: it's right there for the taking, in all its full-blown weirdness. Tunica is real—it's "The Casino Capital of the South." But it's *also* made up, because the business of gambling is nothing if not the successful selling of illusion.

The connection between illusion and reality, lie and truth—and also the gap between them—is one of the leitmotifs that runs through *Tishomingo Blues*. Everything in Tunica is faux, including the whore-in-a-trailer pre-tending to be Barbie, and the "Southern Living Village," a complex in the throes of development where all the dwellings are imitations of something else and the entire operation is a front for the drug trade. The focus of the story is the Tishomingo Lodge & Casino. Its name is ripped off from a real Native American chief; its form is a kitschy tepee; its cocktail waitresses wear fringed fake-buckskin miniskirts; its foyer mural is horrendously inaccurate. But though the decor in Tunica may be fake, the danger is real.

Dennis the diver lands in Tunica because he's talked the manager of the casino into engaging his high-dive act as a customer attraction. Almost immediately he's in trouble. While up on his tower and about to do a test dive, he sees two men down below shoot a third man. They see him seeing them. They're about to pop him, but they get distracted. Robert Taylor, the black criminal, has witnessed the shooting, too. He has also witnessed Dennis witnessing it. They strike up a curious symbiotic palship.

What does each want of the other? What Dennis ought to want is a good-bye handshake and a bus ticket to Nome, Alaska, but he's a bit of an innocent and doesn't know how afraid he ought to be. Also he doesn't want to abandon his tower and his tank. So he sticks around, and Robert Taylor presents himself as a fellow who can help Dennis do that. Without Robert present, we fear, young Dennis's brain will shortly be "red Cream of Wheat," as other brains have been before. So Robert is our man.

But what does Robert Taylor want of Dennis? That's more complicated. First version, he wants Dennis and his diving act to function as the laundry for his drug money, because he plans to take over the market from the local-yokel Dixie Mafia. Second version, he wants to buy Dennis's soul. He puts that right on the table. "You at the crossroads, Dennis. I'm about to make an offer to buy your soul." "Like Faust, man. Sell your soul, you get any-thing you want." If Dennis sells, what he'll get is mojo, and this mojo will enable him to realize his innermost dreams; but he'll have to really believe it—otherwise it won't work—and there's just the one chance to grab it.[3]

For Robert isn't any old gangster. He's invested with more significance than that. He's the Master of the Crossroads, the deceiving prankster born and bred in the briar patch, the man who makes things happen. He's the fast-talking salesman selling himself and riding on a shoeshine and a smile;[4] he's the gambler with his sleeves stuffed with aces. He's the deity you pray to when you want change and action, though there's no guarantee of what kind of action you will get. He's Mercury, god of thieves and com-merce and communication and conductor of souls to the underworld, and he's Anansi, African web-spinner, catcher of flies in traps. He teases Dennis by implying he's the Devil, but if so, he's hardly the Biblical Satan. Instead he's the devil of folklore, whose bargains could work out in your favor, especially if you do what Dennis is urged to do—no matter what you see, keep your mouth shut.[5] Robert is—in other words—a particularly engaging example of a trickster figure.[6] "You gonna miss me, you know it?" he says toward the end of the book, as much to the reader as to the lady he's taking leave of. "You gonna miss the fun."

And he's on solid home ground in Tunica. His roots, he claims, are right here, on the banks of the Mississippi River, the *ur*-river, the Old Man River. The Mississippi divides and binds all elements—North and South, white, black, and Indian, rich and poor, travelers and gamblers. It's the river of *Showboat*, and, yes, Leonard dutifully supplies a beautiful quadroon who's concealing her ancestry. It's the river of Huck and Jim, the first white-black pair out to beat the odds and the scoundrels. It's the river of the King and the Duke, seedy but amusing scammers-for-profit; and it's the river of Melville's Confidence Man, an elusive and ambiguous figure whose masquerades result—sometimes—in good.

Robert Taylor is the inheritor, then, of a long and many-stranded tradition. To watch Leonard in action as he mines this rich lode is a pleasure, though it's somewhat like what Monty Python did with Botticelli's Venus—part humorous travesty, part straight aggression. Robert, for instance, is a history buff. "History can work for you," he says, "you know how to use it," and he does know how. He's gone to college—he paid his tuition by dealing, but he wouldn't sell to students because he figured their minds were already too addled:

> I took eighteen hours of history—ask me a question about it, any-
> thing, like the names of famous assassins in history. Who shot Lin-
> coln, Grover Cleveland. I took history 'cause I loved it, man, not to
> get a job from it. I knew about the Civil War even before I saw it on
> TV, the one Ken Burns did. I stole the entire set of videos from
> Blockbuster.

Robert's first history trick is to get hold of a 1915 souvenir postcard of a lynching, and to tell two different Tunica white bad guys that it's his great-grandpa dangling from the bridge and their great-grandpa doing the hanging:

I thought maybe you already knew your great-granddaddy lynched that man in the picture, my own great-granddaddy, rest his soul. And cut his dick off. Can you imagine a man doing that to another man? . . . I thought to myself, Lookit how our heritage is tied together, going back to our ancestors. Yeah, I'm gonna show him the historical fact of it.

Robert says this to a diehard racist and violent creep. This is *Roots* with a vengeance. "You only used it to set [him] up," says Dennis of the postcard. "That don't mean it ain't real," Robert replies.

Robert's aim is to scam his way as an "African Confederate" into the reenactment of the Battle of Brice's Cross Roads (which will not take place at the real Brice's Cross Roads, needless to say). That way, he can arrange for his opponents to be dispatched with real bullets—putting the history back into History, you might say. The Dixie Mafia's tribute to authenticity, on the other hand, is to attempt to reenact the postcard lynching, with Robert playing the role of dickless corpse. As usual, Leonard has done his research; he has the rules and attitudes of the reenactment movement down pat, and he plays them for all they're worth. If you didn't know about Naughty Child Pie and the Robert E. Lee and Stonewall Jackson salt-and-pepper shakers, and what farbs and hard-cores are, you'll find out here.

Leonard doesn't write whodunits—we always know who done it because we see them doing it. You might say he writes howdunits. His plots are like chess games—the pieces are all out in the open, we can watch the setup, but it's the rapid moves of the endgame that surprise. They're also like Feydeau farces, which is in no way to disparage them. Such performances are very hard to pull off successfully, and timing is everything: Feydeau used to compose with a stopwatch. The reader knows who is in which cupboard and under what bed and behind which bush, but the characters don't know. Then they start figuring it out, and things move very quickly after that. The sleight-of-hand machinery in this book is engineered by Robert, of course: as chief trickster, he is, after all, the Master of Illusion.

But in this world of the amusement park and the dress-ups and the reenactment, of the facade, the disguise, and the sham, where does reality lie, and what's actually worth having, and who has it? I'd say there's one main thing, and that is the respect—not of everyone, because men who want that are vain and foolish—but of a man whose respect counts for something. (These are boys' rules. Women aren't players in the respect game, in the world of *Tishomingo Blues*: they earn favorable attention in other ways.) The ways of obtaining and evaluating this and other kinds of man-to-man respect could form the basis for a dissertation in sociobiology— the male primate stare, for instance, or who looks at whom, and how, and what it means.

Apart from being able to do the stare, you get respect—as far as I can figure out—by being serious about things that count, by not talking too much, by knowing what you're talking about—there's a lot of lore-exchanging in this book, about the blues and their singers; about the Civil War; about how to set up a diving tank; and, rather less enchantingly, about baseball games of yore.[7] If you already have respect, and especially if you're a criminal kingpin, you have to keep the respect by not getting lazy and arrogant, or it'll be the Cream of Wheat brain for you.

But most of all you get the respect by making a hard thing look easy. This is how Dennis gets Robert's respect. "I love to watch people who make what they do look easy. No flaws, nothing sticking out," he says about Dennis's act. A third party comments, "The guy high in the air, twisting and turning, is in control of himself, showing how cool he is. And Robert's cool. He keeps Dennis around because he respects him as a man." Women don't evaluate this kind of behavior in quite the same way. When Dennis douses his clothing in high-test gasoline and torches himself for a fireball jump, Robert says, "Man." But his female companion says, "Big fucking deal." When women do admire Dennis, they're looking at his body—what might be in it for them. But Robert's admiring the guts and the technique.

Billy Darwin, Dennis's employer, has his own version of "big fucking deal." He makes the mistake of thinking that the thing is easy because it looks easy. He belittles what Dennis does, "sounding like a nice guy while putting you in your place, looking down at what you did for a living," and then he tries diving off the tower himself to demonstrate his cool and to show what a snap it is. He comes to grief.

And this, possibly, is our one small peek behind the scenes, to the shadows where the author lurks. Could it be that Mr. Leonard has heard a few too many times that the thing he's done professionally now for four decades, or thirty-seven times, is really easy because he makes it look easy? Just because it's an amusement park and people are entertained by what you do, does that mean it's not a serious skill? Could it be that he'd like to see a few of those kinds of commentators try jumping off the tower themselves? If you've been to the crossroads, and made the deal, and got the mojo—which turns out to be dependent on a great deal of hard work and practice, just like sleight-of-hand—wouldn't you maybe get a trifle riled by that kind of misjudgment from time to time?

Not so as to lose your cool, mind you. Not so much as that.

Notes

1. Le Carré gave these views in his acceptance speech when granted an honorary degree by the University of Edinburgh.

2. "Robert Taylor" was the assumed name of the actor who, besides being a famous romantic lead, starred in a huge number of crime and Western films. He played, for instance, Billy the Kid in the eponymous film in 1941. As someone says in *Tishomingo Blues*, "working for Robert . . . was like being in the fucking movies."

3. It's odd to find the sentiments of the Blue Fairy in *Pinocchio* on the lips of Robert Taylor. But then, wishing upon a star, makes no difference who you are, is partly what distinguishes Taylor from the bad guys: he's dreaming his own version of the American Dream.

4. Robert Taylor is the mirror image of Willy Loman of *Death of a Salesman*. The latter is the dishonest "honest" man, the former the honest dishonest one.

5. See, for instance, the Grimms' tale "The Devil's Sooty Brother." In such stories the hero, if lucky and prompt, can obtain the Devil's bounty and keep his own soul, too, and this is what Dennis does.

6. For much more, see Lewis Hyde's thorough study, *Trickster Makes This World* (Farrar, Straus, & Giroux, 1998). Hyde makes the point, however, that in a nation paved from end to end with snake-oil salesmen, the Trickster doesn't function quite as usual.

7. The character who drones on about baseball is intended to be boring. The trick is to see how he interjects his obsession into any topic whatsoever. If you get tired of it you can do what Dennis does—tune out.

33

Eulogy:

Tiff and the Animals[1]

What do you say when everything has been said? How about: *It won't be the same. We'll miss him. He was creative, extravagantly generous, humane, unique.* What more?

What more? I said to Tiff—figuratively, as I am not yet a truly crazy person out of one of his books. Tiff gave one of those big smoke-filled laughs of his and said, What about the animals?

Well, yes. There were always animals, in the life and in the work. Cats, a lot of those. At Stone Orchard, his farm, a cathouse full. Dogs, sometimes. Birds, occasionally. A bear once. The entire menagerie, in *Not Wanted on the Voyage*. And a whole slew of rabbits.

What's this *thing* you had about Peter Rabbit? I said to Tiff. You did manage to get him in a lot. It wasn't just whimsy, was it? You knew he wasn't a cuddly stuffed toy or a kiddie's milk mug, although you collected those. It's a dark story when you come to think of it. But what was it with you and him, precisely? You even chose him as your banned book, once.

Peter Rabbit, Tiff pronounced, in that voice that was always *his* voice—although he was known to do some wicked imitations of, for instance, me—Peter Rabbit, he pronounced, was Oscar Wilde backward.

---

1. On the occasion of the Timothy Findley Memorial Evening, Convocation Hall, University of Toronto, September 29, 2002.

He must have meant the Oscar who said, I live in fear of not being mis-understood. That, in an age in which being gay was not only a dangerous thing to be but also a crime, as it was when Tiff was young.

And a lot of his work revolves around that—being misunderstood, and also not being misunderstood, which could be even worse. And the fear of both. What to disguise, what to reveal, when to lie and when to blurt, what are the consequences of each? But though this fear is omnipresent in Tiff's writing, it's most often shown in a social context—the context of other people. Being different and going your own way can shatter the family, which sometimes rejects you but sometimes takes you back.

In the very early novel *The Last of the Crazy People*, the young boy bumps off every single one of his relatives, which is one solution. In *The Wars*, the boy shatters the family not only by going off to war but also through a forbidden act; then he escapes into permanent wounded mind-lessness. In *Pilgrim*, the boy-man is a mute in a lunatic asylum. (Being mute—being voiceless—having your voice taken away—being unable to speak, or to speak out—these motifs recur.) However, in the last novel, *Spadework*, the family is shattered by the defection of its husband/father, who falls in love with a man; but then it accepts the shatterer back, and integrates him again into the social group.

This is the Peter Rabbit solution; and in the days of Tiff's adolescence, when gay people were so frequently shunned by their relations and gay-bashing was official state policy, how difficult it was to achieve, and there-fore how desired. It's the wounds of youth that leave the deepest scars.

Consider how the Peter Rabbit story goes. Peter's father is dead. Peter is the sole son in a family consisting of a widow and three conventionally well-behaved daughters. Mother Rabbit issues a taboo—no Mr. McGregor's garden for Peter, no forbidden fruits and especially vegetables, no great big dangerous man with huge boots and a rake with a very, very long handle.

But Peter promptly violates this taboo. In doing so, he runs the risk of devastating the precarious Rabbit family even farther. Off he goes to do the forbidden thing, involving, in his case, lettuces. He comes to grief, and like Oscar Wilde is found out and pursued and incarcerated—not in Reading Jail, but in a watering pot. However, he makes a dash for it, and although by now he's feeling quite ill, he manages to get back to the safety and warmth of his family, where he is cared for and given camomile tea and tucked into bed. And I have to say that nobody has written about the comforting pleasures of clean, fresh, crisp pajamas better than Tiff.

In so many of Tiff's books, the character feels like (and sometimes actually is) a small, helpless animal on the run, excluded by definition, ill or blind, lacerated in body or heart, seeking a place of shelter where he will no longer be alone but part of a loving group; no longer an *I*, but an *us*.

So, there's my interpretation, I said to Tiff. You always wanted more academic literary criticism of your work. D'you buy it?

Not bad about Peter, he said. Though a little overdone about the rake. But you've missed something about animals in general.

What's that? I said. Apart from the simple fact that you were fond of them.

They can't *talk*, he said. They are allowed no *voices*. We don't *listen*. They live in fear of being misunderstood. They are so often . . . *excluded*. They are at our mercy. And we have had the unmitigated *gall* to proclaim that they have no souls!

So, are there any rabbits in Heaven? I said. Now that you're in a position to know. Not to mention cats.

I *demanded* them, said Tiff. It wouldn't have been Heaven without them.

34

To the Lighthouse
by Virginia Wolf

I first read Virginia Woolf's *To the Lighthouse* when I was nineteen. I had to. It was on a course—"The Twentieth-Century Novel," or some such. I got on all right with the nineteenth-century novel—the works of Dickens were, I felt, just as such things should be, at least in England: lots of mad people and fog. Nor did I do too badly with certain twentieth-century novels. Hemingway I could more or less fathom—I'd played war as a child, I'd gone fishing a lot, I knew the approximate rules of both, I was aware that boys were laconic. Camus was depressing enough for the late-adolescent me, with existential angst and gritty, unpleasant sex in the bargain. Faulkner was my idea of what could be possible for—well, for myself as a writer (which was what I wanted to be), hysteria in steaming, bug-infested swamps being my notion of artistic verisimilitude. (I knew those bugs. I knew those swamps, or swamps very like them. I knew that hysteria.) That Faulkner could also be outrageously funny went—at the age I was then—right past me.

But Virginia Woolf was off on a siding as far as my nineteen-year-old self was concerned. Why go to the lighthouse at all, and why make such a fuss about going or not going? What was the book about? Why was everyone so stuck on Mrs. Ramsay, who went around in floppy old hats and fooled around in her garden, and indulged her husband with spoonfuls of tactful acquiescence, just like my surely boring mother? Why would anyone put up with Mr. Ramsay, that Tennyson-quoting tyrant, eccentric disappointed genius though he might be? Someone had blundered, he shouts, but this did not cut any ice with me. And what about Lily Briscoe, who wanted to be an artist and made much of this desire, but who didn't seem to be able to paint very well, or not to her own satisfaction? In Woolfland, things were so tenuous. They were so elusive. They were so inconclusive. They were so deeply unfathomable. They were like the line written by a wispy poet in a Katherine Mansfield short story: "Why must it always be tomato soup?"

At nineteen, I'd never known anyone who had died, with the exception of my grandfather, who'd been old and far away. I'd never been to a funeral. I understood nothing of that kind of loss—of the crumbling of the physical texture of lives lived, the way the meaning of a place could change because those who used to be in it were no longer there. I knew nothing about the hopelessness and the necessity of trying to capture such lives— to rescue them, to keep them from vanishing altogether.

Although I'd been guilty of many artistic failures, such was my callowness that I did not yet recognize them as such. Lily Briscoe suffers the aggression of an insecure man who keeps telling her that women can't paint and women can't write, but I didn't see why she should be so upset about it: the guy was obviously a drip, so who cared what he thought? Anyway, no one had ever said that sort of thing to me, not yet. (Little did I know they would soon begin.) I didn't realize what weight such pronouncements could have, even when uttered by fools, because of the many centuries of heavily respectable authority that lay behind them.

This past summer, forty-three years later, I read *To the Lighthouse* again. No particular reason: I was in that very Canadian space, "the cottage," and so was the book, and I'd read all the murder mysteries. So I thought I'd try again.

How was it that, this time, everything in the book fell so completely into place? How could I have missed it—above all, the patterns, the artistry—the first time through? How could I have missed the resonance of Mr. Ramsay's Tennyson quotation, coming as it does like a prophecy of the First World War? How could I not have grasped that the person painting and the one writing were in effect the same? ("Women can't write, women can't paint.") And the way time passes over everything like a cloud, and solid objects flicker and dissolve? And the way Lily's picture of Mrs. Ramsay—incomplete, insufficient, doomed to be stuck in an attic—becomes, as she adds the one line that ties it all together at the end, the book we've just read?

Some books have to wait until you're ready for them. So much, in reading, is a matter of luck. And what luck I'd just had! (Or so I muttered to myself, putting on my floppy old hat, going out to fool around in my unfathomable garden.)

35

Review:

The Birthday of the World and Other Stories
by Ursula K. Le Guin

*T*he *Birthday of the World* is Ursula K. Le Guin's tenth collection of stories. In it she demonstrates once again why she is the reigning queen of . . . but immediately we come to a difficulty, for what is the fitting name of her kingdom? Or, in view of her abiding concern with the ambiguities of gender, her queendom, or perhaps—considering how she likes to mix and match—her quinkdom? Or may she more properly be said to have not one such realm, but two?

"Science fiction" is the box in which her work is usually placed, but it's an awkward box: it bulges with discards from elsewhere. Into it have been crammed all those stories that don't fit comfortably into the family room of the socially realistic novel or the more formal parlor of historical fiction, or other compartmentalized genres: Westerns, gothics, horrors, gothic romances, and the novels of war, crime, and spies. Its subdivisions include science fiction proper (gizmo-riddled and theory-based space travel, time travel, or cybertravel to other worlds, with aliens frequent); science-fiction fantasy (dragons are common; the gizmos are less plausible, and may include wands); and speculative fiction (human society and its possible future forms, which are either much better than what we have now, or much worse). However, the membranes separating these subdivisions are permeable, and osmotic flow from one to another is the norm.

The lineage of "science fiction," broadly considered, is very long, and some of its literary ancestors are of the utmost respectability. Alberto Manguel has cataloged many in *The Dictionary of Imaginary Places*. Plato's account of Atlantis is among them, and Sir Thomas More's *Utopia* and Jonathan Swift's *Gulliver's Travels*. Accounts of voyages to unknown realms with bizarre inhabitants are as old as Herodotus in his wilder moments, as old as *The Thousand and One Nights*, as old as Thomas the Rhymer. Folk tales, the Norse sagas, and the adventure-romances of chivalry are not-so-distant cousins of such tales, and have been drawn on by hundreds of imitators of *The Lord of the Rings* and/or *Conan the Conqueror*—works that previously fetched their water from the same wells, as did their precursors, George MacDonald and the H. Rider Haggard of *She*.

Jules Verne is probably the best known of the early gizmo-fictionalists, but Mary Shelley's *Frankenstein* could be thought of as the first "science fiction"— that is, the first fiction that had real science in it—inspired as it was by experiments with electricity, in particular the galvanizing of corpses. Some of her preoccupations have stayed with the genre (or genres) ever since: most specifically, what is the price that must be paid by Promethean Man for stealing fire from Heaven? Indeed, some commentators have proposed "science fiction" as the last fictional repository for theological speculation. Heaven, Hell, and aerial transport by means of wings having been more or less abandoned after Milton, outer space was the only remaining neighborhood where beings resembling gods, angels, and demons might still be found. J. R. R. Tolkien's friend and fellow fantasist C. S. Lewis even went so far as to compose a "science fiction" trilogy—very light on science but heavy on theology, the "space ship" being a coffin filled with roses, and the temptation of Eve being reenacted on the planet Venus, complete with luscious fruit.

Rearranged human societies have been a constant in the tradition as well, and they have been used both to criticize our present state of affairs and to suggest more pleasant alternatives. Swift depicted an ideal civilization, although—how English!—it was populated by horses. The nineteenth century, cheered on by its successes with sewage systems and prison reform, produced a number of earnestly hopeful speculative fictions. William Morris's *News from Nowhere* and Edward Bellamy's *Looking*

Backward are foremost among them, but this approach became such a vogue that it was satirized, not only by Gilbert and Sullivan's operetta *Utopia Limited* but also by Samuel Butler's *Erewhon*, where illness is a crime and crime is an illness.

However, as the optimism of the nineteenth century gave way to the Procrustean social dislocations of the twentieth—most notably in the former Soviet Union and the former Third Reich—literary utopias, whether serious or sardonic, were displaced by darker versions of themselves. H. G. Wells's *The Time Machine, The War of the Worlds,* and *The Island of Dr. Moreau* prefigure what was shortly to follow. *Brave New World* and *1984* are of course the best known of these many prescient badlands, with Karel Capek's *R.U.R.* and the nightmarish fables of John Wyndham running close behind.

It's too bad that one term—"science fiction"—has served for so many variants, and too bad also that this term has acquired a dubious if not downright sluttish reputation. True, the proliferation of sci-fi in the twenties and thirties gave rise to a great many bug-eyed-monster-bestrewn space operas that were published in pulp magazines and followed by films and television shows that drew heavily on this odoriferous cache. (Who could ever forget *The Creeping Eye, The Head That Wouldn't Die,* or *The Attack of the Fifty-Foot Woman*? A better question: Why can't we forget them?)

In brilliant hands, however, the form can be brilliant, as witness the virtuoso use of sci-trash material in Kurt Vonnegut's *Slaughterhouse-Five,* or Russell Hoban's linguistically inventive *Riddley Walker,* or Ray Bradbury's *Fahrenheit 451* and *The Martian Chronicles.* (Jorge Luis Borges was a fan of this last book, which is no surprise.) Sci-fi is sometimes just an excuse for dressed-up swashbuckling and kinky sex, but it can also provide a kit for examining the paradoxes and torments of what was once fondly referred to as the human condition: What is our true nature, where did we come from, where are we going, what are we doing to ourselves, of what extremes might we be capable? Within the frequently messy sandbox of sci-fi fantasy, some of the most accomplished and suggestive intellectual play of the past century has taken place.

Which brings us to Ursula K. Le Guin. No question about her literary quality: her graceful prose, carefully thought-through premises, psychological insight, and intelligent perception have earned her the National Book Award, the Kafka Award, five Hugos, five Nebulas, a Newbery, a Jupiter, a Gandalf, and an armful of other awards, great and small. Her first two books, *Planet of Exile* and *Rocannon's World*, were published in 1966, and since then she has published sixteen novels as well as ten collections of stories.

Collectively, these books have created two major parallel universes: the universe of the Ekumen, which is sci-fi proper—space ships, travel among worlds, and so forth—and the world of Earthsea. The latter must be called "fantasy," I suppose, since it contains dragons and witches and even a school for wizards, though this institution is a long way from the Hogwarts of Harry Potter. The Ekumen series may be said—very broadly—to concern itself with the nature of human nature: How far can we stretch and still remain human? What is essential to our being, what is contingent? The Earthsea series is occupied—again, very broadly speaking—with the nature of reality and the necessity of mortality, and also with language in relation to its matrix. (That's heavy weather to make of a series that has been promoted as suitable for age twelve, but perhaps the fault lies in the marketing directors. Like *Alice's Adventures in Wonderland*, these tales speak to readers on many levels.)

Le Guin's preoccupations are not divided into two strictly separate packages, of course: both of her worlds are scrupulously attentive to the uses and misuses of language; both have their characters fret over social gaffes and get snarled up in foreign customs; both worry about death. But in the Ekumen universe, although there is much strangeness, there is no magic apart from the magic inherent in creation itself.

The astonishing thing about Le Guin as a writer is that she managed to create these two realms, not only in parallel but also at the same time. The first Earthsea book, *A Wizard of Earthsea*, appeared in 1968, and *The Left Hand of Darkness*, the famous classic from the Ekumen series, in 1969. Either one would have been sufficient to establish Le Guin's reputation as a mistress of its genre; both together make one suspect that the writer has the benefit of arcane drugs or creative double-jointedness or ambidexterity.

Not for nothing did Le Guin invoke handedness in her fourth title: as soon as we start talking about the *left* hand, all sorts of Biblical connotations gather. (Although the left hand is the sinister one, God, too, has a left hand, so left hands can't be all bad. Should your right hand know what your left hand is doing, and if not, why not? And so forth.) As Walter Benjamin once said, the decisive blows are struck left-handed.

Ursula K. Le Guin has continued to explore and describe and dramatize both of her major fictional realms over the thirty-six years that have passed since her first novel was published. But since the stories in *The Birthday of the World* are Ekumen stories—with two exceptions—it's as well to concentrate on the science-fiction world rather than on the fantasy one. The general premises of the Ekumen series are as follows. There are many habitable planets in the universe. Long, long ago they were "seeded" by a people called the Hainish, space travelers from an Earth-like planet, after which time passed, disruptions occurred, and each society was left alone to develop along different lines.

Now, a benevolent federation called the Ekumen having been established, explorers are being sent out to see what has become of these far-flung but still hominid or perhaps even human societies. Conquest is not the aim, nor is missionary work: noninvasive, nondirective understanding and recording are the functions required of such explorers or ambassadors, who are known as Mobiles. Various gizmos are provided to allow them to function amid the alien corn, and they are provided with a handy widget called the "ansible," a piece of technology we should all have because it allows for instantaneous transmission of information, thus canceling out the delaying effects of the fourth dimension. Also, it never seems to crash like your Internet e-mail program. I'm all for it.

Here it is necessary to mention that Le Guin's mother was a writer, her husband is a historian, and her father was an anthropologist; thus she has been surrounded all her life by people whose interests have dovetailed with her own. The writing connection, through her mother, is obvious. Her husband's historical knowledge must have come in very handy: there's more than an echo in her work of the kinds of usually unpleasant events that change what we call "history." But her father's discipline, anthropology, deserves special mention.

If the "fantasy" end of science fiction owes a large debt to folk tale and myth and saga, the "science fiction" end owes an equally large debt to the development of archaeology and anthropology as serious disciplines, as distinct from the tomb-looting and exploration-for-exploitation that preceded them and continued alongside them. Layard's discovery of Nineveh in the 1840s had the effect of a can opener on Victorian thinking about the past; Troy and Pompeii and ancient Egypt were similarly mesmerizing. Through new discoveries and fresh excavations, European concepts of past civilizations were rearranged, imaginative doors were opened, wardrobe choices were expanded. If things were once otherwise, perhaps they could be otherwise again, especially where clothing and sex were concerned—two matters that particularly fascinated Victorian and early-twentieth-century imaginative writers, who longed for less of the former and more of the latter.

Anthropology arrived a little later. Cultures were discovered in remote places that were very different from the modern West, and rather than being wiped out or subjugated, they were taken seriously and studied. How are these people like us? How are they different? Is it possible to understand them? What are their foundation myths, their beliefs about an afterlife? How do they arrange their marriages, how do their kinship systems work? What are their foods? How about their (a) clothing and (b) sex? Which were usually discovered—through the work of various perhaps overeager inquirers such as Margaret Mead—to be (a) scantier and (b) more satisfactory than ours.

Anthropologists do—or are supposed to do—more or less what the Mobiles in Le Guin's Ekumen construction are supposed to do: they go to distant shores, they look, they explore foreign societies and try to figure them out. Then they record, and then they transmit. Le Guin knows the tricks of the trade, and also the pitfalls: her Mobiles are mistrusted and misled while they are in the field, just as real anthropologists have been. They're used as political pawns, they're scorned as outsiders, they're feared because they have unknown powers. But they are also dedicated professionals and trained observers, and human beings with personal lives of their own. This is what makes them and the stories they tell believable, and Le Guin's handling of them engaging as writing in its own right.

It's informative to compare two of Le Guin's introductions: the one she wrote for *The Left Hand of Darkness* in 1976, seven years after the book was first published, and the foreword she's now written for *The Birthday of the World*. *The Left Hand of Darkness* takes place on the planet of Gethen, or Winter, where the inhabitants are neither men nor women nor hermaphrodites. Instead they have phases: a nonsexual phase is followed by a sexual phase, and during the latter each person changes into whichever gender is suitable for the occasion. Thus anyone at all may be, over a lifetime, both mother and father, both penetrator and penetratee. As the story opens, the "king" is both mad and pregnant, and the non-Gethenian observer from the Ekumen is nothing if not confused.

This novel appeared at the beginning of the hottest period of 1970s feminism, when emotions were running very high on subjects having to do with genders and their roles. Le Guin was accused of wanting everyone to be an androgyne and of predicting that in the future they would be; conversely, of being antifeminist because she'd used the pronoun "he" to denote persons not in "kemmer"—the sexual phase.

Her introduction to *The Left Hand of Darkness* is therefore somewhat brisk. Science fiction should not be merely extrapolative, she says; it should not take a present trend and project it into the future, thus arriving via logic at a prophetic truth. Science fiction cannot predict, nor can any fiction, the variables being too many. Her own book is a "thought-experiment," like *Frankenstein*. It begins with "Let's say," follows that with a premise, and then watches to see what happens next. "In a story so conceived," she says, "the moral complexity proper to the modern novel need not be sacrificed . . . thought and intuition can move freely within bounds set only by the terms of the experiment, which may be very large indeed."

The purpose of a thought-experiment, she writes, is to "describe reality, the present world." "A novelist's business is lying"—lying interpreted in the novelist's usual way—that is, as a devious method of truth-telling. Consequently the androgyny described in her book is neither prediction nor prescription, just description: androgyny, metaphorically speaking, is a feature of all human beings. With those who don't understand that metaphor is metaphor and fiction is fiction, she is more than a little irritated. One suspects she's received a lot of extremely odd fan mail.

The foreword to *The Birthday of the World* is mellower. Twenty-six years later, the author has fought her battles and is an established feature of the sci-fi landscape. She can afford to be less didactic, more charmingly candid, a little scattier. The universe of the Ekumen now feels comfortable to her, like "an old shirt." No sense in expecting it to be consistent, though: "Its Time Line is like something a kitten pulled out of the knitting basket, and its history consists largely of gaps." In this foreword, Le Guin describes process rather than theory: the genesis of each story, the problems she had to think her way through. Typically, she doesn't concoct her worlds: she finds herself in them, and then begins to explore them, just like, well, an anthropologist. "First to create difference," she says, ". . . then to let the fiery arc of human emotion leap and close the gap: this acrobatics of the imagination fascinates and satisfies me as almost no other."

There are seven shorter stories in *The Birthday of the World*, and one that might qualify as a novella. Six of the first seven are Ekumen stories—they're part of the "old shirt." The seventh probably belongs there, though its author isn't sure. The eighth is set in a different universe altogether—the generic, shared, science-fiction "future." All but the eighth are largely concerned with—as Le Guin says—"peculiar arrangements of gender and sexuality."

All imagined worlds must make some provision for sex, with or without black leather and tentacles, and the peculiarity of the arrangements is an old motif in science fiction: one thinks not only of Charlotte Perkins Gilman's *Herland*, where the genders live separately, but also of W. H. Hudson's *A Crystal Age*, featuring an antlike neuter state, or John Wyndham's "Consider Her Ways," also based on a hymenoptera model, or Marge Piercey's *Woman on the Edge of Time*, which tries for absolute gender equality. (Men breast-feed: watch for this trend.) But Le Guin takes things much farther. In the first story, "Coming of Age in Karhide," we see Gethen/Winter not through the eyes of a Mobile but through those of a

Gethenian just coming into adolescence: Which gender will s/he turn into first? This story is not only erotic, but happy. Why not, in a world where sex is always either spectacular or of no concern whatsoever?

Things aren't so jolly in "The Matter of Seggri," where there's a gender imbalance: far more women than men. The women run everything, and marry each other as life partners. The rare boy children are spoiled by the women, but as men they must live a segregated life in castles, where they dress up, show off, stage public fights, and are rented out as studs. They don't have much fun. It's like being trapped in the World Wrestling Federation, forever.

"Unchosen Love" and "Mountain Ways" take place on a world called O, created by Le Guin in *A Fisherman of the Inland Sea*. On O, you must be married to three other people but can have sex with only two of them. The quartets must consist of a Morning man and a Morning woman— who can't have sex—and an Evening man and an Evening woman, who also can't have sex. But the Morning man is expected to have sex with the Evening woman and also the Evening man, and the Evening woman is expected to have sex with the Morning man and also the Morning woman. Putting these quartets together is one of the problems the characters face, and keeping them straight—who's for you, who's taboo—is a problem for both reader and writer. Le Guin had to draw charts. As she says, "I like thinking about complex social relationships which produce and frustrate highly charged emotional relationships."

"Solitude" is a meditative story about a world in which conviviality is deeply distrusted. Women live alone in their own houses in an "auntring" or village, where they make baskets and do gardening, and practice the nonverbal art of "being aware." Only the children go from house to house, learning lore. When girls come of age they form part of an auntring, but boys must go off to join adolescent packs and scratch a living in the wilderness. They fight it out, and those who survive become breeding males, living shyly in hermit huts, guarding the auntrings from a distance, and being visited by the women, who "scout" for purposes of mating. This setup, despite its spiritual satisfactions, would not suit everyone.

"Old Music and the Slave Women" comes very close to home, inspired as it was by a visit to a former plantation in the American South. On the planet of Werel, slavers and antislavers are at war, and sex among the slavers is a matter of raping the field hands. The chief character, an intelligence officer with the Ekumen embassy, gets into arguments over human rights and then bad trouble. Of all the stories, this one comes closest to substantiating Le Guin's claim that science fiction describes our own world. Werel could be any society torn by civil war: wherever it's happening, it's always brutal, and Le Guin, although at times a movingly lyrical writer, has never shied away from necessary gore.

The title story is constructed on an Inca base, with a splash of ancient Egypt. A man and a woman together form God. Both positions are hereditary and created by brother-sister marriage; the duties of God include divination by dancing, which causes the world to be born anew each year. Governance is carried out by God's messengers, or "angels." What happens when a foreign but powerful presence enters this highly structured world and the belief system that sustains it crumbles? You can imagine, or you can read *The Conquest of Peru*. Nevertheless, this delicate story is strangely courageous, strangely hopeful: the world ends, but then, too, it is always beginning.

The last story, "Paradises Lost," continues the note of renewal. Many generations have been born and have died on board a long-distance space ship. During the voyage a new religion has sprung up, whose adherents believe they are actually, now, in Heaven. (If so, Heaven is just as boring as some have always feared.) Then the ship reaches the destination proposed for it centuries earlier, and its inhabitants must decide whether to remain in "Heaven" or to descend to a "dirtball" whose flora, fauna, and microbes are completely alien to them. The most enjoyable part of this story, for me, was the release from claustrophobia: try as I might, I couldn't imagine why anyone would prefer the ship.

Le Guin is on the side of the dirtball, too; and, by extension, of our very own dirtball. Whatever else she may do—wherever her curious intelligence may take her, whatever twists and knots of motive and plot and genitalia she may invent—she never loses touch with her reverence for the immense *what is*. All her stories are, as she has said, metaphors for the one human story; all her fantastic planets are this one, however disguised. "Paradises Lost" shows us our own natural world as a freshly discovered Paradise Regained, a realm of wonder; and in this, Le Guin is a quintessentially American writer, of the sort for whom the quest for the Peaceable Kingdom is ongoing. Perhaps, as Jesus hinted, the kingdom of God is within; or perhaps, as William Blake glossed, it is within a wildflower, seen aright.

The story—and the book—end with a minimalist dance, as an old woman and a crippled old man celebrate—indeed, worship—the ordinary dirt that sustains them after they have left the ship. "Swaying, she lifted her bare feet from the dirt and set them down again while he stood still, holding her hands. They danced together that way."

36

Introduction:

Ground Works,
Christian Bök, editor

G   *round Works* is an anthology of experimental fiction by writers
who emerged on the wilder shores of literature in Canada
almost forty years ago.

I admit to being the instigator of this book. I agitated for it because a
body of work that deserved to be recalled and set within its original frame
was slipping from view, leaving the young with the impression that there
was nothing unorthodox in this country before folks started getting their
tongues pierced. But I did not want to trust my own now somewhat
arthritic judgment, so Christian Bök, a young experimental writer of the
twenty-first century, was asked to do the selecting and arranging, and is
thus the book's primary editor. The result is a sort of Ogopogo Creature:
you've heard the rumors about an invisible, impossible weirdness, now
here's the blurry snapshot. See? There was something down there all along!

The term "experimental fiction" covers a lot of territory. It also makes
me a little nervous, as I grew up with scientists and know their single-
minded ways, and the term itself is a tribute to the early twentieth century's
reverence for that particular branch of human knowledge. The reverence
may have faded somewhat, but the term remains, leaving behind a faint
whiff of formaldehyde and Dr. Frankenstein: the dissection of language
and narrative, and their reassembly into talking monsters, can strike us as
cold-blooded. Dr. Frankenstein himself was not cold-blooded, however; he
was a disrupter of social norms, a breaker of laws, a subversive idealist, a

feverish believer in the new and the potential; and so it is with many "experimental" writers.

In what ways can fiction be "experimental"? On the one hand, all fiction is experimental, in that it ventures into the unknown and attempts to prove a hypothesis. Thus:

Hypothesis: (a) That this piece of fiction can actually be written by the author attempting it, and (b) that it can thereafter hold a reader's attention.

Demonstration: The piece of fiction.

Conclusion: Someone actually reads the book all the way through, without throwing it against the wall.

But that's too broad. What we usually mean by "experimental fiction" is fiction that sets up certain rules for itself—rules that are not the same as those followed by the mainstream fiction of its day—and then proceeds to obey its own new commandments, while subverting the conventions according to which readers have understood what constitutes a proper work of literature. There's a faint air of peeking beneath the skirts, of snooping behind the rhetorical scenes. Pieces like these can border on the parody or the extended joke—Woody Allen's story about the machine that allows real people to get into well-known books as characters, Pozzo's send-up rendition of a sunset description in *Waiting for Godot*, Michael Ondaatje's use of pulp romance conventions to syncopate his Billy the Kid saga—which does not exclude the possibility of their being at the same time deeply unsettling. Accepted narrative lines are turned upside down, language is stretched and pulled inside out, characters don't remain "within character." Thus the writers in this anthology—at least in the works represented here—were more interested in coloring outside the lines than within them, and some even had it in mind to toss the entire coloring book into the fire and start with a whole new sheet of paper.

What was it that made the Canada of the 1960s such fertile ground for this kind of writing? Partly it was a stranger place in many ways than is often supposed—who remembers the LSD that flowed so freely in London, Ontario, in the 1950s—well before the age of Timothy Leary—not to mention the orgies in the cathedral? It was strange in a literary way as well. What other country would have produced a set of Spenserian eclogues spoken in a farmyard by a flock of geese? (*A Suit of Nettles*, James Reaney, 1958.) Partly, also, it was an open field—some might say a vacant lot. Many of the conditions taken for granted today—that there is a Canadian "canon"; that a Canadian writer can be widely known, respected, and solvent; that you can get a grant or a film contract or teach creative writing or win big prizes; that there are such things as book-promotion tours and literary festivals; that it is possible to live in Canada and function as a professional writer with a national—indeed an international—"career"—these conditions scarcely existed in the writing world of the 1950s and 1960s, when the writers collected here had their toes on the starting line. Nature abhors a vacuum, and so does literature. There is nothing more conducive to scribbling than a blank page.

There had been well-known Canadian fiction writers earlier—L. M. Montgomery of *Anne of Green Gables* fame, for instance, or Mazo De La Roche of the Jalna books, or, on higher literary ground, Morley Callaghan—but as a rule these had entered the scene through non-Canadian publishers, and were then distributed in Canada through agents or branch plants. There was, too, a Canadian-owned publishing industry, which even had a cheap-hardback, mass-distribution side to it, but the Depression, the Second World War, and the advent of the United States–controlled paperback industry had kicked large holes in that. After the war, the old order changed: the British Empire as a political force was all but defunct, and any writer associated with it was passé; the new wave of money coming into Canada was American, as was the new wave of widely read writers. This was—with a few exceptions—largely a one-way street.

Morley Callaghan had taken it for granted that a young writer would cut his teeth in the U.S. magazine market and would go on to be published in New York—the route he himself had taken—but this was an increasingly unlikely scenario. Young Canadian "experimental" writers felt cut off—too "Canadian," whatever that meant, to be published internationally, and too radical in their approach to their writing to be published readily in the five or so established but beleaguered Canadian English-language houses functioning at that time. These houses estimated—rightly enough—that in such newly postcolonial times, when the "real" cultural places were thought to be elsewhere, the audience for Canadian writing wasn't large enough to justify their investing in a novel unless a foreign publishing partner could be obtained. But, Canada being viewed in "the States" as the place where the snow came from, and "Canadian writer" being considered an oxymoron by London cultural commentators, foreign partners willing to take the chance were few.

If you were a frustrated young writer who despaired of making a place for yourself in Canada, you could always move, of course; you could live elsewhere and begin publishing there, and that's what some novelists did. Or if you were a poet, you could crank out your own work and that of your friends on small presses and stick it into mimeo magazines, such as *Tish* and *The Sheet*, or even into more beautifully designed productions such as *Emblem Books* and *Alphabet*; there was already a tradition of this sort of publishing in Canada. You could "publish" over the airwaves, on Robert Weaver's show *Anthology*—about the only venue that would pay you actual money. You could—from 1960 or so on—read your poetry out loud, in a few dark, smoky coffeehouses that held reading series; and there you might meet international—usually American—poets who were blowing through town.

Or you could, alone or together with other writers, scrape together a few dollars and start a new small publishing house. And this is what indeed happened, in more or less that order. Contact Press, Coach House Press, House of Anansi Press, Talonbooks, BlewOintment Press, Sono Nis, and Quarry Press were among the many such enterprises that began in this way at that time. Many but not all of the writers sampled here were also poets, and many of the presses that first published them began with poetry, in the early to mid-'60s. The overlaps—poets publishing poets in presses devoted to poetry—were considerable. Michael Ondaatje was for years a member of the Coach House collective; I myself worked as an editor with House of Anansi Press. Andreas Schroeder worked with Sono Nis, George Bowering was associated with *Tish*; and these are just a few examples.

This scene was not idyllic. In my own experience, small-press publishing was a hotbed of jealousy and intrigue and puddles of blood on the floor, second only to Rome under Caligula. Coach House Press got around this in the early days by consuming large amounts of mellowing substances —"Printed in Canada by mindless acid freaks" read their logo, right alongside "Copyright is obsolete"—but at House of Anansi it was not so much drugs as drinking, and no one got out of it without a knife between the shoulder blades. No one but a lunatic, or someone brainwashed by the Girl Guides into thinking she had to do Good Deeds for Others, would have stayed in this situation for long. Which was I? A little of both. But that's another story.

The writers in *Ground Works*, as a group, were born in the 1930s or the 1940s. They were not baby boomers; they preceded that wave. As children they were close to Depression times, and also to war times, when Canada had in fact cut a bit of a dash. They came of intellectual age at the zenith of the postwar French intellectuals; they read the great modernists as a matter of course. Existentialism was the philosophical catchword then; Brecht and Sartre and the Theater of the Absurd were frequently performed on campuses; "experiment" was in the air. This period followed the McCarthy years, transited the Age of the Beatniks, and led into days of the civil rights movement and then into the era of the Vietnam War. It was a time of ferment and change, and out of that cauldron came—at about this time—the idea of cultural nationalism. This was a modest enough thing in Canada, consisting as it did mainly in a proclamation of one's own existence, but it caused a good deal of uproar nonetheless. (Canada was then, and still is, one of those odd places where large doses of patriotism are considered unpatriotic, and where the powers that be are of the firm belief that a rocked boat always sinks.)

This was also, in writing, perhaps the most thoroughly male-dominated period of the past hundred years. Internationally, the great female modernists belonged to the first third of the twentieth century. (Of the Canadians, Elizabeth Smart was then unknown; Mavis Gallant, if noticed at all, was believed to be an American; and Sheila Watson had composed *The Double Hook* some time before its ultimate publication in 1961, when it appeared just in time to perk a lot of us up.) The hot new writers making their debuts in the late '40s and the '50s and the early '60s were almost all men. Many reasons could be given for this state of affairs, but suffice it to say that such was the reality, and it—as well as the observable fact that men have historically been more interested in literature as a game than women have been—accounts for the scarcity of female writers in this collection. More women writers of all kinds would appear in Canada shortly. Margaret Laurence would come to prominence, Alice Munro and Marian Engel would publish at the tail end of the 1960s, and many more would follow, some of whom wrote "experimental" fiction and are included in this book. But writing in the 1960s was pretty much a guy thing, in Canada as elsewhere, in experimental literature as well as in the "mainstream."

It was also an urban thing. The small town, the wilderness, the Native motifs, and the pioneering past of earlier Canadian writing had been tossed out along with the Empire. They'd be back, but they hadn't come back yet.

I've made the literary climate back then sound like inclement weather, and it was. There wasn't much infrastructure or public recognition—writers, when thought about at all, were pictured as bearded maniacs inhabiting some insalubrious bohemia or drafty ivory tower; or, if female, especially if female poets, as half-baked women, the baked half being the head in the oven, for after the recent, spectacular exit of Sylvia Plath, suicide for such was almost de rigueur. Unless you cracked New York—a snowball's chance in Hell—there were scant prospects of being rich and famous. But on the other hand it was an era of tremendous freedom. You didn't have to worry about market forces, because there was hardly any market as such: the numbers for even a Canadian "best seller" were tiny by today's standards. You could travel strange roads, because there were no highways. You didn't feel weighted down by your country's cultural baggage, because—officially, at any rate—there wasn't much of it. You could get lost in the language, because the signposts were few. You could take your influences from wherever you liked, because who was looking?

It was a verbal free-for-all: a rambunctious eclecticism prevailed. There was—strangely enough—a spirit of enormous optimism: not much was actual, therefore everything was potential. All was poised on the verge, about to happen. We felt, for a while, as if we really could stop being who we were often told we were—small, boring, hopelessly provincial—and, like the albatross, go straight from fledgling status to full, soaring flight.

Ground Works allows us to look back on those simmering years.

(After that, of course, everything changed. As is its habit.)

37

Introduction:

Doctor Glas
by Hjalmar Söderberg

Now I sit at my open window, writing—for whom? Not for any friend or mistress. Scarcely for myself even. I do not read today what I wrote yesterday; nor shall I read this tomorrow. I write simply so my hand can move, my thoughts move of their own accord. I write to kill a sleepless hour. Why can't I sleep? After all, I've committed no crime.

Doctor Glas was first published in Sweden in 1905, when it caused a scandal, largely because of its handling of those two perennially scandalous items, sex and death. I first read it in the form of a tattered paperback sent to me by Swedish friends—a reissue of a 1963 translation, published to coincide with the film based on it. On the back of my copy are various well-deserved encomiums from newspaper reviews: "a masterpiece," "the most remarkable book of the year," "a book of rare quality developed with true skill." Nevertheless, *Doctor Glas* has long been out of print in this English version. It's a pleasure to welcome it back.

The uproar around *Doctor Glas* stemmed from the perception that it was advocating abortion and euthanasia, and was perhaps even rationalizing murder. Its protagonist is a doctor, and he has some strong things to say about the hypocrisy of his own society concerning these matters. But Hjalmar Söderberg, its author—already a successful novelist, playwright, and short-story writer—may have been somewhat taken aback by this, because *Doctor Glas* is not a polemic, nor a work of advocacy. Instead it is an elegant, vigorous, and tightly knit psychological study of a complex individual who finds himself at a dangerous but compelling open doorway and can't decide whether to go through it, or why he should.

The novel's protagonist, Doctor Tyko Gabriel Glas, is a thirtyish medical man whose journal we read over his shoulder as he composes it. His voice is immediately convincing: intelligent, wistful, opinionated, dissatisfied, by turns rational and irrational, and unnervingly modern. We follow him through his memories, his desires, his opinions of the mores of his social world, his lyrical praises or splenetic denunciations of the weather, his prevarications, his self-denunciations, his boredom, and his yearning. Glas is a romantic idealist turned solitary and sad, and afflicted with fin-de-siècle malaise—a compound of fastidious aestheticism, longing for the unobtainable, skepticism concerning the established systems of morality, and disgust with the actual. He would like only beautiful things to exist, but has the sordid forced on him by the nature of his profession. As he himself says, he's the last person on earth who should have been a doctor: it brings him into too much contact with the more unpleasant aspects of human carnality.

What he wants above all is action, a feat to perform that might fit the hero he hopes he may carry around inside him. In romances, such deeds often involve a knight, a troll, and a captive maiden who must be rescued, and this is the sort of situation that Fate serves up to Doctor Glas. The troll is a flesh-creepingly loathsome and morally repulsive pastor called Gregorius, whom Glas hates even before he finds he has good reason for his hatred. The maiden in captivity is Gregorius's young and beautiful wife, Helga, who confides to Doctor Glas that she has married Gregorius out of mistaken religious notions, and can no longer stand his sexual attentions. Divorce is impossible: a "respectable" clergyman convinced of his own righteousness, as the Reverend Gregorius is, would never consent to it. Mrs. Gregorius will be enslaved to this toadstool-faced goblin forever unless Doctor Glas will help her.

Doctor Glas has now been given a chance to prove himself. But will he discover that he is a brave knight, an ordinarily timorous nobody, or just as much of a troll as Gregorius, only a murderous one? He contains within himself the possibilities of all three. His name, too, is threefold. *Tyko* refers to the great Danish astronomer Tycho Brahe, who kept his eyes on the stars, far away from the earthiness of Earth—as Doctor Glas so often does throughout the novel. *Gabriel* is the name of the Angel of the Annunciation, proclaimer of the Holy Birth, who is also credited with being the Destroying Angel, sent to wipe out Sodom and Sennacharib, and thought to be the angel of the Last Judgment as well. Thus it's a good name for a medical practitioner who holds the keys to life and death, but it's also a good name for Doctor Glas, who must decide whether to take judgment into his own hands.

And *Glas* is glass: like the diary form itself, it's a reflecting surface, a mirror in which one sees oneself. It's hard and impermeable, but easily shattered; and, from certain angles, it's transparent. This last quality is one of Glas's complaints: he can only fall in love with women who are in love with someone else, because their love makes them radiant; but their love for other men means that Glas himself is invisible to them. So it is with Mrs. Gregorius: she is having an adulterous affair with another man and can't "see" Doctor Glas. She can only see through him, making of him a means to the end she longs for. As for Doctor Glas's nemesis, it's worth noting that although "Gregorius" is the name of a saint and of a couple of popes, it's also the name of a certain kind of telescope. Like Glas, Gregorius is glassy; he wears glasses, and looking into them, Glas sees the reflection of his own bespectacled self. Perhaps he hates Gregorius so much because the man unconsciously reminds Glas of the father who used to punish him, and whose physicality repelled him as a young boy; or perhaps it's because Gregorius is his ogreish double, the sly, whining, selfish, and self-justifying personification of the lust he can't permit himself to act out.

At first glance the structure of *Doctor Glas* is disarmingly casual, almost random. The device of the diary allows us to follow events as they unfold, but allows us also to listen in on Glas's reactions to them. The workings of the novel are so subtle that the reader doesn't notice at first that it has any: so immediate, even blunt, is the voice that we appear to be reading the uncensored thoughts of a real person. Glas promises candor: he won't set down everything, he says, but he will record nothing that isn't true. "Anyway," he adds, "I can't exorcise my soul's wretchedness—if it is wretched—by telling lies." Chance encounters and trivial conversations alternate with fits of midnight scribbling; jokes and pleasant, convivial meals are followed by hours of anguish; night and dreamtime counterpoint the world of purposeful daylight. Unanswered questions punctuate the text—"By the way, why do the clergy always go into church by a back door?"—as do odd moments of hilarity verging on the burlesque, as when Gregorius considers administering the communion wine in the form of pills, to avoid germs. (The pill idea soon recurs in a much more evil form.)

Söderberg had read his Dostoevsky: he, too, is interested in the disgruntlements of underground men, and in charting impulse and rationalization and motive, and in the fine line that runs between the violent thought and the criminal act. He'd read his ghost-ridden Ibsen and that master of bizarre obsession, Poe. He'd also read his Freud, and he knows how to make use of the semiconscious motif, the groundswells of the unspoken. There are two hints in the text that point us toward the book's methods: Glas's meditation on the nature of the artist, who to him is not an originator but an aeolean harp who makes music only because the winds of his own time play over him—thus the discursiveness; and his invocation of Wagner, who used the leitmotif to connect large swathes of disparate music into a unified whole. A tracing of all the red roses—from dead mother to out-of-reach beloved to rejected potential sweetheart—reveals some of these interconnections, as does a survey of all the astronomical images, from moon to stars to sun to the sunny, starry-eyed Mrs. Gregorius. "Truth is like the sun," says Glas's friend Markel, "its value wholly depends upon our being at a correct distance away from it." And so it would be, we suspect, with Mrs. Gregorius: she can be valuable for Glas as an ideal only as long as she is kept at a correct distance.

Doctor Glas is deeply unsettling, in the way certain dreams are—or, no coincidence, certain films by Bergman, who must have read it. The eerie blue northern nights of midsummer combined with an unexplained anxiety, the nameless Kirkegaardean dread that strikes Glas at the most ordinary of moments, the juxtaposition of pale spirituality with an almost comic vulgar sensuality—these are from the same cultural context. The novel launches itself from the ground of naturalism set in place by French writers of the nineteenth century, but goes beyond it. Some of Söderberg's techniques—the mix of styles, the collagelike snippets—anticipate, for instance, *Ulysses*. Some of his images anticipate the Surrealists: the disturbing dreams with their ambiguous female figures, the sinister use of flowers, the glasses with no eyes behind them, the handless watchcase in which Doctor Glas carries around his little cyanide pills. A few decades earlier and this novel would never have been published; a few years later and it would have been dubbed a forerunner of the stream-of-consciousness technique.

Doctor Glas is one of those marvelous books that appears as fresh and vivid now as on the day it was published. As the English writer William Sansom has said, "in most of its writing and much of the frankness of its thought, it might have been written tomorrow." It occurs on the cusp of the nineteenth and the twentieth centuries, but it opens doors the novel has been opening ever since.

38

Introduction:

High Latitudes
by Farley Mowat

T hink back to 1952. The American South was still segregated, World War II had been over for a mere seven years, McCarthyism was at full boil, women professors were scarce as clowns at a funeral, and there was not yet any rock 'n' roll. That was the year Farley Mowat published his first book, *People of the Deer*, an account of the hard times and injustices suffered by those who lived on the "barren lands" of the Canadian North, and who depended on the caribou for their existence. *People of the Deer* was highly successful as a book, but in addition it turned Mowat into an instant and controversial celebrity.

It was also an X in the sand: it marked a crucial turning point in general Canadian awareness. Before it, the only "Eskimos" southern Canadians might recognize were on ice cream bars. Who knew or cared anything about that part of the North? After it, not only was consciousness expanded, conscience was—however sporadically—engaged. *People of the Deer* was to the support for increased autonomy among northern peoples as Rachel Carson's *Silent Spring* was to the environmental movement: a wake-up call, the spark that struck the tinder that ignited the fire from which many subsequent generations of writers and activists have lit their torches, often ignorant of where that spark came from in the first place.

Since 1952, Mowat has written more than thirty-eight books. Over the decades, he's been published in forty countries and translated into twenty-five languages, and has been counted among Canada's most widely read writers. Many of his books have reflected his passionate commitment to the ideal of a caring and attentive life within Nature, and his discouragement in the face of the ongoing slaughter and waste carried out by that dominant but often greedy and untidy primate, *Homo sapiens sapiens*. Many of these books, like *People of the Deer*, have marked Xs in the sand, and have struck their own igniting sparks: numerous writers on Nature, wolves, wilderness travel, and ecology have acknowledged their debts to Mowat.

His rage can be Swiftean, his humor Puckish, but his compassion for all creatures great and small has been consistent. He's been treated as a revered grandfather, a father against whom one must rebel, a sort of dotty uncle with bright but eccentric ideas who might possibly be making bombs in the garage, an icon to be scribbled on, and as a black-sheep juvenile-delinquent cousin, in trouble again and yet again, but the intensity of the reaction to him merely underlines the strong family connections people feel both with the man himself and with his writing. Love him or resent him, he's now an ancestral totem, whether he likes it or not. We might have picked someone less given to howling like a wolf at the dinner table or to doing strange dances in a kilt while making oinking noises, but Canadians have never been too stuck on the idea of inflated notions of stately dignity, so Farley Mowat is right up there on our totem pole. The fact that he's grinning like a goat should fool no one: he has always adopted a prankish public mask, behind which he could live his life as a deeply serious and intensely committed writer.

Now, in *High Latitudes: A Journey*, he chronicles the journey he took across northern Canada in 1966 by various means of transportation, all of them hazardous. In its origins and intentions, this was a salvation escapade—he hoped to write a book that would let northern people speak for themselves, and that would also give the lie to the current political idea that the North was "a bloody great wasteland" with no people in it, and therefore resource developers could go up there and hack apart and pollute whatever they wanted. That book was not the one that appeared back then, for the reasons Mowat describes. But here it is now, with the original conversations recorded by Farley Mowat during that epic journey.

High Latitudes gives us, with passion and insight, a vertical section of time past—the time that preceded our present. The choices that were made then affect our now, just as the choices we make now will determine the future. I'm sure Farley Mowat hopes that politicians today will be smarter than they were then, though he probably isn't betting on it.

It's both depressing and cheering to note the changes that have taken place since 1966. On the one hand, more damage and devastation, both natural and social, with global warming as a contributing factor. On the other hand, an increased optimism, at least among the people of self-governing Nunavut, recently created in the eastern Arctic. Inventiveness and creativity there have been given a big boost. But as Farley Mowat has always known, and as more and more people have come to agree, it's a race against time, and time—not just for the North, but for the planet as well—is running out.

39

Review:

Child of My Heart
by Alice McDermott

hild of My Heart is Alice McDermott's fifth work of fiction. The
fourth, *Charming Billy*, won the National Book Award, and was
a best seller, as was *At Weddings and Wakes*. Both of these novels
explore, subtly but ruthlessly, the same complex world—that of second-
and third-generation emigrant Irish, living angry, ruined, melancholy,
occasionally hopeful lives in and around Brooklyn and Queens, mainly in
the fifties and early sixties, with summer vacations spent on Long Island.
Both show the stories made from events as being coexistent with, different
from, and frequently more important than the events themselves.

Both books are expertly told from multiple points of view—*At Weddings and Wakes* mainly by children but with slices of adult perspective,
Charming Billy mainly by adults, with child's-eye vignettes. *Child of My
Heart* is different; it takes the world of *Billy* and *Weddings* and turns it
inside out. Long Island is not an idyllic interlude—the place where Billy
meets his false true love, the place where the kids can briefly escape the
carpings, weepings, and wranglings of their extended family. Instead it's
almost the entire setting. And *Child of My Heart* has a single narrator; so,
though it's if anything even more focused on stories, and why and how we
make them, and what we make out of them, these stories are all told to us
by a single person.

That person is Theresa, fifteen-year-old babysitter par excellence.
Here it should be mentioned that if your preferred reading is about

trench warfare and serial killers, this book is not for you. It is not a boys' book: there's a good deal too much diaper-changing and bottle-sucking in it for that. The characters are mostly children, and they behave a lot like real children—that is to say, often quite tediously. (Some readers may cherish the subversive hope, at least at moments, that Edward Gorey will turn up and hurl a few of the tinies off a plinth. To put it more kindly, this feeling may simply be a tribute to the author's art.)

One of the noteworthy features about boys' books is the absent center—a center we might call peacefulness, or the maternal principle, or home and hearth. The violent action of boys' books takes place at the periphery, where the male musk oxen stand guard, backs turned to the cows and calves who are nevertheless the point of the exercise. In *Moby-Dick*, the quintessential boys' book, there's a telling interlude (in chapter 87) during which the *Pequod* penetrates to the center of a large gathering of whales, where the mothers are nursing the babies, and where—despite the frenzied slaughter going on around the borders—the whales are mating. Ishmael comments,

> And thus, though surrounded by circle upon circle of consterna-
> tions and affrights, did these inscrutable creatures at the center
> freely and fearlessly indulge in all peaceful concernments; yea,
> serenely reveled in dalliance and delight. But even so, amid the tor-
> nadoed Atlantic of my being, do I myself still for ever centrally dis-
> port in mute calm; and while ponderous planets of unwaning
> revolve around me, deep down and deep inland there I still bathe
> me in eternal mildness of joy.

From the point of view of action and adventure and narrative drive, what happens at the still center is nothing much. From the point of view of the "mute calm" and the "eternal mildness of joy," what happens there is everything. *Child of My Heart* concerns itself with this nothing much, this everything—the almost timeless, action-free lagoon of the spirit, the territory of dalliance and delight—and also with its paradoxes, and also with how to make a story out of it.

Theresa is a storyteller herself, in more ways than one. She opens with an account of the truly outrageous whopper she concocted the previous winter with the collusion of her eight-year-old cousin Daisy, to fascinate and annoy Daisy's numerous siblings—a yarn about a lollipop tree that appears once a year, in honor of a dead little boy. (When Theresa actually creates this lollipop tree later in the book, it carries an ominous charge.) Viewed as unusually competent, well-mannered, and trustworthy by adults, Theresa serves notice on the reader that she is in fact none of these things. Instead she's a fantasist with more than a few secret plans.

Partly because of her ability to enter into their world, Theresa has a special knack with small children and animals. She flourishes during the golden age of babysitting—the fifties, when the baby boom was in full spate and infants were busting out all over, but the dependable, trained, live-in nannies of the twenties and thirties had disappeared; and, unlike the mother whales in *Moby-Dick*, the mothers in *Child of My Heart* have abdicated. At least ten years before the advent of the women's movement, they are in full flight—off to the city, up to no good, getting divorced. The fed-up slamming of their car doors and the wailing of their abandoned kids resounds throughout the book. An entire generation of pubescent and pre-pubescent girls was recruited to fill the gap, leaving many a toddler in the hands of girls only marginally capable of looking after them.

Theresa is made of solider stuff, however, at least in her own eyes, and she's certainly experienced, having begun to babysit at age ten. Her doting parents, viewing her as exceptionally beautiful, have moved to East Hampton, on Long Island, for the express purpose of casting their only child in the way of the rich and eligible Prince Charmings they believe inhabit the place; they push her toward the homes of the affluent, hoping for some matrimonial talent-spotting. Theresa's motives are different; she likes taking care of children because she can cast them in her own inner drama and dress them up for their parts. A lot of attention is thus paid to the weaving of floral garlands, the braiding of beribboned hairdos, and the putting on and taking off of outfits, as well as to hugging and stroking— dalliance and delight, nonsexual, but sensual nonetheless.

Theresa is aptly named. Her patron saint is Theresa of Lisieux, "The Little Flower," author of the *The Story of the Soul*, a book that recounts the coming to God through humble daily activities. (There are certainly a lot of those in this novel.) But there are two other saintly Theresas, each with symbolic possibilities. There's Mother Teresa—we learn on the first page, when our Theresa makes a nest for a clutch of expiring baby rabbits, that this girl is heavily into palliative care. And there's Teresa of Avila, she of the trances and barefoot nuns.

One of Teresa of Avila's major works is *The Castle of Imagination*, which could well act as a subtitle for this book; for imagination is not only Theresa's solace, it is also her weapon. There are no villains in *Child of My Heart*; instead there is mortality. *Et in Arcadia Ego* is a promising slogan for any novelist when things are looking a bit too tranquil, and Death is present even on Long Island, even in the golden summertime; for *Child of My Heart* is—on one level—a meditation on the massacre of the innocents. In the course of the book, Death does away with one cat (squashed by a car), one dog (shot for biting), three newborn rabbits ("Not meant to live"), and one child, also not meant to live. There are a couple of near misses: the five neighboring Moran kids, neglected by their slut of a mother and bursting with chaotic vitality, seem perpetually on the verge of doing one another in or killing themselves by accident; they usually appear dripping with blood, which Theresa mops up. She is young enough to believe that she can actually do something about mortality; she sets herself against it in every way she can. "It was the worst thing," thinks Theresa as she recalls the grisly skull of a recently mangled cat. "It was what I was up against."

The summer the grown-up narrator is describing is "the summer Daisy came." Girls named Daisy have a thin time of it in American literature, in memory perhaps of *Faust*'s Marguerite: James's Daisy Miller dies young of an excess of innocent romanticism; Fitzgerald's Daisy reaches for a star that turns to mud. McDermott links her Daisy to two lesser namesakes: Daisy Mae, the indigent, scantily clad, perennially disappointed ingenue of Al Capp's comic strip of the period, *L'il Abner*; and the sweet, bicycle-built-for-two Daisy of the song, who has answers true but isn't going to get much in the way of prosperity in exchange for them. Daisy—"Margaret Mary"—is thus "poor Daisy" both by literary inheritance and by fate. (We suspect that Hopkins' young Margaret, grieving for Goldengrove unleaving—for time and death, "the blight man was born for"—is lurking somewhere in the vicinity as well.)

Shortly after Daisy arrives, Theresa notices that she has some odd bruises, bruises she at first attributes to the fact that Daisy lives in a rough-and-tumble household with many brothers in it. But the bruises don't fade, and more of them mysteriously appear. What is wrong with Daisy? Theresa doesn't know, but she knows these bruises are the mark of mortality, the mark of her dire enemy. She does her best to cover them up, to erase them, by slathering them in Noxzema, by trying out a little sea-bathing and faith-healing, by telling the worried Daisy comforting fictions and invoking the eventually cured Tiny Tim, and by keeping the bruises secret from the adult world that would only verify catastrophe and take Daisy away. Perhaps her efforts will prove useless: "I had begun to suspect," she tells us, "that God and I . . . weren't seeing eye to eye." "You could reimagine, rename, things all you wanted, but it was flesh, somehow, that would not relent," she realizes later. However, as with the rabbit babies, she struggles on.

Daisy has been invited to visit partly because Theresa feels sorry for her and is a rescuer—it will do Daisy good to get away from her strict, penny-pinching family in Queens and her too-numerous siblings, especially her whiny, attention-grabbing, smart, chubby, blowfish-toothed older sister, Bernadette; and partly because Daisy is enough like Theresa to be a full participant in Theresa's somewhat Gothic inner world, where magical thinking is the order of the day. Another subtitle of this book might be *The Uses of Enchantment*, for references to centaurs, leprechauns, fairies, dragons, spells, ghosts, and charms are sprinkled throughout.

The two emotional poles of the book are represented by two plays of Shakespeare's, plays Theresa has read or acted in at school. The comic pole—where, despite sorrows and confusions, all ends happily—is represented by *A Midsummer Night's Dream*. Theresa is a theatrical girl, and as the book opens, she tells us she's been in the habit of casting herself as Titania, with her infant charges taking the parts of her attendant fairies. (She's actually nicknamed two of them Peaseblosssom and

Cobweb; luckily she knows this is silly and funny, or, like Dorothy Parker's Constant Reader, we might throw up.)

Titania has some peculiar sexual adventures in a wood, and so does Theresa. One of her charges—the only one she actually gets paid for—is Flora, the toddler daughter of a wrinkly but lecherous artist, who lives in a house surrounded by an entangling forest. At first you might think this old goat has been cast in the role of Bottom the Weaver with his donkey's head; certainly the ancient creature has a lot of besotted women inexplicably dancing attendance, including his housekeeper and a party guest who just wanders through. Who has dribbled what sort of magic flower juice into Theresa's eyes to get her to toss away her chance at Prince Charming and assume the horizontal with this avid but crumbling lust-for-life goat? (A goat who wonders out loud, not incidentally, how much extra time on earth he'd get if he were to play the ogre and gobble up not only Daisy and Theresa, but his own daughter as well.)

We suspect that instead of foolish, clumsy Bottom, he represents Oberon, "king of shadows"—far from a reassuring figure, but a potent one, since he is also, by folk tradition, king of the underworld. This man's studio is rendered in terms of shadows, a place of "pale, enchanted light," and he himself evokes for Theresa the dust he will shortly become. If mortality is your enemy and you don't understand it, why not go to the expert? "Dusty death," Theresa quotes, as the emphasis shifts to *Macbeth*, the tragic pole of the story, devoid of happy endings and replete with stains, like Daisy's, that can't be cured. At school, Theresa has acted the role of Macduff, whose children are all slaughtered. Explaining her understated dramatic interpretation to the old painter—her only confidant in the matter of Daisy's illness—she says, "I just said it like it was something he always knew was going to happen. . . . I said, 'Heaven looked on, and would not take their part'—not a question, like he always knew."

The artist understands her concerns, as others have not, because he knows about death. In a sense, he is Dusty Death personified, and Theresa has sex with him—only once—on his daybed, described as a bier. This act is not much like a joyous roll in the hay: no dalliance and delight. Instead, it's more like a ritual. Theresa's motives are not sexual; desire doesn't apply. She once overheard an incoherent version of desire when some of her previous employers had a noisy afternoon quickie—"Oh, what happened? Oh, where is it?" she thought the woman was crying, "but in a language I didn't know"; however, this isn't what she's after. What she wants is a trade: innocence for knowledge, blood for artistic power; for concealed deep within this seemingly artless book is a *bildungsroman,* the title of which might well be "How the Artist Got Her Art," or even "Portrait of the Artist as a Young Babysitter."

For Mr. Unnamed Dusty Death is an artist, and he's got what Theresa wants. Whether his "work" will last or not, he's got the impulse, the drive, the desperation, the key to the kingdom of shadows; and what she feels toward him is not lust, but "complicity." The gift she receives from him is a "dark, sharp jewel"—another of the dark jewels that shine here and there, both in the stories of babies' tears turned into gems that Theresa tells, but also on Daisy's adored but tawdry plastic shoes and in the sounds of overheard sex—precious things, but sinister, too, with pain and loss in them.

Here it's worth mentioning the changes rung on the word "work." Babysitting is work, being happy is work, crying is work, making a lollipop tree is work, and art is work—though perhaps the old artist's pictures may "come to nothing, at all. Not work at all, but play, pretending." What then are the kinds of work that are not pretending, that will indeed come to something? Those that have value in the worlds of the three "St. Theresas," perhaps, which are a lot like many of the things McDermott has put into this book—joy in the "peaceful contentments" of daily life, care for others involving hopeless hope, and especially the Castle of Imagination, made of "clouds" though Theresa knows it to be.

Daisy's death from her illness, the narrator tells us, "while it may well be the end point of this particular story . . . is not, after all, the reason I tell it." What, then, is the reason? Grown-ups cluster around the young Theresa like the good and bad fairies around Sleeping Beauty, making predictions about her future: she will marry well, she will marry a clam digger and have twelve children, she will become a model. We aren't told what has actually become of her in "real life"; what she is for us, however, is the voice that tells the story. Like the yarns Theresa spins when younger, this one is a charm, a spell, and its ambitions are large. The old painter is her model:

> in his kingdom by the sea, where art was what he said it was and the limits of time and age were banished and everything was possible because everything that mattered was inside his head.

As a spell-weaver, Theresa wants nothing less than to reverse time, and to bring Daisy back from the dead.

The narrator knows the ice she's sliding on is risky. Stories about dead children—children too good for this world, or probably, in reality, too exhausted to be naughty—are tricky, growing as they do in the shadow of Little Nell and a fair amount of lugubrious olden-time sentimental glop. She attempts to distance herself from such conventions by having them erased:

> The songs, the foolish tales of children's tragic premonitions. I wanted them scribbled over, torn up. Start over again. Draw a world where it simply doesn't happen. . . . Out of my head and more to my liking: a kingdom by the sea, eternal summer, a brush of fairy wings and all dark things banished, age, cruelty, pain, poor dogs, dead cats, harried parents, lonely children, all the coming griefs, all the sentimental, maudlin tales fashioned out of the death of children.

Not possible, of course. The giveaway is the "kingdom by the sea," quoted from the quintessential dead-girl poem, Poe's "Annabel Lee." The kingdom by the sea, enchanted though it is, contains a tomb. However hard you try, you can't get the Ego out of Acardia.

But you can do the next best thing: you can take out your sharp, dark jewel of art, the one with pain and loss at the center, and you can write a story about a dead child who is not yet dead, and thus have Daisy live again in an eternal summer of your own concoction, and hope things don't get too maudlin and that the spell will hold. It's an old attempt—at least as old as Dante, certainly as old as Proust—and a brave effort. Read as stark realism—a thing Alice McDermott has been much praised for—this richly textured, intricately woven, novella-like novel doesn't altogether come off. But read instead as a work not only of, but also about, the imagination— an imagination that works through oblique reference and pattern and symbolism as much as through observed detail—it's entirely convincing.

40

Napoleon's Two
Biggest Mistakes

In my high-school music appreciation class we listened to Tchaikovsky's *1812 Overture*. We liked it, because there was stuff we could identify: cannons boomed, bells rang, national anthems resounded, and there was a satisfying uproar at the end.

The English—being English—have since produced a version performed by sheep and chickens. Generals screw up, their fiascos get made into art, and then the art gets made into fiascos. Such is the march of progress. We were told that Tchaikovsky's piece celebrated Napoleon Bonaparte's retreat from Moscow, but we weren't told who Napoleon was or what he was doing in Moscow in the first place. So in case you had a similarly vague musical appreciation experience, here's the deep background.

Napoleon was a brilliant soldier who rose like a bubble during a time of unrest and bloodletting, won many battles, and was thus able—like Julius Caesar—to grab near-absolute power. He got hold of Italy and Austria and Prussia and Spain. He replaced the French Republic with an emperor—himself—thus giving rise to much impressive furniture with eagles and columns on it. He also brought in a legal code, still somewhat admired today.

He had laudable motives, or so his spin-doctoring went: he wanted peace, justice, and European unity. But he thought it would be liberating for other countries to have their stifling religious practices junked and their political systems replaced with one like his. To this end, he scrapped the kings of other countries and created new kings, who happened to be members of his own family.

Which brings me to Napoleon's two biggest mistakes.

The first was Spain. Napoleon got Spain treacherously. He had an agreement whereby he could march through it on the way to Portugal, which was bothering him by interfering with his sanctions against trading with the British. Once his armies were in Spain, he took the place over, whereupon his forces engaged in their usual practices of priest-pestering, church-looting, and removing sparkly things and artworks to other locations for safekeeping. Napoleon's big mistake was underestimating the religious feelings of the staunchly Catholic Spanish.

He thought they'd embrace "liberation," but it seems they had a curious attachment to their own beliefs. The British annoyed Napoleon in Spain by winning battles against him, but the real defeat of the French was brought about by widespread guerrilla resistance. Things got very nasty on both sides: the Spaniards cut French throats, the French roasted Spaniards alive, the Spaniards sawed a French general in two.

The Spanish population won—although at enormous cost—because you can kill some of the people all of the time and you can kill all of the people some of the time, but you can't kill all of the people all of the time. When a whole population hates you, and hates you fanatically, it's difficult to rule.

Present leaders take note: never underestimate the power of religious fervor. Also: your version of what's good for them may not match theirs.

Napoleon's second big mistake was invading Russia. There's no one clear explanation for this. He didn't need to do it. Russia wasn't attacking him, though it had in the past and might in the future. Maybe he just wanted to add it to his set. In any case, he invaded. When his horse stumbled as he crossed the Dnieper—a bad omen—a voice said from the shadows, "A Roman would have turned back."

Warfare at that time meant forcing your opponent to stand and fight, resulting in victory on one side or the other. But the Russians merely retreated, burning crops as they went and leading Napoleon deeper and deeper into the same huge Russian landmass and awful Russian weather that also defeated Hitler. When Napoleon reached Moscow, he thought maybe he'd "won": but the Russians burned Moscow, and retreated again. Napoleon hung around in the cinders, expecting the czar to sue for peace, but no message ever arrived. Thus the retreat, and the *1812 Overture*, and the decimation of the Grand Army. As others have learned since, it's very hard to defeat an enemy who never turns up.

The occupation of Japan after the Second World War has been proposed as a model for Iraq. It's not a helpful comparison. First, the religious fervor of the Japanese soldier was attached to the emperor, who thus had the power to order a surrender. Iraq will have no such single authority. Second, Japan is an island: no Russian-style, Afghan-style retreat was possible. Third, Japan had no neighbors that shared its religious views and might aid it. The Japanese had only two choices: death or democracy.

Iraq, on the other hand, has many coreligionist neighbors who will sympathize with it, however repugnant they've previously found Saddam Hussein. A foreign occupation—not immediately, but in the long run—is less likely to resemble Douglas MacArthur in Japan than Napoleon in Spain.

Now you know about the *1812 Overture*. That moment—after which Napoleon plummeted and the French Empire dissolved—was the hinge on which the rest of the nineteenth century turned, as the First World War was the hinge for the twentieth.

When a door swings open, you never know what will come through it. And as Napoleon himself believed, the fortunes of war—being notoriously unpredictable, and riddled with variables—are ruled by the Goddess of Chance.

41

Letter to America

Dear America:

This is a difficult letter to write, because I'm no longer sure who you are. Some of you may be having the same trouble.

I thought I knew you: We'd become well acquainted over the past fifty-five years. You were the Mickey Mouse and Donald Duck comic books I read in the late 1940s. You were the radio shows—Jack Benny, *Our Miss Brooks*. You were the music I sang and danced to: the Andrews Sisters, Ella Fitzgerald, the Platters, Elvis. You were a ton of fun.

You wrote some of my favorite books. You created Huckleberry Finn, and Hawkeye, and Beth and Jo in *Little Women*, courageous in their different ways. Later, you were my beloved Thoreau, father of environmentalism, witness to individual conscience; and Walt Whitman, singer of the great republic; and Emily Dickinson, keeper of the private soul. You were Hammett and Chandler, heroic walkers of mean streets; even later, you were the amazing trio Hemingway, Fitzgerald, and Faulkner, who traced the dark labyrinths of your hidden heart. You were Sinclair Lewis and Arthur Miller, who, with their own American idealism, went after the sham in you, because they thought you could do better.

You were Marlon Brando in *On the Waterfront*, you were Humphrey Bogart in *Key Largo*, you were Lillian Gish in *Night of the Hunter*. You stood up for freedom, honesty, and justice; you protected the innocent. I believed most of that. I think you did, too. It seemed true at the time.

You put God on the money, though, even then. You had a way of thinking that the things of Caesar were the same as the things of God: That gave you self-confidence. You have always wanted to be a city upon a hill, a light to all nations, and for a while you were. Give me your tired, your poor, you sang, and for a while you meant it.

We've always been close, you and we. History, that old entangler, has twisted us together since the early seventeenth century. Some of us used to be you; some of us want to be you; some of you used to be us. You are not only our neighbors; in many cases—mine, for instance—you are also our blood relations, our colleagues, and our personal friends. But although we've had a ringside seat, we've never understood you completely, up here north of the forty-ninth parallel. We're like Romanized Gauls—look like Romans, dress like Romans, but aren't Romans— peering over the wall at the real Romans. What are they doing? Why? What are they doing now? Why is the haruspex eyeballing the sheep's liver? Why is the soothsayer wholesaling the Bewares?

Perhaps that's been my difficulty in writing you this letter: I'm not sure I know what's really going on. Anyway, you have a huge posse of experienced entrail-sifters who do nothing but analyze your every vein and lobe. What can I tell you about yourself that you don't already know?

This might be the reason for my hesitation: embarrassment, brought on by a becoming modesty. But it is more likely to be embarrassment of another sort. When my grandmother—from a New England background—was confronted with an unsavory topic, she would change the subject and gaze out the window. And that is my own inclination: keep your mouth shut, mind your own business.

But I'll take the plunge, because your business is no longer merely your business. To paraphrase Marley's Ghost, who figured it out too late, mankind is your business. And vice versa: when the Jolly Green Giant goes on the rampage, many lesser plants and animals get trampled underfoot. As for us, you're our biggest trading partner: we know perfectly well that if you go down the plughole, we're going with you. We have every reason to wish you well.

I won't go into the reasons why I think your recent Iraqi adventures have been—taking the long view—an ill-advised tactical error. By the time you read this, Baghdad may or may not be a pancake, and many more sheep entrails will have been examined. Let's talk, then, not about what you're doing to other people but about what you're doing to yourselves.

You're gutting the Constitution. Already your home can be entered without your knowledge or permission, you can be snatched away and incarcerated without cause, your mail can be spied on, your private records searched. Why isn't this a recipe for widespread business theft, political intimidation, and fraud? I know you've been told that all this is for your own safety and protection, but think about it for a minute. Anyway, when did you get so scared? You didn't used to be easily frightened.

You're running up a record level of debt. Keep spending at this rate and pretty soon you won't be able to afford any big military adventures. Either that or you'll go the way of the USSR: lots of tanks but no air-conditioning. That will make folks very cross. They'll be even crosser when they can't take a shower because your shortsighted bulldozing of environmental protections has dirtied most of the water and dried up the rest. Then things will get hot and dirty indeed.

You're torching the American economy. How soon before the answer to that will be not to produce anything yourselves but to grab stuff other people produce, at gunboat-diplomacy prices? Is the world going to consist of a few megarich King Midases, with the rest being serfs, both inside and outside your country? Will the biggest business sector in the United States be the prison system? Let's hope not.

If you proceed much farther down the slippery slope, people around the world will stop admiring the good things about you. They'll decide that your city upon the hill is a slum and your democracy is a sham, and therefore you have no business trying to impose your sullied vision on them. They'll think you've abandoned the rule of law. They'll think you've fouled your own nest.

The British used to have a myth about King Arthur. He wasn't dead, but sleeping in a cave, it was said; and in the country's hour of greatest peril, he would return. You, too, have great spirits of the past you may call upon: men and women of courage, of conscience, of prescience. Summon them now, to stand with you, to inspire you, to defend the best in you. You need them.

42

Writing *Oryx and Crake*

*O*ryx and Crake was begun in March 2001. I was still on a book tour for my previous novel, *The Blind Assassin*, but by that time I had reached Australia. After I'd finished the book-related events, my spouse and I and two friends traveled north, to Max Davidson's camp in the monsoon rain forest of Arnheimland. For the most part we were bird-watching, but we also visited several open-sided cave complexes where Aboriginal people had lived continuously, in harmony with their environment, for tens of thousands of years. After that we went to Cassowary House, near Cairns, operated by Philip Gregory, an extraordinary birder; and it was while looking over Philip's balcony at the red-necked crakes scuttling about in the underbrush that *Oryx and Crake* appeared to me, almost in its entirety. I began making notes on it that night.

I hadn't planned to begin another novel so soon after the previous one. I'd thought I might take some time off, write a few short pieces, clean out the cellar. But when a story appears to you with such insistence, you can't postpone it.

Of course, nothing comes out of nothing. I'd been thinking about "what if" scenarios almost all my life. I grew up among the scientists—"the boys at the lab" mentioned in the acknowledgments are the graduate students and postdocs who worked with my father in the late 1930s and early 1940s at his forest-insect research station in northern Québec, where I spent my early childhood. Several of my close relatives are scientists, and the main topic at the annual family Christmas dinner is likely to be intestinal parasites or sex hormones in mice, or, when that makes the nonscientists too queasy, the nature of the universe. My recreational reading—books I read for fun, magazines I read in airplanes—is likely to be pop science of the Stephen Jay Gould or *Scientific American* type, partly so I'll be able to keep up with the family dialogue and maybe throw a curve or two. ("Supercavitation?")

So I'd been clipping small items from the back pages of newspapers for years, and noting with alarm that trends derided ten years ago as paranoid fantasies had become possibilities, then actualities. The rules of biology are as inexorable as those of physics: run out of food and water and you die. No animal can exhaust its resource base and hope to survive. Human civilizations are subject to the same law.

I continued to write away at *Oryx and Crake* during the summer of 2001. We had some other travels planned, and I wrote several chapters of this book on a boat in the Arctic, where I could see for myself how quickly the glaciers were receding. I had the whole book mapped out and had reached the end of part 7 when I was due to go to New York for the paperback publication of *The Blind Assassin*.

I was sitting in the Toronto airport, daydreaming about part 8. In ten minutes my flight would be called. An old friend of mine came over and said, "We're not flying." "What do you mean?" I said. "Come and look at the television," he replied. It was September 11.

I stopped writing for a number of weeks. It's deeply unsettling when you're writing about a fictional catastrophe and then a real one happens. I thought maybe I should turn to gardening books—something more cheerful. But then I started writing again, because what use would gardening books be in a world without gardens, and without books? And that was the vision that was preoccupying me.

Like *The Handmaid's Tale, Oryx and Crake* is a speculative fiction, not a science fiction proper. It contains no intergalactic space travel, no teleportation, no Martians. As with *The Handmaid's Tale*, it invents nothing we haven't already invented or started to invent. Every novel begins with a *what if* and then sets forth its axioms. The *what if* of *Oryx and Crake* is simply, *What if we continue down the road we're already on? How slippery is the slope? What are our saving graces? Who's got the will to stop us?*

"Perfect storms" occur when a number of different forces coincide. So it is with the storms of human history. As novelist Alistair MacLeod has said, writers write about what worries them, and the world of *Oryx and Crake* is what worries me right now. It's not a question of our inventions—all human inventions are merely tools—but of what might be done with them; for no matter how high the tech, *Homo sapiens sapiens* remains at heart what he's been for tens of thousands of years—the same emotions, the same preoccupations. To quote poet George Meredith,

> *In tragic life, God wot,*
> *No villain need be! Passions spin the plot:*
> *We are betrayed by what is false within.*

43

George Orwell:
Some Personal Connections

I grew up with George Orwell. I was born in 1939, and *Animal Farm* was published in 1945. Thus I was able to read it at age nine. It was lying around the house, and I mistook it for a book about talking animals, sort of like *Wind in the Willows*. I knew nothing about the kind of politics in the book—the child's version of politics then, just after the war, consisted of the simple notion that Hitler was bad but dead. So I gobbled up the adventures of Napoleon and Snowball, the smart, greedy, upwardly mobile pigs, and Squealer the spin doctor, and Boxer the noble but thick-witted horse, and the easily led, slogan-chanting sheep, without making any connection with historical events.

To say that I was horrified by this book would be an understatement. The fate of the farm animals was so grim, the pigs were so mean and mendacious and treacherous, the sheep were so stupid. Children have a keen sense of injustice, and this was the thing that upset me the most: the pigs were so *unjust*. I cried my eyes out when Boxer the horse had an accident and was carted off to be made into dog food, instead of being given the quiet corner of the pasture he'd been promised.

The whole experience was deeply disturbing to me, but I am forever grateful to George Orwell for alerting me early to the danger flags I've tried to watch out for since. In the world of *Animal Farm*, most speechifying and public palaver is bullshit and instigated lying, and though many characters are good-hearted and mean well, they can be frightened into closing

their eyes to what's really going on. The pigs browbeat the others with ideology, then twist that ideology to suit their own purposes: their language
games were evident to me even at that age. As Orwell taught, it isn't the
labels—Christianity, socialism, Islam, democracy, Two Legs Bad, Four Legs
Good, the works—that are definitive, but the acts done in their names.

I could see, too, how easily those who have toppled an oppressive power
take on its trappings and habits. Jean-Jacques Rousseau was right to warn
us that democracy is the hardest form of government to maintain; Orwell
knew that in the marrow of his bones, because he's seen it in action. How
quickly the precept "All Animals Are Equal" is changed into "All Animals
Are Equal, but Some Are More Equal Than Others." What oily concern
the pigs show for the welfare of the other animals, a concern that disguises
their contempt for those they are manipulating. With what alacrity do they
put on the once-despised uniforms of the tyrannous humans they have
overthrown, and learn to use their whips. How self-righteously they justify
their actions, helped by the verbal web-spinning of Squealer, their nimble-
tongued press agent, until all power is in their trotters, and pretense is no
longer necessary, and they rule by naked force. A *revolution* often means
only that: a revolving, a turn of the wheel of fortune, by which those who
were at the bottom mount to the top and assume the choice positions,
crushing the former power-holders beneath them. We should beware of all
those who plaster the landscape with large portraits of themselves, like the
evil pig Napoleon.

Animal Farm is one of the most spectacular Emperor-Has-No-Clothes
books of the twentieth century, and it got George Orwell into trouble
accordingly. People who run counter to the current popular wisdom, who
point out the uncomfortably obvious, are likely to be strenuously baa-ed at
by herds of angry sheep. I didn't have all that figured out at age nine, of
course—not in any conscious way. But we learn the patterns of stories
before we learn their meanings, and *Animal Farm* has a very clear pattern.

Then along came *1984*, which was published in 1949. Thus I read it in
paperback a couple of years later, when I was in high school. Then I read
it again, and again: it was right up there among my favorite books, along
with *Wuthering Heights*. At the same time, I absorbed its two companions,
Arthur Koestler's *Darkness at Noon* and Aldous Huxley's *Brave New World.*

I was keen on all three of them, but I understood *Darkness at Noon* to be a tragedy about events that had already happened, and *Brave New World* to be a satirical comedy, with events that were unlikely to unfold in exactly that way. ("Orgy-Porgy," indeed.) But *1984* struck me as more realistic, probably because Winston Smith was more like me—a skinny person who got tired a lot and was subjected to physical education under chilly conditions—this was a feature of my school—and who was silently at odds with the ideas and the manner of life proposed for him. (This may be one of the reasons *1984* is best read when you are an adolescent; most adolescents feel like that.) I sympathized particularly with Winston Smith's desire to write his forbidden thoughts down in a deliciously tempting secret blank book: I had not yet started to write, myself, but I could see the attractions of it. I could also see the dangers, because it's this scribbling of his—along with illicit sex, another item with considerable allure for a teenager of the fifties—that gets Winston into such a mess.

Animal Farm charts the progress of an idealistic movement of liberation toward a totalitarian dictatorship headed by a despotic tyrant; *1984* describes what it's like to live entirely within such a system. Its hero, Winston Smith, has only fragmentary memories of what life was like before the present dreadful regime set in: he's an orphan, a child of the collectivity. His father died in the war that has ushered in the repression, and his mother has disappeared, leaving him with only the reproachful glance she gave him as he betrayed her over a chocolate bar—a small betrayal that acts both as the key to Winston's character and as a precursor to the many other betrayals in the book.

The government of Airstrip One, Winston's "country," is brutal. The constant surveillance, the impossibility of speaking frankly to anyone, the looming, ominous figure of Big Brother, the regime's need for enemies and wars—fictitious though both may be—which are used to terrify the people and unite them in hatred, the mind-numbing slogans, the distortions of language, the destruction of what has really happened by stuffing any record of it down the Memory Hole—these made a deep impression on me. Let me restate that: they frightened the stuffing out of me. Orwell was writing a satire about Stalin's Soviet Union, a place about which I knew very little at age fourteen, but he did it so well that I could imagine such things happening anywhere.

There is no love interest in *Animal Farm*, but there is one in *1984*. Winston finds a soul mate in Julia, outwardly a devoted Party fanatic, secretly a girl who enjoys sex and makeup and other spots of decadence. But the two lovers are discovered, and Winston is tortured for thought crime—inner disloyalty to the regime. He feels that if he can only remain faithful in his heart to Julia, his soul will be saved—a romantic concept, though one we are likely to endorse. But like all absolutist governments and religions, the Party demands that every personal loyalty be sacrificed to it, and replaced with an absolute loyalty to Big Brother. Confronted with his worst fear in the dreaded Room 101, where there's a nasty device involving a cageful of starving rats that can be fitted to the eyes, Winston breaks—"Don't do it to me," he pleads, "do it to Julia." (This sentence has become shorthand in our household for the avoidance of onerous duties. Poor Julia—how hard we would make her life if she actually existed. She'd have to be on a lot of panel discussions, for instance.)

After his betrayal of Julia, Winston Smith becomes a handful of malleable goo. He truly believes that two and two make five and that he loves Big Brother. Our last glimpse of him shows him sitting drink-sodden at an outdoor café, knowing he's a dead man walking and having learned that Julia has betrayed him, too, while he listens to a popular refrain: "Under the spreading chestnut tree/I sold you and you sold me."

Orwell has been accused of bitterness and pessimism—of leaving us with a vision of the future in which the individual has no chance, and the brutal, totalitarian boot of the all-controlling Party will grind into the human face forever. But this view of Orwell is contradicted by the last chapter in the book, an essay on Newspeak—the doublethink language concocted by the regime. By expurgating all words that might be troublesome—"bad" is no longer permitted, but becomes "double-plus-ungood"—and by making other words mean the opposite of what they used to mean—the place where people get tortured is the Ministry of Love, the building where the past is destroyed is the Ministry of Information—the rulers of Airstrip One wish to make it literally impossible for people to think straight. However, the essay on Newspeak is written in standard English, in the third person, and in the past tense, which can only mean that the regime has fallen, and that language and individuality have survived. For whoever has written the essay on Newspeak, the world of *1984* is over. Thus it's my view that Orwell had much more faith in the resilience of the human spirit than he's usually been given credit for.

Orwell became a direct model for me much later in my life—in the real 1984, the year in which I began writing a somewhat different dystopia, *The Handmaid's Tale*. By that time I was forty-four, and I'd learned enough about real despotisms—through the reading of history, through travel, and through my membership in Amnesty International—that I didn't need to rely on Orwell alone.

The majority of dystopias—Orwell's included—have been written by men, and the point of view has been male. When women have appeared in them, they have been either sexless automatons or rebels who've defied the sex rules of the regime. They've acted as the temptresses of the male protagonists, however welcome this temptation may be to the men themselves. Thus Julia, thus the cami-knicker-wearing, orgy-porgy seducer of the Savage in *Brave New World*, thus the subversive femme fatale of Yvgeny Zamyatin's 1924 seminal classic *We*. I wanted to try a dystopia from the female point of view—the world according to Julia, as it were. However, this does not make *The Handmaid's Tale* a "feminist dystopia," except insofar as giving a woman a voice and an inner life will always be considered "feminist" by those who think women ought not to have these things.

In other respects, the despotism I describe is the same as all real ones and most imagined ones. It has a small, powerful group at the top that controls—or tries to control—everyone else, and it gets the lion's share of available goodies. The pigs in *Animal Farm* get the milk and the apples, the elite of *The Handmaid's Tale* get the fertile women. The force that opposes the tyranny in my book is one in which Orwell himself—despite his belief in the need for political organization to combat oppression—always put great store: ordinary human decency, of the kind he praised in his essay on Charles Dickens. The Biblical expression of this quality is probably in the verse "Insofar as you do it unto the least of these, you do it unto me." Tyrants and the powerful believe, with Lenin, that you can't make an omelet without breaking eggs and that the end justifies the means. Orwell, when push came to shove, would have believed—on the contrary—that the means define the end. He wrote as if he sided with the John Donne who said, "Every man's death diminishes me." And so say—I would hope—all of us.

At the end of *The Handmaid's Tale*, there's a section that owes much to *1984*. It's the account of a symposium held several hundred years in the future, in which the repressive government described in the novel is now merely a subject for academic analysis. The parallels with Orwell's essay on Newspeak should be evident.

Orwell has been an inspiration to generations of writers in another important respect—his insistence on the clear and exact use of language. "Prose like a windowpane," he said, opting for plainsong rather than ornament. Euphemisms and skewed terminology should not obscure the truth. "Acceptable megadeaths" rather than "millions of rotting corpses," but hey, it's not us who're dead; "untidiness" instead of "massive destruction"—this is the beginning of Newspeak. Fancy verbiage is what confuses Boxer the horse and underpins the chantings of the sheep. To insist on *what is*, in the face of ideological spin, popular consensus, and official denial: Orwell knew this takes honesty and a lot of guts. The position of odd man out is always an uneasy one, but the moment we look around and find that there are no longer any odd men among our public voices is the moment of most danger—because that's when we'll be in lockstep, ready for the Three Minutes' Hate.

The twentieth century could be seen as a race between two versions of man-made Hell—the jackbooted state totalitarianism of Orwell's *1984*, and the hedonistic ersatz paradise of *Brave New World*, where absolutely everything is a consumer good and human beings are engineered to be happy. With the fall of the Berlin Wall in 1989, it seemed for a time that *Brave New World* had won—from henceforth, state control would be minimal, and all we'd have to do was go shopping and smile a lot, and wallow in pleasures, popping a pill or two when depression set in.

But with the notorious 9/11 World Trade Center and Pentagon attacks in the year 2001, all that changed. Now it appears we face the prospect of two contradictory dystopias at once—open markets, closed minds—because state surveillance is back again with a vengeance. The torturer's dreaded Room 101 has been with us for millennia. The dungeons of Rome, the Inquisition, the Star Chamber, the Bastille, the proceedings of

General Pinochet and of the junta in Argentina—all have depended on secrecy and on the abuse of power. Lots of countries have had their versions of it—their ways of silencing troublesome dissent. Democracies have traditionally defined themselves by, among other things, openness and the rule of law. But now it seems that we in the West are tacitly legitimizing the methods of the darker human past, upgraded technologically and sanctified to our own uses, of course. For the sake of freedom, freedom must be renounced. To move us toward the improved world—the utopia we're promised—dystopia must first hold sway. It's a concept worthy of doublethink. It's also, in its ordering of events, strangely Marxist. First the dictatorship of the proletariat, in which lots of heads must roll; then the pie-in-the-sky classless society, which oddly enough never materializes. Instead we just get pigs with whips.

What would George Orwell have to say about it? I often ask myself.

Quite a lot.

44

Review:

Enough: Staying Human in an Engineered Age by Bill McKibben

*E*nough, by Bill McKibben, is a passionate, succinct, chilling, closely argued, sometimes hilarious, touchingly well-intentioned, and essential summary of the future proposed by "science" for the human race. This is the same Bill McKibben who wrote *The End of Nature*, about how *Homo sapiens* has been rearranging the biosphere with the aid of genetically modified plants to suit what it believes is its own interests, and *Long Distance*, about running marathons, as well as essays for the *New Yorker*, the *New York Times*, the *New York Review*, the *Atlantic*, and others.

Bill McKibben appears to be a smart and thoughtful person, but also kindly and optimistic, as far as can be told from his prose. He likes going for walks in the woods, and he seems very fit, and his jacket photo looks like someone you wouldn't want playing against you at bridge because he'd already know what you had in your hand. In other words, he could qualify for membership in a muscular branch of upper-level-IQ geekhood, and cannot be simply dismissed as a dull-normal Luddite too dumb to understand the nifty customized body-and-brain parts soon to be on offer to you and yours.

On offer for a price, of course. Ah, yes, the price. The traditional fee for this kind of thing was your soul, but who pays any attention to that tattered theological rag anymore, since it can't be located with a brain probe? And hey, the special deal is a super package! How could you refuse? It contains so much that human dreams are made of.

Faust wanted the same sort of stuff. Many have wanted it: eternal youth, godlike beauty, hyperintelligence, Charles Atlas strength. Those of us brought up on the back pages of comic books know the appeal. They'll never laugh again when you sit down at the piano because now you'll have X-Men fingers and Mozart's genius; they won't dare to kick sand in your face at the beach because you'll be built like Hercules; you'll never again be refused a date because of your ugly blackheads, which will have been banished, along with many another feature you could do without. Turning to more adult concerns such as death, you won't have to invest in a cement coffin container, because not only will your loved one be safe tonight, he or she will still be alive, and forever! And so will you.

The line forms to the right, and it'll be a long one. (*Enough* mentions a couple of California artists who set up a piece of conceptual art in the form of a boutique called Gene Genies Worldwide, with printed brochures illustrating what you could buy, and were deluged with serious inquiries.) Anyone who thinks there won't be a demand for what's putatively on sale is hallucinating. But along comes Bill McKibben with his sidewalk-preacher's sandwich board, denouncing the whole enterprise and prophesying doom. There will be catcalls of *killjoy* and *spoilsport*, not to mention *troglodyte*, *naysayer*, and *hand-wringer*. Like Prince Charles, who's just come out against nanotechnology on the ground that it could reduce the world to gray goo, McKibben will be told to keep his nose out of it because it's none of his business.

"Mankind was my business," laments Marley's ghost when it's too late for him. And so says Bill McKibben. Mankind is his business. He addresses the greedy little Scrooge in all of us, and points out to that greedy little Scrooge why he should not want more and more, and more, and, just to top it off, more.

More of what? To that in a minute, but first, a digression on the word *more*. Two emblematic uses of *more* spring to mind. The first is, of course, the echoing "more" pronounced by Oliver Twist when he is being starved in a foundlings' home by venal officials. That "more" is the legitimate response to "not enough." It's the "more" of real need, and only the hard-hearted and wickedly self-righteous Mr. Bumbles of this world can be outraged by it. The second "more" is in the film *Key Largo*, in the remarkable exchange between the Humphrey Bogart hero character and the Edward G. Robinson evil crook. The crook is asked what he wants, and he doesn't know. Humphrey knows, however. "He wants more," he says. And this is what the crook does want: more, and more than he can possibly use; or rather, more than he can appreciate, dedicated as he is to mere accumulation and mere power. For the alternative to "more," in McKibben's book, is not "less," but "enough." Its epigraph might well be that old folk saying, "Enough is as good as a feast."

The "enough" of the title, seen rightly—McKibben implies—is already a feast. It's us as we are, with maybe a few allowable improvements. More than that is too much. These tempting "mores"—for there are many of them—grow on the more and more Trees of Knowledge that crowd the modern scientific landscape so thickly you can't see the forest for them. McKibben takes ax in hand and sets out to clear a path. Which apples should be plucked, which left alone? How hard should we think before taking the fateful bite? And why shouldn't we pig out, and what's our motivation if we do? Is it the same old story—we want to be as the gods? If it's *that* story, we've read it, in its many versions. It's never had a happy ending. Not so far.

The items on the smorgasbord of human alteration divide roughly into three. First, genetic alteration, or gene splicing, whereby parents who are five feet tall and bald can give birth to a six-footer with long blond hair who looks like the next-door neighbor. Well, it'll provide some new excuses. ("Honey, we *chose* that! Remember?") Second, nanotechnology, or the development of single-atom-layer gizmos that can replicate themselves and assemble and disassemble matter. Some of these might be sent into our bodies to repair them, like the miniaturized submarine containing the memorable Raquel Welch in the film *Fantastic Voyage*. Third, cybernetics, or the melding of man with machine, like the bionic man. At least we'll all be able to get the lids off jars.

There's a fourth idea that's glanced at—cryogenics, or getting yourself or your budget-version head flash-frozen until such time as the yellow-brick road to immortality has been built; whereupon you'll be unfrozen and restored to youth and health, and, if the head-only option has been chosen, a new body can be grown for you from a few scrapings of your—or somebody else's—DNA. Investing even a small amount of belief in this scheme puts you in the same league as those who happily buy the Brooklyn Bridge from shifty-looking men in overcoats, for the company—yes, it would be a company—in charge of your frozen head would need to be not only perennially solvent—bankruptcy would equal meltdown—but also impeccably honest.

Every field of human endeavor attracts its quota of con men and scam artists, but this one would seem to be a natural. What's to stop the operators from banking your money, subjecting you to the initial gelatification, and then, pleading electrical failure, dumping your unpleasantly melting self into the trash, or better—waste not, want not, and the shareholders expect a solid bottom line—recycling you for cat food? The pyramids of the mummified Egyptian kings, thoroughly pillaged once the relatives' backs were turned, stand as a gloss on this kind of thinking, as does London's Highgate Cemetery, a Garden of Eternity parceled out in pricey lots that became an overgrown thicket once the money stream petered out.

But McKibben's fervent arguments are of a more clean-cut kind: he is not a novelist or a poet and thus does not descend all the way into the foul rag-and-bone shop of the heart. He assumes a certain amount of sincerity and probity in the less-wacky advocates of these developments, and his appeals are directed to our rational and ethical faculties. We should act, he believes, out of respect for human history and the human race.

He first tackles genetic engineering, already present in soybeans and not so far off for *Homo sapiens* now that we have the luminous green rabbit and the goat/spider. Gene splicing is the modern answer to the eternal urge to make a more perfect model of ourselves. The novel of record is Mary Shelley's *Frankenstein*: we just can't stop tinkering, partly because it's so interesting, and partly because we have a high opinion of our own abilities; but we risk creating monsters.

297

Gene splicing depends on cloning—McKibben explains how—but is not the same. It involves inserting selected genes—of those other than the parents—into an egg, which is then implanted in the usual way (or will be until the bottled babies of *Brave New World* make their appearance, and we can do away with the womb altogether). If we become genetically enhanced in this way—enhanced by our parents before we're born—the joy and mystery will go out of life, says McKibben, because we won't have to strive for mastery. Our achievements won't be "ours" but will have been programmed into us; we'll never know whether we are really feeling "our" emotions, or whether they—like the false memories embedded in the replicants in the film *Blade Runner*—are off the shelf. We won't be our unique selves, we'll just be the sum totals of market whims. We truly will be the "meat machines" that some scientists already term us. Right now about all our parents can pick for us are our names, but what if they could pick everything about us? (And you thought your mother had bad taste in sofas!)

Worse, we'll be caught in a keep-up-with-the-Joneses competition whereby each new generation of babies will have to have all the latest enhancements—will have to be more intelligent, more beautiful, more disease-free, longer-lived, than the generation before. (Babies of the rich, it goes without saying, because there's gold in them thar frills.) Thus each new generation will be *sui generis*—isolated, disconsolate, as out of date as last year's car model before they're even twenty-one, each of them stuck on a lily pad of enhancement a few hops behind the one that follows them. In addition to that, they'll be cut off from history—from their own family tree—because who knows what family trees they'll really be perpetuating? They'll bear little relation to their so-called ancestors. The loneliness and the sense of disconnection could be extreme.

McKibben does not go on to explore the ultimate hell this situation could produce. Imagine the adolescent whining and sulking that will be visited upon the parents who have chosen their children's features out of a catalog, and—inevitably—will have chosen wrong. "I didn't ask to be born" will be replaced by resentments such as "I didn't ask to have blue eyes" or

"I didn't ask to be a math whiz." Burn that gene brochure! If your kid whines about not being enhanced enough, you can just say you couldn't afford it. (The advocates of gene enhancement might respond that since you'll be able to choose your child's temperament as well, naturally you'll pick a type that will never do any adolescent whining or sulking. Pay no attention: these people will not be talking about flesh-and-blood children, but about Stepford Kids.)

Again, McKibben doesn't go all the way down, into the dark realms of envy, cheating, payoffs, and megalomaniacal revenge. What's to prevent your enemy from bribing your gene doctor so that your baby turns out like Hannibal the Cannibal?

But what about heritable diseases? you may reasonably ask. Why should any child get stuck with cerebral palsy, or autism, or schizophrenia, or Huntington's chorea, or the many other maladies that genes are heir to? They shouldn't if there's a remedy, and there is. McKibben points out that these conditions can be eliminated without taking the final step. (After *Enough* was published and before this review was written, a Canadian team cracked the gene for autism. Help is on the way.) Once their genome has been analyzed, parents at risk could be notified of any defects, and could go the in vitro route, with fertilized eggs lacking in the culpable gene chosen for implanting. This "somatic gene therapy" would not involve the addition of anyone else's genes. Plastic surgery, hormones, vitamin pills, and somatic gene therapy are enough, says McKibben; gene splicing is too much.

Next, McKibben delves into nanotechnology, which is also well on the way. The applicable folktale for nanotechnology is "The Sorcerer's Apprentice"—what if you get the process started, but the self-replicating nanobot escapes, and you can't turn the darn thing off? We might create an assembler that makes food—dirt in one end, potatoes out the other—or something that destroys bioforms hostile to us. But what if such a nanobot goes on the rampage and attacks all bioforms? This is where Prince Charles's apprehension about "gray goo" comes in. It's a real fear, and one discussed by McKibben.

Cybernetics and artificial intelligence also get a look-in, as man-and-machine combinations are occupying some of our better-paid minds. Visions of microchips implanted in your brain dance in their heads—well, we already have pacemakers, so what's the difference? Why shouldn't we baptize artificial intelligence doodads, because they can be made to resemble us so much that maybe they have whatever we think merits baptism? Call it a soul; why not? Maybe we can get enhanced smellability, X-ray vision, Spidey Sense, the works. Artificial orgasms, better than the real thing. *Everything* will be better than the real thing! Why shouldn't we have eyes in the backs of our heads? Why do we only have one mouth that has to perform several functions—talking, eating, whistling? If we had several buccal orifices we'd be able to do all these things at once! (Sign here. You owe it to yourself. Because you deserve it.)

There's been quite a lot of chat about the shortcomings we've had to put up with thanks to Mother Nature, the dirty, treacherous cow, and this is the not-so-cleverly-hidden subtext of a lot of *Brave New World*–type thinking. These folks hate Nature, and they hate themselves as part of it, or her. McKibben cites an amazing speech given by Max More (last name chosen by himself) to the Extropian Convention ("extropy," coined as the opposite to "entropy"). This speech took the form of a dissing of Mother Nature, and said, essentially, thanks for nothing and good-bye. Nature has made so many mistakes, the chief one being death. Why do we have to get old and die? Why is man the one creature that foresees his own death?

As in many religions—and the energy propelling the wilder fringes of this "more" enterprise is religious in essence—there has to be a second birth, one that gets around the indignity of having come out of a body—a female body—and, come to think of it, of having a body yourself. All that guck and blood and cells and death. Why do we have to eat? And, by implication, defecate? So messy. Maybe we can fix our digestive tracts so we just slip out a little pellet—say, once a month. Maybe we can be born again, this time out of an artificial head instead of a natural body, and download the contents of our brains into machines, and linger around in cyberspace, as in William Gibson's novels. Though if you've read William Gibson, you'll know the place is a queasy nightmare.

All the enhancements McKibben discusses are converging on the biggie, which is none other than the final nose-thumb at Nature—immortality. Immortality doesn't fare so well in myth and story. Either you get it but forget to request eternal youth, too, and become a crumbling horror (Tithonus, the Sibyl of Cumae, Swift's Struldbrugs), or you seize the immortality and the vitality but lose your soul and must live by feeding on the blood of the innocent (Melmoth the Wanderer, vampires, and so forth). The stories are clear: gods are immortal, men die, try to change it and you'll end up worse off.

That doesn't stop us from hankering. McKibben recognizes the impulse: "Objecting even slightly to immortality," he rightly says, "is a little like arguing against ice cream—eternal life has only been humanity's great dream since the moment we became conscious." But unlike all previous generations, ours might be able to achieve it. This would alter us beyond recognition. We'd become a different species—one living in eternal bliss, in the eyes of its proponents; sort of like—well, angels, or superhuman beings, anyway. It would certainly mean an end to narrative. If life is endless; why tell stories? No more beginnings and middles, because there will be no more endings. No Shakespeare for us, or Dante, or, well, any art, really. It's all infested with mortality and reeks of earthiness. Our new angel-selves will no longer need or understand our art. They might have other art, though it would be pretty bloodless.

But once we're well and truly immortal, what would we do all day? Wouldn't we get tired of the endlessness, the monotony, the lack of meaningful event? Wouldn't we get bored? Nope. We'd sit around and contemplate problems such as: "Where did the universe come from?" "Why is there something rather than nothing?" "What is the meaning of conscious existence?" Is that to be the result of all this admittedly fascinating science—a tedious first-year philosophy seminar? "Not to be impolite," says McKibben, "but for this we trade our humanity?"

That's the good version of the immortal mind. I encountered the bad version in a paperback I received through a high school book-a-month club. *Donovan's Brain* was its title, and the brain in question was being kept

301

alive in a large fish tank and fed on brain food. The hope of the scientists doing this was that the brain would grow in power and strength, and solve problems such as "Why is there something rather than nothing?" and benefit mankind. But Donovan when he had a body was a stock manipulator or the equivalent, and he bent his newfound mind powers in the direction of world domination, zapping people who got in his way. A big brain does not mean a nice brain. This was made clear to me at age twelve, and it's made even clearer in *Enough*. There are some very clever people at work on the parts that will go into making up our immortality, and what they're doing is on some levels fascinating—like playing with the biggest toy box you've ever seen—but they are not the people who should be deciding our future. Asking these kinds of scientists what improved human nature should be like is like asking ants what you should have in your backyard. Of course they would say "more ants."

And while we're on the subject, who exactly is "we"? The "we," that is, who are promised all these goodies. "We" will be the "GenRich," the rich in genes. "We" are certainly not the six billion people already on the planet, nor the ten billion projected for the year 2050—those will be the "Gen-Poor." "We," when we appear, will be a select few, and since our enhanced genes and our immortality are going to be so expensive, and will not survive —for instance—being squashed flat by tanks, we will have to take steps to protect ourselves. Doubtless "we" will devise almost impenetrable walls, as in the Zamyatin novel of the same name, or "we" will live in a castle, with "them"—the serfs and peasants, the dimwits, the mortals—roiling around outside. We will talk like James Dewey Watson; we'll say things like "It's not much fun being around dumb people." In fact, we'll behave a lot like the aristocrats of old, convinced of our own divine right. The serfs and peasants will hate us. Not to throw cold water on it, but if the serfs and peasants are true to form, sooner or later they'll get hold of some pitchforks and torches and storm the barricades. So to avoid the peasants, we'll have to go into outer space. Having fun yet?

The agenda of those who visualize themselves as the GenRich—like Past Lifers, Future Lifers never see themselves playing the role of ditch digger—is being pushed in the name of that magic duo, progress and inevitability, the twins that always make an appearance when quite a few potential shareholders smell megabucks in the air. (Along with them come the usual my-dick-is-bigger adjectives, as McKibben points out—guts and risk-taking and so forth—so if you don't rush out and get your genes spliced and your head frozen, you're some sort of a wuss.) "Progress" has deluded many, but surely its pretensions as a rallying slogan have been exploded by now: progress is not the same as change. As for "inevitability," it's the rapist's argument: the thing is going to happen anyway, so why not just lie back and enjoy it? Resistance is futile. (That was the old advice: now you're told to scream and vomit, thus influencing the outcome. Times change.)

McKibben takes on both of the magic twins, and is particularly moving on "inevitability." We still have choice, he says. Just because a thing has been invented doesn't mean you have to use it. He offers as exemples the atomic bomb; the Japanese samurais' rejection of guns; the Chinese abandonment of advanced sea power; and the Amish, who examine each new technology and accept or reject it according to social and spiritual criteria. We, too, he says, can accept or reject according to social and spiritual criteria. We can, and we should. We must decide as ourselves—as who we already are as human beings. We must decide from the fullness of our present humanity, flawed though it may be. As I've said, McKibben is an optimist. I agree with him about what we should do, but I'm not too sure we'll do it.

The fact is—and this is not a line of thought McKibben pursues—that the argument for the perfectibility of mankind rests on a logical fallacy. Thus: Man is by definition imperfect, say those who would perfect him. But those who would perfect him are themselves, by their own definition, imperfect. And imperfect beings cannot make perfect decisions. The decision about what constitutes human perfection would have to be a perfect decision; otherwise the result would be not perfection, but imperfection. As witness the desire for several different mouths.

Perhaps our striving for perfection should take a different, more Blakean form. Perhaps Infinity can be seen in a grain of sand, and Eternity in an hour. Perhaps happiness is not a goal but a road. Perhaps the pursuit of happiness is that happiness. Perhaps we should take a cue from Tennyson, and separate wisdom and knowledge, and admit that wisdom cannot be cloned or manufactured. Perhaps that admission is wisdom. Perhaps enough should be enough for us. Perhaps we should leave well enough alone.

45

Foreword:

Victory Gardens: A Breath of Fresh Air
by Elise Houghton

When I was small, people had Victory Gardens. This was during the Second World War, and the idea was that if people grew their own vegetables, then the food produced by the farmers would be freed up for use by the army. There was another strong motivator: rationing was in effect for things you were unlikely to be able to grow yourself, such as sugar, butter, milk, tea, cheese, and meat, so the more you could grow, the better you would eat, and the better the soldiers would eat, too. Thus, by digging and hoeing and weeding and watering, you, too, could help win the war.

But people did not live on vegetables and fruit alone. Anything resembling protein or fat was precious. Shortening, margarine, and bacon drippings were cherished; gizzards, livers, feet, and necks were not scorned. Bits and scraps that today would be carelessly tossed into the trash were hoarded and treasured, making their way from their first appearance as, say, a roasted chicken, through various other incarnations as noodle-and-leftovers casseroles, soups and stews, and mystery ingredients in pot pies. A housewife's skill was measured by the number of times she could serve up the same thing without your knowing it.

Careful planning was required; waste was frowned on. This meant that everything, not only from such things as chickens but also from the garden, had to be used, and, if necessary, preserved. Home freezing hadn't arrived yet, so canning and preserving were major activities, especially in the late summer, when the garden would produce more than the family could eat. Housewives cooked up vast quantities of tomato sauce, pickles, green beans, strawberries, applesauce—vegetables and fruits of all kinds. These would be eaten in the winter, along with the cabbages and the winter squash and the root vegetables—beets, carrots, turnips, and potatoes—that had been stored in a cool place.

As children growing up in this era, we knew that every seedling was precious. We were part of the system: we weeded and watered, we picked off cabbage worms and tomato worms and potato bugs. We dug peelings and cores and husks back into the soil; we fended off woodchucks; we sprinkled wood ashes. If lucky enough to be near a source of blueberries, we picked them; and we picked peas and beans, and we dug potatoes. I can't claim that all of this was spontaneous labor, joyfully performed: such tasks were chores. But the connection between tending the vegetables and eating the results was clear. Food did not come wrapped in plastic from the supermarket—there were hardly any supermarkets, anyway. It came out of the ground or it grew on a bush or a tree, and it needed water and sunlight and proper fertilization.

My mother's generation was brought up strictly: children were expected to finish everything on their plates, whether they liked it or not, and if they failed to do this they were made to sit at the dinner table until they did. Frequently they were told to remember other children who were starving—the Armenians, the Chinese. I used to think this was both harsh—why force a child to eat when it wasn't hungry?—and ridiculous— what good would eating your bread crusts do for the Armenians? But this method doubtless had at its heart an insistence on respect. Many people had labored to produce the food on the plate, among them the parents, who had either grown it or paid hard-earned cash for it. You could not snub this food. You should show a proper gratitude. Hence the once-widespread practice of saying grace at meals, which has fallen into disuse. Why be grateful for something now so easy to come by?

In the plotline of life on Earth, gardens are a recent twist. They date back to perhaps ten thousand years ago, when the gathering and hunting that had been the prevailing model for 99 percent of human history could no longer sustain societies in the face of diminishing game and wild food supplies.

When the total population of Earth was less than four million people—before, the experts estimate, about ten thousand years ago—the gathering and hunting way of life was still viable. The myth of the Golden Age appears to have some foundation in fact: food was there in the wild, for the taking, and people didn't have to spend much of their time obtaining it. After that point, conditions became harder, as communities had to adapt more labor-intensive stratagems to feed themselves. "Agriculture" is sometimes used to denote any form of cultivation or domestication—of herd animals for meat and milk, of garden crops and fruit trees, of field crops such as wheat and barley. Sometimes a distinction is made between "agriculture," in which large areas are farmed using the plow to break the ground—traditionally a male activity—and "horticulture," in which smaller, individual garden plots are cultivated, traditionally by women. "Horticulture" is thought to have come first, but all agree that there was a long period of transition in which gathering and hunting, horticulture and agriculture, existed side by side.

Many ills have been ascribed to agriculture. In gathering and hunting cultures, food was—as a rule—obtained and eaten as needed. But once agriculture became firmly established—once crops could be harvested and stored, once surpluses could be accumulated, and, not incidentally, transported, exchanged, destroyed, and stolen—social strata became possible, with slaves at the lower end, peasants above them, and a ruling class on top that made no physical effort in order to eat. Armies could march on surplus food supplies; religious hierarchies could tithe; kings could preside; taxes could be levied. Crop monocultures became widespread, with a dependence on only a few kinds of food, resulting not only in malnutrition but also in famine at times of crop failure.

A city dweller's relation to food is—as a system—closer to the gathering-hunting model than to the horticultural-agricultural one. You don't grow the food yourself, or raise it in the form of an animal. Instead, you go to the place where the food is—the supermarket, most likely. Someone else has done the killing, in the case of animal food, or the primary picking, in the case of vegetables, but essentially the shopper is a gatherer. His or her skills consist in knowing where the good stuff is and tracking it down if it's rare. The shopping experience is given all the trappings of a walk in a magic forest—soft music plays, the colors of packages are supernaturally bright, food is displayed as if it's there by miracle. All you have to do is reach out your hand, as in the Golden Age. And then pay, of course.

Such a system disguises origins. The food in shops is dirt-free, and as bloodless as possible. Yet everything we eat comes—in one way or another—out of the earth.

The first garden I can remember was in northern Québec, where my father ran a small field insect research station. The area was a glacial scrape—a region where the glaciers had removed the topsoil thousands of years ago, scraping down to the granite bedrock. Thousands of years after their retreat, the soil was just a thin layer on top of sand or gravel. My parents used this sandy soil as the basis for their garden. Luckily they had a source of manure, from a lumber camp—in those days, horses were still used in winter, to drag the felled trees down to the lake for eventual transport to the mill by water. My parents ferried boatloads of this manure to their fenced-in sandy patch, where they dug it in. From this unpromising ground they raised—among other things—peas, beans, carrots, radishes, lettuce, spinach, Swiss chard, and even the occasional flower. Nasturtiums are what I remember, and the vivid blossoms of the scarlet runner beans, a favorite with hummingbirds. The moral: almost any patch of dirt can be a garden, with enough elbow grease and horse manure.

That garden occurred in the 1940s, when the war was still going on, horticulture in the form of Victory Gardens was still widely practiced, and every morsel of food was treasured.

After the war the postwar boom set in, and attitudes underwent a major change. After a long period of anxiety and hard work and tragedy, people wanted more ease in their lives. Military production switched off, the manufacture of consumer goods switched on. Home appliances proliferated:

the outdoor clothesline was replaced by the dryer, the wringer washer by the automatic. Supermarkets sprang up. Prepackaging arrived. Simple-minded abundance was the order of the day.

The period from 1950 to 2000 might be characterized as the Disposable Period. Waste—including preplanned obsolescence—was no longer seen as an evil and a sin. It became a positive thing, because the more you threw out, the more you would consume, and that would drive the economy, and everyone would become more prosperous. Wouldn't they?

This model works fine as long as there's an endless supply of goods funneling into the in end of the pipe. But it breaks down when the source of supply becomes exhausted. The ultimate source of supply is the biosphere itself. But in the fifties, that, too, appeared to be inexhaustible. And so the party continued. What a thrill, to eat only half of your hamburger, then toss the rest!

There was an undeniable emotional charge to throwing stuff out. Scrimping, saving, and hoarding make a person feel poor—think of Scrooge, in *A Christmas Carol*—whereas dispensing largesse, whether in the form of a prize goose, as in Scrooge's case, or in the form of filling up your garbage can with junk you no longer want, makes you feel rich. Saving is heavy, discarding is light. Why do we feel this way? Once we were nomads, and nomads don't carry around grand pianos. They don't hoard food; instead, they move to where food is. They leave a light footprint, as the green folk say. Well, it's a theory.

But we can't all be nomads anymore. There isn't enough space left for that.

Many people gave up their gardens after the war. My parents kept on with theirs, because they said fresh food tasted better. (This is actually true.) The age of full-blown pesticides was just arriving, and that may have had something to do with it as well. My father was an early opponent of widespread pesticide use, partly because this was his field of study. According to him, spraying forests to kill infestations of budworm and sawfly simply arrested the infestation, after which the insects would develop a resistance to the poisons used on them and would continue on their rampage. Meanwhile, you'd have killed off their natural enemies, which would no longer be around to fight them. The effects of these poisons on human beings was unknown but could not be discounted. At that time his views were considered quaint.

Thus the second major garden in my life was in Toronto. Again, the soil was unpromising: heavy clay, which was sticky in the rain but would bake to a hard finish during dry spells. The soil was particularly good for growing giant dandelions and huge clumps of couch grass. It took a lot of work to turn it into anything resembling a garden. Kitchen scraps were composted, fall leaves were dug into the ground by the bushel.

By this time I was a teenager, and was expected to do quite a lot of weeding and watering. News for parents: weeding and watering someone else's garden is not quite as engaging as weeding and watering your own. The high points were the time when I shot a marauding woodchuck with my bow (the arrow was a target arrow, not a hunting arrow, so it bounced off), and the other time when I pulled up all of my father's experimental Jerusalem artichokes by mistake.

Once past my teenage years, I gave up gardening for a time. I'd had enough of it. Also, I wasn't in a location that permitted it: I was an itinerant student and sometime teacher and market researcher and writer, and I moved fifteen times in ten years. In the early seventies, however, I found myself on a farm that had a barn with a large supply of well-rotted horse manure, and the temptation was too great to resist. For eight years we grew everything imaginable. To the staples we added corn, kohlrabi, asparagus, currants—red and white—and elderberries. We tried out new methods— potatoes grown in straw, marigolds to catch slugs. We canned, froze, dried; we made sauerkraut, not an experiment I would choose to repeat. We made wine, jams and jellies, beer. We raised our own chickens and ducks and sheep; we buried parsnips in holes in the ground, and carrots in boxes of sand in the root cellar.

It was a lot of work. This is one reason people don't do more home gardening.

The other, of course, is lack of land. The number of pumpkins you can raise on your apartment balcony is finite, and your wheat crop in this location would not be large.

Lack of land. Lack of *arable* land. To that we may add "lack of sea," because the sea's resources are being destroyed as fast as the earth's. Soon we may have to add "lack of fresh water" and even "lack of breathable air." There's no free lunch after all.

As a species, we're suffering from our own success. From a population of four million ten thousand years ago, we've increased to six billion today, and growing. The exponential population explosion that has occurred since 1750 was unprecedented in human history, and it will never be repeated. We must slow our growth rate as a species or face a series of unimaginable environmental and human catastrophes. Arable land is finite, and much of it is rapidly being paved over, eroded, polluted, or depleted. The same rules apply to us as to other animals: no biological population can outlive the exhaustion of its resource base. It's an easy thing to demonstrate to children. Get them an ant farm, feed the ants, watch the ants increase in number. Then cut off the food supply. End of ants.

For *Homo sapiens*, the major question of the twenty-first century will be, *How will we eat?* Already 80 percent of the world's people exist on the starvation borderline. Will we see a sudden, enormous crash, as in the mouse-and-lemming cycle? And if so, what then?

These are alarming thoughts to place in the foreword to a kindly and attractive book on school gardening. Such an admirable demonstration of care and careful planning, so much variety, such a symbol of hope. I don't apologize for these thoughts, however: the world I have just described is the one today's children will be facing unless there are some fairly large changes of direction.

The reasons for encouraging the school gardening movement are many. Gardens are educational, teaching as they do many lessons. Food grows in the ground, not in supermarkets; air, soil, sun, and water are the four necessary ingredients; composting is a fine notion; front lawns are a water-gobbling waste of space; the individual can be an instrument for positive change; unless you're a geologist, plants are more interesting than gravel;

beetles come in many forms; worms are good; nature must be respected; we are part of Nature.

All of these are positive concepts, but fifty years ago—even thirty years ago—they would have been viewed as extra, frilly, prissy, goody-goody. Even now, some in our society would place them in this slot: the hard stuff, the right stuff to grind into the minds of children, is how to make a lot of money.

But money's useless when there's nothing to eat. So there's another set of skills to be learned from school gardens: how to grow your own food. Perhaps today's children will need these skills. Perhaps they'll find themselves in some grim collective dedicated to turning golf courses back into market gardens and superhighways into very long grain fields, and front lawns into potato plots. Perhaps the Victory Garden will make a forced comeback due to scarcity.

Or perhaps our species will solve its problems before droughts and famines become endemic.

Then again, perhaps not.

46

Eulogy:

Carol Shields, Who Died Last Week, Wrote Books That Were Full of Delights

T he beloved Canadian author Carol Shields died on July 16 at her home in Victoria, British Columbia, after a long battle with cancer. She was sixty-eight. The enormous media coverage given to her and the sadness expressed by her many readers paid tribute to the high esteem in which she was held in her own country, but her death made the news all around the world.

Conscious as she was of the vagaries of fame and the element of chance in any fortune, she would have viewed that with a certain irony, but she would also have found it deeply pleasing. She knew about the darkness, but—both as an author and as a person—she held on to the light. "She was just a luminous person, and that would be important and persist even if she hadn't written anything," said her friend and fellow author Alice Munro.

Earlier in her writing career, some critics mistook this quality of light in her for lightness, light-mindedness, on the general principle that comedy—a form that turns on misunderstanding and confusion but ends in reconciliation, of however tenuous a kind—is less serious than tragedy, and that the personal life is of lesser importance than the public one. Carol Shields knew better. Human life is a mass of statistics only for statisticians; the rest of us live in a world of individuals, and most of them are not prominent. Their joys, however, are fully joyful, and their griefs are real. It was the extraordinariness of ordinary people that was Shields's forte, reaching its fullest expression in her novels *Swann*, *The Republic of Love*, and especially *The Stone Diaries*. She gave her material the full benefit of her large intelligence, her powers of observation, her humane wit, and her wide reading. Her books are delightful, in the original sense of the word: they are full of delights.

She understood the life of the obscure and the overlooked partly because she had lived it: her study of Jane Austen reveals a deep sympathy with the plight of the woman novelist toiling incognito, appreciated only by an immediate circle but longing for her due. Born in 1935 in the United States, Shields was at the tail end of the postwar generation of North American college-educated women who were convinced by the mores of their time that their destiny was to get married and have five children. This Carol did; she remained a devoted mother and a constant wife throughout her life. Her husband, Don, was a civil engineer. They moved to Canada, beginning with Toronto in the sixties, a time of poetic ferment in that city. Carol, who was already writing then and attended some readings, said of that time, "I knew no writers." Undoubtedly she felt relegated to that nebulous category "just a housewife," like Daisy in *The Stone Diaries* and like Mary Swann, the eponymous poet who is murdered by her husband when her talent begins to show. (Canadian readers would understand the allusion, but British ones who might consider this plot far-fetched will be interested to know that there was a Canadian woman poet murdered in this way: Pat Lowther, whose best-known collection is *The Stone Diary*.)

After obtaining an M.A. at the University of Ottawa, Shields taught for years at the University of Manitoba, in Winnipeg, where she began publishing in the seventies. But this was the decade of rampant feminism—in the arts, at least. Her early books, including *Others Intersect*, *Small Ceremonies*, and *The Box Garden*, which examined the vagaries of domestic life without torpedoing it, did not make a large stir, although some of their early readers found them both highly accomplished and hilarious. She had her first literary breakthrough—not in terms of quality of writing, but in terms of audience size—in Britain rather than in North America, with her 1992 novel *The Republic of Love*.

Her glory book was *The Stone Diaries*, which was short-listed for the

Booker Prize and won the Canadian Governor General's Award, and then, in 1995, the American Pulitzer Prize, a feat her dual citizenship made possible. Her next novel, *Larry's Party*, won the Orange Prize in 1998. To say that she was not thrilled by success would be to do her an injustice. She knew what it was worth. She'd waited a long time for it. She wore her new-found prominence with graciousness and used it with largesse. One of the last instances of her enormous generosity of spirit may not be well known: she supplied a jacket quotation for Valerie Martin's fine but challenging novel *Property*—a book that went on to win the 2003 Orange Prize. It takes place in the American South during slavery, and none of the characters are "nice," but as Carol remarked in a letter she wrote me, that was the point.

Unless, her last novel, was written in the small space of time she spent in England, after beating cancer the first time and before it came back. It's a hymn to the provisional: the sense of happiness and security as temporary and fragile is stronger than ever. *Unless* was published in 2002, and it was short-listed for just about every major English-language prize. The Munro Doctrine, informally named after Alice Munro, had set in by then—after a certain number of prizes you are shot into the stratosphere, where you circulate in radiant mists, far beyond the ken of juries.

Several months before her death, Carol published—with coeditor Marjorie Anderson—*Dropped Threads 2*, the sequel to the spectacularly successful 2001 anthology *Dropped Threads*. This was a frankly feminist collection, taking "feminist" in its broadest sense: contributors were asked to write about subjects of concern to women that had been excluded from the conversation so far. Those who had heard Carol Shields interviewed were probably surprised by this strain in her character, and by the angry letters addressed to male pundits dismissive of woman writers in *Unless*, because in conversation she was discreet and allusive. The little frown, the shake of the head, said it all.

Possibly feminism was something she worked into, as she published more widely and came up against more commentators who thought excellent pastry was a facile creation compared with raw meat on skewers, and who in any case could not recognize the thread of blood in her work, though it was always there. The problem of the luminous is that their very luminosity obscures the shadows it depends on for its brilliance.

I last saw Carol Shields at the end of April. Her new house was spacious, filled with light; outside the windows, the tulips in her much-loved garden were in bloom. Typically for her, she claimed she couldn't quite believe she deserved to live in such a big and beautiful house. She felt so lucky, she said.

Although she was very ill, she didn't seem it. She was as alert, as interested in books of all kinds, and as curious as ever. She'd recently been reading nonfiction works on biology, she told me: something new for her, a new source of amazement and wonder. We did not speak of her illness. She preferred to be treated as a person who was living, not one who was dying.

And live she did, and live she does, for as John Keats remarked, every writer has two souls, an earthly one and one that lives on in the world of writing as a voice in the writing itself. It's this voice, astute, compassionate, observant, and deeply human, that will continue to speak to her readers everywhere.

47

Review:

Reading Lolita in Tehran:
A Memoir in Books
by Azar Nafisi

A
zar Nafisi's engrossing *Reading Lolita in Tehran* is the sort of book that ruins the sleep of those in charge of placing books in bookstores. Where to shelve it? Under "literary criticism"? No, for although it subjects a number of classics to revealing scrutiny, that would miss much of its point. Under "memoirs"? Similar problems: though its story is intertwined with the life of its author, it is not that life. "Women's issues" or "feminism" would not be entirely out of place—the main characters who both act and suffer in this book are female—but again, in such a classification something would be lacking. A mischievous soul might stash it under "book groups," which would be about as close as my college library's choice of "veterinary medicine" for Hemingway's *Death in the Afternoon*. There is a book group in *Reading Lolita*, but it's more like a life raft than an after-work social gathering.

Reading Lolita needs a category all its own. *An approach to the serious reading of mostly modern Western classics under a fundamentalist Muslim dictatorship, with hanging, shooting, and bombing complications* might be a beginning. Its author, Azar Nafisi, is at present a professor at Johns Hopkins University and a frequent visitor to talk shows, now that Iran is increasingly a subject of conversation, but her situation was not always as secure. She grew up in Iran, in a family not without standing—though her father was imprisoned by Shah Reza Pahlevi at one time—then went to college in the United States in the 1970s. There, at the University of Oklahoma, she explored

Western literature and ideas of freedom—especially freedom for women—and took part in protests against the Shah's brutally repressive regime, where the secret-police organization SAVAK indulged in assassination and torture.

As she describes it, Nafisi found this period of her life confusing. She opposed the shah's regime, but from what position should she oppose it? Should she advocate Western liberalism, which was being attacked for failing to come to the defense of individual rights in her country because it put its own oil interests foremost? Should she veer toward the left, back then when the Soviet Union still existed and was doling out funds and party lines? Or was that too modern, too secular, too materialist? The Shah, after all, was modern and secular and materialist. Some felt Iran should go in the other direction—toward the past, toward some version of Islam that would have the strength to overthrow the Shah's regime, purge the country of corruption, and deliver justice to a people who had been too long deprived of it. But if you were a woman, the Islamic option presented risks. "When I was growing up in the 1960s," she says, "there was little difference between my rights and the rights of women in Western democracies. . . . We all wanted opportunities and freedom. That is why we supported revolutionary change—we were demanding *more* rights, not fewer."

Nafisi became involved with a faction on the left, but claims she was never entirely convinced by any of the ideological lines. Her real loyalties were to her homeland and to literature. But a homeland is never identical with the government of the moment, and literature transcends ideology; thus totalitarianisms have always tried to co-opt national sentiments and censor or harness writers. As Nafisi says in hindsight, "Like all other ideologues before them, the Islamic revolutionaries seemed to believe that writers were the guardians of morality. This displaced view of writers, ironically, gave them a sacred place, and at the same time it paralyzed them. The price they had to pay . . . was a kind of aesthetic impotence."

Filled with idealism and with a passionate faith in the dream of an Iran as it might yet be, Nafisi returned to her country to take up a teaching post at the University of Tehran just at the moment when the Shah's walls came tumbling down. Although she didn't know it, this was like returning to Paris when the French Revolution skidded out of control. Turmoil was the order of the day as various revolutionary groups fought for political power.

On the one hand, everything seemed possible; doors opened, exiles returned, prisoners stepped into the light. On the other hand, the reign of the mullahs was to become worse and worse—bloodier and more corrupt than the Shah's regime had ever been. But many Iranians didn't see this coming. They hoped. They believed.

Into this cauldron stepped Nafisi, armed only with her good intentions, her devotion to literature, and a kind of foolhardy innocence. Hearing of the risks she took, the reader is amazed that she wasn't arrested or killed. As a teacher, she was inspired by her students' thirst for knowledge, though she was also angered by their ignorance and their unwillingness to think for themselves. But as one of her students admonished her—a student who was later murdered by the regime—" 'Most of these girls have never had anyone praise them for anything. . . . Now you come in and confront them, accusing them of betraying principles they have never been taught to value. You should've known better.' "

Almost immediately Nafisi's classroom became a focus for the tensions of Iranian society. Oddly enough, it was the books North American readers might find the most innocuous that caused the wildest clashes. Jane Austen roused the ire of fundamentalist students for the very reason that their Western equivalents might dismiss her with a yawn: she wrote books about private life, private love, and personal choices. But as Nafisi points out, in a totalitarian regime the biggest affront is a nonpolitical book—a book that exists for its own reasons. "It is said that the personal is political. That is not true, of course. At the core of the fight for political rights is the desire to protect ourselves, to prevent the political from intruding on our individual lives. Political and personal are interdependent but not one and the same thing. The realm of the imagination is a bridge between them. . . . It was perhaps not surprising that the Islamic Republic's first task had been to blur the boundaries between the personal and the political, thereby destroying both."

The university quickly became the battleground for warring ideologies. Fundamentalist students attended Nafisi's classes to denounce her choice of subject material. Morality was constantly under discussion, often presented in black-and-white terms. Fitzgerald's *The Great Gatsby* was so contentious that the class put it on trial. It shouldn't be taught at all, claimed the fundamentalist prosecution, because there was drinking and adultery in it. Henry James's *Daisy Miller* was deeply troubling to the students because, like the story's narrator, they couldn't decide whether Daisy was a "good" girl or a "bad" one. "A novel is not an allegory," Nafisi tells the class. "It is the sensual experience of another world. . . . This is how you read a novel: you inhale the experience." Years later, Nafisi met a former student, a woman who had attacked her but is now married and has chosen a "secret" name for her daughter: Daisy, after Daisy Miller. " 'I want my daughter to be what I never was—like Daisy. You know, courageous.' "

While Nafisi was attempting to teach, the fundamentalists were tightening their grip. Women's bodies became highly charged political and religious symbols. When the university demanded that she wear the veil, Nafisi quit, only to find herself shortly in a world in which all women, university folk or not, were forced to veil themselves or face imprisonment and worse. The regime had a nasty habit of "marrying" virgin women to guards, who would rape them before executing them. Why? Because virgins went to heaven. Nafisi says that it was the "persistent lack of kindness"—extended to every sphere of life—that frightened her the most. Similarly, for the novelists she teaches and admires, the worst sin is the failure of empathy—the lack of imagination that must lead inevitably to the "persistent lack of kindness."

As external space became more and more closed to Nafisi and as the religious police stepped up their harassment, she set up a private reading group, which met in her house. The only criterion for membership was a wish to discuss Western literature. It is at this point that *Reading Lolita in Tehran* begins: from this midpoint in its own narrative, it ranges backward and forward in time, filling us in on the events that have lead to the group's formation, and telling us what happened next to its various members. Their identities are disguised to protect them. Only one former student appears as herself, but that is because she is dead. The stories of the women range from horrifying to heartbreaking to touching, with a couple of muted happy endings. Every one of them—even those who were in favor of the government at the outset—feels herself ground down, obliterated.

Reading Lolita provides us with a chilling account of what it feels like to live under such conditions: the heaviness, the constant weighing down—which is what we mean by "oppression"—and at the same time a lightness, a sense of unreality—They can't be doing this!—and a feeling that one is becoming both invisible and fictional. Nafisi's reading group paid so much attention to Nabokov partly because of his absolute fidelity to the primacy of the aesthetic imagination, and partly because they saw, in the fate of the defenseless Lolita at the hands of Humbert, their own position reflected. Lolita was turned into a fantasy object, just as every woman in Iran had become a fantasy object for the regime—a regime that wanted to censor all narratives but its own, and to force everyone else to play a preordained part in it. "The desperate truth of Lolita's story," says Nafisi, "is *not* the rape of a twelve-year-old by a dirty old man but *the confiscation of one individual's life by another.*"

Despite the grimness, the pain and horror, and the human malice that *Reading Lolita* describes, it is enthralling nonetheless. It explores with fervor and conviction the tacit pact among writer, book, and reader. It's also a reminder that reading is subject to the zeitgeist, just as we are told writing is. Nafisi reads T. S. Eliot and Dashiel Hammett as the bombs from Iraq are falling close to her house; she reads *Lolita* with her secret group; she rediscovers Austen in Iran. Reading a book creates a memory of itself, and that memory includes the circumstances under which it was read. Where reading is so curtailed and readers so deprived, the books themselves acquire a heightened value. They become an alternate reality, a source of hope, a matter of life and death. This book causes us to reflect on our own reading habits, which by comparison seem casual and lacking in seriousness. It's the old human story: we don't know what we've got until it's gone.

Nafisi's valued friend—a recluse she calls her "magician"—says to her when she is on the verge of leaving Iran, " 'You will not be able to write about Austen without writing about us. . . . This is the Austen you read here, in a place where the film censor is blind and where they hang people in the streets. . . .' "

"I have a recurring fantasy that one more article has been added to the Bill of Rights: the right to free access to imagination," says Nafisi. *Reading Lolita in Tehran* is both a fascinating account at how she arrived at this belief and a stunning vindication of it. All readers should read it. As for writers, it reminds us, with great eloquence, that our words may travel farther and say more than we could ever guess at the time we wrote them.

48

Introduction:

The Complete Stories, Volume 4
by Morley Callaghan

Morley Callaghan, long considered the most important Canadian story writer of his generation—which he was—has also long been a literary misfit; people never knew quite what to make of him. Doubtless this was how he liked it: he took pleasure in baffling expectation. He's important, he's very important, they say; but why? Even the American critic Edmund Wilson, lavish in his praise of Callaghan in his 1964 book *O Canada*, spends a lot of time scratching his head. Callaghan's effects, he says, are so subtle, so modulated, yet so simple, that it's hard to describe them. And so it has often gone.

For those Canadian writers who began in the early 1960s, cutting their teeth on beatniks and postwar French existentialists and the theater of the absurd, Callaghan was neither fish nor fowl. He wrote of a time before our time, but not so long before that we had no memories of it. In some ways the world he depicted overlapped with our own age—we knew about the squalor of rooming houses; and grubby, Depression-scarred lives lived on the financial margins; and the fear of unwanted pregnancy—but in those instances it represented parts of our lives we wanted to change, or hoped we had escaped. Such things held no glamor for us.

The aesthetics of Callaghan's minimalist style, devoid of fancy words and metaphors—a style he hoped to render "transparent as glass" [1]—had excellent antecedents in the English tradition, from Addison's efforts to divest the eighteenth-century English stage of bombast and superfluous rhetoric, to Wordsworth's attempt, in *Lyrical Ballads*, to get back to the poetic basics, to Orwell's prose like a windowpane, intended to give us an unimpeded view of real life, like so many raw steaks in a butcher's display case. All such purifiers see their efforts as a sort of excavation: a fraudulent accumulation of grotty old barnacles called "the literary" or "the academic" must be scraped away to get to the deep-down freshness and newness of the actual—to truth; to honesty; or, in Callaghan's words, to "the object as it really was." [2]

However, if you're a writer, all this must be done through language, which is—how can the purifier get around it?—man-made and therefore artificial. But if you must have speech, then make it plain speech; if words, then short words. Awkwardness is to be preferred to an overly carved and varnished elegance; and if elegance, then the elegance of a Shaker chair. These tendencies, too, can turn mannerist. Taken too far, you'd end up with a literature of monosyllables that would read like a *Dick and Jane* primer, but Callaghan avoided this trap.

Style in every art swings like a pendulum from the plain to the ornamented and back again, with "nature" and "artifice" being the polarizing catchphrases; but we whippersnappers in the early sixties hadn't thought much about that. To us, the hard-boiled school—decades old by the time we came across it—seemed an almost comic affectation, like talking out of the side of the mouth in gangster films. The young are cruel, and they are most cruel to the quasi-parental generation preceding them, as Callaghan himself was cruel to the aesthetes of the turn of the century—"show-off writers," [3] he termed them, fixated on demonstrating their own cleverness. It's a necessary cruelty, I suppose, or we would all be replicants.

Callaghan's legend—as opposed to the milieu depicted in his work—did have glamour for us, however. He'd been our age in the 1920s, and had written through the Great Depression and the war—eras that were now so far away that they were already furnishing the costumes for fancy-dress parties. In Paris, still thought of as the proper destination for an artist of any kind, he'd consorted with Hemingway and Fitzgerald—writers we'd studied in school, and who for that reason alone had an aura of semidivinity, while at the same time being ridiculously hoary. Unlike those two, however, he'd become neither a drunk nor a suicide, and was said to be living in Toronto—Toronto!—an unromantic, second-rate city in which no real writer—surely—would live by choice. Why wasn't he stowed away in Paris or New York, where we wouldn't have to bother about him? Why did he stick around, like a burr?

What was it about Callaghan that made us uncomfortable? For one thing, he was doing something thought to be impossible: he was making a living in Canada, as a writer, albeit through sales in the United States and in England. That was a challenge, since it was a truism among us that you'd have to leave the country to get anywhere. We were—of course—provincials, who believed that the Great Good Place was somewhere else; and he was a nonprovincial who understood the provincial—having once partaken of it—and who had chosen this very provinciality as his material. (He was a student of—among others—Flaubert and de Maupassant, who had done the same.) We youngsters weren't the only folk made nervous by this. As Edmund Wilson said in 1960,

> The reviewer . . . is now wondering whether the primary reason for the current underestimation of Morley Callaghan may not be a general incapacity—apparently shared by his compatriots—for believing that a writer whose work may be mentioned without absurdity in association with Chekhov's and Turgenev's can possibly be functioning in Toronto.[4]

Northrop Frye was another to put his finger on the Canadian uneasiness with Callaghan. After having stated that by 1929 Callaghan had established himself as perhaps the best short-story writer in Canada, he later said:

> Morley Callaghan's books, I think I am right in saying, were sometimes banned by the public library in Toronto—I forget what the rationalization was, but the real reason could only have been that if

a Canadian were to do anything so ethically dubious as write, he should at least write like a proper colonial and not like someone who had lived in the Paris of Joyce and Gertrude Stein.[5]

Not surprisingly, Callaghan—who was nothing if not a scrapper—kicked against the pricks. He took the piss out of what he saw as the back-scratching mediocre sham literati in Canada, calling them—among other things—"local medicine men feasting and having a big cultural pow-wow,"[6] and homegrown critics took the piss out of him for it, and he took the piss out of them back. One of these fracases took place live on television, after Callaghan had been praised by Edmund Wilson, and then predictably denounced for it by a two-bit academic, live on a talk show. Callaghan, no stranger to rancorous debate, did not take this sitting down. It was an object lesson in self-respect to the young, and one we needed; for at that time, in Canada, to be a writer was to be thought next door to a junk-bond salesman: shifty, not above pinching the silver, to be sneered at and viewed with suspicion.

Self-respect. Respect. Respectability. These are key concepts in Callaghan's work: in fact, *respect* is the last word in the last story in this collection. Almost every Callaghan character desires to have and to earn "respect," the admiration of others. "Self-respect"—that quality of inner integrity, the ability to hold up your head when you look in the mirror—is also highly valued. "Respectability" is ambiguous. You need it to get and hold a job, which connects you with money—the ability to earn a living, to show a girl a good time, and to buy coveted objects—often articles of clothing, for people were judged very much by their wardrobes in those days. Money is never out of the picture, because, for Callaghan's characters, it doesn't grow on trees. But "respectability" is also a negative. It's the lack of joie de vivre, the absence of passion and energy; it's conformity; it's hypocrisy; it's mediocrity; it's a dingy, gray, stifling fog. It's also next door to self-righteousness, and self-righteousness was not a quality Callaghan admired, although it occupied him greatly as a subject.

Callaghan has frequently been compared with Hemingway and

Fitzgerald, yet the concerns of the three are very different. In a Western shoot-out saga, Fitzgerald would have been interested in the cattle barons hiring the gunmen, Hemingway in the gunmen themselves; but Callaghan, though he might have paid some attention to both of the other groups, would have focused on the jittery townsfolk crouching behind the dry-goods counter. Fitzgerald was drawn to rich people, Hemingway to adventurous people, but Callaghan to people—men, usually—who might long to be rich and adventurous but who cannot actualize their longings, either because life has not provided them with the scope or because their own makeup defeats them. Their sense of their own worth is tenuous, as is their sense of their own bravery: both can stand or fall on an accident, an incident, a misunderstanding, an added pressure brought to bear. We identify with such characters because we've known people like them, but also because, given a change in circumstances, we could so easily find ourselves in their shoes.

As a story writer, Callaghan has been likened to many: Chekhov and Turgenev, Sherwood Anderson, Katherine Mansfield, de Maupassant, the Joyce of *Dubliners*, even O. Henry. His specialties were the small and thwarted life and the brief but exactly sketched state of emotion. Typically, his characters live in rooming houses or cramped apartments; they're unemployed, or in danger of losing their jobs or modest businesses. They borrow money they can't repay, or they get drunk and blow it, or they skirt the edge of minor criminality. If they are women, their husbands may have run off, or—and Callaghan's sense of gender interaction is exact for his times—they may be resented and even physically abused for having jobs when their men do not. If they are children or young people, adults let them down. If they are dogs, they are unfortunate.

Most of them indulge in irrational hopes and yearn for better things, but it's not likely they'll get them. They see themselves reflected in the eyes of others, and the reflection does not please them unless they are puffed up by a soon-to-be-deflated vainglory. Desiring to be looked up to, they more often feel belittled or small; size does matter. Occasionally someone will score points—the boy in "The New Kid" gains status through combat, the umpire in "Mother's Day at the Ball Park" is cheered by the crowd— confusingly for him, because he's punched a mother-insulting heckler.

Amid the malice and the disappointment and the rage and the bitterness in these lives there are moments of generosity and joy, however unfounded; but such states of grace, we know, are temporary.

In literature, irony is a mode in which the reader guesses more accurately about the character's fate than he does himself, and in this sense Callaghan is a profoundly ironic writer. Life is not only a struggle, it's a puzzle. Another puzzle is why Callaghan, in *That Summer in Paris*, would claim to applaud the art he admires—his example is Matisse—as "a gay celebration of things as they were."[7] "Why couldn't all people have the eyes and heart that would give them this happy acceptance of reality?" he continues. Happiness and gaiety and acceptance of things as they are may have belonged to the author of Callaghan's stories, but they are not frequently found among his characters. Perhaps the stories are, in part, an attempt by Callaghan to answer his own question—to provide a "because" to go with the "why"—with the lamentable scarcity of the right kinds of hearts and eyes.

The next four words in the curious passage quoted above are "The word made flesh." The context might lead us to believe that this is an endorsement of a philosophy of immanence, of the divine *isness* of things—"The appleness of apples. Yet just apples," as Callaghan had just said of Cézanne. Yet they are also a signpost pointing toward Callaghan the Christian writer.[8]

This side of Callaghan is not obtrusive or doctrinaire, and yet it's there—the ground beneath the house, not always seen but necessary. It's more obvious in the novels, and unavoidable in "The Man with the Coat," the last short fiction Callaghan ever wrote—a transitional form, termed a novel in the 1955 issue of *Maclean's* magazine in which it appeared, but really a novella. Callaghan expanded it and changed the plot, and this version later appeared as *The Many-Coloured Coat*.

"The Man with the Coat" is an adroitly constructed piece in which several characters take turns sneering at and belittling one another. Scorn is handed from character to character, like the hot object in a game of Pass the Package, until the sequence of blame leads to a tragic consequence. The motion is not circular, but spiral: its end is not its beginning. It's possible that this story was written as an attempt to work out a problem: how to write a tragedy in the age of the common man. Arthur Miller's *Death of a Salesman*, for instance, is pathetic rather than tragic in its effect, because the salesman can't fall from a high place, having never achieved one. The true tragic hero must plummet like a falling star, and his descent must be due in part to a weakness or flaw in his own character. Or so went the theory. Callaghan was widely read, and perfectly aware of the requirements. As he was a Christian writer, the flaw needed to be a flaw in Christian terms: more a sin than a flaw.

The story begins with a trial and ends with one. The description of the physical ambience—the smell of wet wool, the annoying whoosh of galoshes, every little thing—is spot-on, as is usual in Callaghan. Harry Lane, the hero, starts out as a sort of Timon of Athens before his reversal of fortune, or a Hamlet before the black-suit phase: he's the observed of all observers. He's a celebrated war hero, handsome, well off, easygoing, generous, careless in a lily-of-the-field way, admired by all, and with a top-of-the-line girlfriend. The initial event in the plot is driven, like the acts of Cassius in *Julius Caesar*, by envy: a bank manager named Scotty uses Harry as the cat's-paw in a fraudulent transaction, hoping to profit by it himself. But he gets caught, and is put on trial, and then kills himself, and Harry—undeservedly—has the moral guilt pinned on him. People look down on him. They expect him to feel small. They no longer respect him. For a Callaghan protagonist, this is awful.

Struggling to regain the esteem of his society, Harry passes the parcel of scorn to Scotty's friend, a tailor and ex-pugilist named Mike Kon. The vehicle is a coat with a faulty lining, made by Kon, interpreted by Harry as a gesture of disrespect toward himself. By spreading its story and wearing it everywhere, Harry makes Kon appear dishonest and a fool. (Kon passes on the scorn in his turn, and so does Molly, the upper-class girl with the cold heart who has thrown Harry over due to his disgrace.) But neither Harry nor Kon can resolve the conflict between them, because both suffer from the sin of pride. Both demand "justice."

The plot develops in rounds, like the boxing match that signals the climax of the action. In the course of vindicating themselves, defending their self-respect, and standing up for their honor, the characters wallop another—both verbally and physically, and are walloped in turn. There are three arbiters, or umpires, who stand outside the ring. One is the owner of the prestigious bar where all gather, or want to. He's the social arbiter: he decides who's in, who's out, who's hot, who's not. The second is Michael Kon's father, an old man who's suffered a stroke. He's the spiritual arbiter. He can't talk, but he can write, and he delivers himself of a shakily printed oracle that probably says: *Judge not.* The rest of the phrase, not supplied by the old man, is "Lest ye be judged." And so it is: all who judge are indeed judged.

The third arbiter is Annie Laurie, a woman of large heart and easy morals, who unfortunately—like mermaids—has a jinx on her. Annie Laurie, in the song about her, gives promises true, and Callaghan's Annie also tells the truth, because, having no respectability, she has nothing to lose. She's got those coveted Callaghan qualities, honesty and the ability to show the object as it really is. But Annie Laurie also has this effect on men who stay too long with her: they end up prone and breathless. Are we intended to see her as a sort of femme fatale? I think not: she is connected with truth, not poisonous wiles. Possibly one way of understanding her place in this story is to refer back to Everyman, that other Christian tale of a man's progress toward the grave. Most of Everyman's companions—Kin, Good Fellowship, and the like—desert him when times get tough, as Harry's pals do. The one left at the end is female, and her name is Knowledge. It could be that Annie Laurie is no fatal woman, but instead a trustworthy companion in Harry's time of need, which is also his fated journey. She does try to warn him away from the paths of pride. But he won't listen.

It is Annie who is present when Harry is killed, and Annie who testifies at the trial. Like many a prophetess, she isn't much believed—in her case, because of her dubious sexual reputation. It's Mike Kon, Harry's erstwhile enemy and slayer, who—exonerated by the same legal system that earlier caused Harry so much grief—ends up as the shield-bearer, the Horatio figure, the teller of dead Harry's story. He has learned what it is to judge and to be judged, and has opted for the hidden alternative to justice, which is mercy. It's a conclusion both deeply ironic and oddly compassionate.

Which—underneath everything else—would seem to be the appleness of apples at the very bottom of the Callaghan barrel. Irony and compassion. The Callaghanness of Callaghan. Yet just Callaghan. The object as it really is.

Notes

1., 2., 3. From *That Summer in Paris*, as reprinted in *Canadian Novelists and the Novel*, ed. Douglas Daymond and Leslie Monkman (Ottawa: Borealis Press, 1981), pp. 143–46.

4. Edmund Wilson, *O Canada: An American's Notes on Canadian Culture* (New York: Farrar, Straus, & Giroux, 1964), p. 21.

5. *Northrop Frye on Canada*, ed. Jean O'Grady and David Staines (Toronto: University of Toronto Press, 2003), p. 549.

6. From "The Plight of Canadian Fiction" (1938), reprinted in Daymond and Monkman, *That Summer in Paris*, p. 150.

7. Daymond and Monkman, *That Summer in Paris*, p. 146.

8. Right after this, Callaghan makes a dismissive remark about St. Paul. Christians often see themselves as having to choose between the road of St. Paul, which leads to Rome, and that of Christ, which leads to Cavalry. Not much doubt about which Callaghan preferred.

49

Review:

Hope Dies Last:
Keeping the Faith in Difficult Times
by Studs Terkel

I f Studs Terkel were Japanese, he'd be a Sacred Treasure. As John Kenneth Galbraith has said of him, "Studs Terkel is more than a writer, he is a national resource." *Hope Dies Last* is the latest in the series of American oral histories he's been publishing since *Division Street, America* appeared in 1967. In the thirty-six years between then and now, he's covered, in separate books, the Great Depression, World War II, race relations, working, the American Dream, and aging. For each book, he interviewed an amazing variety of people—where does he meet some of these folks, anyway?—and the entire oeuvre has an exhaustiveness and monumentality that will make it necessary reading for future social historians of the American twentieth century.

The arrangement of subjects begins to took less serendipitous than schematic. Books about youth and middle age—initiation, ordeal, and daily life in action—were followed by books about contemplation and stock-taking. The second-to-last was titled *Death: Will the Circle Be Unbroken?* (2001), which carried us into the unknown: will there be an afterlife? (The general consensus: maybe, maybe not.) The series now resembles a planned cycle, like the cycles of mystery plays put on in medieval towns. You'd think *Death* would have ended it, but with the addition of *Hope Dies Last*, the pattern is now similar to that of Armistice Day ceremonies, where taps, the sundown signal, is followed by reveille, the wake-up call, symbolizing the Resurrection. Death and hope are paired as well on many Christian tombstones, which have the words *In Spe*. No coincidence then that Terkel kicks off his book with an upward-tending sentiment: "Hope has never trickled down. It has always sprung up." First the dead body, then the young, green leaves of grass.

It's very Terkelesque—by now, the man requires an adjective of his own—that after death should come hope, for Terkel's optimism has seldom failed him. His lifetime of ninety-one years has spanned the boom times of the twenties, the Depression, World War II, the McCarthy Red-hunting era, the civil rights movement, the hippie activists of the late sixties, and on into present times. He grew up in Chicago in the 1920s, eavesdropping on the arguments that went on in the lobby of the workingmen's hotel run by his widowed mother—arguments that pitted old Wobblies from the International Workers of the World against anti-unionists, with ordinary working stiffs who "didn't gave a hoot one way or the other" putting their oars in, too. This was the perfect education for a man who was to become the American interviewer par excellence: Terkel became a practiced listener. He learned how to take the measure of what he was hearing and to assess who was saying it.

He spent three dispiriting years at the University of Chicago Law School, then took up acting in radio soap operas to avoid being a lawyer— "I was always typecast as a Chicago gangster," he says. Then he became a disc jockey—classical, jazz, and folk—and, with the advent of television, an unorthodox talk show host. On *Studs's Place* he ran a version of the entertaining hotel lobby debates of his youth—improvised, filmed live, scrappy, unpredictable. His kind of TV was known as "TV, Chicago style"; it had its own manner, a rough-and-tumble ambience with a whiff of Carl Sandburg's famous Chicago poem about it: City of the Big Shoulders, "with lifted head singing so proud to be alive and coarse and strong and cunning," not to mention the fearless, defiant, brawling, dusty-faced, white-teethed laughter to which Sandburg gives pride of place.

Terkel was always a laugher in this sense, though of the puckish kind rather than the brawling, white-teethed variety; and he was never afraid of putting himself on the line. Naturally, he got involved with picket lines and petitions—"I never met a picket line or a petition I didn't like," he says, with daunting Pickwickian geniality. Needless to say, he found himself an object of repeated scrutiny during the McCarthy era. FBI agents used to visit him in solemn twosomes, and though his wife was cool toward them, he himself was "always hospitable. Remember, I was an innkeeper's boy." When an emissary from NBC showed up, demanding that he say he was "duped by the Communists," he refused. "Suppose Communists come out against cancer. Do we have to come out *for* cancer?" he asked. "That is *not* very funny," said the NBC official, like many a schoolmarm before him.

Terkel was then blacklisted for several years, during which he made a living lecturing to women's clubs about jazz. (He's proud of these women's clubs, for they, too, were fearless Chicago-style laughers: though warned off him, not one club ever canceled an engagement.) In the mid-fifties he was finally rescued by Mahalia Jackson, who insisted he be the host of her weekly CBS radio show. When an emissary from the network turned up with a loyalty oath, insisting Studs sign it or else, Mahalia said, "If they fire Studs . . . go find another Mahalia." "In saying no," says Terkel, Mahalia Jackson "revealed more self-esteem, let alone what our country is all about, than . . . all the sponsors and agencies rolled into one."

Those who have had the pleasurable workout of being interviewed by Studs Terkel during his long-running book program on NPR will agree that it was an interview experience like no other. Unlike some, Studs would always read the book. Then he'd reread it. When you arrived for the interview, there would be Studs, hugging your book, which would look as if he'd been rolling around on the floor with it. It would be underlined in different pens and pencils, cross-referenced, with little bits of colored paper sticking out all over it. Then he'd start in—"I stayed up all night reading this, I couldn't put it down"—and you'd realize that he knew more about your book than you did yourself. This knowledge was not used to make you look like an idiot, but to prop you up. The enthusiasm, the energy, the excitement were put across with a verve that had you reeling out of the place feeling you'd just participated in a rafter-raising musical comedy in which Studs had given you the role of star tap dancer without your having auditioned for it.

While conducting the interviews for his oral history series, Terkel evidently drew on many of the same skills, though he concerned himself not with books but with people. He has made himself into a conduit through which voices have flowed—familiar voices, powerful voices, but also obscure voices, ordinary voices, voices that otherwise might not have been heard. It's been a huge amount of work, in aid of which he's traveled all over the country. In his later years it can't have been physically easy for him—he recounts with appreciation his trip, while visiting a Chicago tycoon, up a flight of stairs in an electric armchair—and it must also have been hard in other ways: the stories he's recorded have not been without their conflicts and defeats, the lives celebrated have often been tough, and not all of them have had happy endings. Some of those he interviewed for this book were old and ill. Their wives had died, or they'd had a stroke, or they were using a walker, or they were in a wheelchair. The two people to whom the book is dedicated are the lawyer Clifford Durr and his Southern belle wife, Virginia Durr, of Montgomery, Alabama, who spearheaded the civil rights movement there in the fifties, against fearful odds. Both are dead.

What drove Terkel on? Partly it was the same kind of alert and open curiosity that led him to interviewing in the first place. "I've always wondered what made Virginia and Clifford Durr tick," he muses, without coming up with a definitive theory. But it's more than simple wondering. The answers to such questions, he implies, are in the stories, and he lets his subjects tell these stories for themselves.

It's perhaps helpful to think of Studs Terkel as the inheritor of the same strain of American idealistic romanticism that produced Walt Whitman, and Mark Twain's Huckleberry Finn, and John Dos Passos, and John Steinbeck, and many more. According to this tradition, "democracy" is a serious idea—indeed, an article of belief—rather than a snippet of election-year rhetoric or Oscar Wilde's wisecrack about the bludgeoning of the people, by the people, for the people. For those who still keep faith with the early, bright-eyed concept of American democracy, all men really are created equal, and to treat any human being as less than human is a heresy. No coincidence that Terkel quotes Tom Paine, that eighteenth-century gadfly and apologist for the rights of man, and finds his words appropriate in the America of 2003:

> Freedom had been hunted round the globe; reason was considered as rebellion; and the slavery of fear had made men afraid to think. But such is the irresistible nature of truth that all it asks, and all it wants, is the liberty of appearing. . . . In such a situation, man becomes what he ought. He sees his species, not with the inhuman eye of a natural enemy, but as a kindred.

"One's-Self I sing, a simple separate person,/Yet utter the word Democratic, the word En-masse," says Whitman . . .

> *One of the great nation, the nation of many*
> *nations, the smallest the same,*
> *and the largest the same. . . .*
> *Of every hue and caste am I, of*
> *every rank and religion,*
> *A farmer, mechanic, artist,*
> *gentleman, sailor, quaker;*
> *A prisoner, fancy-man, rowdy,*
> *lawyer, physician, priest.*

This could almost be a prospectus for Terkel's life's work: the bringing together of diverse voices until they join in harmony and counterpoint, the goal being a unified whole in which every individual nevertheless remains distinct. "It's . . . like a legion of Davids, with all sorts of slingshots. It's not one slingshot that will do it," says Terkel.

But there are problems with a legion of Davids. An aroused and rightfully annoyed society is not the same thing as a mob on the rampage, but how do you keep the one from turning into the other? And if the Davids win, won't some of them become Goliaths in their turn, as witness the histories of some unions? *E pluribus unum*, says the Great Seal of the United States, but it doesn't say what kind of one is to be made out of the many, or how you keep the country from becoming a de facto dictatorship, ruled by fear, with everybody snooping on everybody else. These are the difficulties faced by a pluralistic, individualistic, market-driven, yet officially democratic society like that of the United States. "The price of liberty is eternal vigilance," said Thomas Jefferson. Terkel might amend this to "The price of liberty is eternal slingshots." But does liberty mean you can do whatever you like as long as you don't get caught? At what point does the liberty of one depend on the serfdom of another? And what Goliaths, exactly, ought the Davids to shoot at with their slingshots? Any Goliaths who forget that liberty entails responsibility. Terkel would probably reply: walk on people and you're fair game.

The subject of *Hope Dies Last* isn't just any kind of hope, such as "Hope you're feeling better," "Hope for the best," or even "I hope you die." Lots of things have been said about hope; nor has it always had a good press. For some, hope is a phantom, a deluding will-o'-the-wisp, luring men away from reality—presupposed to be grim—and into attractive but deadly swamps. For some, Camus included, it's the dirty trick at the bottom of Pandora's box, the deceptive gizmo that keeps Sisyphus rolling the stone up the hill. "Hope sustains us, to be replaced sooner or later by a walking stick," said the Bulgarian epigrammatist Kouncho Grosev. "There is an abundance of hope, but none for us," said Franz Kafka. "I can't go on, I have to go on, I'll go on," says Beckett in *The Unnameable.*

Terkel knows his Camus and his Beckett and the Greek myths, but does not change course for them. Two of his subjects refer to Emily Dickinson's poem:

> *"Hope" is the thing with feathers—*
> *That perches in the soul—*
> *And sings the tune without the words—*
> *And never stops—at all—*
>
> *And sweetest—in the Gale—is heard—*
> *And sore must be the storm—*

That could abash the little Bird—
That kept so many warm.

This is the kind of hope Terkel means, the hope that persists in the face of discouragement. All but a few of the people he interviews in his book have been chosen because they did not cease from mental fight, or let their swords sleep in their hands: they took up their bows of burning gold and their arrows of desire, and let fly.

If there are Biblical echoes here it's not by accident. "Studs . . . you have such a big mouth, you should have been a preacher," Terkel quotes a pal as saying. But he is a sort of preacher. One branch of Christianity has always led to activism; according to it, all souls are equal before God, the first shall be last and the last shall be first, and you must love your neighbors as yourself and visit them when they are sick and in prison, and if you do bad things unto the least of these, you do them unto God. (There's another branch of Christianity that rests on the verse about those who have getting more, and those who have not being deprived even of what they have, which these folks interpret financially; but that's another story.) A number of the subjects in this book started out along the path of religion: among them are priests, seminarians, Quakers, Methodists, Baptists.

As for hope, it goes hand in hand—Biblically—with faith and charity; you might say faith is the belief, hope is the emotion made possible by it, and charity is the action required. Terkel's hope is not vain hope, but is one with the kindly light that leads amid the encircling gloom: it's hope for something better. The book's title comes from a saying that was current among the Spanish-speaking farm workers organized by Cesar Chavez— "*La esperanza muere última*"—but is cited by others in the book as well. Terkel comments, "It was a metaphor for much of the twentieth century." He quotes Kathy Kelly of the Voices in the Wilderness project: "I'm working toward a world in which it would be easier for people to behave decently."

It's possible to get swept away by what at times resembles an inspirational revival meeting. The spirit moves you; Good Samaritan kindly feelings suffuse you; you feel like rushing out and joining something. Perhaps a caveat is in order: one person's hope-inspired activism is another's pain in the neck. Who's to choose what "a better world" is, and how to best bring it about? There's a point of view that might characterize various well-intentioned activities as misguided obstructionism, illegal interference, subversive undermining of the social order, godless communism, and so on. Should actions be judged by the sincerity of their intentions? Yes, say the romantics; no, say the historians, they should instead be judged, like wars, by their outcomes. As for good intentions, we know what Hell's paved with. Were the Resistance fighters behind the German lines in World War II brave heroes striking a blow for freedom, or were they criminal thugs? Depends on who's doing the labeling.

Hope respects no national boundaries, and it crosses ideological lines at will. Terkel's book dodges this issue, though his inclusion of Paul Tibbetts— pilot of the *Enola Gay*, the plane that dropped the bomb that wiped out Hiroshima—makes us sit up and blink. To be sure, Tibbetts says he was motivated by hope of a kind—he hoped his action would end the war and "save a lot of lives." American lives, it's understood, for his attitude toward the Japanese civilians who were snuffed out is cavalier: "That's their tough luck for being there." As Lenin famously remarked, you can't make an omelet without breaking eggs, but what kind of omelet is needed will always be a matter of dispute, and there's no long line of candidates anywhere for the position of egg.

That said, *Hope Dies Last* captures the reader, though the choices will not be to everyone's taste. Terkel's main emphasis is on people from the parts of society familiar to him: old lefties, workers in housing projects and among the poor, students who fought on behalf of custodial staff during the sit-in at Harvard in 2001, union activists as well as activists against corruption in unions, civil rights workers, peace workers, teachers in difficult neighborhoods. No surprise that quite a few of these are from Chicago.

But there are surprises of other kinds. In one section—"Easy Riders"—the interviewees share only the fact that they ride around on bicycles. One is a courier, living in the moment. Another is a doctor who goes

> a half day every week out into Golden Gate Park on my bicycle with medicines. . . . Usually, if you work in a clinic, people come to you.

Whereas if you're doing outreach in the park, you go up and offer your services. It's a different kind of playing field.

Another section, "Immigrants," contains a sound engineer of Iraqi origin; two undocumented Guatemalans whose hope consists in the hope of not being found out; and a man of Japanese descent who describes how, as a high school senior, he was put in a detention camp with his family after Pearl Harbor and has since worked with the movement to redress the harm done to the Japanese. Will American Iraqis one day have their own redress movement? After September 11, Mr. Usama Alshaibi told Terkel,

> I was very worried because the government took three thousand men and put them in detention centers. They weren't officially charged. . . . I wouldn't be surprised right now if they grabbed me and just started asking me a bunch of questions.

The unpleasant surprises include many horror stories—jailings, beatings, murders. Among them are the account of wheelchair-ridden Dierdre Merriman, a recovering alcoholic whose neck was broken by an ex-boyfriend and who now lives in a single room in a large Chicago apartment building and works as a rape victim advocate, and that of Leroy Orange, tortured with electrodes to obtain a confession of murder during a police department reign of terror in Chicago, wrongfully convicted, and finally pardoned by Governor George Ryan in 2003 after a courageous legal campaign.

By no means all of Terkel's subjects are from the bottom crust of the social pie. John Kenneth Galbraith contributes a pithy statement to the section called "Concerning Enronism":

> As things now stand, we allow enormous incompetence and enormous compensation to those who have power. I see that as a great unsolved problem of our time. And since it is all quite legal, I call it the likelihood of innocent fraud. I entered the world of politics at a time when there were Fifth Amendment communists, and I've reached the age of ninety-four, when there are Fifth Amendment capitalists.

339

He's followed by Wallace Rasmusson, who worked his way up through the Depression to become the president and CEO of Beatrice Foods, a company worth $7.8 billion when he retired in 1975:

> What's happened at Enron and WorldCom—cooking books—is criminal. A great country lasts about four hundred years. We're in the declining-morality period. That is what ruined Rome. . . . Greed . . . I always said, "In God we trust, everything else we audit."

There are several kinds of activism that might seem obvious to some readers but that are not much represented in *Hope Dies Last*. The women's movement marks one of the most noteworthy social shifts of the past two centuries, but it is barely present here. There are women interviewed, yes—seventeen out of fifty-eight—and intrepid women at that. One of those mentioned is anonymous—an old white woman who kept a sit-in at a Woolworth's lunch counter in Nashville from becoming a massacre, purely through force of character and through believing that some ways are no way to behave—a case of Miss Manners to the rescue. "I just came in to buy an egg poacher" was her story.

> She walked up and down between the students seated and the mob that would come up and put out a cigarette on them, spit on a young woman's neck and all. The students just sat, they didn't protest. This old woman . . . [would] go up and talk to these young white thugs. "How would you feel if that was your sister?" And they would kind of, "Oh, I didn't mean nothing." Then they'd go back in the mob and someone else would take over.

Some of the women are among Terkel's bravest subjects—women such as Kathy Kelly, jailed for planting corn on missile silos, and Mollie McGrath, who worked to reform sweatshops and took part in protests against the World Trade Organization—but they are included because they were involved in movements of other kinds. Why is that? Terkel has nothing against women; in fact, so nondiscriminatory is he toward them that he doesn't appear to view them as a special category, or not one needing a

movement of their own. Maybe he has the somewhat bashful attitude—
so common among men once—of not wanting to butt in on a hen party.
Maybe he can't quite believe in oppression by a gender, of a gender,
because of gender. There are no gay activists here, either.

With Mollie McGrath the antiglobalization movement gets a look-in,
but no more than that. The Green movement is touched on through Pete
Seeger, folk singer to a generation, now busily trying to clean up the
Hudson River; also through Frances Moore Lappé. Many will remember
Lappé fondly as the author of *Diet for a Small Planet*. How would we ever
have known about soy flour without her? *Hope Dies Last* is so filled with
quotable quotes you sometimes think you're reading *Bartlett's*, and Lappé
has some ringers. "Hunger is not caused by a lack of food, it's caused by a
lack of democracy," she says.

> My daughter, Anna, loves to say, "I used to think that hope was for
> wimps." Hope is not for wimps; it's for the strong-hearted who can rec-
> ognize how bad things are and yet not be deterred, not be paralyzed.

Hope is not something we find, hope is something we become.

> This is the first generation to know that the choices we're making
> have ultimate consequences. It's a time when you either choose life
> or you choose death. . . . Going along with the current order means
> that you're choosing death. We're just a drop in the bucket. . . . If
> you have a bucket, those raindrops fill it up very fast. . . . Our work
> is helping people see that there is a bucket. There are all these people
> all over the world who *are* creating this bucket of hope.

If we were picking teams—the Hopes vs. the Despairs—Lappé would be
my first choice for captain of the Hopes. Her outlook is global, she knows
where we stand as a species, she's tough as a week-old soy flour biscuit,
and she's looking ahead, not back.

And Studs Terkel would be the umpire. No, I'll rethink that: he'd be too
biased on the side of the Hope team. He'd have to be the coach. He'd bring
to the task many decades of experience, the ability to galvanize, lots of

anecdotal lore, and a store of energy to help out during the hard parts. That's what *Hope Dies Last* is, in essence: not just a social document, not just fascinating American history, but a coach's manual, complete with a number of model pep talks that may get you out of your armchair and propel you right into Blake's mental fight. It's all the more impressive that Terkel was putting this book together in the days after September 11 and before the invasion of Iraq, when it might have looked as if he'd be preaching to the sea. Now many will find the words he's collected both inspiring and timely: Representative Dennis Kucinich speaks for many in *Hope Dies Last* when he says,

We're challenged to insist even more strongly on the basic freedoms that we have, because it is through those freedoms that we're vindicated. If we lose those freedoms, we're not America anymore.

50

Mortifications

Mortifications never end. There is always a never-before-experienced one waiting just around the corner. As Scarlett O'Hara might have said, "Tomorrow is another mortification." Such anticipations give us hope: God isn't finished with us yet, because these things are sent to try us. I've never been entirely sure what that meant. Where there is blushing, there is life? Something like that.

While waiting for the mortifications yet to come, when I'll have dentures and they'll shoot out of my mouth on some august public occasion, or else I will topple off the podium or be sick on my presenter, I'll tell you of three mortifications past.

Early Period

Long, long ago, when I was only twenty-nine and my first novel had just been published, I was living in Edmonton, Alberta, Canada. It was 1969. The Women's Movement had begun, in New York City, but it had not yet reached Edmonton, Alberta. It was November. It was freezing cold. I was freezing cold, and I went about wearing a secondhand fur coat—muskrat, I think—that I'd bought at the Salvation Army for $25. I also had a fur hat I'd made out of a rabbit shruggie—a shruggie was a sort of fur bolero—by deleting the arms and sewing up the armholes.

My publisher arranged my first-ever book signing. I was very excited. Once I'd peeled off the muskrats and rabbits, there I would be, inside the

Hudson's Bay Company Department Store, where it was cozily warm—this in itself was exciting—with lines of eager, smiling readers waiting to purchase my book and have me scribble on it.

The signing was at a table set up in the Men's Socks and Underwear Department. I don't know what the thinking was behind this. There I sat, at lunch hour, smiling away, surrounded by piles of a novel called *The Edible Woman*. Men in overcoats and galoshes and toe rubbers and scarves and earmuffs passed by my table, intent on the purchase of boxer shorts. They looked at me, then at the title of my novel. Subdued panic broke out. There was the sound of a muffled stampede as dozens of galoshes and toe rubbers shuffled rapidly in the other direction.

I sold two copies.

Middle Period

By this time I'd achieved a spoonful or two of notoriety, enough so that my U.S. publisher could arrange to get me onto an American TV talk show. It was an afternoon show, which in those days—could it have been the late seventies?—meant variety. It was the sort of show at which they played pop music, and then you were supposed to sashay through a bead curtain, carrying your trained koala bear, or Japanese flower arrangement, or book.

I waited behind the bead curtain. There was an act on before me. It was a group from the Colostomy Association, who were talking about their colostomies, and about how to use the colostomy bag.

I knew I was doomed. No book could ever be that riveting. W. C. Fields vowed never to share the stage with a child or a dog; I can add to that, "Never follow the Colostomy Association." (Or any other thing having to do with frightening bodily items, such as the port-wine-stain removal technique that once preceded me in Australia.) The problem is, you lose all interest in yourself and your so-called work—"What did you say your name was? And tell us the plot of your book, just in a couple of sentences, please"—so immersed are you in picturing the gruesome intricacies of . . . but never mind.

Modern Period

Recently I was on a TV show in Mexico. By this time I was famous, insofar as writers are, although perhaps not quite so famous in Mexico as in other places. This was the kind of show where they put makeup on you, and I had eyelashes that stood out like little black shelves.

The interviewer was a very smart man who had lived—as it turned out—only a few blocks from my house in Toronto, when he'd been a student and I'd been elsewhere, being mortified at my first book signing, in Edmonton. We went merrily along through the interview, chatting about world affairs and such, until he hit me with the F-question. The do-you-consider-yourself-a-feminist question. I lobbed the ball briskly back over the net ("Women are human beings, don't you agree?"), but then he blind-sided me. It was the eyelashes: they were so thick I didn't see it coming.

"Do you consider yourself *feminine?*" he said.

Nice Canadian middle-aged women go all strange when asked this by Mexican talk-show hosts somewhat younger than themselves, or at least I did. "What, at my age?" I blurted. Meaning: *I used to get asked this in 1969 as part of being mortified in Edmonton, and after thirty-four years I shouldn't have to keep on dealing with it!* But with eyelashes like that, what could I expect?

"Sure, why not?" he said.

I refrained from telling him why not. I did not say: *Geez, Louise, I'm sixty-three and you still expect me to wear pink, with frills?* I did not say: *Feminine, or feline, pal? Grr, meow.* I did not say: *This is a frivolous question.*

Whacking my eyelashes together, I said: "You really shouldn't be asking *me*. You should be asking the men in my life." (Implying there were hordes of them.) "Just as I would ask the women in *your* life if you are masculine. They'd tell me the truth."

Time for the commercial.

A couple of days later, still brooding on this theme, I said, in public, "My boyfriends got bald and fat and then they died." Then I said, "That would make a good title for a short story." Then I regretted having said both.

Some mortifications are, after all, self-inflicted.

51

Review:

A Story as Sharp as a Knife: The Classical Haida Mythtellers and Their World
by Robert Bringhurst

S uppose you grow up in a culturally rich and economically stable
society. All around you are the vividly carved symbols of the invisible spirits that inform your dealings with the natural and human
worlds. Living inside your village is like living inside a Norman cathedral,
crossed with a medieval castle, crossed with a network of Stonehenge ley
lines. Your ancestry in all its intricate twists and turns and its relation to
the spirit world is posted—literally—outside your home, like a wooden,
vertical coat of arms. This is an oral society: it has a highly developed
system of signs, but it does not have writing as such.

As in any culture, children are gifted in different ways. You yourself
have a talent for remembering stories, and for combining them in surprising patterns that yield novel meanings. You become a mythteller. You
perform the stories to an appreciative audience, one that holds its breath
during the scary parts, and identifies the allusions, and laughs at the jokes.
These performances are yours in the same way as, say, Olivier's *Hamlet* was
his—so much in a performance is carried by tone of voice, by expression,
by the spaces left in speech—but more so, since you have put the performances together in unique ways.

Then catastrophe strikes. A mysterious disease sweeps through your
community. The mortality rate is 95 percent. The houses and their deco-
rations crumble away. At the same time, an influx of strangers with nasty
weapons and odd convictions appears, ready to destroy the ceremonial

objects and to suppress the ancient customs, and to tell you that your stories are obsolete or evil.

You yourself survive the disease. You remember your performances, but
you have no apprentice; you can't hand your work on. And even if you
could, is there anyone left who can understand it?

This was the plight of two remarkable poets, Skaay and the younger
Ghandl, who had been blinded by the disease. Both were from the Haida,
one of the many cultures that flourished along the northwest coast of
North America before the arrival of the smallpox-carrying, Gospel-bearing
Europeans in the nineteenth century. Their land was—and is—an island
cluster some five hundred miles north of Vancouver. At the beginning of
the nineteenth century the population was twelve thousand. At its end,
some eight hundred were left.

A last-ditch possibility presented itself to Skaay and Ghandl. When
Skaay was seventy-three and Ghandl was about fifty, they encountered an
ethnographer/linguist. His name was John Reed Swanton. Unwittingly, he
acted as a messenger to the future: he was collecting stories, as a way into
learning a language. Skaay and Ghandl performed their creations, not for
Swanton—he couldn't speak Haida—but through a Haida-speaking inter-
mediary, who wrote them down phonetically.

To the poets themselves this must have seemed as desperate an act as
putting a jewel into a bottle and flinging it into the sea. It's the sort of
despairing gamble taken by those who wrote down the Mayan *Popol Vuh*
when the Spaniards were at their doorstep. Hope against hope; and yet, in
both cases, something did survive.

Skaay and Ghandl died in the early years of the twentieth century.
Their stories gathered dust in libraries for almost a hundred years. Then
along came Robert Bringhurst, American turned Canadian, poet in his
own right, expert on typography, and easy to confuse with the sort of
obsessive-compulsive, nit-picking polymath that turns up in post-
Romantic fiction. Think of Sherlock Holmes as a self-taught reader of
Haida phonetic transliterations, crossed with someone like Shelley or
Chopin to supply the large dollop of passionate enthusiasm, and you'll
have some idea.

For twelve years Bringhurst—with the aid of many helpers—hacked his way through the brambles of the staggeringly difficult language, rubbed the tarnished old lamp, pried the cork out of the bottle. Count the metaphors here, figure out how many of them would mean nothing to you if you hadn't read any European/Arabian fairy tales, then estimate your chances of understanding very much about Haida symbol systems without help. In any case, Bringhurst labored. Finally, as in the tale of Sleeping Beauty, those who seemed dead, awoke. As in a story by Ghandl or Skaay, bones rubbed with medicine plants came back to life. As in the tale of Aladdin, out came the genie. And one humdinger of a genie it is.

Like a lot of genies, it's a book. Actually, it's three of them. You can get them singly, or in a boxed set called *A Story as Sharp as a Knife: Masterworks of the Classical Haida Mythtellers*. Volume 1 is *A Story as Sharp as a Knife: The Classical Haida Mythtellers and Their World*. This is the one you need to start with, or you'll be like someone looking at the aforesaid Norman cathedral and its Creation-to-Last-Judgment picture sequences without any knowledge of the Bible or of Christian symbolism. Volume 2—*Nine Visits to the Mythworld*—is devoted to the works of Ghandl, and *Being in Being*, volume 3, to the works of Skaay. Each includes biographical and historical material that locates the poets in time and space and aids in an evaluation of their achievements. Each volume is also illustrated—happily, since the visual art of the culture was an extension of the stories, and vice versa.

An astonishing fact: this is the first time the name of any North American oral poet has ever appeared on the front of a book as the author of what's between the covers. It's the same with most of the oral material that's come to us. As soon as it got written down—as soon as the tale became separable from the telling—the names of the individual creators had a habit of vanishing, to be subsumed by the well-known Anonymous or treated as the collective creation of a tribe. As Bringhurst says, "[O]thers have written at great length on the nature of oral culture, but rarely in such works do we encounter an actual oral text. Still less often do we meet an actual speaker. The result is that the real human beings who inhabit oral cultures disappear, and stereotypes replace them. Native American oral poets have so often been mistreated in this way that their namelessness has come to seem routine."

Bringhurst is the editor and translator of these two poets, but he's a good deal more than that. He has thought long and carefully about the many issues involved in his task, and he has an agenda. On it is a long list of things I can't begin to summarize, but here are a few of them.

Oral poetry is poetry, and the people who made it are poets. The *Iliad* and the *Odyssey* are oral poetry written down, and so is much of the Bible, and so are the poem cycles of Skaay and Ghandl. Oral poetry is different in nature from the poetry produced by a society in which writing is the norm. It depends on individual performance and therefore on audience. It is heard in the way that music is heard, and it employs many of the same devices. It is embedded in land forms and bears witness to a close interaction with what we call Nature. It is profoundly local.

This doesn't mean that the work of these two poets is provincial, or limited in interest. No, it can stand with the best, because it goes beyond its culture of origin to stand side by side with the great myth-based artistic creations of the world. Thus the anger of certain factions who claim that Bringhurst, being white, has no business messing with stories that are "owned" by the Haida—though in some ways understandable, considering the havoc wreaked and the thefts committed in the past by strangers—is misplaced. As well to say nobody should translate Tolstoy because he is "owned" by the Russians. Tolstoy could not have existed without the Russians, true, but should nobody else be permitted to read him?

To continue with the Bringhurst fiats: for North Americans, these poems and others like them should be part of the great stack of building blocks in what we call our "identity," our "history," our "story." Why should our groundworks come from Greece and Rome and the Bible and European sagas, and not also from the places where we actually live? These are questions not without interest for the inhabitants of, for instance, the United States and Australia and New Zealand and South America and Mexico. As Bringhurst says, "Isn't it just possible that if we listened to the stories and the voices native to the place, we'd be a bit less eager to strip-mine it, clearcut it, pave it, and pollute it in the name of making money?"

Furthermore, these are not "just poems." They are—especially in the case of Skaay—works of philosophy. So claims Bringhurst.

Hang on a minute, you say. You mean to tell me that a story about

Raven eating the cranberries in his own excrement is part of a philosophical meditation on the nature of Being? Well, actually, yes. But this is an argument that must be followed closely by those more skilled at such arguments than I. I'll merely add that, though philosophy in our own time is far removed from religion, the two used to be joined at the hip, and both were inseparable from narrative. "Being" is what it does, and what it does is embodied in the often violent and upsetting stories about it, not in a set of abstract propositions. Nor can you depend on Being to act the way you think it should. (This set of concepts is a lot more modern than the hierarchies and certainties and pieties of the Victorians, which were what Skaay and Ghandl were up against.) If we can deal with the "I Am That I Am" of Exodus as a legitimate comment on the mystery of Being, we ought to be able to grasp Voicehandler, whose face cannot be seen and who behaves toward men much as God did to Job.

Why has Canada produced so many thinkers concerned with the same matters that have caught Bringhurst's attention—with such spectacular, and, at times, such peculiar results? Why Edmund Carpenter and the 1950s magazine *Explorations*, which went hand in hand with Marshall McLuhan and his great book on the effects of literacy, *The Gutenberg Galaxy*? ("The medium is the message" = "Oral is not the same as written.") Why was Leonard Cohen's first poetry collection called *Let Us Compare Mythologies*? Why Northrop Frye and his exhaustive studies of myth and literature? Why—more recently—Sean Kane and his widely praised book *The Wisdom of the Mythtellers*, which deals with Haida myths, among others?

Anyone who came of age reading Canadian poetry will remember the title "A Country without a Mythology"—a challenge if there ever was one. We so dislike being told that there's a desirable cultural goodie we haven't got. Either we do have it, and it's been overlooked—the Bringhurst response—or we have to make it ourselves, which was the task undertaken by the Canadian poets and writers of the generations just before his. But in making it—anytime, anywhere—how much of other people's "we" should we include in our "we"?

There's a brawl going on over the word "we," of course. Shall "we" become bigger or smaller? Shall "we" include all of humanity, or would that be to share "our" secrets with a lot of dunderheads who will degrade and rob us? Who gets into our magic circle, and by what tokens? Do poems belong to those who compose them, or to those who appreciate them? It's one of the features of such battles that each side often wounds its own champions.

You can follow the back-and-forth in a small pamphlet that comes with the three-volume magnum opus, and in which Bringhurst gives his thorny answers to the thorny questions that have been thrust on him. But such territorial squabbling cannot obscure the fact that Bringhurst's achievement is gigantic as well as heroic. It's one of those works that rearranges the inside of your head—a profound meditation on the nature of oral poetry and myth, and on the habits of thought and feeling that inform them. It restores to life two exceptional poets we ought to know. It gives us some insight into their world—in Bringhurst's words, "the old-growth forest of the human mind"—and, by comparison, into our own. In our march toward the secular, the orderly, the urban, the mechanized, what have we lost?

52

Review:

The Mays of Ventadorn
by W. S. Merwin

W S. Merwin's *The Mays of Ventadorn* is an enchanting book. I use that word in its original sense: to be enchanted implied that you'd been put under a spell by a magical song. This short but potent book is enchanting in itself, and it's also about enchantment.

It is, however, the sort of book that poses a problem for classifiers: What shelf to put it on? Is it a memoir? Not exactly, but sort of. Is it a rumination upon memory? Yes and no. Is it about poetry? Not only.

It's part of the *National Geographic*'s Directions series, ostensibly dedicated to capturing "the spirit of travel and place" and "bringing fresh perspective and renewed excitement to the art of travel writing," but anyone who expects a standard travel book—what quaint hotel to stay in and so forth—needs a *Michelin Guide* instead. As Merwin says of himself, "Reading a guidebook and then glancing up to identify what the résumé has been summarizing is likely to seem to me, quite soon, as an exercise in alienation." There are places in this book, of course, and there's travel; but the places cannot be visited now, not in the form that holds their most vivid life, and the travels took place long ago. Those who would take this voyage must follow the Paths of the Dead.

But if you think about *The Mays of Ventadorn* not as travel writing but as a book about the transformation and mutation of poetry, then all comes clear. It's written by a poet and a translator, and one for whom these concerns have always been central. How does the poem work its way through the mind of a dead man into the mind of a living one? How is translation possible, or is it possible at all? How can one move "across the silence between languages"? How does the torch get passed from hand to hand—distant hands, then our hands? National borders and lapsed years do not stop the blowing of that wind of the passing of that flame.

The gateways to the journey—a space-travel journey but also a time-travel one—are positioned by Merwin at the very beginning of his book. The first is the ruins of the château of Ventadour (or, in its original Occitane, Ventadorn) in southern France—"jagged shards and ramparts and towers standing by themselves on their steep hilltop." Even those ruins overlap with many pasts, including the one from just before Merwin's own first glimpse of them, one recorded in the odd old photograph. "The human figures, whose originals had long since departed by the time I saw their likenesses, stare at the then-visible camera with fixed belief, far away in the knowledge that the picture of them, even as it is being taken, belongs to another life, and that they will never see that glass eye again."

The second gateway is the entrance to St. Elizabeth's Hospital in Washington, D.C., the asylum where Ezra Pound was locked up after his ignominious return to America from conquered Fascist Italy. "A dingy entrance, and at the top of a flight of stairs an attendant opened a heavy, metal-covered door." Browning's *Childe Roland* could have supplied the first bit of architecture, with its ruins and towers, and Dante's *Inferno* the second. If we're alert, and if we know our folktales or our classics or our Jung, we expect a Wise Old Man or Sybil or prophet of Virgil-like guide who will give our young hero—Merwin himself, as the student he was then—a piece of talismanic advice he will need for his difficult quest. He is setting out to be a poet, and then, in postwar America—actually, at any time and in any place—this was, and remains, a dangerous thing to do. Many have lost their way in the word mazes.

We do get the Wise Old Man, who turns out to be Pound himself, in his disguise as a lunatic. He is not, for Merwin, the sackful of deplorable politics and zany monetary theories he was for many. Instead, Pound provides an example of how to take up a vocation under impossible circumstances. "He was an American—middle-class and in every sense provincial, as I was—who had set out from the beginning to be an artist, a poet. And

353

to do it without money." But he gives Merwin the key piece of advice he does not yet know he needs: he tells him to go back to the source, where the freshness and originality might be found, the inspiration to "make it new." The source, for Pound, was the troubadours, who wrote in what was then called "the Provençal."

Pound makes his entrance and his exit via a spiral staircase "that looked like the bottom of a circling staircase in a tower," and it is the spiral—so beloved of Yeats, and of Tennyson before him, and especially of Merwin's beloved Dante—that is the organizing geometrical shape for this book. Ascending and descending a spiral staircase, you revolve around a core, sometimes a core of emptiness; you keep passing the same points, but you see them from different perspectives. And this is how Merwin's book proceeds. It is not chronologically arranged. Instead it unwinds, rewinds, unwinds again. This is part of enchantment: enchantments often involve weaving and winding, and the sense of being lost in a tangled wood. It's no accident that the grown-up Merwin became the translator, not only of the troubadours, but also of that quintessential tale of woodland enchantment, *Sir Gawain and the Green Knight.* The search for "the Provençal" took the young Merwin back in time, first to the story of Richard Coeur-de-Leon and his betrayal and imprisonment during his return from the Crusades, and the famous troubadour song he composed at that time. But it also took Merwin to France, where, as a very young man, he bought—on impulse, using a small legacy left to him by an aunt—a deserted house in the Quercy, near the ruins of Ventadorn. What made him do it? The motivation—he speculates—is perhaps in his childhood experiences of remote, entrancing natural locations, now long vanished; or perhaps it's his preference for "imagining what it might be like to spend time in a given spot, to get to know the sounds and the light . . . and how some of it had come to look the way it did."

Merwin lived for many years in this region, exploring its places, its ruins, its people as they were then, and also its history. The Quercy was the land of the troubadours, and Merwin recounts some of their histories— what can be deduced, what is long, what was invented—and also the history of his involvement with them, as fellow poet and translator. They're a fascinating bunch, and equally fascinating is the debt they owed to what was then the epitome of culture and civilization—the courts of the Sultans of the Middle East. Diseases and loot were not the only things the Crusaders brought back with them; they also brought back poetic techniques, poetic attitudes, poetic influences of many kinds. How odd to think of the links between the Courtly Love Convention and that other civilization we often assume is so far from it.

Merwin's favorite troubadour poet is Bernart de Ventadorn—hence the title of the book. The "Mays" of Ventadorn are both the many springs that have passed over it—hundreds of years of them, by now—but also the flower that preceded the rose as the poets' flower of youth and love par excellence. Unraveling Bernart's life and frequently high times is a quest in itself. Was Eleanor of Aquitaine the lady to whom his love poems are addressed? Were they lovers? Time will not tell.

The poet of Ventadorn leads Merwin into the history of the château of Ventadorn itself, and the history of the family. Both have been long, colorful, and often gloomy. This is where Merwin's spiral design leads downward, until we come to the darkest point of all. During the German occupation of France, a descendant of Bernart—who had evidently inherited his courteous spirit—was involved in the Resistance, was betrayed like Richard Coeur-de-Leon, was tortured and imprisoned, and died in a Nazi camp.

If one were to draw parallels with Dante, this one corresponds to the low point of the *Inferno*. But Merwin has not read his Dante—and his Eliot—for nothing. The way down is the way up, and the ascent to light is both sudden and surprising. The spirit and the words of the poet who once lived at Ventadorn did not die there, says Merwin: "A rather flimsy, anomalous wire fence and gate now protect what remains of the great citadel, but what the walls themselves once fostered and heard has gone everywhere."

Thus we readers emerge from our enchantment, bearing its gifts.

355

53

Review:

Snow
by Orhan Pamuk

S *now,* the seventh novel by the Turkish writer Orhan Pamuk, is not only an engrossing feat of tale-spinning, but essential reading for our times.

In Turkey, Pamuk is the equivalent of rock star, guru, diagnostic specialist, and public-affairs pundit: the Turkish public reads his novels as if taking its own pulse. He is also highly esteemed in Europe: his sixth novel, the lush and intriguing *My Name Is Red,* carried off the 2003 Dublin Impac Award, adding to his long list of literary prizes.

He deserves to be better known in North America, and no doubt he will be, as his fictions turn on the conflict between the forces of "Westernization" and those of the Islamists. Although it's set in the 1990s and written before September 11, 2001, *Snow* is eerily prescient, both in its analyses of fundamentalist attitudes and in the nature of the repression and rage and conspiracies and violence it depicts.

Like Pamuk's other novels, *Snow* is an in-depth tour of the divided, hopeful, desolate, mystifying Turkish soul. It's the story of Ka, a gloomy but appealing poet who hasn't written anything in years. But Ka is not his own narrator; by the time of the telling he has been assassinated, and his tale is pieced together by an "old friend" of his who just happens to be named Orhan Pamuk.

As the novel opens, Ka has been in political exile in Berlin, but has returned to Istanbul for his mother's funeral. He's making his way to Kars, an impoverished city in Anatolia, just as a severe snowstorm begins. (*Kar* is "snow" in Turkish, so we have already been given an envelope inside an envelope inside an envelope.) Ka claims to be a journalist interested in the recent murder of the city's mayor and the suicides of a number of young girls forced by their schools to remove their headscarves, but this is only one of his motives. He also wants to see Ipek, a beautiful woman he'd known as a student. Divorced from a onetime friend of Ka's turned Islamist politician, she lives in the shabby Snow Palace Hotel, where Ka is staying.

Cut off from escape by the snow, Ka wanders through a decaying city haunted by its glorious former selves—architectural remnants of the once-vast Ottoman Empire; the grand Armenian church standing empty, testifying to the massacre of its worshipers; ghosts of Russian rulers and their lavish celebrations; pictures of Ataturk, founder of the Turkish Republic and instigator of a ruthless "modernization" campaign, which included—not incidentally—a ban on headscarves.

Ka's pose as a journalist allows Pamuk to put on display a wide variety of opinions. Those not living in the shrunken remains of former empires may find it hard to imagine the mix of resentful entitlement (We ought to be powerful!), shame (What did we do wrong?), blame (Whose fault is it?), and anxiety about identity (Who are we really?) that takes up a great deal of head room in such places and thus in *Snow*.

Ka tries to find out more about the dead girls but encounters resistance: he's from a bourgeois background in cosmopolitan Istanbul, he's been in exile in the West, he has a snazzy overcoat. Believers accuse him of atheism; the secular government doesn't want him writing about the suicides—a blot on its reputation—so he's dogged by police spies; common people are suspicious of him. He's present in a pastry shop when a tiny fundamentalist gunman murders the director of the institute that has expelled the headscarf girls. He gets mixed up with his beloved's former husband, the two of them are arrested, and he witnesses the brutality of the secularist regime. He manages to duck his shadowers long enough to meet with an Islamist extremist in hiding, the persuasive Blue, said to be behind the director's murder. And so he goes, floundering from encounter to encounter.

In *Snow*, the line between playful farce and gruesome tragedy is very fine. For instance, the town's newspaper publisher, Serder Bey, prints an article describing Ka's public performance of his poem "Snow." When Ka protests that he hasn't written a poem called "Snow" and is not going to perform it in the theater, Serder Bey replies, "Don't be so sure. There are those who despise us for writing the news before it happens. . . . Quite a few things happen only because we've written them up first. This is what modern journalism is all about." And sure enough, inspired by the love affair he begins with Ipek and happier than he's been in years, Ka begins to write poems, the first of them being "Snow." Before you know it, there he is in the theater, but the evening also includes a ridiculous performance of an Ataturk-era play, *My Fatherland or My Headscarf.* As the Religious School teenagers jeer, the secularists decide to enforce their rule by shooting the audience.

The twists of fate, the plots that double back on themselves, the trickiness, the mysteries that recede as they're approached, the bleak cities, the night prowling, the sense of identity loss, the protagonist in exile—these are vintage Pamuk, but they're also part of the modern literary landscape. A case could be made for a genre called "The Male Labyrinth Novel," which would trace its ancestry through De Quincy and Dostoevsky and Conrad and would include Kafka, Borges, Marquez, Don DeLillo, and Paul Auster, with the Hammett-and-Chandler noir thriller thrown in for good measure. (It's mostly men who write such novels and feature as their rootless heroes, and there's probably a simple reason for this: send a woman out alone on a rambling nocturnal quest and she's likely to end up a lot deader a lot sooner than a man would.)

Women—except as idealized objects of desire—have not been of notably central importance in Pamuk's previous novels, but *Snow* is a departure. There are two strong female characters, the emotionally battered Ipek and her sister, the stubborn actress Kadife. In addition, there's a chorus: the headscarf girls. Those scrapping for power on both sides use these dead girls as symbols, having put unbearable pressure on them while they were alive. Ka, however, sees them as suffering human beings.

It wasn't poverty or helplessness that Ka found shocking in these sto-ries. Neither was it the constant beatings to which these girls were subjected, or the insensitivity of fathers who wouldn't even let them go outside, or the constant surveillance of jealous husbands. . . . [It] was the way these girls had killed themselves: abruptly, without ritual or warning, in the midst of their everyday routines. . . . .

Their suicides are like the other violent events in the novel: sudden eruptions of violence thrown up by relentless underlying forces.

The attitudes of men toward women drive the plot in *Snow*, but even more important are the attitudes of men toward one another. Ka is always worrying about whether other men respect or despise him, and that respect hinges not on material wealth but on what he is thought to believe. Since he himself isn't sure, he vacillates from one side to another. Shall he stick with the Western enlightenment? But he was miserable in Berlin. Shall he return to the Muslim fold? But, despite his drunken hand-kissing of a local religious leader, he can't fit in.

If Ka were to run true to the form of Pamuk's previous novels he might take refuge in stories. Stories, Pamuk has hinted, create the world we per-ceive: instead of "I think, therefore I am," a Pamuk character might say, "I am because I narrate." It's the Scheherezade position in spades. But poor murdered Ka is no novelist; it's up to "Orhan Pamuk" to act as his Horatio.

Snow is the latest entry in Pamuk's longtime project: narrating his country into being. It's also the closest to realism. Kars is finely drawn, in all its touching squalor, but its inhabitants resist "Pamuk's" novelizing of them. One of them asks him to tell the reader not to believe anything he says about them because " 'No one could understand us from so far away.' " This is a challenge to Pamuk and his considerable art, but it is also a chal-lenge to us.

54

Review:

From Eve to Dawn
by Marilyn French

*F*rom *Eve to Dawn* is Marilyn French's enormous three-volume
history of women. It runs from prehistory until the present and
is global in scope: the first volume alone covers Peru, Egypt,
Sumer, China, India, Mexico, Greece, and Rome, as well as religions from
Judaism to Christianity and Islam. It examines not only actions and laws,
but also the thinking behind them. It's sometimes annoying, in the same
way that Fielding's *Amelia* is annoying—enough suffering!—and it's
sometimes maddeningly reductionist; but it can't be dismissed. As a reference work it's invaluable: the bibliographies alone are worth the price.
And as a warning about the appalling extremes of human behavior and
male weirdness, it's indispensable.

Especially now. There was a moment in the 1990s when, it was
believed, history was over and utopia had arrived, looking very much like
a shopping mall, and "feminist issues" were supposed dead. But that
moment was brief. Islamic and American right-wing fundamentalisms are
on the rise, and one of the first aims of both is the suppression of women—
their bodies, their minds, the results of their labors: women, it appears, do
most of the work around this planet—and last but not least, their
wardrobes.

From Eve to Dawn has a point of view, one that will be familiar to the
readers of French's phenomenally best-selling 1977 novel *The Women's
Room*. "The people who oppressed women were men," French claims.

"Not all men oppressed women, but most benefited (or thought they benefited) from this domination, and most contributed to it, if only by doing nothing to stop or ease it."

Women who read this book will do so with horror and growing anger: *From Eve to Dawn* is to Simone de Beauvoir's *The Second Sex* as wolf is to poodle. Men who read it may be put off by the depiction of the collective male as brutal psychopath, or puzzled by French's idea that men should "take responsibility for what their sex has done." (How responsible can you be for Sumerian monarchs, Egyptian pharaohs, or Napoleon Bonaparte?) However, no one will be able to avoid the relentless piling up of detail and event—the bizarre customs, the woman-hating legal structures, the gynecological absurdities, the child abuse, the sanctioned violence, the sexual outrages—millennium after millennium. How to explain them? Are all men twisted? Are all women doomed? Is there hope? French is ambivalent about the twisted part, but—being a peculiarly American kind of activist—she insists on the hope.

Her project started out as a sweeping television series, like *The History of Civilization*. It would have made riveting viewing. Think of the visuals—witch-burnings, rapes, stonings to death, Jack the Ripper clones, bedizened courtesans, and martyrs from Joan of Arc to Rebecca Nurse. The television series fell off the rails, but French kept on, writing and researching with ferocious dedication, consulting hundreds of sources and dozens of specialists and scholars, although she was interrupted by a battle with cancer that almost killed her. The whole thing took her twenty years.

Her intention was to put together a narrative answer to a question that had bothered her for a long time: How had men ended up with all the power—specifically, with all the power *over women*? Had it always been like that? If not, how was such power grasped and then enforced? Nothing she had read had addressed this issue directly. In most conventional histories, women simply aren't there. Or they're there as footnotes. Their absence is like the shadowy corner in a painting where there's something going on that you can't quite see.

French aimed to throw some light into that corner. Her first volume—*Origins*—is the shortest. It starts with speculations about the kind of egalitarian hunter-gatherer societies also described by Jared Diamond in his classic *Guns, Germs, and Steel.* No society, says French, has ever been a matriarchy—that is, a society in which women are all-powerful and do dastardly things to men. But societies were once matrilineal—that is, children were thought to descend from the mother, not the father. Many have wondered why that state of affairs changed, but change it did; and as agriculture took over and patriarchy set in, women and children came to be viewed as property—men's property, to be bought, sold, traded, stolen, or killed.

As psychologists have told us, the more you mistreat people, the more pressing your need to explain why your victims deserve their fate. A great deal has been written about the "natural" inferiority of women, much of it by the philosophers and religion-makers whose ideas underpin Western society. Much of this thinking was grounded in what French calls, with wondrous understatement, "men's insistent concern with female reproduction." Male self-esteem, it seemed, depended on men not being women. All the more necessary that women should be forced to be as "female" as possible, even when—especially when—the male-created definition of "female" included the power to pollute, seduce, and weaken men.

With the advent of larger kingdoms and complex and structured religions, the costumes and interior decoration got better, but things got worse for women. Priests—having arguably displaced priestesses—came up with decrees from the gods who had arguably replaced goddesses, and kings obliged with legal codes and penalties. There were conflicts between spiritual and temporal power brokers, but the main tendency of both was the same: men good, women bad, by definition. Some of French's information boggles the mind: the "horse sacrifice" of ancient India, for instance, during which the priests forced the raja's wife to copulate with a dead horse. The account of the creation of Islam is particularly fascinating: like Christianity, it was woman-friendly in the beginning, and was supported and spread by women. But not for long.

The Masculine Mystique (Volume 2) is no more cheerful. Two kinds of feudalism are briskly dealt with: the European and the Japanese. Then it's on to the appropriations by Europeans of Africa, of Latin America, of North America, and thence to the American enslavement of blacks, with women at the bottom of the heap in all cases. You'd think the Enlightenment would have loosened things up, at least theoretically, but at the salons run by educated and intelligent women the *philosophes* were still debating—while hoovering up the refreshments—whether women had souls, or were just a kind of more advanced animal. In the eighteenth century, however, women were beginning to find their voices. Also they took to writing, a habit they have not yet given up.

Then came the French Revolution. At first, women as a caste were crushed by the Jacobins despite the key role they'd played in the aristocracy-toppling action. As far as the male revolutionaries were concerned, "Revolution was possible only if women were utterly excluded from power." Liberty, equality and fraternity did not include sorority. When Napoleon got control "he reversed every right women had won." Yet after this point, says French, "women were never again silent." Having participated in the ovethrow of the old order, they wanted a few rights of their own.

Infernos and Paradises is the third and longest volume. It takes us through the growing struggle for the emancipation of women in the nineteenth and twentieth centuries, with the gains and reverses, the triumphs and backlashes, played out against a background of imperialism, capitalism, and world wars. The Russian Revolution is particularly gripping—women were essential to its success—and particularly dispiriting as to the results. "Sexual freedom meant liberty for men and maternity for women," says French. "Wanting sex without responsibility, men charged women who rejected them with 'bourgeois prudery.' . . . To treat women as men's equals without reference to women's reproduction . . . is to place women in the impossible situation of being expected to do everything men do, and to reproduce society and maintain it, all at the same time and alone."

It's in the final three chapters that French comes into her home territory, the realm of her most personal knowledge, and her deepest enthusiasms. "The History of Feminism," "The Political Is Personal, The Personal Is Political," and "The Future of Feminism" make up the promised "dawn" of the general title. These sections are thorough and thoughtful. In them, French covers the contemporary ground, including the views of antifeminist and conservative women, who, she argues, see the world much as feminists do—half of humanity acting as predators on the other half—but differ in the degree of their idealism or hope. (If gender differences are "natural," nothing is to be done but to manipulate the morally inferior male with your feminine wiles, if any.) But almost all women, she believes—feminist or not—are "moving in the same direction along different paths."

Whether you share this optimism or not will depend on whether you believe Titanic Earth is already sinking. A fair chance and a fun time on the dance floor for all would be nice in theory. In practice it may be a scramble for the lifeboats. But whatever you think of French's conclusions, the issues she raises cannot be ignored. Women, it seems, are not a footnote after all: they are the necessary center around which the wheel of power revolves; or, seen another way, they are the broad base of the triangle that sustains a few oligarchs at the top. No history you will read, post-French, will ever look the same again.

55

To Beechy Island

The tourist is part of the landscape of our times, as the pilgrim was in the Middle Ages.

—V. S. Pritchett, *The Spanish Temper*

A week before my pilgrimage began, my partner Graeme Gibson and I found a dead crow in the backyard. "West Nile virus," we thought. We put it in the freezer and called the Humane Society. They took the frozen crow away, but said they would not be informing us of the diagnosis, as they did not want panic to spread. At about this time it occurred to me that I ought to have put on some DEET before pruning the rosebushes: there had been a few mosquitoes.

The day before my departure, I noticed some pink blotches around my waist. I put them down to a Thai spring roll I'd eaten. Perhaps I had an allergy.

Soon the blotches were more numerous, and spreading outward. I checked my tongue for furriness, my brain for light-headedness, my neck for stiffness. I did feel peculiar, although no one else seemed to be noticing. By this time I was on a plane bound for Greenland, and then, suddenly— time passes quickly when you're infested with microbes—I found myself on a Russian Arctic-research vessel called the *Akademic Ioffe*. I was a temporary staff member of an outfit called Adventure Canada, which sublet the Russian research ship from Peregrine, an Australian tour company that leased the boat for Antarctic cruises. On board with me were a mixed bunch: the Russian crew, the Australian folks who ran the "hotel" aspects of the trip, and the Canadians who planned and executed the daily programs for the sake of the hundred or so eager adventurers who had booked passage. My job was to give a couple of talks on northern exploration as shaped by literary and artistic concepts—a job that, in my virus-addled state, I felt ill equipped to perform.

Soon we were sailing down the long, long Sonderström Fjord—a fjord being, as our onboard geologist explained, a valley originally scooped out by glaciers and subsequently filled by the sea. Then we turned north and skirted the western coast of Greenland, cruising among huge and spectacular icebergs. The sea was blue, the sky was blue, the icebergs were blue as well, or their recently sheared surfaces were: an unearthly blue, inklike, artificial. As we cruised among them in our rubber Zodiacs, thousand-year-old ice fizzed in the water as its compressed air escaped.

We were bound—eventually—for Baffin Bay, then Lancaster Sound, and finally for Beechy Island, where the first three members of the doomed 1845 Franklin expedition were buried. Was I fated to join them? I wondered as the mountains rose to the right, and the dazzling ice-filled sea stretched out to the left, and the sunsets went on for hours. Was my head about to explode, for reasons that would appear mysterious to those observing? Was history poised to repeat itself, and would I perish of unknown causes, to be followed shortly by the entire passenger list and crew, just as in the Franklin expedition? I shared these thoughts with no one, although I felt it might be fitting to make a few illegible but poignant notes, to be discovered later, in a tin can or plastic pill container, like the garbled scrap that survived the Franklin debacle: *Oh, the dire sad.*

But the subject is pilgrimages, or a pilgrimage. I was supposed to be writing about one—this one, the one I was on. But in my blotchy state— the blotches had now reached my wrists and possibly my brain—I couldn't quite focus on the general idea. What was a pilgrimage? Had I ever made one before? Could what I was doing now be considered one? And if so, in what sense?

I'd made some literary pilgrimages in my youth, of a sort. I'd thrown up beside the road in Wordsworth country; I'd inspected the Brontë manse and marveled at the tiny size of its famous inhabitants; I'd been to Dr. Johnson's house in London, and to the House of the Seven Gables, in Salem, Massachusetts. But did such visits count? All of them had been accidents: I happened to be passing by. How much of the essence of a pilgrimage resides in the intention, rather than in the journey as such?

The dictionary provides some flexibility: a pilgrim can mean simply a wanderer, a sojourner; or it can mean one who travels to a sacred place as an act of religious devotion. Motion is involved, relics not necessarily. But the motion has to be protracted—a stroll to the corner store for a loaf of bread wouldn't qualify. It also has to be—surely—noncommercial in nature. Marco Polo, although a magnificent traveler, was not a pilgrim. Also, a pilgrimage was supposed to be good for you: good for your health (Temples of Asclepius, Lourdes, the heart of Brother André, with its trail of abandoned crutches), or good for the state of your soul (purchase an indulgence, get time off in Purgatory; become a Pilgrim Father, found the righteous New Jerusalem somewhere in the Boston area).

Needless to say, not all pilgrimages work out as advertised. Consider the Crusades.

When I thought of pilgrims, however, I thought first of literature. Most of the pilgrims I'd known had been encountered there.

There's Chaucer, of course: his Canterbury pilgrims are a sociable batch, making their trip together because it's spring, and they've got wanderlust, and they want to have fun. Whatever religious gloss they may put upon it, what they really enjoy is traveling in a merry company, and observing one another's wardrobes and foibles, and telling tales.

There's the seventeenth-century variety of pilgrim, exemplified by those in Bunyan's *Pilgrim's Progress*. For these hardy Protestants, the pilgrim's journey took him, not to a shrine, but through this mortal vale of tears and spiritual battles toward his goal, the heavenly home to be gained after his death.

The eighteenth century went on grand tours and sentimental journeys rather than pilgrimages, but with the Romantic age the pilgrimage was back. Consider Lord Byron's long poem *Childe Harold's Pilgrimage*.

Its hero is a wastrel, though filled with restless longing for he knows not what. But the sacred places he visits are not churches; they are sublime landscapes, with many a cliff and chasm, and the poem ends with a panegyric to the immensity of the sea, which contains this frequently quoted stanza:

> *Roll on, thou deep and dark blue ocean—roll!*
> *Ten thousand fleets sweep over thee in vain;*
> *Man marks the earth with ruin—his control*
> *Stops with the shore;—upon the watery plain*
> *The wrecks are all thy deed, nor doth remain*
> *A shadow of man's ravage, save his own,*
> *When for a moment, like a drop of rain*
> *He sinks into thy depths with bubbling groan,*
> *Without a grave, unknell'd, uncoffin'd and unknown.*

Putting all these varieties of pilgrimages together, what do we get? At first glance, nothing very consistent. However, there are a few links. For instance, a pilgrim—it seems—is never first on the ground. Someone else has always been there before him, and has come to an unfortunate (though heroic or saintly) end. It is in honor of these forerunners that the pilgrim takes up his staff. Chaucer's jolly company is headed to Canterbury, scene of the murder of Thomas à Becket. Bunyan's pilgrims are following in the footsteps of the crucified Christ; and even Byron's *Childe Harold* ends with the contemplation of a myriad tragic shipwrecks and drownings. A dead body, it seems, usually precedes the live pilgrim.

The journey I undertook had elements of all three sorts of pilgrimages. I sojourned with a merry company, and told tales, and listened to them as well. I observed sublime landscapes, and sublime seascapes, too, and meditated on dead sailors and drowned vessels.

As for spiritual battles, although I myself did not engage in any, those who'd given the route its haunted notoriety had most certainly engaged in them. We were taking the same sea road traveled by Franklin and his crew when they set out to discover the Northwest Passage in 1845 and were never seen again. Between their hopeful departure and the discovery of their silverware and gnawed bones, much anguish must have occurred.

But Franklin himself was not the direct object of my pilgrimage. My immediate agenda concerned a friend of mine, fellow poet Gwendolyn MacEwen. In the early 1960s, when she was in her early twenties, she'd written a remarkable verse drama for radio about the Franklin expedition, named after Franklin's two ships: the *Terror* and the *Erebus*. I'd heard this play when it was first broadcast, and had been very impressed by it—all the more so because Gwen had never been to the Arctic, had never reached Beechy Island, had never visited the Franklin expedition's three poignant graves. She had sailed these seas in imagination only, and had died in her midforties without ever seeing an iceberg.

My pilgrimage—if it can be called that—was undertaken for her. I would go where she'd been unable to go, stand where she had never stood, see what she had seen only with the mind's eye.

A sentimental gesture; but then, pilgrimages are sentimental by nature.

The voyage proceeded. Elements of the Chaucerian pilgrimage manifested themselves at mealtimes, with merry tales, and jests involving Viking outfits and kilts and false beards, and, on one memorable occasion, fur sunglasses and fur jockstraps. The Protestant-style soul-searching spiritual journey was an individual matter, as such things are: there was a lot of journal-keeping aboard ship. Ruminations on the human state and the state of nature were frequent: anxiety, not over the life to come, but over the near future, for it was evident even to an untrained eye that the glaciers are receding at a rapid pace.

The Byronic version of the pilgrimage was experienced on the bridge, or—with mittens—out on deck, as the—where are the adjectives? *Spectacular, grand,* and *sublime* hardly do it—as the indescribable scenery drifted past. "Look at that iceberg/cliff/rockface," people would say, entranced. "It looks just like a Lawren Harris painting." And yes, it did, only better, and so did that one, and the amazing one over there, purple and green and pink in the sunset, and then indigo and an unearthly yellow color. You found yourself just standing, with eyes and mouth open, for hours

369

By the time of my first talk on board ship, the original pink blotches were fading, but more had appeared. (Considerately, they stopped at the neckline.) The disorganization of my discourse was probably set down to the scrambled state in which "creative" people are thought to exist on a daily basis. I considered explaining about my curious disease, but then people might have thought they were on a plague ship and jumped overboard, or gotten themselves airlifted. Anyway, I was still walking and talking. It's just that I didn't appear to myself to be entirely responsible for what was coming out of my mouth. "Was that all right?" I asked Graeme. But he had been up on the bridge, watching fulmars.

What did I say? I think I began by remarking to my audience that Voltaire would have considered them all mad. To pay money for a voyage, not to some center of civilization where the proper study of mankind would be—as it ought to be—man, or even to some well-tended château with symmetrical plantings surrounding it, but to an icy waste with very large amounts of rock, water, and sand in it—this would have seemed to Voltaire the height of folly. Men did not risk their lives in such places unless there was a reason—money to be made, for instance. What changed between Voltaire and us—or between Voltaire and, for instance, Hilary uselessly climbing Mount Everest and Scott uselessly freezing himself in the Antarctic? A changed worldview. Burke's idea of the Sublime became a Romantic yardstick, and the sublime could not be the Sublime without danger. The history of Arctic exploration in the nineteenth century was seen through this glass, and those who went north and described and painted these landscapes did so with the Romantic hero looking over their shoulders.

Franklin's expedition, I think I said, occurred at a sort of hinge in time, the moment when such risky explorations ceased to be undertaken in hope of gain—no one deeply believed, by 1845, that the Northwest Passage would be the key to China and would make Britain very, very rich—and began to be undertaken in the spirit of heroic enterprise, as a sort of barrel trip over Niagara Falls. What was being defied by derring-do explorers and potential martyrs was not pagans, but Nature herself. "They forged the last link with their lives," reads the inscription on Franklin's memorial in Westminster Abbey—an inscription for which Lady Jane

Franklin, the widow, worked long and hard, as she worked to ensure that Franklin was seen as a hero in the Christian Romantic mode. But the last link of what? Of an idea. For as Ken McGoogan so ably demonstrates in his book *Fatal Passage*—a book I was reading as I was ferried blotchily across Baffin Bay—Franklin didn't really find the Northwest Passage. He found a body of water that was always choked with ice, instead, which ought not to have counted.

After he died, and after his ships had been locked in the ice for three years, his men set out overland, cooking and eating one another as they went. When the first news of these culinary activities reached England, brought by the intrepid explorer John Rae, Lady Franklin was most distressed; for if Franklin had indulged in cannibalism, he would not be a hero, but only a sort of chef. (John Rae, we now know, was right about the cannibalism, though Franklin himself had undoubtedly died before it got under way.)

Sometime during this admittedly rambling talk, I read from Gwendolyn's verse drama, in which she suggests that Franklin created the Northwest Passage by an act of imagination and will:

> *Ah, Franklin!*
> *To follow you, one does not need geography.*
> *At least not totally, but more of that*
> *Instrumental knowledge the bones have,*
> *Their limits, their measurings.*
> *The eye creates the horizon,*
> *The ear invents the wind,*
> *The hand reaching out from a parka sleeve*
> *By touch demands that the touched thing be.*

A fitting motif for pilgrimages: for what inspires them if not a purely imaginative link between place and spirit?

Having crossed Baffin Bay, we traveled through Lancaster Sound, and finally along the wild, and—again, adjectives fail—oddly Egyptian-looking sandstone cliffs of Devon Island. Devon is the largest uninhabited island in the world. Was it here we saw two polar bears eating a dead walrus, while groups of seals swam in the little harbor? I find I have recorded the event and the date—September 1—but not the exact location. There were several sites from the Thule people—those who preceded the present Inuit— and our on-ship archaeologist explained them to us. The huge whale ribs that once acted as roof beams were still there.

The sun shone, the breezes blew. Although it was autumn, several small Arctic flowers were still in bloom. Pakak Inukshuk and Aaju Peters, Inuit culture resource people, drum-danced and sang. At such moments the Arctic is intensely alive. It seems a benign landscape, mild and hazy and welcoming, a place of many delights.

The next day it was colder and the wind was up. We reached the westernmost end of Devon Island and dropped anchor in the harbor of Beechy Island, a small knob at the western end of Devon. Franklin's two ships, the *Terror* and the *Erebus*, spent their first winter there, protected from the crush of ice. The shore, once the edge of a warmer sea where marine life thrived, is now fossil-strewn, barren, windswept. Many have visited since Franklin's day; many have posed for the camera beside the three graves there; many have pondered.

Some years ago the three bodies were disinterred, in an attempt to learn more about the expedition. The scientists engaged in this venture—as recorded in John Geiger's book *Frozen in Time*—discovered that high levels of lead poisoning from canned food must have made a substantial contribution to the disaster. The tin cans themselves can still be seen on the beach: lead as thick as candle drippings closes their seams. The dangers of eating lead were not well understood then, and the symptoms mimicked scurvy. Lead attacks the immune system, and causes disorientation and lapses in judgment. The supplies that were supposed to keep the expedition members alive were in fact killing them.

We disembarked from the *Akademic Ioffe* in zodiacs and walked along the beach. I was blotch-free by this time; nevertheless I felt quite weightless. After visiting the graves—the markers are replicas now, as the originals suffered from the pilgrim's urge to chip off a piece of the action—Graeme and I sat on the shingle, near an old coal depot where ships used to leave supplies for other ships until polar bears tore the storage building apart. We ate a piece of chocolate, hoarded by me for this occasion, and toasted Gwen in water from our water bottles, and Graeme sang "The Ballad of Lord Franklin," the words swallowed up by the wind. Further along the beach, some bag-piping was underway, so faint we could scarcely hear it.

"Inchoate thoughts about spaces, emptiness, gaps; jumping across crevasses," I wrote in my notebook. "Words travelling across."

The next day we were beset by drifting pack ice, just like Franklin. It was astonishing how quickly the ice moved, and with what strength. We had to go seventy miles around to get away from it.

Pilgrims have traditionally brought something back with them from their journeys. Sometimes it was a cockle shell to show they'd been to Jerusalem, or an expensive splinter claiming to be a piece of the true cross, or the alleged fingerbone of a saint. Modern-day pilgrims, disguised as tourists, bring photos of themselves sticking out their tongues in front of the Eiffel Tower, or postcards, or purchased mementos—coffee spoons with the crests of cities on them, baseball caps, ashtrays.

There was no stand selling bits of explorer's finger or T-shirts with *Souvenir of Beechy Island* on them, so I brought back a pebble. It was identical with the millions of other pebbles on the beech—dun-colored sandstone, no distinguishing features. This pebble traveled with me to Toronto in a makeup kit.

I called my doctor as soon as I arrived and described my symptoms. "I think I've had West Nile virus," I said. "Hard to tell," was his reply. Worse come to worst, at least I wouldn't have been buried in the permafrost. I'd have been popped into the ship's freezer kept specially for that one purpose, so as not to get the bodies mixed up with the beef Stroganoff.

On a hot, dry day in mid-September, I put the Beechy Island pebble into my pocket, took a serving spoon from the kitchen, and walked over to Gwendolyn MacEwen Park, imagining to myself the rather sardonic poem Gwen might have made, both out of the park and out of the pebble event in which I was about to indulge. Accompanying me was David Young, one of whose plays, *Unimaginable Island,* deals with the unsung heroes of the Scott Antarctic expedition—unsung because they'd had the dubious taste to survive. To be a hero—at least in the nineteenth and early twentieth centuries—it was almost mandatory to be dead.

When we got to the park, David looked the other way while I dug a dusty hole with my spoon and inserted the pebble. So now, somewhere in the heart of darkest Toronto, its exact location known only to me, there's a tiny piece of geology brought all the way from Beechy Island. The only link between the two places is an act of the imagination, or perhaps two acts—Franklin's imagining of the Northwest Passage, and the twenty-two-year-old Gwendolyn MacEwen's imagining of Franklin.

> *So I've followed you here*
> *Like a dozen others, looking for relics*
> *   of your ships, your men.*
> *Here to this awful monastery,*
> *   where you, where Crozier died,*
> *   and all the men with you died,*
> *Seeking a passage from imagination to reality.*

56

Introduction:

Frozen in Time:
The Fate of the Franklin Expedition
[revised edition]
by Owen Beattie and John Geiger

*F*rozen in Time is one of those books that, having once entered our imaginations, refuses to go away. As I've been writing this intro-duction, I've described the project to several people. "*Frozen in Time*," I say. They look blank. "The one with the picture of the Frozen Franklin on the front," I say. "Oh yes. *That* one," they say. "I read that!" And off we go on a discussion of forensic anthropology under extreme conditions. *Frozen in Time* made a large impact, devoted as it was to the astonishing revelations made by Dr. Owen Beattie—including the high probability that lead poisoning had contributed to the annihilation of the 1845 Franklin expedition.

I read *Frozen in Time* when it first came out. I looked at the pictures in it. They gave me nightmares. I incorporated story and pictures as a subtext and extended metaphor in a short story called "The Age of Lead," published in a 1991 collection called *Wilderness Tips*. Then, some nine years later, during a boat trip in the Arctic, I met John Geiger, one of the authors of *Frozen in Time*. Not only had I read his book, he had read mine, and it had caused him to give further thought to lead as a factor in northern exploration and in unlucky nineteenth-century sea voyages in general.

Franklin, said Geiger, was the canary in the mine, although unrecog-nized as such at first: until the last years of the nineteenth century, crews on long voyages continued to be fatally sickened by the lead in tinned food. He has included the results of his researches in this expanded version of *Frozen in Time*. The nineteenth century, he said, was truly an "age of lead." Thus do life and art intertwine.

Back to the foreground. In the fall of 1984, a mesmerizing photograph grabbed attention in newspapers around the world. It showed a young man who looked neither fully dead nor entirely alive. He was dressed in archaic clothing and was surrounded by a casing of ice. The whites of his half-open eyes were tea-colored. His forehead was dark blue. Despite the soothing and respectful adjectives applied to him by the authors of *Frozen in Time*, you would never have confused this man with a lad just drifting off to sleep. Instead he looked like a blend of *Star Trek* extraterrestrial and B-movie victim of a curse—not someone you'd want as your next-door neighbor, especially if the moon was full.

Every time we find the well-preserved body of someone who died long ago—an Egyptian mummy, a freeze-dried Incan sacrifice, a leathery Scandinavian bogperson, the famous iceman of the European Alps—there's a similar fascination. Here is someone who has defied the general ashes-to-ashes, dust-to-dust rule and who has remained recognizable as an individual human being long after most have turned to bone and earth. In the Middle Ages, unnatural results argued unnatural causes, and such a body would either have been revered as saintly or staked through the heart. In our age, try for rationality as we may, something of the horror classic lingers: the mummy walks, the vampire awakes. It's so difficult to believe that one who appears to be so nearly alive is not conscious of us. Surely, we feel, a being like this is a messenger. He has traveled through time, all the way from his age to our own, to tell us something we long to know.

The man in the sensational photograph was John Torrington, one of the first three to die during the doomed Franklin expedition of 1845. Its stated goal was to discover the Northwest Passage to the Orient and claim it for Britain; its actual result was the obliteration of all participants. Torrington had been buried in a carefully dug grave, deep in the permafrost on the shore of Beechy Island, Franklin's base during the expedition's first winter. Two others—John Hartnell and William Braine—were given adjacent graves. All three had been painstakingly exhumed by anthropologist Owen Beattie and his team, in an attempt to solve a long-standing mystery: why had the Franklin expedition ended so disastrously?

Beattie's search for evidence of the rest of the Franklin expedition, his excavation of the three known graves, and his subsequent discoveries gave rise to a television documentary, and then—three years after the photograph first appeared—to the book you are holding in your hands. That the story should generate such widespread interest 140 years after Franklin filled his freshwater barrels at Stromness in the Orkney Islands before sailing off to his mysterious fate was a tribute to the extraordinary staying powers of the Franklin legend.

For many years the mysteriousness of that fate was the chief drawing card. At first, Franklin's two ships, the ominously named *Terror* and *Erebus*, appeared to have vanished into nothingness. No trace could be found of them, even after the graves of Torrington, Hartnell, and Braine had been found. There is something unnerving about people who can't be located, dead or alive. They upset our sense of space—surely the missing ones have to be somewhere. But where? Among the ancient Greeks, the dead who had not been retrieved and given proper funeral ceremonies could not reach the Underworld; they lingered in the world of the living as restless ghosts. And so it is, still, with the disappeared: they haunt us. The Victorian Age was especially prone to such hauntings, as witness Tennyson's *In Memoriam*, its most exemplary tribute to a man lost at sea.

Adding to the attraction of the Franklin story was the Arctic landscape that had subsumed leader, ships, and men. In the nineteenth century very few Europeans—apart from whalers—had ever been to the Far North. It was one of those perilous regions attractive to a public still sensitive to the spirit of literary Romanticism—a place where a hero might defy the odds, suffer outrageously, and pit his larger-than-usual soul against overwhelming forces. This Arctic was dreary and lonesome and empty, like the windswept heaths and forbidding mountains favored by aficionados of the Sublime. But the Arctic was also a potent Otherworld, imagined as a beautiful and alluring but potentially malign fairyland, a Snow Queen's realm complete with otherworldly light effects, glittering ice palaces, fabulous beasts—narwhals, polar bears, walruses—and gnomelike inhabitants dressed in exotic fur outfits. There are numerous drawings of the period that attest to this fascination with the locale. The Victorians were keen on fairies of all sorts—they painted them, wrote stories about them, and sometimes went so far as to believe in them. They knew the rules: going to an otherworld was a great risk. You might be captured by nonhuman beings. You might be trapped. You might never get out.

Ever since Franklin's disappearance, each age has created a Franklin suitable to its needs. Prior to the expedition's departure there was someone we might call the "real" Franklin, or even the Ur-Franklin—a man viewed by his peers as perhaps not the crunchiest biscuit in the packet, but solid and experienced, even if some of that experience had been won by bad judgment (as witness the ill-fated Coppermine River voyage of 1819). This Franklin knew his own active career was drawing toward an end, and saw in the chance to discover the Northwest Passage the last possibility for enduring fame. Aging and plump, he was not exactly a dream vision of the Romantic hero.

Then there was Interim Franklin, the one who came into being once the first Franklin failed to return and people in England realized that something must have gone terribly wrong. This Franklin was neither dead nor alive, and the possibility that he might be either caused him to loom large in the minds of the British public. During this period he acquired the adjective "gallant," as if he'd been engaged in a military exploit. Rewards were offered, search parties were sent out. Some of these men, too, did not return.

The next Franklin, one we might call Franklin Aloft, emerged after it became clear that Franklin and all of his men had died. They had not just died, they had perished, and they had not just perished, they had perished miserably. But many Europeans had survived in the Arctic under equally dire conditions. Why had this particular group gone under, especially since the *Terror* and the *Erebus* had been the best-equipped ships of their age, offering the latest in technological advances?

A defeat of such magnitude called for denial of equal magnitude.

Reports to the effect that several of Franklin's men had eaten several others were vigorously squelched; those bringing the reports—such as the intrepid John Rae, whose story was told in Ken McGoogan's 2002 book *Fatal Passage*—were lambasted in the press; and the Inuit who had seen the gruesome evidence were maligned as wicked savages. The effort to clear Franklin and all who sailed with him of any such charges was led by Lady Jane Franklin, whose social status hung in the balance: the widow of a hero is one thing, but the widow of a cannibal quite another. Due to Lady Jane's lobbying efforts, Franklin, in absentia, swelled to blimplike size. He was credited—dubiously—with the discovery of the Northwest Passage, and was given a plaque in Westminster Abbey and an epitaph by Tennyson.

After such inflation, reaction was sure to follow. For a time in the second half of the twentieth century we were given Halfwit Franklin, a cluck so dumb he could barely tie his own shoelaces. Franklin was a victim of bad weather—the ice that usually melted in the summer had failed to do so, not in just one year, but in three—but in the Halfwit Franklin reading, this counted for little. The expedition was framed as a pure example of European hubris in the face of Nature: Sir John was yet another of those Nanoodles of the North who came to grief because they wouldn't live by Native rules and follow Native advice—"Don't go there" being, on such occasions, advice number one.

But the law of reputations is like a bungee cord: you plunge down, you bounce up, though to diminishing depths and heights each time. In 1983, Sten Nadolny published *The Discovery of Slowness*, a novel that gave us a thoughtful Franklin, not exactly a hero but an unusual talent, and certainly no villain. Rehabilitation was on the way.

Then came Owen Beattie's discoveries, and the description of them in *Frozen in Time*. It was now clear that Franklin was no arrogant idiot. Instead he became a quintessentially twentieth-century victim: a victim of bad packaging. The tins of food aboard his ships had poisoned his men, weakening them and clouding their judgment. Tins were quite new in 1845, and these tins were sloppily sealed with lead, and the lead had leached into the food. But the symptoms of lead poisoning were not recognized at the time, being easily confused with those of scurvy. Franklin can hardly be blamed for negligence, and Beattie's revelations constituted exoneration of a kind for Franklin.

There was exoneration of two other kinds as well. By going where Franklin's men had gone, Beattie's team was able to experience the physical conditions faced by the surviving members of Franklin's crews. Even in summer, King William Island is one of the most difficult and desolate places on earth. No one could have done what these men were attempting— an overland expedition to safety. Weakened and addled as they were, they didn't have a hope. They can't be blamed for not making it.

The third exoneration was perhaps—from the point of view of historical justice—the most important. After a painstaking, finger-numbing search, Beattie's team found human bones with knife marks and skulls with no faces. John Rae and his Inuit witnesses, so unjustly attacked for having said that the last members of the Franklin crew had been practicing cannibalism, had been right after all. A large part of the Franklin mystery had now been solved.

Another mystery has since arisen: why has Franklin become such a Canadian icon? As Geiger and Beattie report, Canadians weren't much interested at first: Franklin was British, and the North was far away, and Canadian audiences preferred oddities such as the well-known midget Tom Thumb. But over the decades, Franklin has been adopted by Canadians as one of their own. For example, there were folk songs such as "The Ballad of Sir John Franklin"—a song not much remembered in England—and Stan Rogers's well-known "Northwest Passage." Then there were the contributions of writers. Gwendolyn MacEwen's radio drama " *Terror* and *Erebus*" was first broadcast in the early 1960s; the poet Al Purdy was fascinated by Franklin; the novelist and satirist Morecai Richler considered him an icon ripe for iconoclasm, and, in his novel *Solomon Gursky Was Here*, added a stash of cross-dresser women's clothing to the contents of Franklin's ships. What accounts for such appropriation? Is it that we identify with well-meaning nongeniuses who get tragically messed up by bad weather and evil food suppliers? Perhaps. Or perhaps it's because—as they say in china shops—if you break it, you own it.

Canada's North broke Franklin, a fact that appears to have conferred an ownership title of sorts.

It's a pleasure to welcome *Frozen in Time* back to the bookshelves in this revised and enlarged edition. I hesitate to call it a groundbreaking book, as a pun might be suspected, but groundbreaking it has been. It has contributed greatly to our knowledge of a signal event in the history of northern journeying. It also stands as a tribute to the enduring pull of the story—a story that has passed through all the forms a story may take. The Franklin saga has been mystery, surmise, rumor, legend, heroic adventure, and national iconography; and here, in *Frozen in Time*, it becomes a detective story, all the more gripping for being true.

57

Review:

Acquainted with the Night: Excursions Through the World After Dark by Christopher Dewdney

C hristopher Dewdney's intriguing new book, *Acquainted with the Night*, is what its subtitle says it is: a series of excursions through the twelve hours of every twenty-four that we spend where the sun doesn't shine. It's a fascinating miscellany of things you might bump into when the lights are out; or, conversely, of things that might bump into you. Who has never been mesmerized by the night? Who's never been afraid of it? No hands go up. Night is a universal experience—everyone everywhere has been through it—and thus a universal symbol; although, like all such symbols, it has its positive and its negative variants.

A reviewer should have nothing up her sleeves, so I must reveal here that I know the author. His father, Selwyn Dewdney, was a canoe-tripping pal of my father's. Thus I was aware of Christopher Dewdney when I was more or less grown up and he was still a boy. The kinds of things that caught his fancy when he was much younger—Why do rotten logs glow in the dark? Why are sunsets red? What is the green flash? What happens if you sample the well-known poisonous mushroom the Fly Agaric? Why do moths desire lightbulbs? What is your liver doing when you are asleep but it is awake?—such items still catch his fancy. Perhaps that's why this book is so full of boyish enthusiasm.

Christopher Dewdney came to my mother's ninetieth birthday party. Others brought chocolates and flowers; Dewdney brought a rock. It was from an inland ridge that marked an ancient shore of Lake Superior; he'd picked it up almost forty years before, on a canoe trip with my mother. Who hasn't carted such rocks home as mementos and then forgotten where they came from? But Dewdney remembered, and presented the rock, along with a few words on what kind of rock it was, geology being one of his excitements. Set a mind like that loose on a subject like "night" and you get this book.

People like Chistopher Dewdney collect stuff, and then they arrange the stuff in cabinets. When they are showing you the cabinets, they tell you how they came across the snail or bug or saint's toenail or whatever, and why it's important, and what it suggests in the greater scheme of things. And so it is with *Acquainted with the Night*: it interweaves personal experience with speculations and unexpected factoids, arranged according to the twelve hours of night. But this is not a Victorian museum, with everything dry and labeled and under glass, because Dewdney is also a poet. *Acquainted with the Night* brings together his two main strengths—his gift for language, and his insatiable curiosity about almost everything. The prose moves from the strictly informative to the lyrical to the charming to the amusing to the odd to the strangely moving without batting an eye. Dracula? Ordeals at the sleep clinic? Astronomy? Goddesses of Night? Dreaming? The Manson family and their nocturnal creepings about? Bioluminescence? Film noir? Fireworks festivals? Eat-in-the-dark restaurants? Werewolves? The circadian rhythm? UFO sightings? Painters of nocturnes? Goatsuckers? It's all here, stuck with quotations from a lot of well-known poets and writers, and—this being Dewdney—from many others nobody else has heard of.

Dewdney begins with a common childhood experience: sneaking out at night and wandering around in the darkness. Almost everyone I know used to do that. (Almost every Canadian, that is: in most of Canada, there are no venomous snakes. A child from a tropical climate would have to think twice.) We can still recall the magic of those innocently illicit but thrilling escapades, and these are words that recur in Dewdney's book: magic, illicit, thrilling. The words for night items enthrall him:

Night is profoundly in our souls and minds, our hearts and bodies. It is woven into our language. There are a thousand and one Arabian nights and each night has a thousand eyes. There is music in the night and a nightingale sings in Barclay Square. Night crawlers glisten on residential lawns, while downtown, night owls rub shoulders with fly-by-nights. . . . There are night watchmen, night-walkers, and night stalkers. Ladies of the night come and go.

(Dewdney has dutifully collected some ladies of the night; prostitutes are here, and famous courtesans; but they are not a main attraction for him. Given the choice between a ravishing lady of the night and a ravishing beetle of the night, one suspects he would take the beetle.)

Each of the chapters in this book has both an hour and a title. Thus 8:00 P.M. is "The Children's Hour." Within each chapter there are also subchapters, and it would have conveyed a greater sense of the book's range and richness had these been listed on the contents page. "The Children's Hour," for instance, has three subsections in addition to its introductory pages: "Victorian Europe and the Birth of Children's Literature," "The Bridge to Dreams: Four Children's Night Classics," and "Night Games." The second of these subsections contains a beautiful analysis of the Margaret Wise Brown classic *Goodnight Moon*: its eerie but comforting effects, and how it obtains them. Hint to readers: this is a browser's book. You can go back and forth in it. But don't skip any of the chapters without checking the subsection headings first, or you may miss a gem.

I could go on. And Dewdney does go on, occasionally a little too long, but there's something for everyone in his Cabinet of Dr. Callidewdney, and some readers will want to know more about, for instance, the acetylcholine-flooded pons or the noctilucent clouds or the eyeless American cavefishes or the life story of Galileo than others will. He could hardly have left anything out, or roars would have arisen. Some roars will arise anyway. For instance, he says that "contrary to the *Lord of the Rings* trilogy," dwarfs cannot go out by day or they will turn to stone. Every Ringhead in Middle Earth will be on his case: surely nothing can be contrary to *Lord of the Rings!* Imagine the hate mail. But before licking that stamp, ask yourself: Who else would have told you that the Panzer divisions invading Poland were on bennies? Or that a vampire bat consumes 60 percent of its own weight at one feed? Or that our sensitivity to dust peaks at 11:00 P.M.? It all balances out.

"Part of the process of writing about night was trying to gain a perspective that made it new, not commonplace," says Dewdney. He found it helpful to imagine that he was a being from another planet, one that had no night. Quite possibly this isn't the first time he's pictured himself as an extraterrestrial. In any case, his method worked: as you read these pages, your life will change, because the way you see half of it will change. The night we're all familiar with will emerge as a fresh thing, deeper, fuller, older, younger, more evocative, more intimate, larger, more spectacular, and yes, more magical, and much more thrilling.

58

Introduction:

Ten Ways of Looking at
The Island of Doctor Moreau
by H. G. Wells

H. G. Wells's *The Island of Doctor Moreau* is one of those books that, once read, is rarely forgotten. Jorge Luis Borges called it an "atrocious miracle," and made large claims for it. Speaking of Wells's early tales—*The Island of Doctor Moreau* among them—he said, "I think they will be incorporated, like the fables of Theseus or Ahasuerus, into the general memory of the species and even transcend the fame of their creator or the extinction of the language in which they were written." [1]

This has proved true, if film may be considered a language unto itself. *The Island of Doctor Moreau* has inspired three films—two of them quite bad—and doubtless few who saw them remembered that it was Wells who authored the book. The story has taken on a life of its own, and, like the offspring of Mary Shelley's *Frankenstein*, has acquired attributes and meanings not present in the original. Moreau himself, in his filmic incarnations, has drifted toward the type of the Mad Scientist, or the Peculiar Genetic Engineer, or the Tyrant-in-Training, bent on taking over the world; whereas Wells's Moreau is certainly not mad, is a mere vivisectionist, and has no ambitions to take over anything whatsoever.

Borges's use of the word "fable" is suggestive, for—despite the realistically rendered details of its surface—the book is certainly not a novel, if by that we mean a prose narrative dealing with observable social life. "Fable" points to a certain folkloric quality that lurks in the pattern of this curious work, as animal faces may lurk in the fronds and flowers of an Aubrey Beardsley design. The term may also indicate a lie—something fabulous or invented, as opposed to that which demonstrably exists—and employed this way it is quite apt, as no man ever did or ever will turn animals into human beings by cutting them up and sewing them together again. In its commonest sense, a fable is a tale—like those of Aesop—meant to convey some useful lesson. But what is that useful lesson? It is certainly not spelled out by Wells.

"Work that endures is always capable of an infinite and plastic ambiguity; it is all things for all men," says Borges, ". . . and it must be ambiguous in an evanescent and modest way, almost in spite of the author; he must appear to be ignorant of all symbolism. Wells displayed that lucid innocence in his first fantastic exercises, which are to me the most admirable part of his admirable work."[2] Borges carefully did not say that Wells employed no symbolism, only that he appeared to be ignorant of doing so.

Here follows what I hope will be an equally modest attempt to probe beneath the appearance, to examine the infinite and plastic ambiguity, to touch on the symbolism that Wells may or may not have employed deliberately, and to try to discover what the useful lesson—if there is one—might be.

Ten Ways of Looking at The Island of Doctor Moreau

1. *Elois and Morlocks*

The Island of Doctor Moreau was published in 1896, when H. G. Wells was only thirty years old. It followed *The Time Machine*, which had appeared the year before, and was to be followed two years later by *The War of the Worlds*, this being the book that established Wells as a force to be reckoned with at a mere thirty-two years of age.

To some of literature's more gentlemanly practitioners—those, for instance, who had inherited money, and didn't have to make it by scribbling—Wells must have seemed like a puffed-up little counter-jumper, and a challenging one at that, because he was bright. He'd come up the hard way. In the stratified English social world of the time, he was neither working-class nor top crust. His father was an unsuccessful tradesman; he himself apprenticed with a draper for two years before wending his way, via school-teaching and a scholarship, to the Normal School of Science. Here he studied under Darwin's famous apologist Thomas Henry Huxley. Wells graduated with a first-class degree, but he'd been seriously injured by one of the students while teaching, an event that put him off school-mastering. It was after this that he turned to writing.

The Time Traveler in *The Time Machine*—written just before *The Island of Doctor Moreau*—finds that human beings in the future have split into two distinct races. The Eloi are pretty as butterflies, but useless; the grim and ugly Morlocks live underground, make everything, and come out at night to devour the Eloi, whose needs they also supply. The upper Classes, in other words, have become a bevy of Upper-Class Twitterers and have lost the ability to fend for themselves, and the working classes have become vicious and cannibalistic.

Wells was neither an Eloi nor a Morlock. He must have felt he represented a third way, a rational being who had climbed up the ladder through ability alone, without partaking of the foolishness and impracticality of the social strata above his nor of the brutish crudeness of those below.

But what about Prendick, the narrator of *The Island of Doctor Moreau*? He's been pootling idly about the world—for his own diversion, we assume—when he's shipwrecked. The ship is called the *Lady Vain*, surely a comment on the snooty aristocracy. Prendick himself is a "private gentleman" who doesn't have to work for a living, and, though he—like Wells—has studied with Huxley, he has done so not out of necessity but out of dilettantish boredom—"as a relief from the dullness of [his] comfortable independence." Prendick, though not quite as helpless as a full-fledged Eloi, is well on the path to becoming one. Thus his hysteria, his lassitude, his moping, his ineffectual attempts at fair play, and his lack of common sense— he can't figure out how to make a raft because he's never done "any carpentry or suchlike work" in his life, and when he does manage to patch something together, he's situated it too far from the sea and it falls apart when he's dragging it. Although Prendick is not a complete waste of time—if he were, he wouldn't be able to hold our attention while he tells his story—he's nonetheless in the same general league as the weak-chinned curate in the later *War of the Worlds*, that helpless and driveling "spoiled child of life." [3]

His name—Prendick—is suggestive of "thick" coupled with "prig," this last a thing he is explicitly called. To those versed in legal lore, it could suggest "prender," a term for something you are empowered to take without it having been offered. But it more nearly suggests "prentice," a word that would have been floating close to the top of Wells's semiconsciousness, due to his own stint as an apprentice. Now it's the upper-class's turn at apprenticeship! Time for one of them to undergo a little degradation and learn a thing or two. But what?

2. Signs of the Times

The Island of Doctor Moreau comes not only midway in Wells's most fertile period of fantastic inventiveness; it also comes during such a period in English literary history. Adventure romance had taken off with Robert Louis Stevenson's *Treasure Island* in 1882, and Rider Haggard had done him one better with *She*, in 1887. This latter coupled straight adventure —shipwreck, tramps through dangerous swamps and nasty shrubbery, encounters with bloody-minded savages, fun in steep ravines and dim grottoes—with a big dollop of weirdness carried over from earlier gothic traditions, done up this time in a package labeled "Not Supernatural." The excessive powers of She are ascribed not to a close encounter with a vampire or god, but to a dip in a revolving pillar of fire, no more supernatural than lightning. She gets her powers from Nature.

It's from this blend—the grotesque and the "natural"—that Wells took his cue. An adventure story that would once have featured battles with fantastic monsters—dragons, gorgons, hydras—keeps the exotic scenery, but the monsters have been produced by the very agency that was seen by many in late Victorian England as the bright, new, shiny salvation of mankind: science.

The other blend that proved so irresistible to readers was one that was developed much earlier, and to singular advantage, by Jonathan Swift: a plain, forthright style in the service of incredible events. Poe, that master of the uncanny, piles on the adjectives to create "atmosphere"; Wells, on the other hand, follows R. L. Stevenson and anticipates Hemingway in his terse, almost journalistic approach, usually the hallmark of the ultrarealists. *The War of the Worlds* shows Wells employing this combination to best effect—we think we're reading a series of news reports and eyewitness accounts, but he's already honing it in *The Island of Doctor Moreau*. A tale told so matter-of-factly and with such an eye to solid detail surely cannot be—we feel—either an invention or a hallucination.

3. *Scientific*

Wells is acknowledged to be one of the foremost inventors in the genre we now know as "science fiction." As Robert Silverberg has said, "Every time-travel tale written since *The Time Machine* is fundamentally indebted to Wells. . . . In this theme, as in most of science fiction's great themes, Wells was there first."[4]

"Science fiction" as a term was unknown to Wells; it did not make its appearance until the 1930s, in America, during the golden age of bug-eyed monsters and girls in brass brassieres.[5] Wells himself referred to his science-oriented fictions as "scientific romances"—a term that did not originate with him, but with a lesser-known writer named Charles Howard Hinton.

There are several interpretations of the term "science." If it implies the known and the possible, then Wells's scientific romances are by no means scientific; he paid little attention to those boundaries. As Jules Verne remarked with displeasure, *"Il invente!"* The "science" part of these tales is embedded instead in a worldview that derived from Wells's study of Darwinian principles under Huxley, and has to do with the grand study that engrossed Wells throughout his career: the nature of man. This, too, may account for his veering between extreme Utopianism (if man is the result of evolution, not of Divine creation, surely he can evolve yet further?) and the deepest pessimism (if man came from the animals and is akin to them, rather than to the angels, surely he might slide back the way he came?). *The Island of Doctor Moreau* belongs to the debit side of the Wellsian account book.

Darwin's *On The Origin of Species* and *The Descent of Man* were profound shocks to the Victorian system. Gone was the God who spoke the world into being in seven days and made man out of clay; in its place stood millions of years of evolutionary change, and a family tree that included primates. Gone, too, was the kindly Wordsworthian version of Mother Nature that had presided over the first years of the century; in her place was Tennyson's "Nature, red in tooth and claw/With ravine." The devouring femme fatale that became so iconic in the 1880s and 1890s owes a lot to Darwin. So does the imagery and cosmogony of *The Island of Doctor Moreau.*

4. *Romance*

So much for the "scientific" in "scientific romance." What about the "romance"?

In both "scientific romance" and "science fiction," the scientific element is merely an adjective; the nouns are "romance" and "fiction." In respect to Wells, "romance" is more helpful than "fiction."

"Romance," in today's general usage, is what happens on Valentine's Day. As a literary term it has slipped in rank somewhat—being now applied to such things as Harlequin Romances—but it was otherwise understood in the nineteenth century, when it was used in opposition to the term "novel." The novel dealt with known social life, but a romance could deal with the long ago and the far away. It also allowed much more latitude in terms of plot. In a romance, event follows exciting event at breakneck pace. As a rule, this has caused the romance to be viewed by the high literati—those bent more on instruction than on delight—as escapist and vulgar, a judgment that goes back at least two thousand years.

In *The Secular Scripture*, Northrop Frye provides an exhaustive analysis of the structure and elements of the romance as a form. Typically a romance begins with a break in ordinary consciousness, often—traditionally—signaled by a shipwreck, frequently linked with a kidnapping by pirates. Exotic climes are a feature, especially exotic desert islands; so are strange creatures.

In the sinister portions of a romance, the protagonist is often imprisoned or trapped, or lost in a labyrinth or maze, or in a forest that serves the same purpose. Boundaries between the normal levels of life dissolve: vegetable becomes animal, animal becomes quasi-human, human descends to animal. If the lead character is female, an attempt will be made on her virtue, which she manages miraculously to preserve. A rescue, however improbable, restores the protagonist to his or her previous life and reunites him or her with loved ones. *Pericles, Prince of Tyre*, is a romance. It's got everything but talking dogs.

The Island of Doctor Moreau is also a romance, though a dark one. Consider the shipwreck. Consider the break in the protagonist's consciousness—the multiple breaks, in fact. Consider the pirates, here supplied by the vile captain and crew of the *Ipecacuanha*. Consider the name *Ipecacuanha*, signifying an emetic and purgative: the break in consciousness is going to have a nastily physical side to it, of a possibly medicinal kind. Consider the fluid boundaries between animal and human. Consider the island.

5. *The Enchanted Island*

The name given to the island by Wells is Noble's Island, a patent irony as well as another poke at the class system. Say it quickly and slur a little, and it's *no blessed island.*

This island has many literary antecedents and several descendants. Foremost among the latter is William Golding's island in *Lord of the Flies*—a book that owes something to *The Island of Doctor Moreau*, as well as to those adventure books *Coral Island* and *The Swiss Family Robinson*, and of course to the great original shipwreck-on-an-island classic, *Robinson Crusoe*. *Moreau* could be thought of as one in a long line of island-castaway books.

All those just mentioned, however, keep within the boundaries set by the possible. *The Island of Doctor Moreau* is, on the contrary, a work of fantasy, and its more immediate grandparents are to be found elsewhere. *The Tempest* springs immediately to mind: here is a beautiful island, belonging at first to a witch, then taken over by a magician who lays down the law, particularly to the malignant, animal-like Caliban, who will obey only when pain is inflicted on him. Doctor Moreau could be seen as a sinister version of Prospero, surrounded by a hundred or so Calibans of his own creation.

But Wells himself points us toward another enchanted island. When Prendick mistakenly believes that the beast-men he's seen were once men, he says: "[Moreau] had merely intended . . . to fall upon me with a fate more horrible than death, with torture, and after torture the most hideous degradation it was possible to conceive—to send me off, a lost soul, a beast, to the rest of [the] Comus rout."

Comus, in the masque of that name by Milton, is a powerful sorcerer who rules a labyrinthine forest. He's the son of the enchantress Circe, who in Greek myth was the daughter of the Sun and lived on the island of Aeaea. Odysseus landed there during his wanderings, and Circe transformed his crew into pigs. She has a whole menagerie of other kinds of animals—wolves, lions—that were also once men. Her island is an island of transformation: man to beast (and then to man again, once Odysseus gets the upper hand).

As for Comus, he leads a band of creatures, once men, who have drunk from his enchanted cup and have turned into hybrid monsters. They retain their human bodies, but their heads are those of beasts of all kinds. Thus changed, they indulge in sensual revels. Christina Rosetti's *Goblin Market*, with its animal-form goblins who tempt chastity and use luscious edibles as bait, is surely a late offshoot of Comus.

As befits an enchanted island, Moreau's island is both semi-alive and female, but not in a pleasant way. It's volcanic, and emits from time to time a sulfurous reek. It comes equipped with flowers, and also with clefts and ravines, fronded on either side. Moreau's beast-men live in one of these, and since they do not have very good table manners, it has rotting food in it and it smells bad. When the beast-men start to lose their humanity and revert to their beast natures, this locale becomes the site of a moral breakdown that is specifically sexual.

What is it that leads us to believe that Prendick will never have a girlfriend?

6. *The Unholy Trinity*

Nor will Doctor Moreau. There is no Mrs. Moreau on the island. There are no female human beings at all.

Similarly, the God of the Old Testament has no wife. Wells called *The Island of Doctor Moreau* "a youthful piece of blasphemy," and it's obvious that he intended Moreau—that strong, solitary gentlemen with the white hair and beard—to resemble traditional paintings of God. He surrounds Moreau with semi-Biblical language as well: Moreau is the lawgiver of the island; those of his creatures who go against his will are punished and tortured; he is a god of whim and pain. But he isn't a real God, because he cannot really create; he can only imitate, and his imitations are poor.

What drives him on? His sin is the sin of pride, combined with a cold "intellectual passion." He wants to know everything. He wishes to discover the secrets of life. His ambition is to be as God the Creator. As such, he follows in the wake of several other aspirants, including Doctor Franken-stein and Hawthorne's various alchemists. Doctor Faustus hovers in the background, but he wanted youth and wealth and sex in return for his soul, and Moreau has no interest in such things; he despises what he calls "materialism," which includes pleasure and pain. He dabbles in bodies but wishes to detach himself from his own. (He has some literary brothers: Sherlock Holmes would understand his bloodless intellectual passion. So would Oscar Wilde's Lord Henry Wooton, of that earlier fin de siècle transformation novel *The Picture of Dorian Gray*.)

But in Christianity, God is a trinity, and on Moreau's island there are three beings whose names begin with M. *Moreau* as a name combines the syllable "mor"—from *mors, mortis*, no doubt—with the French for "water," suitable in one who aims at exploring the limits of plasticity. The whole word means "moor" in French. So the very white Moreau is also the Black Man of witchcraft tales, a sort of anti-God.

Montgomery, his alcoholic assistant, has the face of a sheep. He acts as the intercessor between the beast folk and Moreau, and in this function stands in for Christ the Son. He's first seen offering Prendick a red drink that tastes like blood, and some boiled mutton. Is there a hint of an ironic Communion service here—blood drink, flesh of the Lamb? The com-munion Prendick enters into by drinking the red drink is the communion of carnivores, that human communion forbidden to the beast folk. But it's a communion he was part of anyway.

The third person of the Trinity is the Holy Spirit, usually portrayed as a dove—God in living but nonhuman form. The third M creature on the island is M'Ling, the beast creature who serves as Montgomery's attendant. He, too, enters into the communion of blood: he licks his fingers while preparing a rabbit for the human beings to eat. The Holy Spirit as a deformed and idiotic man-animal? As a piece of youthful blasphemy, *The Island of Doctor Moreau* was even more blasphemous than most commentators have realized.

Just so we don't miss it, Wells puts a serpent beast into his dubious garden: a creature that was completely evil and very strong, and that bent a gun barrel into the letter S. Can Satan, too, be created by man? If so, blas-phemous indeed.

7. The New Woman as Catwoman

There are no female human beings on Moreau's island, but Moreau is busily making one. The experiment on which he's engaged for most of the book concerns his attempt to turn a female puma into the semblance of a woman.

Wells was more than interested in members of the cat family, as Brian Aldiss has pointed out. During his affair with Rebecca West, she was "Panther," he was "Jaguar." But "cat" has another connotation: in slang, it meant "prostitute." This is Montgomery's allusion when he says—while the puma is yelling under the knife—"I'm damned . . . if this place is not as bad as Gower Steet—with its cats." Prendick himself makes the connection explicit on his return to London when he shies away from the "prowling women [who] would mew after me."

"I have some hope of her head and brain," says Moreau of the puma. ". . . I will make a rational creature of my own." But the puma resists. She's almost a woman—she weeps like one—but when Moreau begins torturing her again, she utters a "shriek almost like that of an angry virago." Then she tears her fetter out of the wall and runs away, a great bleeding, scarred, suffering, female monster. It is she who kills Moreau.

Like many men of his time, Wells was obsessed with the New Woman. On the surface of it he was all in favor of sexual emancipation, including free love, but the freeing of Woman evidently had its frightening aspects. Rider Haggard's *She* can be seen as a reaction to the feminist movement of his day—if women are granted power, men are doomed—and so can Wells's deformed puma. Once the powerful, monstrous sexual cat tears her fetter out of the wall and gets loose, minus the improved brain she ought to have courtesy Man the Scientist, look out.

8. The Whiteness of Moreau, the Blackness of M'Ling

Wells was not the only nineteenth-century English writer who used furry creatures to act out English sociodramas. Lewis Carroll had done it in a whimsical way in the *Alice* books, Kipling in a more militaristic fashion in *The Jungle Book*.

Kipling made the Law sound kind of noble in *The Jungle Book*. Not so

Wells. The Law mumbled by the animal-men in Moreau is a horrible parody of Christian and Jewish liturgy; it vanishes completely when the language of the beasts dissolves, indicating that it was a product of language, not some eternal God-given creed.

Wells was writing at a time when the British Empire still held sway, but the cracks were already beginning to show. Moreau's island is a little colonial enclave of the most hellish sort. It's no accident that most (although not all) of the beast folk are black or brown, that they are at first thought by Prendick to be "savages" or "natives," and that they speak in a kind of mangled English. They are employed as servants and slaves—in a regime that's kept in place with whip and gun—they secretly hate the real "men" as much as they fear them, and they disobey the Law as much as possible, and kick over the traces as soon as they can. They kill Moreau and they kill Montgomery and they kill M'Ling, and, unless Prendick can get away, they will kill him, too, although at first he "goes native" and lives among them, and does things that fill him with disgust and that he would rather not mention.

White Man's Burden, indeed.

9. The Modern Ancient Mariner

The way in which Prendick escapes from the island is noteworthy. He sees a small boat with a sail and lights a fire to hail it. It approaches, but strangely: it doesn't sail with the wind, but yaws and veers. There are two figures in it, one with red hair. As the boat enters the bay, "Suddenly a great white bird flew up out of the boat, and neither of the men stirred nor noticed it. It circled round, and then came sweeping overhead with its strong wings outspread." This bird cannot be a gull: it's too big and solitary. The only white seabird usually described as "great" is the albatross.

The two figures in the boat are dead. But it is this death boat, this life-in-death coffin boat, that proves the salvation of Prendick.

In what other work of English literature do we find a lone man reduced to a pitiable state, a boat that sails without a wind, two death figures, one with unusual hair, and a great white bird? The work is, of course, *The Rime of The Ancient Mariner*, which revolves around man's proper relation to Nature, and concludes that this proper relation is one of love. It is when he manages to bless the sea serpents that the Mariner is freed from the curse he has brought upon himself by shooting the albatross.

The Island of Doctor Moreau also revolves around man's proper relation to Nature, but its conclusions are quite different, because Nature itself is seen differently. It is no longer the Nature eulogized by Wordsworth, that benevolent motherly entity who never did betray that heart that loved her, for between Coleridge and Wells came Darwin.

The lesson learned by the albatross-shooting Mariner is summed up by him at the end of the poem:

> *He prayeth well, who loveth well*
> *Both man and bird and beast.*

> *He prayeth best, who loveth best*
> *All things both great and small;*
> *For the dear God who loveth us,*
> *He made and loveth all.*

In the Ancient Mariner–like pattern at the end of *The Island of Doctor Moreau*, the "albatross" is still alive. It has suffered no harm at the hands of Prendick. But he lives in the shadow of a curse anyway. His curse is that he can't love or bless anything living: not bird, not beast, and most certainly not man. He has another curse, too: the Ancient Mariner is doomed to tell his tale, and those who are chosen to hear it are convinced by it. But Prendick chooses not to tell because, when he tries, no one will believe him.

10. *Fear and Trembling*

What then is the lesson learned by the unfortunate Prendick? It can perhaps best be understood in reference to *The Ancient Mariner*. The god of Moreau's island can scarcely be described as a dear God, who makes and loves all creatures. If Moreau is seen to stand for a version of God the Creator who "makes" living things, he has done—in Prendick's final view—a very bad job. Similarly, if God can be considered as a sort of Moreau, and if the equation "Moreau is to his animals as God is to man" may stand, then God himself is accused of cruelty and indifference—making man for fun and to satisfy his own curiosity and pride, laying laws on him he cannot understand or obey, then abandoning him to a life of torment.

Prendick cannot love the distorted and violent furry folk on the island, and it's just as hard for him to love the human beings he encounters on his return to "civilization." Like Swift's Gulliver, he can barely stand the sight of his fellow men. He lives in a state of queasy fear, inspired by his continued experience of dissolving boundaries: as the beasts on the island have at times appeared human, the human beings he encounters in England appear bestial. He displays his modernity by going to a "mental specialist," but this provides only a partial remedy. He feels himself to be "an animal tormented . . . sent to wander alone."

Prendick forsakes his earlier dabblings in biology, and turns instead to chemistry and astronomy. He finds "hope"—"a sense of infinite peace and protection" in "the glittering hosts of heaven." As if to squash even this faint hope, Wells almost immediately wrote *The War of the Worlds*, in which not peace and protection, but malice and destruction, come down from the heavens in the form of the monstrous but superior Martians.

The War of the Worlds can be read as a further gloss on Darwin. Is this where evolution will lead—to the abandonment of the body, to giant, sexless, blood-sucking heads with huge brains and tentaclelike fingers? But it can also be read as a thoroughly chilling coda to *The Island of Doctor Moreau*.

Notes

1. Borges, Jorge Luis. Weinberger, Eliot (ed.), Allen, Esther (trans.), *The Total Library: Non-Fiction 1992–1986* (London: Allen Lane, Penguin Press, 1999).

2. Borges, Jorge Luis, *Other Inquisitions 1937–1952* (New York: Clarion, 1968).

3. Wells, H. G., *War of the Worlds* (New York: Airmont, 1964).

4. Wells, H. G., *The Island of Doctor Moreau* (New York: Everyman, 1993).

5. Silverberg, Robert, (ed.), *Voyages in Time: Twelve Great Science Fiction Stories* (New York: Tempo, 1970).

6. The "brass brassiere" is from an oral history of science fiction prepared by Richard Wolinsky for Berkeley's KPFA-FM.

7. Frye, Northrop, *The Secular Scripture: A Study of the Structure of Romance* (Massachusetts: Harvard University Press, 1976).

ACKNOWLEDGMENTS

My thanks to all who have contributed to this book. To Philip Turner, of Carroll & Graf, who read a great many things and helped to select; to Phoebe Larmore, my agent; to Adrienne Leahey, for her concept of the book, and for her work in pulling it together; to Jen Osti-Fonseca, my assistant, and to Surya Bhattacharya, who helped to track things down; to Gene Goldberg, who is full of bright ideas; and to Coleen Quinn, who kept me in working order. Thanks also to Martha Sharpe, of House of Anansi Press in Canada, who kept me on the path. There are many, many newspaper and magazine editors with whom I've worked over the years: thank you to all.

And to Graeme Gibson, who has so often and so wisely said, "I wouldn't write that if I were you"; and to Jess Gibson, constant reader, who is sometimes able to correct my slang.

The publisher wishes to thank Sarah Maclachlan and Martha Sharpe of House of Anansi Press, Graham Fidler and Kevin Williams of Publishers Group Canada, and Michael Martin.

BIBLIOGRAPHY

Part One: 1983–1989

1. "Wondering What It's Like to Be a Woman." Review of *The Witches of Eastwick* by John Updike. *New York Times Book Review*, 13 May 1984.

2. "Atwood on Pornography." *Chatelaine* (September 1983).

3. "The Sorcerer as Apprentice." Review of *Difficult Loves* by Italo Calvino. *New York Times Book Review*, 13 May 1984.

4. "That Certain Thing Called the Girlfriend." *New York Times Book Review*, 11 May 1986.

5. "True North." *Saturday Night*, Vol. 102, No. 1 (January 1987).

6. "Haunted by Their Nightmares." Review of *Beloved* by Toni Morrison. *New York Times Book Review*, 13 September 1987.

7. Afterword to *A Jest of God* by Margaret Laurence (Toronto: M&S, 1988).

8. "Great Aunts." From *Family Portraits: Remembrances by Twenty Distinguished Writers*, ed. Carolyn Anthony (New York: Doubleday, 1989).

9. Introduction: "Reading Blind." Introduction to *The Best American Short Stories, 1989*, eds. Margaret Atwood and Shannon Ravenel (New York: Houghton, 1989).

10. Introduction to *Women Writers at Work: The Paris Review Interviews*, ed. George Plimpton (New York: Penguin, 1989).

11. "The Public Woman as Honorary Man." Review of *The Warrior Queens* by Antonia Fraser. *Los Angeles Times Book Review*, 2 April 1989.

12. Writing Utopia. Unpublished speech, 1989.

Part Two: 1990–1999

13. "Nine Beginnings." From *The Writer on Her Work, Volume 1,* ed. Janet Sternburg (New York: Norton, 1990, 2000).

14. "A Slave to His Own Liberation." Review of *The General in His Labyrinth* by Gabriel García Márquez. *New York Times Book Review,* 16 September 1990.

15. Afterword to *Anne of Green Gables* by Lucy Maud Montgomery (Toronto: M&S, 1992).

16. "Why I Love *Night of the Hunter.*" Review of *The Night of the Hunter,* dir. Charles Laughton (1955). *The Guardian,* 19 March 1999.

17. Spotty-handed Villainesses: Problems of Female Bad Behaviour in the Creation of Literature. An address delivered in the Cheltenham Lecture Series, University of Gloucester, 8 October 1993.

18. "The Grunge Look." *Writing Away: The PEN Canada Travel Anthology,* ed. Constance Rooke (Toronto: M&S, 1994).

19. "Not So Grimm." The Staying Power of Fairy Tales. Review of *From the Beast to the Blonde: On Fairy Tales and Their Tellers* by Marina Warner. *Los Angeles Times Book Review,* 29 October 1995.

20. "A Rich Dessert from a Saucy Carter." Review of *Burning Your Boats: The Collected Short Stories* by Angela Carter. *Globe and Mail,* 6 April 1996.

21. "'Little Chappies With Breasts.'" Review of *An Experiment in Love* by Hilary Mantel. *New York Times Book Review,* 2 June 1996.

22. In Search of *Alias Grace:* On Writing Canadian Historical Fiction. An address given at Bronfman Lecture Series (Ottawa: November 1996), Smithsonian Institute (Washington: 11 December 1996), Chicago Library Foundations (6 January 1997), Oberlin College Friends of the Library (8 February 1997), City Arts & Lectures (San Francisco: 5 March 1997). Reprinted in *American Historical Review,* Vol. 103, No. 5 (December 1998).

23. "Masterpiece Theatre." Review of *Trickster Makes This World: Mischief, Myth and Art* and *The Gift: Imagination and the Erotic Life of Property* by Lewis Hyde. *Los Angeles Times Book Review,* 25 January 1998.

Part Three: 2000–2005

24. "First Job, Waitressing." *New Yorker,* 23 April 2001.

25. "Mordecai Richler: 1931–2001: Diogenes of Montreal." *Globe and Mail,* 4 July 2001.

26. "A Novel Worthy of a Queen(ey)." Review of *According to Queeney* by Beryl Bainbridge. *Globe and Mail,* 4 August 2001.

27. Introduction to *She* by H. Rider Haggard (New York: Random House, 2002).

28. "When Afghanistan Was at Peace." *New York Times Magazine,* 28 October 2001.

29. "Mystery Man." Review of: *The Selected Letters of Dashiell Hammett, 1921– 1960,* eds. Richard Layman and Julie Rivett; *Dashiell Hammett: A Daughter Remembers* by Jo Hammett; and *Dashiell Hammett: Crime Stories & Other Writings,* ed. Steven Marcus. *New York Review of Books,* Vol. 49, No. 2 (14 February 2002).

30. "Of Myths and Men." Review of *Atanarjuat: The Fast Runner,* dir. Zacharias Kunuk (2001). *Globe and Mail,* 13 April 2002.

31. Review of *Life of Pi* by Yann Martel. *Sunday Times,* 12 May 2002.

32. "Cops and Robbers." Review of *Tishomingo Blues* by Elmore Leonard. *New York Review of Books,* Vol. 49, No. 9 (23 May 2002).

33. Tiff and the Animals. An address delivered on the occasion of the Timothy Findley Memorial Evening, University of Toronto, 29 September 2002.

34. "The Indelible Woman." Essay on Virginia Woolf's *To the Lighthouse. The Guardian,* 7 September 2002.

35. "The Queen of Quinkdom." Review of *The Birthday of the World and Other Stories* by Ursula K. Le Guin. *New York Review of Books,* Vol. 49, No. 14 (26 September 2002).

36. Introduction to *Ground Works: Avant-Garde for Thee,* ed. Christian Bök (Toronto: Anansi, 2002).

37. Introduction to *Doctor Glas* by Hjalmar Söderberg, trans. Paul Britten Austin (New York: Anchor, 2002).

38. Introduction to *High Latitudes: An Arctic Journey* by Farley Mowat (North Royalton, Vermont: Steerforth, 2002).

39. "Castle of the Imagination." Review of *Child of My Heart* by Alice McDermott. *The New York Review,* Vol. L, No 1, 16 January 2003.

40. Napoleon's Two Biggest Mistakes. From "Bonaparte to Bush: You'll be Sorry." *Globe and Mail,* 1 March 2003.

41. Letter to America. *The Nation,* 14 April 2003.

42. Writing *Oryx and Crake.* Book of the Month Club/Bookspan (January 2003).

43. George Orwell: Some Personal Connections. An address broadcast on the BBC Radio 3 on 13 June 2003. Reprinted as "Orwell and Me," *The Guardian,* 16 June 2003.

44. "Arguing Against Ice Cream." Review of *Enough: Staying Human in an Engineered Age* by Bill McKibben. *New York Review of Books,* 12 June 2003.

45. Victory Gardens. Foreword to *A Breath of Fresh Air: Celebrating Nature and School Gardens* by Elise Houghton (Toronto: Sumach Press, 2003).

46. Carol Shields, Who Died Last Week, Wrote Books That Were Full of Delights. From "Lives & Letters: Carol Shields." *The Guardian,* 26 July 2003.

47. "The Book Lover's Tale." Review of *Reading Lolita in Tehran: A Memoir in Books* by Azar Nafisi. *Literary Review of Canada* (September 2003).

48. Introduction to *The Complete Stories, Volume 4* by Morley Callaghan (Toronto: Exile Editions, 2003).

49. "He Springs Eternal." Review of *Hope Dies Last: Keeping the Faith in Difficult Times* by Studs Terkel. *New York Review of Books,* 6 November 2003.

50. "Mortification." From *Mortifications: Writers' Stories of Their Public Shame,* ed. Robin Robertson (London: Fourth Estate, 2003).

51. "Uncovered: An American Iliad." Review of *A Story as Sharp as a Knife: The Classical Haida Mythtellers and Their World* by Robert Bringhurst. *The Times Weekend Review,* 28 February 2004.

52. Review of *The Mays of Ventadorn* by W. S. Merwin. *American Poetry Review,* Vol. 33, No. 3 (May/June 2004).

53. "Headscarves to Die For." Review of *Snow* by Orhan Pamuk, trans. Maureen Freely. *New York Times Book Review,* 15 August 2004.

54. "Handmaids' Tales." Review of *From Eve to Dawn: Vol 1 Origins; Vol 2 The Masculine Mystique; Vol 3 Infernos and Paradises* by Marilyn French. *The Times,* 21 August 2004.

55. To Beechy Island. From *Solo: Writers on Pilgrimage,* ed. Katherine Govier (Toronto: M&S, 2004).

56. Introduction to *Frozen in Time: The Fate of the Franklin Expedition* (rev. ed.) by Owen Beattie and John Geiger (Vancouver: Greystone, 2004).

57. Review of *Acquainted with the Night: Excursions through the World After Dark* by Christopher Dewdney (New York: Bloomsbury, 2004).

58. Ten Ways of Looking at *The Island of Doctor Moreau*. Introduction to *The Island of Doctor Moreau* (London: Penguin, 2005).

INDEX

A

According to Queeney (Bainbridge), 194–197

Achebe, Chinua, *Anthills of the Savannah*, 70

Acid Rain Dinner, 36–37

Acquainted with the Night: Excursions Through the World After Dark (Dewdney), 382–385

activism, social, 337–339, 340–342. see also environmentalism; women's movement

addiction, to pornography, 17–18

advocacy writing, xv

Afghanistan, 3, 205–207, xiv

African American authors, 46–51

African Americans, 26–27

African Queen (film), 122

Agee, James
   The African Queen, 122
   A Death in the Family, 122
   Let Us Now Praise Famous Men, 122

Alcott, Louisa May, *Little Women*, 280

Alias Grace (Atwood), 104
   writing of, 170–176

All Souls (Marias), 162–163

Allan Quartermain (Haggard), 198

Allen, Woody, 255

Alone of All Her Sex (Warner), 147

American culture, 228–229, 331–342
   corporate, 339–340
   early twentieth century, 331–332
   political, 187–188, 280–283, 333–336

American Spelling Book (Webster), 214

Ana Historic (Marlatt), 167

Anderson-Dargatz, Gail, *The Cure for Death by Lightning*, 167

Anderson, Sherwood, 214

Angel Walk (Govier), 167

Angelou, Maya, 86–87

Animal Farm (Orwell), 289–290

"Annabel Lee" (Poe), 275

Anne of Green Gables (Montgomery), 115–120
   character development in, 118–120

anorexia, 156–157

Anthills of the Savannah (Achebe), 70

Anthology (radio show), 257

anthropology, 248, 350

Apprenticeship of Duddy Kravitz (Richler), 193

Arabian Nights, 147

archaeology, 248

"Ashputtle or The Mother's Ghost. A

Victorian Fable (with Glossary)"
    (Carter), 152
At Weddings and Wakes (McDermott),
    268
Atanarjuat: The Fast Runner (Kunuk),
    220–223
Atlantic magazine, 294
Atwood, Margaret
    Alias Grace, 104, 170–176
    awards won, 52–53, 186
    The Blind Assassin, 185–186
    Bodily Harm, 12
    Cat's Eye, 3, 4–5
    childhood and family, 56–67,
        159–160
    The Circle Game, 52
    early career, 57–58, xiv
    education, 200–201
    embarassing moments of,
        343–345
    first job, 189–191
    Good Bones, 104
    The Handmaid's Tale, 3, 4, 5,
        96–100, 207, 284, xvi
    "In Search of Alias Grace", 104,
        158–176
    The Journals of Susanna Moodie,
        166, 170
    meets Margaret Laurence, 53
    Morning in the Burned House, 104
    Murder in the Dark, 104
    Negotiating with the Dead, 186
    Oryx and Crake, 186, 284–286
    recreational reading material, 285
    The Robber Bride, 103, 104
    Second Words: Selected Critical Prose,
        xvi
    "Spotty-Handed Villainesses", 103,
        125–138
    Strange Things, 104
    "The Age of Lead", 375

tours Europe, 140–145
    Wilderness Tips, 103, 375
"Aunt Moon's Young Man" (Hogan), 78
Austen, Jane, 24
    Pride and Prejudice, 128
Away (Urquhart), 167

B
bad women, in literature, 125–126,
    134, 135–138, 149–150, 154–157
Bainbridge, Beryl
    According to Queeney, 194–197
    works of, 194
Bantam Books, 27
Barney's Version (Richler), 193
Beaches (Dart), 27–28
Bear (Engel), 32, 167
Beattie, Owen, and John Geiger,
    Frozen in Time, 373, 375–381,
    379–380
Beckett, Thomas
    Knapp's Last Tape, 162
    The Unnameable, 336
Beechy Island, 372–373
Bellamy, Edward, Looking Backward,
    94, 244–245
Beloved (Morrison), 46–51, 136
Berlin Wall, fall of, 5, 292
Bettelheim, Bruno, The Uses of
    Enchantment, 148
Bible, The, 50, 291, 337
    Book of Genesis, 54
    Book of Jeremiah, 54
    Book of Revelations, 93–94
    Book of Ruth, 22
    Old Testament, 99, 393–395
    as oral tradition, 349
    women in, 22, 136, 137
Birthday Boys (Bainbridge), 194
Birthday of the World and Other Stories
    (Le Guin), 243–253

Birthday of the World (Le Guin), 249, 250

Bishop, Elizabeth, 81

"Black Hand Girl" (Boyd), 77

Black Mask (magazine), 211, 213

Blackboard Jungle (film), 121–122

Blackrobe (Moore), 167

Blade Runner (film), 298

BlewOintment Press, 257

Blind Assassin (Atwood), 185–186

Bluest Eye, The (Morrison), 70

Bly, Robert, 177

Blyton, Enid, 23

Boadicea, 89–90, 91

Bodily Harm (Atwood), 12

Bolivar, Simon, 111–114

Book of Laughter and Forgetting (Kundera), 162

Booker Prize, 4, 186, 315

Bottle Factory Outing, Sweet William (Bainbridge), 194

Bowen, Elizabeth, 86

Bowering, George, 257
  Burning Waters, 167

"Boy on the Train" (Robinson), 76–77

Boyd, Blanche McCrary, "The Black Hand Girl", 77

Bradbury, Ray, novels of, 245

Brave New World (Huxley), 94, 95, 288–289, 291, 292, 298

Bringhurst, Robert, *A Story as Sharp as a Knife*, 346–351

Bronte, Charlotte
  Jane Eyre, 23, 116, 137–138
  Shirley, 23

Bronte, Emily, 69
  Wuthering Heights, 24, 47

Brown, Larry, "Kubuku Rides (This Is It)", 77

Brown, Mary, 17

Brown, Rita Mae, *Rubyfruit Jungle*, 23

Browning, Robert, *Childe Roland*, 353

Buckler, Ernest, *The Mountain and the Valley*, 63, 64–64

Burnett, Frances Hodgson, 116

Burning Waters (Bowering), 167

Burning Your Boats (Carter), 151–153

Butler, Samuel, *Erewhon*, 94, 245

Byron, *Childe Harold's Pilgrimage*, 367–368

C

Cagney and Lacey (TV show), 27

Calasso, Roberto, 103

Callaghan, Morley, 256
  The Complete Stories, Volume 4, 322–330
  "Man With the Coat", 327–329
  That Summer in Paris, 327

Calvino, Italo
  Difficult Loves, 19–21
  Invisible Cities, 19

Camus, Albert, 240, 336

Canada, 31–45
  1837 Rebellion, 172–173
  Canadian Shield, 38–39
  environmentalism, 36–37, 42–43, 265–267
  hazards of, 39–40
  landscape, 37, 38–40, 43
  logging industry, 35–36
  native peoples, 265–267, 346–351
  Nova Scotia, 59
  relationship with United States, 280–282
  tourist areas, 44
  U. S. border, 34–35

Canada House, London, 140, 141

Canadian Authors' Association, 57–58

Canadian Governor General's Award, 315

Canadian historical fiction, 158–175

Canadian publishers, 257–258

Canadian writers, 255–259, 265–267, 324–325, 350–351

Cannes Film Festival, 220

Capp, Al, *L'il Abner*, 271

Carmilla (Le Fanu), 24–25, 29, 202

Carpenter, Edmund, 350

Carroll, Lewis, 395

Carson, Rachel, *Silent Spring*, 265

Carter, Angela
  "A Very, Very Great Lady and Her Son at Home", 152
  "Ashputtle or The Mother's Ghost. A Victorian Fable (with Glossary)", 152
  Burning Your Boats, 151–153
  "The Company of Wolves", 151

Castle of Imagination (Saint Teresa of Avila), 271, 274

Catherine the Great, 90, 91

Cat's Eye (Atwood), 3, 4–5

censorship, 13–14

Centaur, The (Updike), 6

chador, 206–207

Chandler, Raymond, 214
  The Simple Art of Murder, 73, 209

Charlie's Angels (TV show), 216

Charming Billy (McDermott), 268

Chase, Joan, *During the Reign of the Queen of Persia*, 23

Chaucer, Geoffrey, 367–368, 369

Chicago, Judy, "Dinner Party", 91

Child of My Heart (McDermott), 268–276

Childe Harold's Pilgrimage (Byron), 367–368

Childe Roland (Browning), 353

children, portrayal of, 76–77

Christianity. *see also* Bible, The
  and social activism, 337–338
  and utopianism, 93–94

Christmas Carol (Dickens), 163, 295, 309

Churchill, Winston, 96

Circle Game, The (Atwood), 52

Civil Rights Congress Bail Fund, 209

Civil Rights movement, 340

Civil War reenactments, 234–235

cloning, 297–298

Coach House Press, 257, 258

Cohen, Leonard, *Let Us Compare Mythologies*, 350

Cold War, 44, 103

Coleridge, Samuel Taylor, *Rime of the Ancient Mariner*, 396–397

Color Purple, The (Walker), 26, 27, 49

"Coming of Age in Karhide" (Le Guin), 250–251

communism, failure of, 103, 292

Complete Stories, Volume 4 (Callaghan), 322–330

"Concert Party" (Gallant), 78

Conrad, Joseph, *Heart of Darkness*, 203

"Consider Her Ways" (Wyndham), 250

consumerism, post WWII, 308–309

Contact Press, 257

Cooper, Fenimore, *Leatherstocking Tales*, 214

Corey, Giles, 218

crime, and American culture, 227–230, 233–234

crime novels, 228–229. *see* Hammett, Daschiell; Leonard, Elmore

criminals, as heroes, 229

Crucible, The (Miller), 218

cryogenics, 296–297

Crystal Age (Hudson), 94, 95, 250

Cunningham, Michael, "White Angel", 75

Cure for Death by Lightning (Anderson-Dargatz), 167

Custom of the Country, The (Wharton), 137
cybernetics, 296, 300
Cymbeline (Shakespeare), 203

D
Dain Curse, The (Hammett), 211
Daisy Miller (James), 271, 320
Dali, Salvador, *The Persistence of Memory*, 162
Dante Allegieri, 94
  Inferno, 353, 355
Daoud, Muhammad, xiv
Darkness at Noon (Koestler), 96, 288–289
Dart, Iris Rainer, *Beaches*, 27–28
Darwin, Charles
  Descent of Man, 390–391
  Origin of the Species, 390–391
Dashiell Hammett: A Daughter Remembers (Hammett), 210
Dashiell Hammett: Crime Stories & Other Writings (Marcus), 210, 215
Davies, Robertson, 159
  Murther and Walking Spirits, 167
de Beauvoir, Simone, 53
  The Second Sex, 357
De La Roche, Mazo, 256
death and loss, 241, 271–275
Death in the Family (Agee), 122
Death of a Salesman (Miller), 328
Death: Will the Circle be Unbroken (Terkel), 331
DeMarinis, Rick, "The Flowers of Boredom", 76
democracy, 334–336
Descent of Man (Darwin), 390–391
Devil, The, 232–233, 393–394, 394
Dewdney, Christopher, *Acquainted with the Night*, 382–385
dialects, 214

Diamond, Jared, *Guns, Germs, and Steel*, 361–362
Dickens, Charles, 240
  A Christmas Carol, 163, 295, 309
  Great Expectations, 116
  Oliver Twist, 116, 295–296
  A Tale of Two Cities, 164
Dickinson, Emily, 128
  "Hope is the thing with feathers", 336–337
dictatorship, genesis of, 98
Dictionary (Johnson), 195
Dictionary of Imaginary Places (Manguel), 244
Didion, Joan, 84
Diet for a Small Planet (Lappe), 341
Difficult Loves (Calvino), 19–21
"Dinner Party" (Chicago), 91
Dionne Quints Museum, 34
Discovery of Slowness (Nadolny, Sten), 379
"Disneyland" (Gowdy), 76
Disorderly Conduct: Visions of Gender in Victorian America (Smith-Rosenberg), 24
"Displacement" (Louie), 77–78
Diviners, The (Laurence), 13, 54, 167
Division Street, America (Terkel), 331
Doctor Glas (Soderberg), 260–264
Doerr, Harriet, "Edie: A Life", 77
Donne, John, 291–292
Donovan's Brain (Siodmak), 301–302
Double Hook (Watson), 258
Down among the Women (Weldon), 22, 26
Dr. Faustus (Marlowe), 394
Dracula (Stoker), 131, 202
Dreyer, Benjamin, 186
Dropped Threads 2 (Shields), 315
Dulac, Edmund, 147
During the Reign of the Queen of Persia (Chase), 23

dystopias, 93–95, 291–292. *see also*
The Handmaid's Tale (Atwood)
sexuality in, 95
social purposes of, 94–95, 95
women in, 291

E
Edel, Leon, 161
"Edie: A Life" (Doerr), 77
editors, 187–188
1812 Overture (Tchaikovsky),
277–279
Eliot, George, 69
Middlemarch, 24, 164
The Mill on the Floss, 24
Eliot, T. S., 56
Elizabeth I, Queen of England, 90, 91
enchanted island, as literary device,
392–393
End of Nature, The (McKibben), 294
Engel, Marian, 259
Bear, 32, 167
English Patient, The (Ondaatje), 167
Englishman's Boy (Vanderhaeghe),
167–168
Enola Gay, 338
Enough (McKibben), 294–304
Enron, 339, 340
environmentalism, 282, 284–286, 341
Canadian, 36–37, 42–43, 265–267
and food production, 309–310,
310–311
and overpopulation, 311
Erewhon (Butler), 94, 245
eulogies
Carol Shields, 313–316
Mordecai Richler, 192–193
Timothy Findley, 237–239
Euripides, Medea, 136
Every Man For Himself (Bainbridge),
194

evolution, Darwinian, 390–391
evolution, of societies, 305–308,
362–364
Experiment in Love (Mantel), 154–157
experimental fiction, 254–259
Explorations (magazine), 350
Extropian Convention, 300

F
Fahrenheit 451 (Bradbury), 245
fairy tales, 134–135, 147–150
Fall on Your Knees (MacDonald), 167
Farmer's Rebellion (Salutin), 166
Fatal Passage (McGoogan), 371, 379
Faulkner, William, 69, 240
Felix Krull, Confidence Man (Mann),
137
feminism, 201–202, 356–359. *see also*
Women's Movement
influence on literature, 131–134,
148, 249, 395
Findley, Timothy
eulogy, 237–239
works of, 167, 238
Finishing School, The (Godwin), 28–29
Fire-Dwellers, The (Laurence), 54
Fisherman of the Inland Sea (Le Guin),
251
Fitzgerald, F. Scott, 325–326
The Great Gatsby, 319–320
Flaubert, Gustave, *Madame Bovary,*
137
"Flowers of Boredom" (DeMarinis), 76
food production, history of, 305–308
Fowles, John, *A Maggot,* 112
Frankenstein (Shelley), 244, 297, 386
Franklin expedition, 366–381
Franklin, John, 378–381
Fraser, Antonia, *The Warrior Queens,*
89–91
French, Marilyn

From Eve To Dawn, 360–364
The Women's Room, 26, 356–357
Freudian psychiatry, 25, 162, 202–203
friendships, women's, 22–30
  African American, 26–27
  lesbian, 28
  Victorian era, 23–25
From Eve to Dawn (French), 360–364
From the Beast to the Blonde: On Fairy tales and Their Tellers (Warner, 147–150
"From the Menoirs of a Private Detective" (Hammett), 213
Frost in May (White), 23
Frozen in Time (Geiger and Beattie), 373, 375–381, 379–380
Frye, Northrop, 324–325, 350
  The Secular Scripture, 202, 391
Fugitive Pieces (Michaels), 167

G
Galbraith, John Kenneth, 331, 339–340
Gallant, Mavis, "Concert Party", 78
Gandhi, Indira, 90
Garcia Marquez, Gabriel, *The General and His Labyrinth*, 111–114
gardening and food production, 305–312
Gardner, Erie Stanley, 208
Geiger, John, and Owen Beattie, *Frozen in Time*, 373, 375–381, 379–380
gender, reader's
  boys' vs. girls' books, 269
  and perspective, 82
gender, writer's, 358–359
  and perspective, 72, 82
  and social role, 82–88, 106
  and style, 82
General and His Labyrinth, The (Garcia Marquez), 111–114
Genesis, Book of, 54

genetic engineering, 294–304
  cryogenics, 296–297
  gene splicing, human, 296, 297–299
  nanotechnology, 299
  and religion, 300
Genie Awards, 220
Germany, reunification of, 5, 103
ghosts, 46–47, 49
Gibson, Graeme, Perpetual Motion, 167, 168
Gibson, William, 300
Gide, Andre, 127–129
Gilbert, Sandra and Susan Gubar, *No Man's Land*, 201–202
Giles Corey of the Salem Farms (Longfellow), 218
Gilman, Charlotte Perkins, *Herland*, 94, 250
Gish, Lillian, 121
Glass Key (Hammett), 211
Glover, Douglas, "Why I Decide to Kill Myself and Other Jokes", 77
Go-Between, The (Hartley), 168
Goblin Market (Rosetti), 393
Godwin, Gail, 23
  The Finishing School, 28–29
Golding, William, *Lord of the Flies*, 392
Gone With the Wind (Mitchell), 28
Good Bones (Atwood), 104
Gordimer, Nadine, 84
Governor General's Award for Poetry, Atwood wins, 52–53
Govier, Katherine, *Angel Walk*, 167
Gowdy, Barbara, "Disneyland", 76
Great Expectations (Dickens), 116
Great Gatsby (Fitzgerald), 319–320
greed, 295–296
Greene, Graham, *The Lawless Roads*, 76
Greene, Graham, *The Ministry of Fear*, 161
Grimms' Fairy Tales, 134, 147

Grosev, Kouncho, 336
Ground Works, 254–259
Group, The (McCarthy), 25–26, 157
Grubb, Davis, 122
  Night of the Hunter, 229
Grumback, Doris, *The Ladies*, 23
Guardian, xiv
Gubar, Susan and Sandra Gilbert, *No Man's Land*, 201–202
Gulliver's Travels (Swift), 94, 244
Guns, Germs, and Steel (Diamond), 361–362
Gutenberg Galaxy (McLuhan), 350

H
Haggard, H. Rider, *She*, 186, 198–204, 244, 388
Haggard, Rider, novels of, 198
Haida people, 346–351
Hall, Radclyffe, *Well of Loneliness*, 23
Hammett, Dashiell, 208–219
  early life, 211
  ill health, 217
  literary silence, 217–218
  novels of, 211, 213
  and red scare, 209, 211–212, 218
  Selected Letters of Dashiell Hammett (Rivett and Layman), 212–213
  The Thin Man, 215, 217
  "ZigZags of Treachery", 218
Hammett, Josephine, *A Daughter Remembers*, 210
Handmaid's Tale, The (Atwood), 3, 4, 284, xvi
  and *1984*, 291–292
  film, 5
  genesis of dictatorship in, 97–98
  polygamy in, 98–99
  as science fiction, 92–93
  surrogate motherhood in, 99, 99–100
  writing of, 92–100, 207

hard-boiled crime fiction, 215
Hardy, Thomas, *Tess of the D'Urbervilles*, 136
Hartley, L. P., *The Go-Between*, 168
Harvard Graduate School, 200–201
Harvard University, 52, xiv
Harvard University Graduate School, 96
hate literature, pornography as, 15–16
Hawthorne, Nathaniel, *The Scarlet Letter*, 137, 170
Heart of Darkness (Conrad), 203
Hebert, Anne, *Kamouraska*, 167
Hellman, Lillian, 210–211
  Little Foxes, 25
  Pentimento, 209
Hemingway, Ernest, 214, 240, 325–326
Herland (Gilman), 94, 250
Hiassen, Carl, 214
High Latitudes (Mowat), 265–267
Hilton, James, 203
historical novels, 158–175, 163–164
  and the past, as safe, 168–169
history, recording of, 171–172
Hoban, Russell, *Riddley Walker*, 245
Hogan, Linda, "Aunt Moon's Young Man", 78
Homer, 220
  The Iliad, 349
  The Odyssey, 349
hope, 335–336
Hope Dies Last: Keeping the Faith in Difficult Times (Terkel), 331–342
"Hope is the thing with feathers" (Dickinson), 336–337
Houghton, Elise, *Victory Gardens: A Breath of Fresh Air*, 305–312
House of Anansi Press, 257, 258
Housekeeping (Robinson), 23
Huckleberry Finn (Twain), 214, 233, 280

Hudson, W. H., *A Crystal Cage*, 94, 250
hunting, irresponsible, 42–43
Hutchinson, Anne, 6
Huxley, Aldous
    Brave New World, 94, 95, 288–289,
        292, 298
    Point Counter Point, 138
Hyde, Lewis
    *The Gift: Imagination and the Erotic
        Life of Property*, 177–179
    *Trickster Makes This World: Mischief,
        Myth, and Art*, 179–181

I
Idylls of the King (Tennyson), 201
If on a Winter's Night a Traveler
    (Calvino), 19
Il Postino (film), 176
Iliad (Homer), 349
immortality, 300–302
In Memoriam (Tennyson), 377
"In Search of Alias Grace" (Atwood),
    104, 158–176
In the Skin of a Lion (Ondaatje), 167, 168
Inferno (Dante), 353, 355
intent, meanings of, 75, xvii
Inuit culture, 221–222
Invisible Cities (Calvino), 19
Iran, political upheaval, 317–321
Iraq, invasion of, 187–188, 282–283
Isabella, Queen of Spain, 90
Islamic fundamentalism, 318–321,
    356–359
Island of Dr. Moreau (Wells), 245,
    386–398
Ivanhoe (Scott), 164

J
Jackson, Mahalia, 333
James, Henry
    Daisy Miller, 271, 320

    Portrait of a Lady, 24
    The Turn of the Screw, 130–131
    Wings of the Dove, 24
Jane Eyre (Bronte), 23, 116, 137–138
Jeremiah, Book of, 54
Jest of God, A (Laurence), 52–55
Jinga, Queen of Angola, 90
Johnson, Samuel
    Dictionary, 195
    Lives of The English Poets, 195
joke, qualities of, 74
Jonas, George, 171
Jones, Doug, 166
Journals of Susanna Moodie (Atwood),
    166, 170
Joyce, James, 69
    Portrait of the Artist as a Young Man,
        181
Jungle Book, The (Kipling), 395–396

K
Kafka, Franz, 336
Kamouraska (Hebert), 167
Kane, Sean, *The Wisdom of the
    Mythtellers*, 350
Kate and Allie (TV show), 27
Keats, John, 316
Kelly, Kathy, *Voices of the Wilderness
    Project*, 337, 340
Kennedy, Ted, 37
Key Largo (film), 296
King Lear (Shakespeare), 136
King, Makenzie, 165–166
King Solomon's Mines (Haggard), 198
Kipling, Rudyard, 202
    The Jungle Book, 395–396
Knapp's Last Tape (Beckett), 162
Koestler, Arthur, *Darkness at Noon*, 96,
    288–289
"Kubuku Rides (This Is It)" (Brown),
    77

Kucinich, Dennis, 342
Kundera, Milan, *The Book of Laughter and Forgetting*, 162

L
Ladies, The (Grumback), 23
Lady Chatterley's Lover (Lawrence), 13
Lang, Andrew, 147
language, American, 214, 216
language, foul, 227–228
language, spoken, 71–72, 73
and oral traditions, 346–351
Lappe, Frances Moore, *Diet for a Small Planet*, 341
Larry's Party (Shields), 315
Last of the Crazy People (Findley), 238
Laughton, Charles, 121
Laurence, Margaret, 259
  The Diviners, 13, 54, 167
  The Fire-Dwellers, 54
  A Jest of God, 52–55
  meets Margaret Atwood, 53
  The Stone Angel, 52, 158
Lawless Roads, The (Greene), 76
Lawrence, D. H., 203
  Lady Chatterley's Lover, 13
Le Carre, John, 227–228
Le Fanu, Sheridan, 152
  Carmilla, 24–25, 29, 202
Le Guin, Ursula
  awards, literary, 246
  Birthday of the World, 249, 250
  The Birthday of the World and Other Stories, 243–253
  A Fisherman of the Inland Sea, 251
  The Left Hand of Darkness, 246, 249
  Planet of Exile, 246
  Rocannon's World, 246
  short stories, 250–251, 251, 252
  "Solitude", 251
  A Wizard of Earthsea, 246

lead poisoning, 379–380
Leatherstocking Tales (Cooper), 214
Left Hand of Darkness (Le Guin), 246, 249
Leonard, Elmore, 214
  Tishomingo Blues 227–236
lesbians, 23–24, 26, 28
Let Us Compare Mythologies (Cohen), 350
Let Us Now Praise Famous Men (Agee), 122
Lethem, Jonathan, *Motherless Brooklyn*, 215
"Letter Writer, The" (Sharif), 77
Lewis, C. S., 203, 244
Life in the Clearings (Moodie), 171
Life of Pi (Martel), 224–226
L'il Abner (Capp), 271
Little Foxes (Hellman), 25
Little Women (Alcott), 280
Lives of The English Poets (Johnson), 195
logging industry, Canadian, 35–36
Lolita (Nabokov), 321
Long Distance (McKibben), 294
Longfellow, Henry Wadsworth
  Giles Corey of the Salem Farms, 218
  "The Children's Hour", 218
Looking Backward (Bellamy), 94
Lord of the Flies (Golding), 392
Lord of the Rings (Tolkien), 203, 384
Los Angeles Times, 4
loss and death, 241, 271–275
Louie, David Wong, "Displacement", 77–78
Luce, Clare Booth, *The Women*, 25

M
Macbeth (Shakespeare), 126, 136, 273
MacDonald, Anne Marie, *Fall on Your Knees*, 167
MacDonald, George, 152

MacEwen, Gwendolyn, 373
  Terror and Erebus, 166, 369, 371, 374, 380
Mackenzie, William Lyon, 172–173
Maclean's magazine, 327
MacLeod, Allistair, 286
Mad Trapper of Rat River, 40
Madame Bovary (Flaubert), 137
Maggot, A (Fowles), 112
Magnificent Spinster, The (Sarton), 28
Maltese Falcon (Hammett), 211
"Man With the Coat" (Callaghan), 327–329
"Management of Grief" (Mukherjee), 78
Manguel, Alberto, Dictionary of Imaginary Places, 244
Mann, Thomas, Felix Krull, Confidence Man, 137
Mansfield, Katherine, 86
Mantel, Hilary, An Experiment in Love, 154–157
Marias, Javier, All Souls, 162–163
Marks, Grace, 171–175
Marlatt, Daphne, Ana Historic, 167
Marlowe, Christopher, Dr. Faustus, 394
Martel, Yann, Life of Pi, 224–226
Martian Chronicles (Bradbury), 245
Martin, Valerie, Property, 315
Marxism, as utopian, 93
Master Georgie (Bainbridge), 194
Maud (Empress), 90
Mays of Ventadorn (Merwin), 352–355
McCarthy, Mary
  The Group, 25–26, 157
  interview, 85–86
McCarthyism, 209, 211–212, 333
McCullers, Carson, 152
McDermott, Alice
  Charming Billy, 268
  Child of My Heart, 268–276
  At Weddings and Wakes, 268

McGoogan, Ken, Fatal Passage, 371, 379
McGrath, Mollie, 341
McKibben, Bill
  The End of Nature, 294
  Enough, 294–304
  Long Distance, 294
McLuhan, Marshall, 129–130
  The Gutenberg Galaxy, 350
Medea (Euripides), 136
Meir, Golda, 90
Melville, Herman, Moby-Dick, 269
memory, 161–163
"Meneseteung" (Munro), 78–79
Meredith, George, 286
Merwin, W. S., The Mays of Ventadorn, 352–355
Michaels, Anne, Fugitive Pieces, 167
Middlemarch (Eliot), 24, 164
Midsummer Night's Dream (Shakespeare), 272–273
Mill on the Floss, The (Eliot), 24
millenium, new, 185
Miller, Arthur, 280
  The Crucible, 218
  Death of a Salesman, 328
Miller, Perry, 96
Milton, John, 94
Ministry of Fear (Greene), 161
Mitchell, Margaret, Gone With the Wind, 28
Mitchum, Robert, 121
Moby-Dick (Melville), 269
Modest Proposal, A (Swift), 10
Montgomery, Lucy Maud, 118
  Anne of Grees Gables, 115–120
Monuments and Maidens (Warner), 147
Moodie, Susannah
  Life in the Clearings, 171
  Roughing it in the Bush, 170–171
Moore, Brian, Blackrobe, 167

Moore, Marianne, 84–85
More, Max, 300
More, Thomas, 93
   Utopia, 93, 94, 244
Morning in the Burned House
   (Atwood), 104
Morris, James, 83
Morris, Jan, 83
Morris, William, *News From Nowhere*,
   94, 244–245
Morrison, Toni, 23
   Beloved, 46–51, 136
   The Bluest Eye, 70
   interview, 87
   Sula, 26–27
mortality, 270–274, 300–302
Mother Goose, 148, 149
Mother Teresa, 271
Motherless Brooklyn (Lethem), 215
Mountain and the Valley, The (Buckler),
   63, 64–65
"Mountain Ways" (Le Guin), 251
Mowat, Farley
   High Latitudes, 265–267
   People of the Deer, 265, 266
Mukherjee, Bharati, "The Manage-
   ment of Grief", 78
Munro, Alice, 259
   "A Wilderness Station", 167
   "Meneseteung", 78–79, 167
Munro Doctrine, 315
Murder in the Dark (Atwood), 104
Murther and Walking Spirits (Davies),
   167
Muslim fundamentalism, 318–321
My Name is Red (Orhan), 356

N
Nabokov, Victor, *Lolita*, 321
Nadolny, Sten, *The Discovery of Slow-*
   ness, 379

Nafisi, Azar, *Reading Lolita in Tehran*,
   317–321
nanotechnology, 296, 299
Napoleon Bonaparte, 277–279
Nation, The, 187
National Book Award, 268
National Geographic's Directions
   Series, 352
native peoples, of North America,
   265–267, 346–351, 372
Nature, concepts of, 7, 40, 43, 202,
   300, 390–391
Navasky, Victor, 187
Nazi Germany, 245
Negotiating with the Dead (Atwood),
   186
New York Review of Books, 187, 294, xiv
New York Times, 294
New Yorker magazine, 294
News From Nowhere (Morris), 94
Night and Fog (film), 162
Night of the Hunter (film), 121-124, 280
Night of the Hunter (novel, Davis), 229
1984 (Orwell), 4, 18, 94, 95, 162,
   288–289, 289–291
No Man's Land (Gilbert and Gubar),
   201–202
North Bay, 34
nostalgia, 41–42, 169
Nova Scotia, 59
   Atwood visits, 62–63
novel, the, 125-138
   Canadian historical fiction,
      158–175
   character development, 132–134
   characteristics of, 127–129,
      161–162
   plot development, 130–131

O
O Canada (Wilson), 322

Oates, Joyce Carol, 23, 84
  interview, 88
  Solstice, 29
Odyssey (Homer), 349
"Old Music and the Slave Women" (Le Guin), 252
Old Testament, 99, 393–395
Oliver Twist (Dickens), 116, 295–296
Ondaatje, Michael, 255, 257
  The English Patient, 167
  In the Skin of a Lion, 167, 168
Ontario Board of Film Censors, 12, 17
oral traditions, 346–351
Orange Prize, 315
Origin of the Species (Darwin), 390–391
orphans, 116–117
Orwell, George, 287–293
  1984, 4, 18, 94, 289–291
  Animal Farm, 287–288, 289–290
Orwell, George, *1984*, 95, 162
Oryx and Crake (Atwood), 186
  writing of, 284–286
Ottawa River, 34
Oxford University, 104

P
Pahlevi, Reza, 317, 318
Paine, Thomas, 335
Pamuk, Orhan, *Snow*, 356–359
"Paradises Lost" (Le Guin), 252
Paris Review, 82
Parker, Dorothy, interview, 83, 88
Parsifal (Wagner), 201
Pater, Walter, *Mona Lisa*, 201
"Pelican, The" (Wharton), xv
Penthouse magazine, 13
Pentimento (Hellman), 209
People of the Deer (Mowat), 265, 266
Perez-Reverte, Arturo, 215
Perpetual Motion (Gibson), 167, 168
Perrault, Charles, 152

Persistence of Memory (Dali), 162
Phillips, Dale Ray, "What Men Love For", 76
Piano Man's Daughter (Findley), 167
Picture of Dorian Gray (Wilde), 394
Piercy, Marge, *Women on the Edge of Time*, 94, 95, 250
pilgrimages, 366–374
Pinter, Harold, 5
Planet of Exile (Le Guin), 246
Plath, Sylvia, 259
Plato, 244
Plato's *Republic*, 93–94
plot development, of the novel, 130–131
Poe, Edgar Allan, 152
  "Annabel Lee", 275
poetry, 352–353
Point Counter Point (Huxley), 138
Polar Sea (icebreaking ship), 37
political issues, 187–188, 280–283, 333–336
political topics, writing on, xv
politics, women in, 91
polygamy, in *The Handmaid's Tale*, 98–99
pornography, 12–18
  as addiction, 17–18
  as hate literature, 15–16
  as sex education, 16–17
  and the women's movement, 13, 14–15
Porter, Katherine Anne, 85
Portrait of a Lady (James), 24
Portrait of the Artist as a Young Man (Joyce), 181
Pound, Ezra, 85, 354–355
power
  absolute, 48
  male, 357
Pratt, E. J., 166

Pride and Prejudice (Austen), 128
profanity, 227–228
Property (Martin), 315
Proust, Marcel, 162
publishers, Canadian, 257–258
Pulitzer Prize, 315
Purdy, Al, 166
Puritans, 96–97, 218
Pynchon Thomas, *V,* 215

Q
Quarry Press, 257
Queen, Ellery, 208

R
race relations, and slavery, 48–49
race, writers', 86–87
Rackham, Arthur, 147
Rae, John, 379, 380
Rani of Jhansi, 90
Rasmusson, Wallace, 340
Ravenel, Shannon, 68–69
reader, perspective of, 241–242
    and gender, 82
reading aloud, 71
reading blind, 69, 70
Reading Lolita in Tehran (Nafisi),
    317–321
Reaney, James, 166
    A Suit of Nettles, 256
Rebel Without a Cause (film), 121–122
Red Harvest (Hammett), 211
red scare, 209, 211–212, 218, 333
religion
    and genetic engineering, 300
    and philosophy, 349–350
    and social activism, 337–338
    social force of, 97
    and utopianism, 93–94
religious fundamentalism, 318–321,
    356–359

Republic of Love (Shields), 314
Revelations, Book of, 93–94
reviewing, of books, 129–130, xv
    short stories, 68–69
reviews
    According to Queeney (Bainbridge),
        194–197
    Acquainted with the Night
        (Dewdney), 382–385
    Anne of Green Gables (Mont-
        gomery), 115–120
    Atanarjuat: The Fast Runner
        (Kunuk), 220–223
    *From the Beast to the Blonde: On
        Fairy Tales and Their Tellers*
        (Warner, 147–150
    *The Birthday of the World and Other
        Stories* (Le Guin), 243–253
    Burning Your Boats (Carter),
        151–153
    Child of My Heart (McDermott),
        268–276
    Dashiell Hammett, 207
    Enough (McKibben), 294–304
    From Eve to Dawn (French),
        360–364
    An Experiment in Love (Mantel),
        154–157
    The General and His Labyrinth
        (Garcia Marquez), 115–120
    *The Gift: Imagination and the Erotic
        Life of Property* (Hyde), 177–179
    *Hope Dies Last: Keeping the Faith in
        Difficult Times* (Terkel),
        331–342
    Life of Pi (Martel), 224–226
    The Mays of Ventadorn (Merwin),
        352–355
    Night of the Hunter (film), 121–124
    Reading Lolita in Tehran (Nafisi),
        317–321

Snow (Orhan), 356–359

A Story as Sharp as a Knife (Bringhurst), 346–351

Tishomingo Blues (Leonard), 227–
236

*Trickster Makes This World: Mis-
chief, Myth, and Art* (Hyde),
179–181

Richard, Mark, "Strays", 76

Richardson, John, *Wacousta,* 163–164

Richler, Mordecai, 186, xvi

eulogy, 192–193

novels of, 193, 380

riddle, qualities of, 74

Riddley Walker (Hoban), 245

Riel, Louis, 166

Rime of the Ancient Mariner
(Coleridge), 396–397

Robber Bride, The (Atwood), 103, 104

Robinson, Arthur, "The Boy on the
Train", 76–77

Robinson, Marilynne, *Housekeeping,*
23

Rocannon's World (Le Guin), 246

romance, 391–392

Romans, Book of, 50

Romeo and Juliet (Shakespeare), 23

Rosetti, Christina, *Goblin Market,*
393

Roughing it in the Bush (Moodie),
170–171

Rubyfruit Jungle (Brown), 23

Rule, Jane, 52

This is Not For You, 28

Russia, 3

Ruth, book of, 22, 23, 25

S

Sahgal, Nayantara, 83

Salutin, Rick, *The Farmer's Rebellion,*
166

Sarton, May, *The Magnificent Spinster,*
28

Satan, 232–233, 393–394, 394

Scarlet Letter (Hawthorne), 137, 170

Schlorndorff, Volker, 5

Schroeder, Andreas, 257

science fiction, 243–253

and anthropology and archaeology,
248

films, 245

and H. G. Wells, 390–391

The Handmaid's Tale as, 92–93

sexuality in, 249–251

social purposes of, 245, 249–250

Scientific American, 285

Scorched Wood People (Wiebe), 167,
167–168

Scotland, landscape of, 37–38

Scott, Walter, *Ivanhoe,* 164

Second Sex, The (de Beauvoir), 357

Second Words: Selected Critical Prose
(Atwood), xvi

Secret Garden, The (Burnett), 116

*Secular Scripture: A Study of the Struc-
ture of Romance* (Frye), 202, 391

Seeger, Pete, 341

Selected Letters of Dashiell Hammett
(Rivett and Layman), 209–210,
212–213

September 11, 2001, 186, 284–285

sequelae, 292–293, 339

sex education, pornography as, 16–17

sexuality, in utopian literature, 95

Shakespeare, William, 128

Cymbeline, 203

King Lear, 136

Macbeth, 126, 136, 273

A Midsummer Night's Dream,
272–273

Romeo and Juliet, 23

The Tempest, 392

Sharif, M. T., "The Letter Writer", 77
She (Haggard), 186, 198–204, 244, 388
  and Freudian psychiatry, 202–203
Shelley, Mary, 152
  Frankenstein, 244, 297, 386
Shields, Carol
  eulogy, 313–316
  other novels by, 314–315
  The Stone Diaries, 167, 314, 314–315
Shirley (Bronte), 23
short stories, 68–79
Silent Spring (Carson), 265
Silvers, Robert, 187
Simple Art of Murder, The (Chandler),
  73, 209
Siodmak, Curt, *Donovan's Brain*,
  301–302
Sir Gawain and the Green Knight, 354
Slaughterhouse-Five (Vonnegut), 245
slavery, 47–49
  and race relations, 48–49
Smith-Rosenberg, Carroll, 28
  Disorderly Conduct: Visions of
  Gender in Victorian America, 24
Snow (Orhan), 356–359
Snow White and the Seven Dwarfs, 134
societies, evolution of, 305–308,
  362–364
Soderberg, Hjalmar, *Doctor Glas*,
  260–264
"Solitude" (Le Guin), 251
Solomon Gursky Was Here (Richler),
  193, 380
Solstice (Oates), 29
Sono Nis, 257
South America, 111–114
Soviet Union, 3, 245
spiral staircase, as metaphor, 354
"Spotty-Handed   Villainesses"
  (Atwood), 103, 125–138
spy novels. *see* Leonard, Elmore

Stevenson, Robert Louis, *Treasure
  Island,* 164, 388
Stoker, Bram, 152
  Dracula, 131, 202
Stone Angel, The (Laurence), 52, 158
Stone Diaries (Shields), 167, 314,
  314–315
stories, evaluating, 68–69, 73–74
  criteria for, 68, 73, 74–76
stories, overheard, 71–72, 73
Story as Sharp as a Knife (Bringhurst),
  346–351
Story of a Soul (Saint Theresa of
  Lisieux), 270–271
story, voice of, 70–71
Strange Things (Atwood), 104
"Strays" (Richard), 76–77
"Suggestions   to   Detective   Story
  Writers" (Hammett), 213
Suit of Nettles (Reaney), 256
Sula (Morrison), 26–27
Sunday Times (London), 187
Swift, Jonathan, *A Modest Proposal*, 10
Swift, Jonathan, *Gulliver's Travels*, 94,
  244

T
Tale of Two Cities (Dickens), 164
Talonbooks, 257
Tamara, Queen of Georgia ("The Lion
  of The Caucasus"), 90
Tchiakovsky's 1812 Overture, 277–279
Temiscaming, Canada, 35
Tempest (Shakespeare), 392
Temptations of Big Bear (Wiebe), 167
Tennyson, Alfred, 161
  The Idylls of the King, 201
  In Memoriam, 377
Tenth Clew (Hammett), 213
Teresa, Saint of Avila, *The Castle of
  Imagination*, 271, 274

Terkel, Studs
  career, 331–334
  Death: Will the Circle be Unbroken, 331
  Division Street, America, 331
  Hope Dies Last: Keeping the Faith in Difficult Times, 331–342
Terror and Erebus (MacEwen), 166, 369, 371, 374, 380
Tess of the D'Urbervilles (Hardy), 136
Thackeray, William M., *Vanity Fair*, 24, 137–138, 164
That Summer in Paris (Callaghan), 327
Thatcher, Margaret, 90, 91
"The Age of Lead" (Atwood), 375
"The Children's Hour" (Longfellow), 218
"The Company of Wolves" (Carter), 151
The Gift: Imagination and the Erotic Life of Property (Hyde), 177–179
"The Matter of Seggri" (Le Guin), 251
theocracy, 97
Theresa, Saint of Lisieux, *The Story of a Soul*, 270–271
Thin Man, The (Hammett), 215, 217
This is Not For You (Rule), 28
Thomson, Tom, 40
Thousand and One Nights, The, 244
Tibbett, Paul, 338
time, and context, xiii–xiv
Time Machine (H. G. Wells), 94, 245, 387, 388, 389
Time magazine, 136
Times (London), xiv
Tishomingo Blues (Leonard), 227–236
To the Lighthouse (Woolf), 240–242
Tolkien, J. R. R., *Lord of the Rings*, 203, 384
Treasure Island (Stevenson), 164, 388

Trickster Makes This World: Mischief, Myth, and Art (Hyde), 179–181
Trung Nhi, 90
Trung Trac, 90
Tunica, Mississippi, 229
Turkey, 356-359
Turn of the Screw (James), 130–131
Twain, Mark (Samuel Clemens), 213
  Huckleberry Finn, 214

U
"Unchosen Love" (Le Guin), 251
Unimaginable Island (Young), 373–374
United States, culture, 228–229, 280–283, 331–342
  corporate, 339–340
  early twentieth century, 331–332
  political, 187–188, 280–283, 333–336
University of Alabama, 4
Unless (Shields), 315
Unnameable, The (Beckett), 336
Updike, John
  The Centaur, 6
  The Witches of Eastwick, 6–11
Urquhart, Jane
  Away, 167
  The Whirlpool, 167
Uses of Enchantment (Bettelheim), 148
USSR (United Soviet Socialist Republics), 3
utopia, definition, 93
Utopia Limited (Gilbert and Sullivan), 245
Utopia (More), 93, 94, 244
utopias
  propensity for, and culture, 93–94
  sexuality in, 95
  social purposes of, 94–95, 95, 244–245

V

V (Thomas), 215

vampires, 202

Vanderhaeghe, Guy, *The Englishman's Boy*, 167, 167–168

Vanity Fair (Thackeray), 24, 137–138, 164

vernacular, 214, 216

Verne, Jules, 244

"Very, Very Great Lady and Her Son at Home" (Carter), 152

Victoria, Queen of England, 23–24

Victorian era
and archaeology, 200–201
concepts of Nature, 390–391, 395–396
and moral virtue, 133
Romanticism of, 377–378
women's friendships, 23–25

Victory Gardens: A Breath of Fresh Air (Houghton), 305–312

violence
nineteenth century, 49
and pornography, 12–18

Virginian, The (Wister), 214

Vogue magazine, 104

voice, of the story, 70–71

Vonnegut, Kurt, *Slaughterhouse-Five*, 245

W

Wacousta (Richardson), 163–164

Wagner, Erica, 187

Wagner, Richard, *Parsifal*, 201

Walker, Alice, 23
The Color Purple, 26, 27, 49

War of the Worlds (Wells), 245, 388, 398

Warner, Marina
Alone of All Her Sex, 147
From the Beast to the Blonde: On

Fairy Tales and Their Tellers, 147–150
Monuments and Maidens, 147

Warner, Sylvia Townsend, 152

Warrior Queens (Fraser), 89–91

Wars, The (Findley), 167

Washington Post, xiv

Watson, Sheila, *The Double Hook*, 258

Weaver, Robert, *Anthology*, 257

Webster, Mary, 97

Webster, Noah, *The American Spelling Book*, 214

Weldon, Fay, *Down among the Women*, 22, 26

Well of Loneliness (Hall), 23

Wells, H. G., 387–388
influence on science fiction, 390–398
The Island of Dr. Moreau, 245, 386–398
Time Machine, 94, 245, 387, 388, 389
War of the Worlds, 94, 388, 398

Welty, Eudora, 86

West, Nathanael, 214

Western genre, 214

Wharton, Edith
The Custom of the Country, 137
"The Pelican", xv

"What Men Love For" (Phillips), 76

Whirlpool, The (Urquhart), 167

"White Angel" (Cunningham), 75

White, Antonia, *Frost in May*, 23

"Why I Decide to Kill Myself and Other Jokes" (Glover), 77

Wiebe, Rudy
Scorched Wood People, 167, 167–168
The Temptations of Big Bear, 167–168

Wilde, Oscar, 152
The Picture of Dorian Gray, 394

"Wilderness Station" (Munro), 167
Wilderness Tips (Atwood), 103, 375
Wilson, Edmund, 324
  O Canada, 322
Wings of the Dove (James), 24
Winters, Shelley, 121
Wisdom of the Mythtellers (Kane), 350
Wister, Owen, 214
  The Virginian, 214
witchcraft trials, 218
Witches of Eastwick, The (Updike), 6–11
Wizard of Earthsea (Le Guin), 246
Wizard of Oz, 80, 229
women. *see also* feminism; women's movement
  history of, 360–364
  opressed, 320–321, 356–359
  warriors, 89–91
women characters, 130–138, 291
  bad, 125–126, 134, 135–138, 149–150, 154–157
Women on the Edge of Time (Piercey), 94, 95, 250
Women, The (Luce), 25
women writers
  Canadian, 258–259
  interviews, collection of, 80–88
  social roles, 82–85
  style of, 82
Women Writers At Work, 82
women's friendships, 22–30, 24–25
  African American, 26–27
  lesbian, 28
  Victorian era, 23–25
women's movement, 201–202. *see also* Feminism
  influence on literature, 7–8, 131–134, 148
  and pornography, 13, 14–15

Women's Room, The (French), 26, 356–357
women's weeds, 22
Woolf, Virginia, 83–84, 86
  To the Lighthouse, 240–242
World Trade Center attacks, 186, 285
  sequelae, 292–293, 339
writers, 72
  African American, 86–87
  Canadian, 255–259, 265–267, 324–325, 350–351
  gender of. *see* gender, writer's interviewing, 80–81
  women. *see* women writers
writing, 79, 87–88
  book reviews, xv–xvi
  character development, 118–120, 127
  criteria for evaluating, 68, 73, 74–76
  historical fiction, 158–175
  novels, 125–138
  from others' point of view, 69–70, 72
  plot development, 130–131, 224–226
  on political topics, xv
  process of, 106–107, 110
  purpose and motivation for, 105–110, 217–218
  styles, 82, 322–323
Wuthering Heights (Bronte), 24, 47
Wyndham, John, "Consider Her Ways", 250

Y

You Went Away (Findley), 167
Young, David, *Unimaginable Island*, 373–374

Z

Zenobia, 90
"ZigZags of Treachery" (Hammett), 218

ABOUT THE AUTHOR

M argaret Atwood's books have been published in more than thirty-five countries. She is the author of nearly forty books of fiction, poetry, and criticism. In addition to *The Handmaid's Tale,* her novels include *Cat's Eye,* shortlisted for the Booker Prize; *Alias Grace,* which won the Giller Prize in Canada and the Premio Mondello in Italy; *The Blind Assassin,* winner of the 2000 Booker Prize; and *Oryx and Crake,* which was shortlisted for seven awards, including the Man Booker Prize, the Giller Prize, and the Orange Prize. Her earlier collection of essays and reviews was *Second Words,* published in 1982. Margaret Atwood lives in Toronto with writer Graeme Gibson.

4/05

ML